Professional
Visual Basic
Windows® CE Programming

Larry Roof

Wrox Press Ltd.

Professional Visual Basic Windows CE Programming

© 1998 Wrox Press

Published by Wrox Press Ltd. 30 Lincoln Road, Olton, Birmingham, B27 6PA
Printed in CANADA
1 2 3 4 5 TRI 99 98

ISBN 1-861001-62-2

Credits

Author
Larry Roof

Development Editor
Dominic Shakeshaft

Editors
Craig Berry
Darren Gill

Index
Diane Brenner

Technical Reviewers
Arnold Cota
Mike Crowe
Daniel M. Laby M.D
Thomas Lewis
Scott Mason
William Moore
Boyd Nolan
Tihan Seale
Richard Veith

Cover/Design/Layout
Andrew Guillaume

Copy Edit
Alex Zoro
Barney Zoro

CONTENTS

Table of Contents

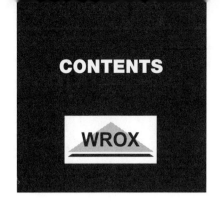

Introduction   **1**

Part 1: Working With Visual Basic For Windows CE   **7**

Chapter 1: Getting Started   **9**

Setting Up Your System   9
> Visual Basic for Windows CE Toolkit   9
> Windows CE Platform SDK   10
> Windows CE Services   10

Requirements of the VBCE Toolkit   10
> The Hardware Requirements   10
> The Software Requirements   11

Getting Up and Running   11
> The Installation Process   11
>> The Foundation – Windows NT   12
>> Add Visual Basic   12
>> Installing the Visual Basic for CE Toolkit   12
>>> Part 1 – The Visual Basic for Windows CE Toolkit   13
>>> Part 2 – The Windows CE Platform SDK   14
>>> Part 3 – The Windows CE Services   14

What is Included with the VBCE Toolkit?   20
> A New Project Type   21
> Modifications to the VB Menu Structure   21
>> The File Menu   22
>> The Project Menu   22
>> The Debug Menu   22
>> The Run Menu   22
>> The Tools Menu   22
>> The Windows CE Menu   22
>>> Application Install Wizard   23
>>> Books Online   23
>>> Download Runtime Files   23
>>> Control Manager   23
>>> Heap Walker   24
>>> Process Viewer   24
>>> Registry Editor   24
>>> Spy   25
>>> Zoom   25
> Changes to the VB Toolbar   26
> A New Debug Dialog Window   26

The Differences Between VB and VBCE   27

     VB and VBCE Use Different ActiveX Controls   27

     There is a Single Data Type in VBCE   27

     VBCE Uses a Different Method to Exit Your Applications   27

     VBCE is Limited to a Single .BAS Module   27

     The Absence of OLE in VBCE   28

     There Are No MDI Forms or Class Modules in VBCE   28

     You Cannot Unload Forms in VBCE   28

     There are Differences Between Form and Code Modules   28

     VBCE Has Limited Error Handling Capabilities   28

     VBCE Language Errors are Handled at Runtime   28

     There is No Support for API Calls in VBCE   28

     You Cannot Access Help from Your VBCE applications   28

     The Debug Object is Not Supported in VBCE   28

     Absence of the Database Support   29

     VBCE Uses different Methods of File I/O   29

     VB Functions That Are Missing From VBCE   29

Summary   29

Chapter 2: Creating A Handheld Application   **31**

The CE Application Creation Process   31

Time Manager – A Step-By-Step Example   32

     Step-By-Step Projects – The Recipe   32

     Time Manager – The Completed Project   33

       Using Time Manager   33

     Time Manager – The Requirements   34

     Time Manager – The Design   34

     Time Manager – The Construction   34

Summary   55

Chapter 3: Designing Applications For Windows CE   **57**

How to Design an Effective CE Application   57

     Designing For The Handheld Display   58

       Larry Roof's Display Rule Number One – Bigger is Better   58

       Larry Roof's Display Rule Number Two – Less is More   60

       Larry Roof's Display Rule Number Three –

              The Snapshot Test   61

     Designing for Handheld Input   61

       Larry Roof's Input Rule Number One – Bigger is Better   61

       Larry Roof's Input Rule Number Two –

              To Each Their Own   62

       Larry Roof's Input Rule Number Three – Do it for Them   63

     Designing for Handheld Usage   63

       Larry Roof's Usage Rule Number One –

              Does it Work There?   64

Larry Roof's Usage Rule Number Two –
It Has to Work There 64
Larry Roof's Usage Rule Number Three –
The Hardware Blues 64
Larry Roof's Usage Rule Number Four –
Right Here, Right Now 64

Enhancing Time Manager 65
What is Wrong with Time Manager? 65
Display Problems 65
Input Problems 65
Usage Problems 65

Time Manager – The Revised Project 66
Using the Revised Time Manager 66
Time Manager – The Requirements 67
Time Manager – The Design 67
Time Manager – The Construction 68
Auto-Sizing the Form 77
Summarizing the Revised Time Manager 78

Converting Your Desktop Applications 78
Handling Errors in Your Applications 79
The On Error Resume Next Statement 79
The Err.Number Property 80
Runtime Errors in Visual Basic for Windows CE 81
Adding Error Handling to Time Manager 82
The Programmer's 'Safety Chute' 82
Handling Formatting Errors 84

Summary 85

Chapter 4: ActiveX Controls For Windows CE – Interface Tools 87

ActiveX Controls for Windows CE 88
Controls Included with the Toolkit 88
What is in the Control Pack 88
The Windows CE ActiveX Interface Controls 89
The Grid Control 89
The File System Control 89
The Image Control 89
The ImageList Control 90
The ListView Control 90
The PictureBox Control 90
The TabStrip Control 90
The TreeView Control 90
The VBCE.com Utility Control 91

Working with ActiveX Controls 91
Adding Them to Your Project 91
The Control Manager 92
Installing a Control on the Emulator 93

Installing a Control on Your H/PC	94
Removing Controls	94
Distributing Controls with Your CE Apps	95
The Sample Applications	95
Application One – The CEWizard	95
Features Found in the CEWizard Application	96
Using the CEWizard	96
Building the CEWizard	98
Closing Thoughts on the CEWizard	112
The DataDisplay Example Application	112
Features Found in the DataDisplay Application	112
Using DataDisplay	113
Building DataDisplay	114
Closing Thoughts on DisplayData	120
The Explorer Example Application	120
Features Found In The Explorer Application	120
Using Explorer	121
Building Explorer	122
Closing Thoughts On Explorer	131
Summary	131

Chapter 5: ActiveX Controls For Windows CE – Data Tools   133

The Windows CE ActiveX Data Tool Controls	133
The Comm Control	133
The Common Dialog Control	134
The File System Control	134
The Finance Control	134
The Winsock Control	134
The VBCE.com Utility Control	135
Working with ActiveX Controls	135
The Sample Applications	135
The Chat Example Application	136
Features Found in the Chat Application	136
Using Chat	136
Building Chat	139
Closing Thoughts on Chat	145
The Utility Example Application	145
Features Found in the Utility Program	145
Using the Utility Program	146
Building the Utility Program	147
Closing Thoughts on the Utility Program	159
The HTML Viewer Example Application	159
Features Found in HTML Viewer	160
Using the HTML Viewer	160
Building the HTML Viewer	161
Summary	165

Chapter 6: Working With Files   167

Using Files with Your Applications   167
Working with the File Control   168
   Working with Sequential Files   168
      Opening Sequential Files   169
         Opening a Text File for Input   169
         Opening a Text File for Output   170
         Opening a Text File for Append   171
      Writing to Sequential Files   171
         Writing Text, a Note or a Memo to a Sequential File   172
         Writing Data Items to a Sequential File   172
      Reading from Sequential Files   173
         Reading Text, a Note or a Memo From a Sequential File 173
         Reading Data Items in from a Sequential File   175
      Closing Sequential Files   176
   Working with Random Access Files   176
      Opening Random Access Files   177
         Opening a Random Access File for Reading and Writing   177
      Writing to Random Access Files   178
      Reading from Random Access Files   179
      Closing Random Access Files   180
   Working with Binary Files   180
      Opening Binary Files   181
         Opening a Binary File for Reading and Writing   181
      Writing to Binary Files   182
      Reading from Binary Files   183
      Closing Binary Files   184
Working with the File System Control   184
   Obtaining a Directory Listing   185
   Creating a New Directory   186
   Deleting a Directory   186
   Copying a File   187
   Moving a File   187
   Deleting a File   188
   Retrieving the File Date and Time Stamp   188
   Determining The Size of a File   189
   Retrieving File Attributes   190
   Setting File Attributes   191
EasyEdit – A Step-By-Step Example   192
   EasyEdit – The Completed Project   192
   EasyEdit – The Requirements   194
   EasyEdit – The Design   194
   EasyEdit – The Construction   195
      Starting and Stopping EasyEdit - The Form Events   197
      Working Around a Text Box Bug   203
      Implementing the EasyEdit Menu - The File Menu   207
      The Edit Menu   211

The Options Menu   214
The Help Menu   215
Summarizing EasyEdit   216
Summary   217

Chapter 7: Working With Databases   219

What Does the ADO Provide?   219
What Does the ADO Not Provide?   220
Acquiring the ADO CE SDK   220
Installing the ADO CE SDK   220
Requirements for Using the ADO CE   220
For the Development Machine   221
For the Client Machine   221
The Installation Procedure   221
Known Setup Bugs   223
Working with the ADO CE Tools   224
Copying Databases from the Desktop PC   224
Copying Databases from the H/PC   227
Copying Data to an ODBC Data Source   228
Copying Databases with Code   229
The Synchronization Process   229
Programming with the ADO CE SDK   230
Creating a Table   230
Creating an Index   232
Determining if a Table Exists   233
Dropping a Table   234
Opening a Table   235
Managing Your Recordsets   236
Selecting the Records to Return   237
Restrictions of the WHERE Clause   237
Sorting The Recordset   238
Navigating Through A Recordset   238
MoveFirst, MoveLast, MoveNext and MovePrevious   238
BOF and EOF Properties   239
Adding A Record   240
Using The SQL INSERT Statement   241
Using AddNew Method   241
Handling the Absence of AutoNumbering   242
Modifying Records   242
Deleting Records   243
Using SQL DELETE Statement   243
Using The Delete Method   243
TableView – A Step-By-Step Example   244
TableView – The Completed Project   244
Using TableView   244

TableView – The Requirements 245
TableView – The Design 245
TableView – The Construction 245
Summarizing TableView 251
Distributing Programs That Use ADO 251
Updating Time Manager 252
Using Time Manager 252
Using The Revised Time Manager 253
Time Manager – The Requirements 253
Time Manager – The Design 253
Time Manager – The Construction 254
Summarizing the Revised Time Manager 264
Summary 264
Further Information On The ADO CE 264

Chapter 8: Moving Data Between Devices **267**

Options for Moving Data 267
Using the Synchronized Files Folder 268
Working with the Synchronized Files Folder 268
Checking the Synchronized Files Folder 269
Using the Check Files Program 269
Examining the Check Files Program 270
Using this Method in Your Applications 272
Step 1 - Checking for a Previous File 272
Step 2 – Deleting a Previous Version of the File 272
Step 3 – Opening the File 272
Step 4 – Writing to the File 272
Step 5 – Closing the File 272
Summarizing the Synchronized Files Method 272
Letting ADO Handle It 273
Using This Method in Your Applications 273
What you need to do to Your CE Databases 273
Primary Keys and AutoNumbering 273
Summarizing the ADO Synchronization Method 274
Copying Tables via the ADO CE 274
Adding ADO CE Functionality to Mobile Devices 274
Using the Manual Method 275
Using the Programmatic Method 275
Using the Copy Tables Program 275
Leveraging the ADO CE API 276
Copying Tables to the H/PC 276
Copying Tables from the H/PC 278
Summarizing the ADO CE Table Copy Method 280
Over the Internet 280
Writing Web-Enabled CE Applications 280
The ASP Client Example 280

Using the ASP Client Program   281
Using the Winsock control   282
Sending Data to an ASP Page   282
Requesting Data from an ASP Page   283
Parsing HTML for Data   285
Summarizing the Internet Method   287
Via the Serial Communications Port   288
Creating Communication-Enabled CE Applications   288
Using the Comm Control   288
Establishing Connection   289
Communicating Instructions   289
Passing Data   289
Confirming Successful Data Transmission   290
Handling Errors in your Communication Routines   290
Summarizing the Serial Port Method   290
Summary   291

Chapter 9: Using Help Files With Your CE Applications   293

Windows CE Help Files   293
Ways to Access CE Help   294
Using CE Help   294
The Components of the CE Help System   295
The Contents File   295
The Topic File   297
HTML Tags Supported by CE Help   299
Building Successful CE Help Systems   300
Accessing Help From Your CE App   300
With the Utility Control   301
The Utility Control Example   301
With the Common Dialog Control   301
The Common Dialog Control Example   302
Adding Help to EasyEdit   302
Using The Revised EasyEdit   302
EasyEdit – The Requirements   303
EasyEdit – The Design   303
EasyEdit – The Construction   304
Summarizing the Revised EasyEdit   313
Adding Help to Time Manager   313
Testing Out the Revised Time Manager   321
Summary   322

Part 2: Case Studies   **325**

Chapter 10: The Inventory Manager: Scanning and Recording Data 327

The Application Specifications   327
The Inventory Manager – Step-By-Step   327
   Using the Inventory Manager   328
     Installing the Inventory Manager   328
     Installing Optional Hardware   328
     Running the Inventory Manager   328
   Removing the Inventory Manager   330
   The Inventory Manager - The Requirements   330
   The Inventory Manager - The Design   330
   The Inventory Manager - The Construction   331
     Implementing the Operation Menu   343
     Implementing the Help Menu   344
   Other Uses for the Inventory Manager   349
Barcode Scanners for Windows CE   350
Summary   351

Chapter 11: The Note Manager   **353**

The Application Specifications   353
Note Manager – Step-By-Step   353
   Using Note Manager   354
     Installing Note Manager   354
     Running Note Manager   354
   Removing Note Manager   358
   Note Manager - The Requirements   358
   Note Manager - The Design   358
     The User Interface   359
     Data Storage   359
   Note Manager - The Construction   360
     The ADO Declarations File   363
     The General Declarations Section   363
     Starting Note Manager – The Form_Load Procedure   364
     The Form_Unload Procedure   371
     The TreeView Control Event Procedures   374
     The txtNote Text Box Control Event Procedures   377
     Implementing the Note Manager Menu   378
     The Edit Menu   388
     The Options Menu   389
     The Help Menu   390
Note Manager – The Final Word   398
   Enhancing Note Manager   399
   Reusing Note Manager Techniques   399
Summary   399

Appendix A: The Examples   **401**

    Getting the Samples and Examples   401
        Extracting the Setup   403
        Installing the Example Files   403
    Using the Sample Code   403
        Shortcuts to Projects   405
        Uninstalling the Samples   405
    Copying Files to the Emulator   405

Appendix B: The Bugs   **407**

    Bugs and Solutions   407
    The Left Function Failure   407
    The Text Box Cursor Keys Failure   408
    The VBCEUtility Control Loading Failure   413
    Lost Events in Framed Controls   413
    The Winsock Control Problems   414

Appendix C: Further Information   **417**

    Web Sites   417
    Newsgroups   419

Index   **423**

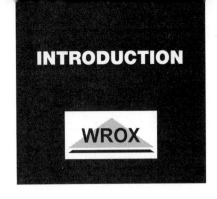

What is this Book About?

Visual Basic for Windows CE (VBCE) is the latest development tool from Microsoft for the Windows CE operating system. As the popularity of handheld computers running Windows CE has increased, so has the need for an easy-to-use application development tool. There can be no easier way to develop just such a tool than by extending the popular Visual Basic environment to include the capability to design, test, and deploy Windows CE applications.

In this book, you'll learn everything you need to know about using VBCE - from how to install Visual Basic for Windows CE, through a series of topics that present techniques you would commonly use in creating CE applications, and then creating several case studies that show you complete CE programs. By the end of this book, you'll be ready to create your own fully functional applications for the Windows CE operating system.

Who is this Book for?

This book is intended for developers who are interested in creating applications for the Windows CE platform. It's designed to give someone who has had previous experience working with Visual Basic all the information that they would need to create commercial quality CE applications. Whether you're working as part of a corporate Information Systems department, or as a self-employed consultant, you'll find that the combination of concepts and projects presented in this book will help you quickly become productive with VBCE.

What Does this Book Cover?

This book is divided into two parts. The first part of the book focuses on the how-to of VBCE. It provides the inexperienced reader with a foundation for working with VBCE by introducing the reader to:

- Working with the Visual Basic for CE add-in, from creation of a new project, through testing, to distribution
- Building easy-to-use applications for the Windows CE platform
- Ways to store data on the handheld, including CE databases, sequential, random and binary files
- How to create help systems for your CE applications

But wait, that's not all! You will find nestled into the first part of the book, two complete programs: **EasyEditor,** a Notepad-type application, and **Larry Roof's Time Manager**, a utility for tracking and billing your time. You will follow along as I build these two applications to demonstrate the concepts and techniques of programming professional applications in VBCE.

The second part of the book presents complete CE applications. These case studies give the experienced reader examples of techniques that can be used to solve common programming problems in the Windows CE environment. Included in this section are the following case studies:

Project 1 – Inventory Manager demonstrates how the handheld computer can be used to streamline and simplify the process of taking inventories. It shows ways to tailor your applications to meet the needs of a user that is moving about while using a handheld computer. Inventory Manager also shows you how to interface a barcode scanner into your Visual Basic for Windows CE programs.

Project 2 – Note Manager shows that Visual Basic for CE can be used to create utilities for the CE operating system. This program can be used to replace post-it notes, To Do lists, grocery lists and other forms of simple notes. It demonstrates another way to handle data in your CE applications.

So altogether, you get four complete applications: two in the first part of the book, along with two case studies in the second part of the book. These applications are yours to dissect, embellish, and reuse! And these are not like those simple, no-feature applications that you would find in other books. What you have here are commercial quality applications complete with help files and installation programs!

What Isn't Covered in this Book

This book shows you how to create applications using VBCE. It doesn't explain the details of the VBCE language. To make best use of this book, you will need to be familiar with one of the Visual Basic programming languages. This could be Visual Basic, Visual Basic for Applications (VBA), or VBScript. Preferably, your experience would be with Visual Basic - since VBCE is an add-in for Visual Basic.

What You Need to Use this Book

To create applications for the Windows CE platform using VBCE, you will need the following for your desktop computer:

- Either the Professional or Enterprise edition of Visual Basic version 5
- The Visual Basic for CE toolkit, which includes the Windows CE Platform SDK and Windows CE Services
- A system running either Windows NT Workstation
- PC with a 486/66 MHz or higher processor
- 24 MB of RAM with 32 MB recommended
- 40 MB of hard-disk space

In addition to the items above, you will need the following for your handheld computer:

- A handheld computer running Windows CE version 2.0. While you can test your applications using the emulator, I would recommend that you also test on a handheld.
- The VBCE.com Utility control which provides you with workarounds for several bugs within the VBCE Toolkit.

How to Use this Book

To get the most out of this book I would recommend that you start at the beginning and work through the first half. Build the example programs **EasyEdit** and **Time Manager** as you work along. This will give you a solid foundation in what Visual Basic for Windows CE offers and how you work with it. The second half of the book can then be reviewed in any order, as the case studies are independent of each other.

Step-by-Step Projects

This book uses step by step projects to demonstrate how to create applications with VBCE. Each project presented in this book follows this plan:

- **Viewing the Completed Project** – A project starts by showing you a completed example. This way you get to see what you are building before you begin.

- **List of Requirements** – Next there is a detailed list of the requirements for the application.

- **Designing the Application** – For each project, we will walk through a design - including any special considerations for the CE environment.

- **Development of the Application** – The development of each application will be examined in detail so that you aren't left on your own to figure out how a program works.

- **Testing** – With each project you will learn testing techniques that you can apply to your own projects.

- **Deployment** - No CE application would be complete without an installation routine. Each of the applications presented in this book includes an installation program.

Using this step by step methodology for each of this book's four applications provides you with a solid understanding of the how to create CE applications.

Where You Will Find the Sample Code

The examples presented in this book are provided as compressed files on the Wrox web site:

`http://www.wrox.com`

On the Wrox web site you will also find additional material and example applications which we just didn't have the time or room to fit into this book.

Detailed instructions on downloading and installing the examples are included in Appendix A.

Conventions Used in this Book

We've used a number of different styles of text and layout in the book to help differentiate between kinds of information. Here are examples of the styles we use and an explanation of what they mean:

> **Important, not to be missed information appears in boxes like this.**

Advice, hints, or background information is presented like this.

- **Important Words** are in a bold type font
- Words that appear on the screen in menus like the File or Window menu are in a similar font to what you see on screen
- Keys that you press on the keyboard, like *Ctrl* and *Enter*, are in italics
- Visual Basic code has two fonts. If it's a word that we're talking about in the text, for example, when discussing the **For...Next** loop, it's in a bold font. If it's a block of code that you can type in as a program and run, then it's also in a gray box:

```
Private Sub cmdQuit_Click()
    End
End Sub
```

Sometimes you'll see code in a mixture of styles, like this:

```
Private Sub cmdQuit_Click()
    End
End Sub
```

- There are two reasons why this might be so. In both cases we want you to consider the code with the gray background. The code with a white background is either code we've already looked at and that we don't wish to examine further, or when you're typing code in, this is code that Visual Basic automatically generates and doesn't need typing in.
- Sometimes you will find that we have split a line of code over two or more lines. We have tried to use the VB line continuation character (_) when we can - but in some instances we have used ✎ on the line below.

Tell Us What You Think

We've worked hard on this book to make it useful. We've tried to understand what you're willing to exchange your hard-earned money for, and we've tried to make the book live up to your expectations.

Please let us know what you think about the book. Tell us what we did wrong, and what we did right. This isn't just a marketing pitch, we really do huddle around the email to find out what you think. If you don't believe it, then send us a note. We'll answer, and we'll take whatever you say on board for future editions. The easiest way to send us your comments is via email at:

feedback@wrox.com

You can also find more details about Wrox Press on our web site. There, you'll find code from our latest books, sneak previews of forthcoming titles, and information about the authors and editors. You can order Wrox titles directly from the site, or find out where your nearest local bookstore with Wrox titles is located. The address to our web site is:

http://www.wrox.com

Customer Support

If you find a mistake, please have a look at the errata page for this book on the Wrox web site first.

If you can't find the answer there, tell us about the problem and we'll do everything we can to answer promptly!

Just send us an email to **support@wrox.com.**

Or fill in the form on our web site.

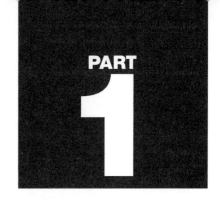

Working with Visual Basic for Windows CE

Well here it is, all in one package, the how-to for creating Windows CE applications using Visual Basic for Windows CE. In this first part of the book you will learn how to create CE applications from the ground up. By working through the step-by-step examples, you will learn everything that you need to know to construct your very own CE programs.

We start out in Chapter 1 by learning how to install and configure the Visual Basic for Windows CE development environment. This environment includes a desktop PC, an emulator, and a handheld computer - so it's important to get everything set up right before we can begin building applications.

Chapter 2 walks you through the process of creating a handheld application from start to finish. Every step is presented in detail so that you have a clear understanding of the process. It's here that you'll first be introduced to my **Time Manager** application.

CE applications have different requirements than desktop programs. In Chapter 3, you'll learn how to design your applications for the CE environment - taking into consideration keyboard and screen restrictions.

Custom controls are the subject of Chapters 4 and 5. You'll see how they play an important role in Visual Basic for Windows CE, extending the limited functionality of language to allow you to create robust applications. Included in these chapters is a listing of the controls that are included with VBCE, what features they provide, and how to incorporate them into your programs. Here you'll also be introduced to the extremely useful VBCE.com Utility ActiveX control, which you'll find invaluable in developing CE applications.

Chapter 6 demonstrates how to incorporate files into your CE applications. You will learn about the File and File System controls, and see how these two controls are used in combination to provide support for sequential, random access and binary files. Here you'll develop most of the **EasyEdit** application.

No discussion of creating applications for the handheld would be complete without examining the database structure provided by the Windows CE environment. Chapter 7 starts with an overview of the structure of CE databases. By the end of the chapter you will have learned how to extend your VBCE applications to create, access and update a database.

Chapter 8 takes the discussion data to the next level by showing you how to synchronize data between your handheld and a desktop PC. You'll see how to streamline the data gathering process by incorporating handheld data into your company's information systems.

Whether it's on the desktop, or the handheld, no application is complete without a help file. In Chapter 9, you'll learn about CE help files. Let's just say that if you're comfortable with HTML then you're going to feel right at home creating CE help files.

By the time you have completed these first 9 chapters, you will have a solid understanding of how to create full-featured, data-integrated, easy-to-use applications for the Windows CE environment using Visual Basic for CE. Sound too good to be true? See for yourself. Just jump on in. I think you'll be pleasantly surprised.

CHAPTER
1

Getting Started

The Visual Basic for Windows CE (VBCE) Toolkit is Microsoft's answer to simplifying the process of creating applications for handheld computers. By augmenting their popular Visual Basic product with the VBCE add-in, Microsoft has provided a tool that enables anyone experienced with Visual Basic to immediately begin to develop handheld applications.

In this chapter I will introduce you to the Visual Basic for Windows CE Toolkit. I will briefly describe how to set up your desktop PC for use as the development platform for your VBCE applications, and then I will walk you through the process of installing the VBCE Toolkit, the Windows CE platform SDK (Software Development Kit) and finally the Windows CE Services.

Once you have the VBCE Toolkit up and running, we will then turn our attention to the Toolkit itself, looking at the features it has on offer and how the Visual Basic design environment has been supplemented to provide you with the ability to create applications for Windows CE.

Finally, we wrap up the chapter by looking at some of the key differences between Visual Basic and VBCE. If you are an experienced VB developer you'll want to keep this list handy, as you'll find that many of your favorite features are missing from the VBCE add-in.

So let's get right at it. The sooner you get the Visual Basic for Windows CE Toolkit installed, the sooner you will be creating your own CE applications.

Setting Up Your System

The VBCE Toolkit is after all, just an add-in to Visual Basic, and as such is fairly easy to install. The installation routines that are provided with the Toolkit are solid and walk you through the process of installing and configuring each of the three components that are required to create CE applications. The components that will be installed on your system are:

- Visual Basic for Windows CE Toolkit
- Windows CE Platform SDK
- Windows CE Services

Just what is the purpose of each of these components?

Visual Basic for Windows CE Toolkit

This toolkit is an add-in for the Visual Basic design environment. It modifies and augments the VB IDE to provide the tools that you will use to create CE applications.

Windows CE Platform SDK

The CE Platform SDK, or Software Development Kit, is a set of tools that enables you to create CE applications. For the most part it is providing a foundation on which to construct your VBCE applications. While you will seldom be aware of its existence during your work, it does, however, provide the CE emulator, which you will use to test your applications.

Windows CE Services

The CE Services provide the necessary communication between your desktop computer and your handheld device. The services allow you to:

▲ View and manage files on the hand-held

▲ Transfer files to the hand-held

Requirements of the VBCE Toolkit

Setting up a system to develop Windows CE applications with the VBCE Toolkit requires a significant investment in both hardware and software. The requirements of each are detailed in the sections following.

The Hardware Requirements

The system on which you will be installing the VBCE Toolkit needs to meet the following hardware requirements:

▲ A 486DX/66 MHz or higher processor. However I wouldn't recommend anything less than a Pentium processor.

▲ 24 MB of RAM. 32 MB is recommended, but I've found that 64 MB is more suitable for running Windows NT, Visual Basic 5, the Windows CE desktop emulator and Windows CE Services all at the same time.

▲ 30 MB of hard disk space is the minimum requirement for the Toolkit. Plan for 115 MB for the complete installation and 220 MB if you want to include the online documentation.

▲ A VGA or higher resolution monitor. I would recommend using a minimum of a 17 inch monitor that along with the video card would allow you to run in a 1024 x 768 resolution. Why? Because the Visual Basic design environment is made up of a group of windows that require a large amount of screen space to display.

▲ A Microsoft compatible mouse.

▲ A CD-ROM drive to install the software.

The Software Requirements

In addition to the VBCE Toolkit you will need the following software:

- Windows NT Workstation version 4.0

- Service Pack 3 for Windows NT

- Visual Basic 5.0, either the Enterprise or Professional Edition

- A web browser is needed to read many of the help and documentation files that are included with the development kit. Version 3.02 of Microsoft's Internet Explorer is included on the Visual Basic for Windows CE Toolkit CD.

Getting Up and Running

Setting up an environment for developing VBCE applications involves installing the VBCE Toolkit, the Windows CE Platform SDK and the Windows CE Services. They need to be loaded on a machine that is running Microsoft Windows NT Workstation.

> **I would recommend that you start with an empty system. This eliminates the occurrence of problems that may be caused by existing configurations.**

Don't have a free system lying around? Try stopping by your local computer store and asking for mounting hardware that allows you to switch the hard drive in use in your system. For a few hundred dollars you can have a fresh system on which to build.

The Installation Process

If you were building a system from scratch here are the installation steps you would need to perform:

- Microsoft Windows NT version 4

- Service Pack 3 for Windows NT

- Microsoft Visual Basic version 5

- Microsoft Visual Basic for Windows CE Toolkit

- Microsoft Windows CE SDK

- Microsoft Windows CE Services

The following sections will present step-by-step instructions on the installation process.

The Foundation – Windows NT

The VBCE Toolkit is designed for use with the Windows NT operating system. While you can install the Toolkit under Windows 95, this is not a supported configuration, thus will be error prone and lacking in several of the key features.

After installing NT you will need to add Service Pack 3 for Windows NT which is available from Microsoft's web site at **http://www.microsoft.com/ntworkstation**. You need to follow the Downloads hyper link to get to the Service Pack download page.

Add Visual Basic

You need to have either the Enterprise or Professional Edition of Visual Basic 5 installed before installing the VBCE Toolkit. The options that are provided with the Typical installation of Visual Basic will suffice.

Installing the Visual Basic for CE Toolkit

As I mentioned earlier, the installation procedure that comes with the VBCE Toolkit handles the installation of three separate components:

- The Visual Basic for Windows CE Toolkit
- The Windows CE Platform SDK
- The Windows CE Services

> **If you already have the Windows CE Services installed on your system you do not need to reinstall them unless you are upgrading from an older version.**

To initiate the installation simply insert the Windows CE Toolkit for Visual Basic CD and run the **Setup** program that can be found in the root directory of the CD:

The opening screen, shown above, will be displayed. This will launch directly into the first of three parts of the installation routine for the VBCE Toolkit.

Part 1 – The Visual Basic for Windows CE Toolkit

The installation procedure for the VBCE Toolkit requires little more of you than clicking a few buttons. The steps of this process are:

- An opening dialog is displayed informing you that this is the installation procedure for the VBCE Toolkit.

- A dialog containing the software license for the Toolkit is next. To accept this agreement click the Yes button.

- The user information dialog will be displayed. Enter your name and company name.

- In the CD Key dialog enter the key off the back of the CD case and click the OK button.

- The installation will begin. A progress meter will keep you informed on the installation.

- At this point you may be prompted to reboot your computer. If you are then do so.

Shortly after a setup completion dialog will be displayed. On this dialog is a check box used to specify whether you want to view the **readme** file for the Toolkit. I would recommend that you view this file as it documents the sample files, creating ActiveX controls for use with VBCE, problems that exist with the Toolkit and general information on the use of the Toolkit.

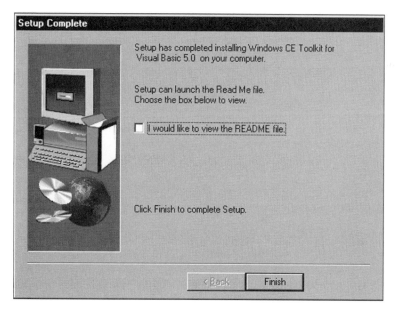

That's all there is to installing the Toolkit. Now let's look at the second part of the installation: the Windows CE Platform SDK.

13

Part 2 – The Windows CE Platform SDK

Although it wouldn't seem possible, the installation procedure for the Windows CE Platform SDK is far simpler than even the VBCE Toolkit. There is nothing for you to do. Just select to install the Platform SDK and sit back. A dialog will be displayed upon its completion:

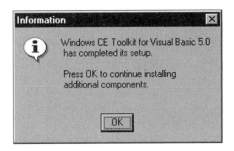

Part 3 – The Windows CE Services

The final component to be installed is the Windows CE Services. While it is by far the longest and most involved installation of the three, it still requires little involvement from you. In addition to installing the CE Services software, this part also:

- Installs the Windows NT Remote Access Service (RAS) if it's not already installed on your system
- Configures RAS
- Establishes the partnership between the desktop and handheld computers

The complete installation process for Windows CE Services is as follows:

- After the Windows CE Platform SDK installation has completed you will be prompted to install the Windows CE Services. If you have already installed these services a dialog will be displayed giving you the option to reinstall, change, remove or configure synchronization for the current version. If you already have these services installed on your system you only need to update them if you have an older version.

- You will receive a warning that Service Pack 3 may need to be re-installed as a result of installing CE Services:

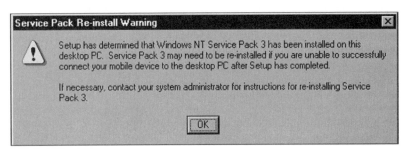

You should remember this warning as it can save you a lot of stress later if you have communication problems between your two machines.

▲ The licensing dialog will be displayed. Click on the <u>Y</u>es button to accept the agreement and continue the installation.

▲ The user information dialog is next. Enter your name and company name.

▲ The setup type dialog will be displayed as shown in the screenshot below. This dialog allows you to control which CE Services components are installed:

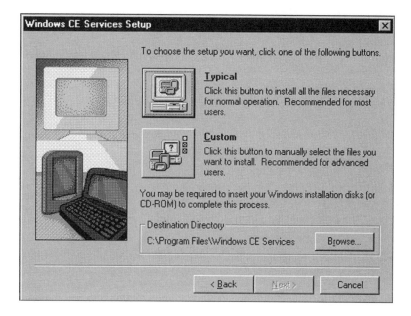

Select the <u>C</u>ustom setup. It will present you with the dialog shown below from which you can pick individual components of the CE Services to install. That way you know exactly what you are getting and what is available.

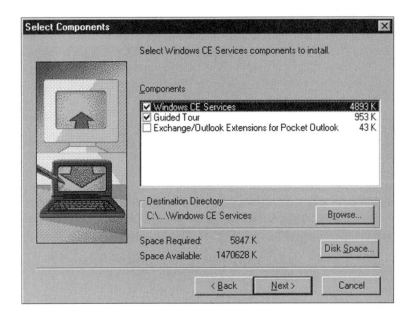

The three components that are available with the Windows CE Services installation are:

- Windows CE Services – Provides communication and synchronization services between the desktop and handheld computers. You must install this option.

- Guided Tour – This HTML based tour walks you through the functionality that is provided by the Windows CE Services including synchronization and use of the Mobile Devices window. I would recommend that first time users select this option.

- Exchange/Outlook Extensions for Pocket Outlook – This component, as well as the Guided Tour, are not required for developing CE applications. These extensions simply provide synchronization support between Pocket Outlook and your desktop Exchange/Outlook.

Continuing on with the details of the setup:

- After selecting what components to install you will be asked how you want the CE Services to appear in the Windows Start menu.

- A confirmation window will be shown listing the install options that you chose in the previous screens.

- The process of copying files to your system will be performed. The display will be updated as the installation progresses.

- At this point, the copying of files for the installation has completed. The remaining part of the installation will handle the configuration of the services that are used by the Windows CE Services.

- A dialog will be displayed informing you that the Windows NT Remote Access Service (RAS) is going to be installed and configured. You will need to provide your NT source media if you have not previously installed RAS.

▲ After completing the RAS installation and configuration you will be asked if you want to create a desktop shortcut for Mobile Devices. The Mobile Devices utility allows you to interface with your handheld's file system.

▲ A setup completion dialog will be displayed.

▲ A dialog will inform you that you need to reboot your computer.

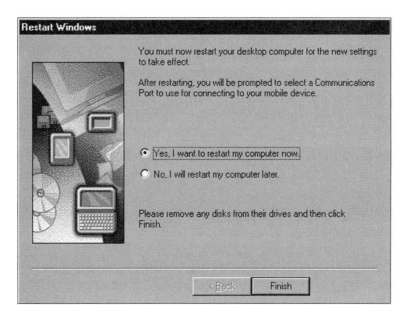

After rebooting your system the process of establishing communications between your desktop and handheld computers should be automatically performed. At the start of this process the Get Connected dialog, as shown below, will be displayed:

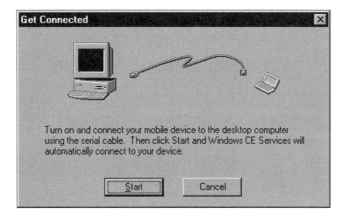

> If this dialog is not displayed you may have to manually install and configure the NT remote access service (RAS) on your system. Refer to your NT help system for further information on the use and configuration of this service.
>
> You may also need to manually configure the connection to your H/PC if you are sharing a communication port between the Windows CE Services and other functions.
>
> I would also recommend reinstalling Service Pack 3 if you run into problems.

▲ The process of establishing communication requires no involvement from you. The utility will search through the serial ports on your desktop computer to determine where your handheld computer is connected. Upon finding the correct port it will perform the needed configurations. You should see activity on the display of your handheld as this step progresses.

▲ Finally the Mobile Devices window will be displayed on your desktop as shown in the screenshot below. This signifies that communication has been established between your two computers:

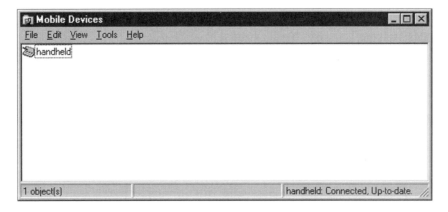

Note that in this screenshot handheld *was the name I assigned to be used for my handheld computer during the establishment of a partnership between my desktop and handheld computers.*

▲ The final step that needs to be performed as part of the installation of the Windows CE Services is to configure the partnership relationship between your desktop and handheld computers. This begins with the displaying of the New Partnership Wizard as shown below:

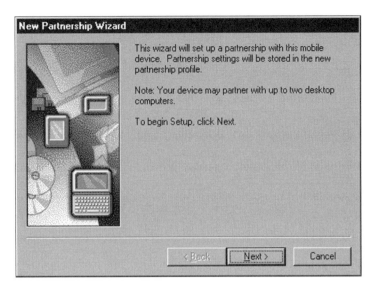

The steps involved with this part of the installation are:

▲ The New Partnership Wizard is displayed.

▲ Next you will be prompted for the device name and description.

▲ The partnership will be established between the two computers.

▲ You will be informed that ActiveSync is now running. This process is responsible for synchronizing data between your desktop and handheld computers.

▲ The New Partnership Wizard will complete and give you the option to view the Guided Tour if you chose to install it:

That's it. Your system is now configured and waiting for you to begin developing applications for Windows CE.

> You must establish communication between the desktop and handheld computers before continuing. You will be unable to transfer and test applications on your handheld computer without this functionality being available.
>
> If you are unable to establish a connection between your handheld and desktop computers try working through the **Communications Troubleshooter** under the Mobile Devices **Help** menu. It walks you through a diagnostic process in an attempt to rectify your communcation problem.
>
> If the troubleshooting tips don't help try shutting off your handheld, shutting down your desktop, resetting your handheld and rebooting your desktop. It's just a general reboot of everything, but it seems to work and causes far less damage than a swift kick.
>
> If you still cannot establish communication between the two computers, try reinstalling Service Pack 3. Failing this, manually install and configure the RAS Service. Start by de-installing Windows CE Services and removing the Windows NT Remote Access Service. Then re-install and configure RAS manually. Finally re-install the Windows CE Services.

What is Included with the VBCE Toolkit?

So now you have this 'Toolkit' installed on your system. What you might be wondering at this point is just what does it gives me? The answer is that it modifies the Visual Basic integrated design environment, or IDE, to provide a set of tools for creating CE applications.

In this section you are going to be introduced to the additions and modifications that have been made to the Visual Basic IDE. You will learn which Visual Basic menus have been altered, what has been removed and what the new tools enable you to do.

> While installing the VBCE Toolkit adds functionality to the Visual Basic IDE it does not remove all existing functionality that is not applicable for use when creating CE applications. For instance the syntax checker is still for the VB5 language and it will allow you to use statements, functions and objects that are not part of the Toolkit language. Remember just because the IDE allows you to do something doesn't mean that it is going to work under Windows CE.

A New Project Type

The first contact that you will have with the VBCE Toolkit occurs when you start Visual Basic. As the VB IDE is loaded the New Project dialog is displayed. This dialog, shown below, contains a new project type, the Windows CE Project:

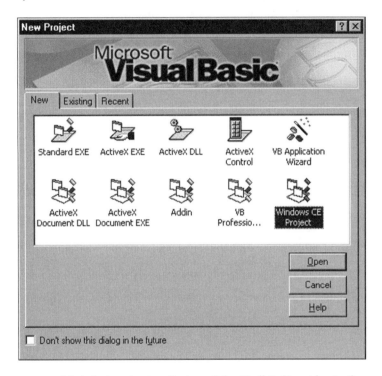

This new project type was added during the installation of the Toolkit. It resides in the **\Template\Projects** folder located under the Visual Basic folder. It is the selection of this project type that results in the use of the VBCE Toolkit within the VB IDE.

Modifications to the VB Menu Structure

Of all of the modifications that the VBCE Toolkit makes to the Visual Basic IDE the most notable are those that are made to the menu structure. Several of the menus – the File, Project, Debug, Run and Tools menu, either contain new items or have had items removed. Plus, there is a whole new menu, Windows CE, which incorporates a set of tools that aid in the development of CE applications.

> **This modified menu structure only appears when you are working with a Windows CE project.**

In this following section we will take a look at how each of these menus has been modified.

The File Menu

The addition made by the VBCE Toolkit to the File menu is minimal. It simply added the Make item that is used to create the project file that will be transferred, along with the VBCE runtime, and ActiveX controls that you use, to the handheld device. Optionally you can make your CE projects using the Make button that can be found on the VB IDE toolbar.

The Project Menu

The changes made by the Toolkit to the Project menu were to remove the capability to add project components that are not supported by the Visual Basic for Windows CE toolkit. These include MDI forms, class modules, user controls, property pages, user documents and the ActiveX designer. Also access to the References dialog has been removed.

The Debug Menu

The Debug menu is all but removed by the VBCE Toolkit. All that remains is the Step Into item. The rest of the debug functionality has been moved to the Debug window that will be discussed later in this chapter.

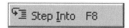

The Run Menu

The Run menu also is pared down under the VBCE Toolkit. All that remains is the Start item. Items like Start With Full Compile and Restart do not have a purpose within the Toolkit.

The Tools Menu

On the Tools menu, the Add Procedure item has been removed.

The Windows CE Menu

The most notable addition to the Visual Basic IDE is the Windows CE menu. The bulk of the new tools and references are incorporated here. It is the items that comprise this menu that we will look at next.

Application Install Wizard
Books Online
Download Runtime Files
Control Manager
Heap Walker
Process Viewer
Registry Editor
Spy
Zoom

Application Install Wizard

This wizard creates an installation program for your CE applications. Just as it is with Visual Basic applications, not only do you need to distribute your program, you also need to send the VBCE runtime and supporting files as well. We will be looking at the Application Install Wizard in far greater detail in Chapter 2.

Books Online

This item provides access to a comprehensive reference for both VBCE and the Windows CE Platform SDK. It provides a searchable index that enables you to locate information more quickly and easily. You will find that it is an excellent source for determining if a particular feature of VB is supported in VBCE.

Download Runtime Files

The purpose behind this menu item is to load runtime files on to the CE emulator or download them to a handheld device. While this is a critical procedure, the VB IDE will prompt you if it's unable to locate the appropriate runtime files on the target device.

Control Manager

The Control Manager is without question one of the most helpful tools that is provided with the VBCE Toolkit. This utility provides everything that you will need for managing ActiveX controls between the desktop computer, the CE emulator and the handheld computer.

When this utility is started it queries each of the three environments: desktop, emulator and handheld, to obtain a list of ActiveX controls that are present on each. It then allows you to install, uninstall and synchronize controls between the environments. An example of the Control Manager interface is shown in the screenshot below:

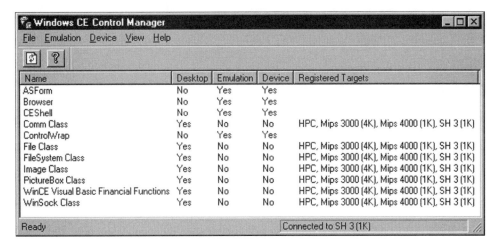

A more detailed discussion of this utility will be provided in Chapter 4.

Heap Walker

The Heap Walker will probably be the tool that you use the least from the VBCE Toolkit. It allows you to view Heap IDs and Flags information for processes that are running on your connected handheld computer. This tool can be helpful in determining if a CE application is handling memory allocation correctly.

Process Viewer

The Process Viewer provides information on the processes and threads that are currently running on your connected handheld computer. The display for this utility is divided into three separate components: process, thread and module information. An example of the Process Viewer is shown in the screenshot below. This utility will be of more benefit to those developing in Visual C++ rather than Visual Basic.

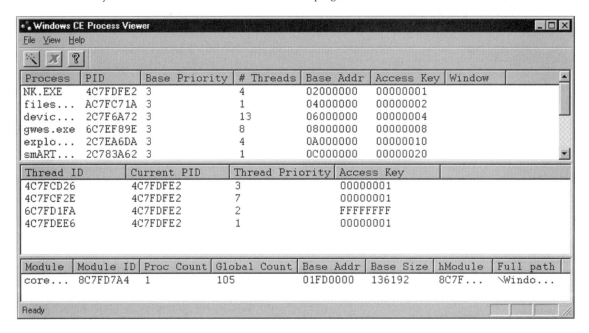

Registry Editor

The Registry Editor allows you to view and modify the contents of the registry for your desktop computer, the CE emulator and your handheld computer. Along with the Control Manager, this is one tool that you will want to understand intimately. If you are comfortable using the Registry Editor for either Windows NT or Windows 95 you shouldn't have any problems with this version. An example of this utility is shown in the screenshot below:

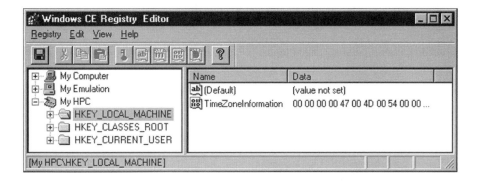

Spy

The Spy utility provides two functions:

- It allows you to view the windows that are open on a connected handheld device

- To monitor the messages that are being sent to a specific window. This utility, like the Heap Walker, will probably have limited usefulness to the typical developer, as Windows messages are not accessible to a VBCE application.

Zoom

The Zoom utility is simply a tool that allows you to do screen captures of a connected handheld computer. It is handy in any situations where you may need a picture of an application's interface while it is running on a handheld computer. All of the application screen shots in this book were obtained using Zoom.

With Zoom you can zoom in and out, print and copy images. An example of this utility is shown below, it shows the screen of a handheld computer that is running Pocket Internet Explorer.

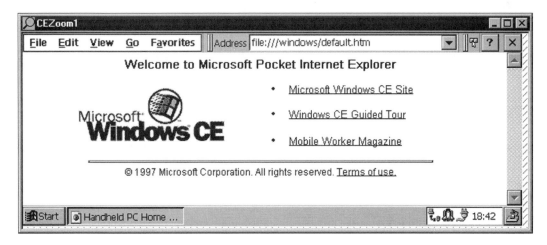

Changes to the VB Toolbar

The VBCE Toolkit provides minimal modification to the standard VB toolbar. What it does modify is to remove the Break and End buttons, since they have no use with a CE application, and to add the Make button.

A New Debug Dialog Window

The last part of the VBCE Toolkit that we will be examining is the Debugger dialog Window. This addition to the VB IDE provides a subset of the debugging tools found in Visual Basic. It allows you to debug applications on either the CE emulator or on a connected handheld device.

The CE debugger allows you to walk through your CE applications step-by-step to help you identify errors in your programming logic. It will be of benefit to you to take the time to gain a solid understanding of this debugging tool. An example of the Debugger dialog Window is shown in the screenshot below. It demonstrates working through a procedure while monitoring the value of a combo box property.

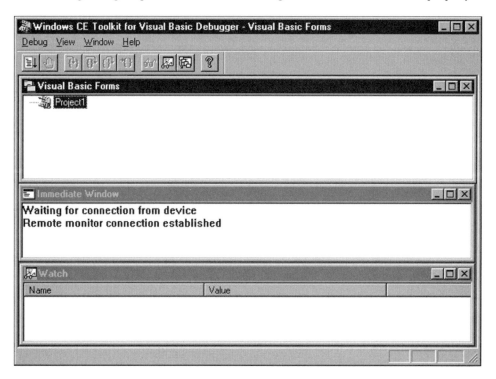

The Differences Between VB and VBCE

As an experienced VB developer, it would be a mistake on your part to think that Visual Basic for Windows CE is the same product as the Visual Basic that you have been working with. VBCE is a new language. Yes, it does share a common core language with VB, but as this section will show, there are many differences between the two languages. These differences will impact how you go about creating CE applications.

This section will focus on informing the experienced VB developer on what is missing from, or different in, VBCE. It is not intended to be a detailed language discussion, but instead a listing of the key differences between the two development tools.

VB and VBCE Use Different ActiveX Controls

While VB and VBCE share some common types of controls, there are a number of controls included with VB that are missing from VBCE. The controls themselves are physically different and in many cases have different properties, methods and events. The rule here is: don't get caught assuming that the VBCE control will work just like the equivalent VB control does.

> **Controls developed for use with Visual Basic under Windows 95 or Windows NT cannot be used in the CE environment. This is due to the differences in hardware and operating systems between these platforms.**

Also, the VBCE Toolkit does not allow you to create ActiveX controls like VB 5 does. You need Visual C++ to create ActiveX controls for use with Windows CE.

There is a Single Data Type in VBCE

VBCE supports only a single data type: variant. Variants are special in the fact that they can hold a variety of types of data. They are not the most efficient method of storing data as they not only have to store the data but also information as to what type of data they contain. When working with variants you will want to get familiar with the **Is** family of functions as in **IsDate**, **IsNumeric**, etc. which are used to determine what type of data is contained within a variant.

VBCE Uses a Different Method to Exit Your Applications

There are no **End** or **Unload** statements in VBCE. So how do you exit your programs? By using the **End** method of the **App** object. An example of this is:

```
Sub cmdExit_Click()
    App.End
End Sub
```

VBCE is Limited to a Single .BAS Module

While in VB you can incorporate numerous **.BAS** modules into a project, a VBCE project is limited to a single **.BAS** file. What this means to you as a developer is that you must create a single, large, generic **.BAS** routine in VBCE in place of the small, specific **.BAS** routines you would use in VB.

The Absence of OLE in VBCE

Neither OLE automation nor insertable OLE objects are supported in VBCE.

There Are No MDI Forms or Class Modules in VBCE

Visual Basic for Windows CE does not provide either MDI forms or class modules.

You Cannot Unload Forms in VBCE

You might want to think twice before creating multiform applications using VBCE. Since the `Unload` statement is not supported there is no way to get rid of forms once they are loaded. The best you can do is to hide them which, given the memory limitations of the handheld computer, is not always a wise decision.

There are Differences Between Form and Code Modules

Be careful when attempting to reuse forms and code modules that you created for Visual Basic with VBCE. The differences between the controls and languages can cause problems. You are better off creating new form templates and standard routines specifically for use with VBCE.

VBCE Has Limited Error Handling Capabilities

VBCE provides only a single method for handling runtime errors, the `On Error Resume Next` statement. While VB allows you to set up error handlers, in VBCE you are forced to use inline error handling instead. This approach can result in significant amounts of additional error-checking code. We will look at the VBCE error handling capabilities in more detail in Chapter 3.

VBCE Language Errors Are Handled at Runtime

One 'feature' that will certainly irritate the experienced VB developer is the fact that VBCE does not check for language errors until they are encountered at runtime. What this means is that at design time you will be allowed to use statements and keywords that are not supported by VBCE and it won't be until runtime that you will be informed, by a runtime error, that there is a problem.

There is No Support for API Calls in VBCE

VBCE, unlike VB, does not provide support for incorporating calls to APIs into your applications. So how do you extend the capabilities of VBCE? By adding ActiveX controls created with tools such as Visual C++. For an example of this, take a look at the Utility control included with this book's source code.

You Cannot Access Help from Your VBCE applications

While it is pretty easy to create Visual Basic applications that incorporate help, VBCE does not provide the same functionality. For your CE applications you must use an ActiveX control to add this functionality. There is just such a control included with the source code for this book. See the chapter on adding help to your applications for more details.

The Debug Object is Not Supported in VBCE

The debug object is not provided in VBCE. While there are debug tools provided with VBCE you do not have the popular `debug.print` method to use for displaying information while a program runs.

Absence of the Database Support

The VBCE Toolkit does not include any form of support for databases. Neither the Data Access Object nor Data control found in Visual Basic are included. So just how do you incorporate databases into your VBCE applications? Either by purchasing an ActiveX control or with the ADO CE. A detailed discussion of the ADO is provided in Chapter 7.

VBCE Uses different Methods of File I/O

While both VBCE and VB provide support for sequential, random and binary files, they use different methods. VBCE provides two controls, the **File** and **File System** controls for this purpose. Chapter 6 will give you all the information you need on working with these controls.

VB Functions That Are Missing From VBCE

There are a number of functions found in VB that are not included with VBCE. In some cases there have been similar functions provided in place of the missing functions. An example of this would be the family of **Format** functions (**FormatCurrency, FormatDateTime, FormatNumber,** and **FormatPercent**) provided in place of the VB **Format** function. Your best bet is to familiarize yourself with the list of the functions in the VBCE Toolkit's Books Online. Even then, chances are still good that you will encounter runtime errors trying to use a function from VB that is not in VBCE.

Summary

This chapter focused on preparing your system for developing VBCE applications, what the VBCE Toolkit has to offer and how VB and VBCE differ. As I showed you, installing the Toolkit, while involving several applications, is fairly straightforward. The three software packages that are needed to develop in Visual Basic for Windows CE are the Visual Basic for Windows CE Toolkit, the Windows CE Platform SDK and the Windows CE Services. The VBCE Toolkit provides an environment Add-In that modifies the Visual Basic IDE. This incorporates development tools and removes functions that are not supported as part of VBCE. The chapter concluded by providing an overview of how VBCE differs from Visual Basic. As this final section detailed, VBCE is a different product from VB. Consequently you need to adjust your application development techniques accordingly.

CHAPTER 2

Creating a Handheld Application

In this chapter I will introduce you to a process that you can use to create applications with Visual Basic for Windows CE. While this process is similar to ones you might have used to create applications with Visual Basic for Windows 95 or Windows NT, it does includes some steps unique to the handheld computer.

Through the course of this chapter I will walk you through this complete development process, from the creation of a new project, to the deployment of the finished application. Along the way you will learn how to use the key components of the VBCE Toolkit. If you are an inexperienced VB developer, I would recommend that you work through this chapter from beginning to end, using the step-by-step instructions as a guide to building this chapter's example program. On the other hand, an experienced VB developer may simply wish to skim through the chapter, focusing on the parts of the development process that are unique to CE applications. Either way, upon finishing this chapter you should be comfortable with:

 The process used to create applications using the VBCE Toolkit

 How to use the key components of the Toolkit

At the heart of this chapter is a nine-step process I use to create applications with the VBCE Toolkit. This will take you through everything from creating a new project, via testing in both the CE emulator and a handheld computer, to deploying your application using the Application Install Wizard. So let's get right at it. The completion of your first CE application is only a chapter away.

The CE Application Creation Process

As I have said, the process of creating applications for Windows CE has many similarities to the process used to create applications for Windows 95 or NT. Tasks such as creating the project, building the user interface and coding event procedures are identical between Visual Basic and the VBCE Toolkit. At the same time, however, some steps (like testing in the emulator and on the handheld computer) are unique to the CE environment. The focus of this chapter is, therefore, to detail each step in the development process and to provide you with step-by-step instructions so that you may become familiar with this process.

The nine-step process we will be using to create a Visual Basic for Windows CE application is as follows:

 Create a new project

 Set the project properties

 Construct the user interface

 Set the properties of the forms and controls

- ▲ Add code to specify what the application is to perform
- ▲ Test and debug the program in the CE emulator
- ▲ Test and debug the program on a handheld computer
- ▲ Create an installation program
- ▲ Test the installation program

Rather than providing a theoretical overview of each of these steps, we will instead look at each step as they are applied to an application that we will be constructing. This will, in fact, be the focus of the remainder of this chapter.

Time Manager – A Step-By-Step Example

In the demonstration of the CE application creation process we'll be building an example program, called Larry Roof's Time Manager. This application is a simple time billing program that allows you to track, categorize and bill your time; incorporating a timer that can be started, paused and stopped. This example will be enhanced as we proceed through the first part of this book to incorporate access to a CE database and a help file.

Step-By-Step Projects – The Recipe

As was detailed in the Introduction to this book, step-by-step projects will be presented in the following format:

- ▲ **Viewing the Completed Project:** I will start a project by showing you a completed example. This way you get to see what you are building before you begin.

- ▲ **List of Requirements:** Next I will provide you with a detailed list of the requirements for the application.

- ▲ **Designing the Application:** For each project we will then walk through the design, especially noting any special considerations for the CE environment.

- ▲ **Development of the Application:** The development of each application will be examined in detail so that you aren't left on your own to figure out how a program works.

- ▲ **Testing:** With each project you will learn testing techniques that you can apply to your own projects.

- ▲ **Deployment:** No CE application would be complete without an installation routine. Each of the applications presented in this book includes an installation program.

Three of these items; development of the application, testing and deployment are the nine-step application creation process itself.

Time Manager – The Completed Project

Before we start constructing the Time Manager application, let's take a look at the completed project. I use this approach because I believe that seeing the finished product aids in understanding discussions on its development.

> **You must have already downloaded and run the setup for the software included with this book to perform this step.**

To install the initial version of my Time Manager on your handheld computer follow these steps:

▲ Establish a connection between your desktop and handheld computers

▲ Using the instructions laid out in Appendix A find the version of Larry Roof's Time Manger for Chapter 2

▲ Follow the installation directions

Using Time Manager

Once you have completed the installation of this example, run it on your handheld computer. The Time Manager interface should be displayed as shown in the screenshot below:

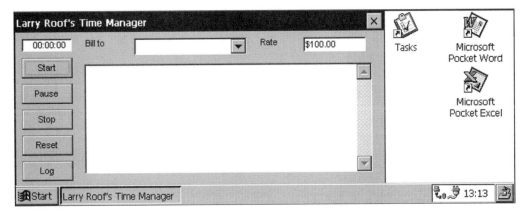

Test out the features of this application. While this version of my Time Manager provides minimal functionality it does support basic timing with the Timer control. To see this use the command buttons to start, pause, stop and reset the timer.

Time Manager – The Requirements

This initial version of my Time Manager application is primarily intended to demonstrate the creation of a simple application using the VBCE Toolkit. As such, the functionality it needs to provide is minimal. The only requirements for this version are to provide:

- A working timer that can be started, paused, stopped and reset
- Ability to select a client to bill for this time
- Ability to specify an hourly rate at which to bill
- Simple note taking capability

Time Manager – The Design

Version 1 of my Time Manager application has a fairly simple design. There is minimal functionality provided with this version. All that it will do is allow the user to time a session. It will not calculate or store billing information. Subsequent versions of the Time Manager will incorporate a CE database and a help file. The design of this version will thus be limited to:

- A single form
- Five command buttons for starting, pausing, stopping, resetting and logging time
- A combo box from which client names can be selected (we'll add the names in Chapter 7)
- A text box in which an hourly rate can be entered
- A multi-line text box for notes

Now that you have an understanding of what the Time Manager application is and what capabilities it has to offer we will turn our attention to the process of constructing the application.

You may want to remove this initial version of the Time Manager program from your handheld computer at this time. The easiest way to accomplish this is through the Start menu, then Settings, Control Panel and finally Remove Programs.

Time Manager – The Construction

In the pages that follow I will lead you through all nine steps of the creation process using the Time Manager application as a demonstration. I would suggest that you work along with the instructions to create your own copy of the Time Manager.

The file Chapter 2 version of **TimeManager.vbp** *in the source code contains a completed version of this project. Refer to Appendix A for instructions on downloading and installing the examples included in this book.*

Step 1 - Starting a New Project

This first step creates a new Windows CE project.

Start Visual Basic. The Visual Basic Integrated Design Environment, or IDE, will be displayed along with the New Project dialog as shown below:

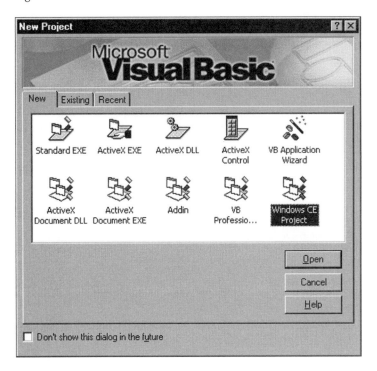

Select the Windows CE Project from the New Tab of this dialog. The template for this new project type was added to your system during the installation of the VBCE Toolkit.

Click the Open button to create the new Windows CE project. The default CE project will be loaded into the Visual Basic IDE.

Step 2 - Setting the Project Properties

The first thing that you want to do with a new project is to set its **Project Properties**. Much of this step will be new even to the experienced VB developer as it relates solely to CE applications. The Windows CE project template lends a hand here by automatically displaying the Project Properties dialog upon creation of a new Windows CE project. You can return to this dialog later by selecting the Project Properties menu item from the Project menu.

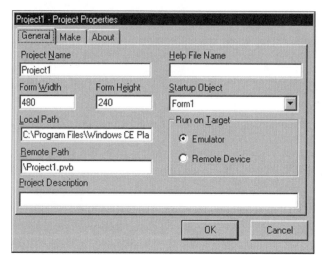

For our Time Manager example program we will use the following settings:

Set the Project Name to TimeManager.

Leave the default Form Width and Height values. Normally you would set these properties to match your needs. Typically, CE applications are run full screen, which means your form size should match the size of the display of your target handheld device. For newer handhelds this would typically be 640 x 240 but for older units this would be 480 x 240. We will see in Chapter 3 how you can adjust the form size at runtime to match the display of the system on which the application is running.

Make sure that you set the form size that you want in this opening dialog. The form size settings on the Project Properties dialog do not affect the size of the form after the project is created. If you want to change the size of the form later you must do so by setting the Width property of the form.

Modify the Local Path value by changing the filename at the end of the path from **Project1.pvb** to **TimeManager.pvb**. This is a work area where a copy of your project will be stored before being run from within the VB IDE.

Set the Remote Path value to **\TimeManager.pvb**. This is where the application will be sent to when downloaded to a connected handheld device.

Set the Project Description to Larry Roof's Time Manager app, Chapter 2. This property has little use other than for the developer.

Leave the Help File Name empty. This property is not used by the VBCE Toolkit.

Leave the Startup Object as Form1. This setting is used to specify which form to load initially in multi-form applications.

Leave the Run on Target option box as Emulator. This configuration controls where your application will be run when it is executed from within the VB IDE. The options are either in the CE emulator or on a connected handheld device.

Your completed Project Properties dialog should now match this screenshot:

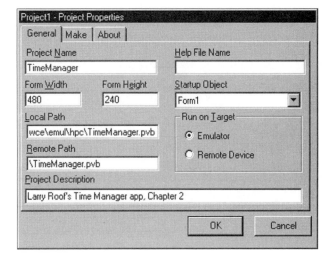

Click the OK button to close the Project Properties dialog.

Finish this step by saving your new project. This process is identical to how it would be done in Visual Basic. Under the File menu select Save Project. Save the form to the file **TimeManager.frm** and the project to the file **TimeManager.vbp**.

Step 3 - Constructing the User Interface

You now have a new project that is comprised of a single form – pretty much what you are used to. The primary difference with this project is that the form has been set to the size you specified in the Project Properties dialog:

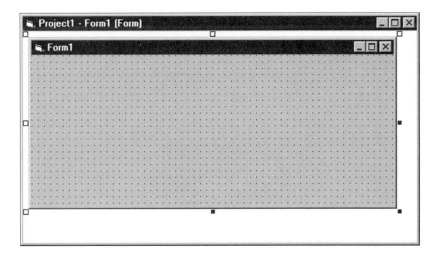

In this step you will be constructing the user interface for the Time Manager application. The process you will use is just like what you would use for any other VB application.

If you closed it open the **Form1** form.

Add controls to the interface so that it looks like this:

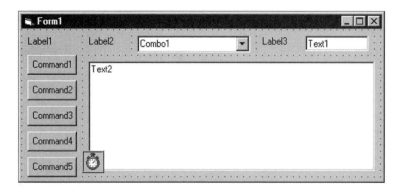

> The Visual Basic IDE does not prohibit you from adding controls to the toolbox that are not intended for use with Windows CE. However, it will stop you from placing a copy of the unsupported control onto a form.

Finish this step by saving your project.

Step 4 - Setting the Form and Control Properties

Now that you have added the controls to the interface of the Time Manager, let's turn our attention to configuration of the form and the control properties. Again, the process used here is identical to that used in Visual Basic.

Set the properties for the form and controls to match the following table:

Object	Property	Value
Form (Form1)	Name	**frmTimeManager**
	Caption	Larry Roof's Time Manager
Time display label (Label1)	Name	**lblTimeDisplay**
	Alignment	2 – Center
	BackColor	&H00FFFFFF& (white)
	BorderStyle	1 – Fixed Single
	Caption	00:00:00

Object	Property	Value
Bill to label (Label2)	Caption	Bill to:
Bill to combobox (Combo1)	Name	**cboBillTo**
	Text	\<Blank\>
Rate label (Label3)	Caption	Rate:
Rate textbox (Text1)	Name	**txtRate**
	Text	\<Blank\>
Start command button (Command1)	Name	**cmdStart**
	Caption	Start
Pause command button (Command2)	Name	**cmdPause**
	Caption	Pause
Stop command button (Command3)	Name	**cmdStop**
	Caption	Stop
Reset command button (Command4)	Name	**cmdReset**
	Caption	Reset
Log command button (Command5)	Name	**cmdLog**
	Caption	Log
Note textbox (Text2)	Name	**txtNotes**
	MultiLine	True
	ScrollBars	2 – Vertical
	Text	\<Blank\>
Timer control (Timer1)	Name	**tmrClock**
	Enabled	False
	Interval	**500** (a half-second)

At this point your form should have an appearance similar to this one:

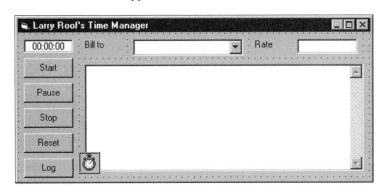

Finish this step by saving your project.

> Normally you might test your interface out on a handheld device at this point,
> before proceeding any further with the development of your application. What you
> will find is what looks good to you on your large desktop monitor might not work
> as well on the targeted system. If possible involve an end user of your application
> in this evaluation process as well. As this is the first time through the process we
> will wait until Step 7 - Testing on a Handheld Computer to try out our interface on
> a handheld.

Step 5 - Adding Your Coding

The next step in our development process is to add the code that will define how our application
performs. For experienced Visual Basic programmers, this step is just the same as the process used to
create desktop applications.

Add the following code to the General Declarations section of the form module:

```
Option Explicit

Const DEFAULTRATE = 100   ' The standard rate to charge clients
Dim mdtmElapsedTime       ' Used to track the time that has elapsed
Dim mdtmStartTime         ' Holds the time that the timer was started
```

> If you are an experienced Visual Basic programmer, you will have to get used to
> working with the VBCE Toolkit's single data type – variant.

Add the following code to the **Form_Load** event procedure that displays the default rate to bill clients:

```
Private Sub Form_Load()

' Initialize the controls on the form
  txtRate.Text = FormatCurrency(DEFAULTRATE)

End Sub
```

> *This procedure demonstrates the use of the VBCE's* **FormatCurrency** *function. Included in the*
> *Toolkit language is a set of* **Format** *functions, which take the place of Visual Basic's more flexible*
> **Format** *function. You will see another of the* **Format** *functions in a moment.*

Add the following code to the **cmdStart_Click** event procedure, which handles the starting of the timer:

```
Private Sub cmdStart_Click()

' Adjust the time as needed to take care of the differences between
' "paused" and "stopped" modes.
  If (cmdStop.Enabled = False) Then
```

```
      mdtmElapsedTime = 0
   End If
   mdtmStartTime = Now

' Set the availability of buttons.
   cmdStart.Enabled = False
   cmdPause.Enabled = True
   cmdStop.Enabled = True
   cmdReset.Enabled = False
   cmdLog.Enabled = False

' Turn on the clock.
   tmrClock.Enabled = True

End Sub
```

The **If** statement at the beginning of this procedure is used to handle the differences in calculating time between starting from scratch and restarting the timer after it has been paused. We tell what mode we are currently in by checking the **Enabled** property of the **cmdStop** control. If it has a value of **False** we are stopped, a value of **True** means we are paused.

Add the following code to the **cmdStop_Click** event procedure, which handles the stopping of the timer:

```
Private Sub cmdStop_Click()

' Set the availability of buttons.
   cmdStart.Enabled = False
   cmdPause.Enabled = False
   cmdStop.Enabled = False
   cmdReset.Enabled = True
   cmdLog.Enabled = True

' Turn off the clock.
   tmrClock.Enabled = False

End Sub
```

Add the following code to the **cmdPause_Click** event procedure, which handles the pausing of the timer:

```
Private Sub cmdPause_Click()

' Set the availability of buttons.
   cmdStart.Enabled = True
   cmdPause.Enabled = False
   cmdStop.Enabled = True
   cmdReset.Enabled = False
   cmdLog.Enabled = False

' Save the time that has elapsed up to this point and stop the clock.
   mdtmElapsedTime = Now - mdtmStartTime + mdtmElapsedTime
   tmrClock.Enabled = False

End Sub
```

Add the following code to the **cmdReset_Click** event procedure, which handles resetting the controls on the form. This procedure would be used to clear the values from a previous billing session before starting a new session:

```
Private Sub cmdReset_Click()

' Reset all of the controls.
  cboBillTo.ListIndex = -1
  txtRate.Text = FormatCurrency(DEFAULTRATE)
  txtNotes.Text = ""
  lblTimeDisplay.Caption = "00:00:00"

' Set the availability of buttons.
  cmdStart.Enabled = True
  cmdPause.Enabled = False
  cmdStop.Enabled = False
  cmdReset.Enabled = False
  cmdLog.Enabled = False

End Sub
```

Add the following code to the **cmdLog_Click** event procedure, which after the chapter on CE databases will handle the saving of information from the current billing session. Presently, it does nothing more than set buttons:

```
Private Sub cmdLog_Click()

' Set the availability of buttons.
  cmdStart.Enabled = False
  cmdPause.Enabled = False
  cmdStop.Enabled = False
  cmdReset.Enabled = True
  cmdLog.Enabled = False

End Sub
```

Add the following code to the **tmrClock_Timer** event procedure, which handles the calculation and display of the running time:

```
Private Sub tmrClock_Timer()

  Dim dtmCurrentTime
  Dim strTempString
  Dim strTimeString

' Update the time display. The two format strings are used to provide the
' leading "00:" effect that I wanted for the display.
  dtmCurrentTime = Now
  strTimeString = FormatDateTime(dtmCurrentTime - mdtmStartTime + _
            mdtmElapsedTime, vbShortTime)
  strTempString = FormatDateTime(dtmCurrentTime - mdtmStartTime + _
            mdtmElapsedTime, vbLongTime)
' Test to see which time format is being used.
  If Right(strTempString, 1) = "M" Then
```

```
            strTimeString = strTimeString & Mid(strTempString, _
                    Len(strTempString) - 5, 3)
        Else
            strTimeString = strTimeString & Mid(strTempString, _
                    Len(strTempString) - 2, 3)
            lblTimeDisplay.Caption = strTimeString
        End If

    End Sub
```

You will notice that I have included an **If** statement which tests to see what the result of formatting with **vbLongTime** is. This is because there are two basic ways of formatting the date. In the US, for example, the **vbLongTime** constant adds an AM or PM onto the end of the time. In Europe, however, these additional characters are not there. Thus in order for my program to work correctly all around the world I needed to check the result of the formatting with **vbLongTime**.

Finish this step by saving your project.

> **Until you are familiar with the differences between the Visual Basic and the VBCE languages I would suggest that you incrementally test your code. Since the VB IDE does not prohibit you from using statements and keywords that are not part of the Toolkit language, it won't be until you run your program that you will become aware of these problems. Read on to find out how to test your code.**

Step 6 - Testing in the CE Emulator

Finally, you are ready to test your application. Most of what you have done up to this point has been nearly identical to the steps you would have taken in creating a normal Visual Basic application. Here, you will be introduced to something new – testing in the CE emulator.

The Windows CE emulator is an application that runs on your desktop machine and emulates an operating CE machine. What it provides to you, as a developer, is an environment in which you can quickly test your CE applications. Also, because of this CE emulator, you do not actually need to have a handheld computer to build applications for a handheld computer.

The CE emulator is for all practical purposes a functional CE machine sitting on your desktop. It has a registry that can be configured, supports the CE object store for database functionality (more on this in Chapter 7) and allows you to add and use ActiveX controls (more on this in Chapter 4).

The general rule of thumb is to do the bulk of your testing using the CE emulator. It is simply quicker and easier to accomplish than testing on a connected handheld computer. Then once you have your program running as desired in the emulator you can switch your testing to a handheld computer for final adjustments.

Follow this process to test your application in the CE emulator:

First you need to configure your project to run in the CE emulator. Under the Project menu select TimeManager Properties (This should be the last menu item under the Project menu). On the Project Properties dialog confirm that the Emulator option button from the Run on Target configuration is selected.

Where your application will run during testing is controlled by the Run on Target setting that is located on the Project Properties dialog.

Before you can use the CE emulator to test for the first time you need to download the VBCE Toolkit runtime files. Under the Windows CE menu, select Download Runtime Files. A download status dialog will be displayed which will inform you of the download progress.

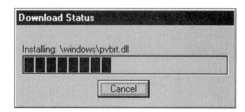

This step should not need to be performed again for future testing unless the emulator's supporting files are deleted or corrupted. You will be prompted to perform this step if you have not already done so.

The Windows CE emulator will be displayed as shown in the screenshot below:

While the CE emulator is automatically started when you run a program from within the VB IDE, it can also be manually started when VB is not running. Using the Start menu find the Windows CE Platform SDK folder and select Desktop Handheld PC Emulation.

To run the Time Manager application in the CE emulator select Start from under the Run menu. You may be warned that there is no startup form. To correct this problem set the Startup Object under the Project Properties Dialog.

A step is performed automatically for you when you select to Start your program. The Make project step is included into the Start process. Make project is responsible for placing a copy of your **.pvb** file in the location specified by the Project Properties dialog.

The Debugger Window will be displayed. If you have the Immediate Window visible within the Debugger Window you will see the statements Waiting for connection from device and Remote monitor connection established displayed.

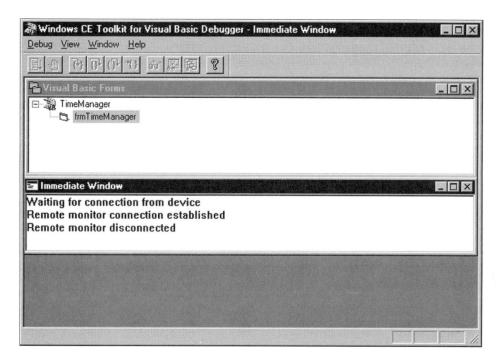

The Time Manager application will be run in the emulator. An example of this is shown in the screenshot below:

Try out the application. Click on the Start command button. The time display should start to increment. Test the other buttons as well. To exit the test, click on the X in the upper right corner of the window. You will be asked if you want to exit the debugger. Select Yes.

To exit the emulator, select Suspend under the Start menu on its interface.

Your version of the Time Manager program is now resident in the CE emulator. To run it again at a later time simply select Run from under the Start menu on the emulator, then enter **TimeManager.pvb** *in the Run dialog Open: combo box and click the OK button.*

> **You do not need to exit the emulator after each test. Simply leave the emulator window open and switch back to the Visual Basic IDE.**

Step 7 - Testing on a Handheld Computer

Well, while the CE emulator is pretty cool, the whole purpose of this book is to show you how to create applications for the handheld computer. In this step you will learn how to run your CE program on your handheld PC.

To configure your project to run on the CE handheld device, under the Project menu select TimeManager Properties. On the Project Properties dialog confirm that the Remote Device option button from the Run on Target configuration is selected.

Before you can use the connected handheld computer to test for the first time you need to download the VBCE runtime files. If you forget to perform this step it will be done automatically for you. Under the Windows CE menu, select Download Runtime Files. A message will be displayed informing you that a connection is about to be made to the remote device. Then a download status dialog will be displayed which will inform you of the download progress.

> *This step should not need to be performed again for future testing unless the handheld computer is hard reset or the supporting files are deleted or corrupted.*

Run your project by selecting Start from under the Run menu.

A message will be displayed informing you that a connection is about to be made to a remote device. The Debugger Window will be displayed. If you have the Immediate Window visible within the Debugger Window you will see the statements Waiting for connection from device and Remote monitor connection established displayed.

After a short delay the Time Manager application will be run on your handheld computer. An example of this is shown in the screenshot below:

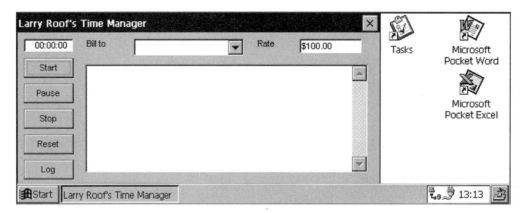

Try out the application. Click on the Start command button. The time display should start to increment. Test the other buttons as well. To exit the test, click on the X in the upper right corner of the window. On your desktop computer you will be asked if you want to exit the debugger. Select Yes.

The screenshot above demonstrates a problem that you may encounter in your CE applications, where the form does not make complete use of the display. In this example the form will only take up approximately 75 percent of a 640 x 240 display. You will learn how you can work around this problem in the next chapter.

Your version of the Time Manager program is now resident on your handheld computer. To run it again at a later time simply select Run from under the Start menu on the handheld, then enter **TimeManager.pvb** in the Run dialog Open: combo box and click the OK button.

Step 8 - Creating an Installation Program

Now that we have a completed application, the next step is to create an installation program. This program will handle the downloading of your application and its supporting files to a handheld device. In this step you will be led through the Application Install Wizard that is included with the VBCE toolkit.

From within the Visual Basic IDE select Application Install Wizard from under the Windows CE menu. The following dialog will be displayed:

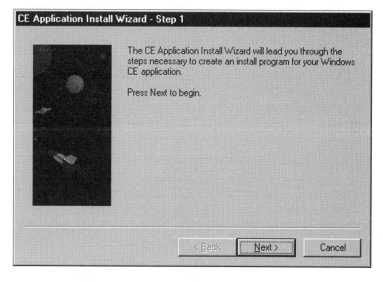

The CE Application Install Wizard is similar to the Application Setup Wizard that is included with Visual Basic. Through a series of dialogs, you define what should be included with your application, where and how it should be installed and any additional files to include with the installation.

> *The CE Application Install Wizard can also be run from outside of the Visual Basic IDE. From the* Start *menu navigate through your folders until you find the* Windows CE *folder and select* Application Install Wizard.

The second dialog in the Application Install Wizard prompts you to enter the path to where you have created the **.pvb** file for your program. Click the Browse button to display the file dialog. It should be set to the folder you specified to use to create the project file in the Project Properties dialog. If not, you will have to navigate to that folder.

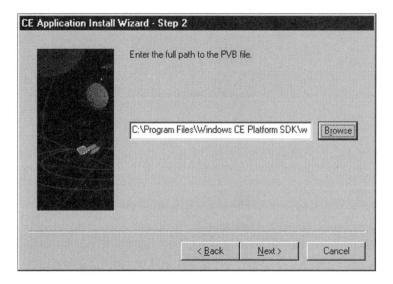

> Make sure that your project file is up to date before creating the installation. Unlike the wizard used by Visual Basic to create installations, this wizard does not give you the option to rebuild your program during the process of generating the installation kit.

To do this, while you are within the VB IDE with your project loaded, select Make TimeManager... from under the File menu to generate a **.pvb** file.

The third dialog in the CE Application Install Wizard prompts you for a path on your desktop computer to use to store the installation files. I prefer to create a subfolder under the folder where your project is stored. For example:

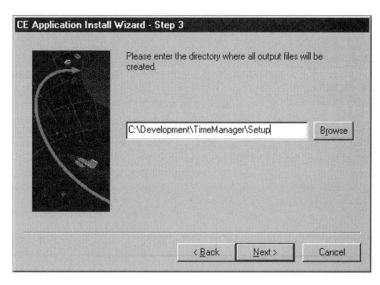

The CE Application Install Wizard functions similar to the Visual Basic Application Setup Wizard configured to produce its output to a directory. In both cases a set of files are generated to the specified directory and are used to install the application from there.

The fourth dialog in the CE Application Install Wizard is used to select the target platforms for which to create installation kits. While your project file is the same for all three platforms, the Pocket Visual Basic runtime files are not.

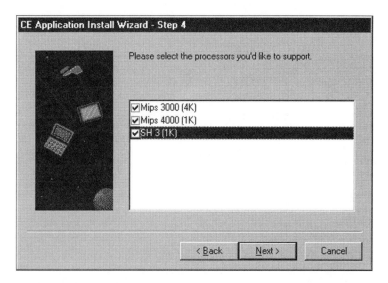

Until you are comfortable with understanding the purpose of each of the files and folders generated by the installation kit and also know which files to include for each platform, you may wish to generate three separate installations, one for each platform.

The fifth dialog of the CE Application Install Wizard is used to specify any ActiveX controls that you have used within your application and as such should be included in the installation kit.

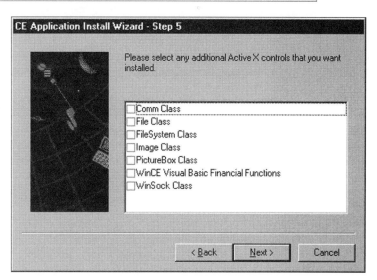

Unlike the Visual Basic Application Setup Wizard that checks your project file to determine what ActiveX controls your project makes use of, the CE Application Install Wizard requires you to specify what controls to include.

> **The ActiveX controls shown on the screenshot above include only those controls that were shipped with the Visual Basic for Windows CE Toolkit. Any third party or self-written controls that your application uses will have to be included using the next dialog.**

The sixth dialog of the CE Application Install Wizard allows you to include files other than your project file, standard ActiveX controls and the VBCE Toolkit runtime files, with the installation kit. You may use this feature to include help files, data files or any other files that are used with your application.

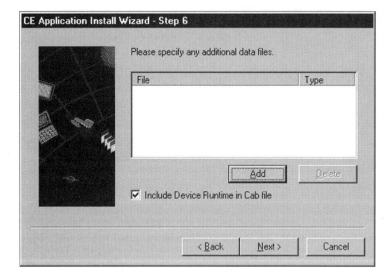

The Include Device Runtime in Cab file checkbox allows you to control whether or not the Toolkit runtime files are included with the installation kit. If you are developing an application to be used with devices that already have the Toolkit runtime files installed, you would clear this checkbox so that the runtime files would not be included. This would minimize the size of the installation kit.

> *What happens if you download a copy of the VBCE Toolkit runtime files to a device that has the runtime files already on ROM? The version that you download will be used. This allows you to update the runtime files at the cost of the space the runtime files use in RAM.*

The seventh dialog of the CE Application Install Wizard is used to specify information on where and how your application should be installed on the handheld computer.

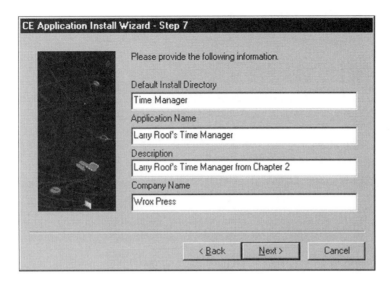

The two important items in this dialog are the installation directory and the application name.
Default Install Directory - For the installation directory, specify the folder that you would like your application placed on the handheld computer. The installation process will append **Program Files** to the front of whatever you enter. In the example below the installation directory will thus be **Program Files\Time Manager**.

Application Name – This is the name that will be given to your application when it's installed on the handheld computer.

The eighth dialog of the CE Application Install Wizard is nothing more than a "Okay, let's do it". Click the Create Install button to begin the process of generating the installation kit.

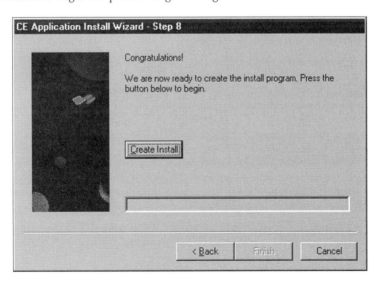

The Finish command button will be enabled to signify the completion of the process of generating the installation kit.

The CE Application Install Wizard, unlike the Application Setup Wizard included with Visual Basic, does not provide the capability of saving the settings that you use to create an installation kit. Instead, it provides instructions in a file named **Readme.txt** for rebuilding the **.cab** files used by the installation. This file can be found in the directory in which the setup was created, as shown in the figure below.

An example of the output generated from the CE Application Install Wizard can be seen in the screenshot below:

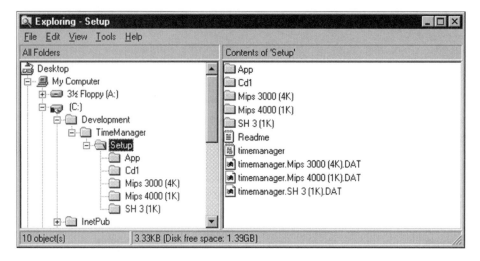

The folders generated by this process are:

- ▲ **App** Folder – Contains the project file for your application. In the case of this example that is the file **TimeManager.pvb**.

- ▲ **Cd1** Folder – Contains the VBCE Toolkit runtime files (if they were specified to be included), the setup program, and initialization file used by the setup program and **CAB** files for each target platform you specified to include with the installation kit.

- ▲ **Mips 3000**, **Mips 4000**, **SH 3** Folders – Contains processor specific files for each target platform you specified to include with the installation kit.

*The contents of the **Setup** folder can be copied to a diskette or compressed into a zip file for distribution.*

Step 9 - Test the Installation Program

With the completed installation in hand, you are ready to test just how well it works. In this step you will be led through the installation process to see how the kit performs.

To start the installation process, open Windows Explorer and navigate to the directory where you created the installation kit.

In this directory you will see a folder named **Cd1**. Enter that directory.

In the **Cd1** directory you will find the setup program, **Setup.exe**, that will perform the installation. Run the program and you will see the following dialog:

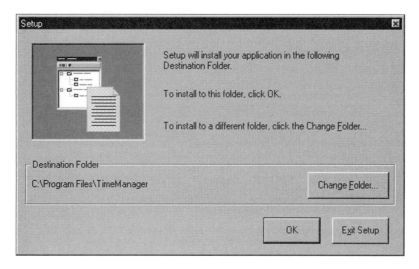

This first dialog provides you with the capability of overriding the default installation folder. For our purposes the default folder will be fine so click the OK button to continue. The following informational dialog will be displayed while information is retrieved from your handheld device:

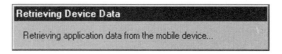

Upon completion of the retrieval of application data from your handheld device, the following dialog will be displayed which gives you one last chance to change where your application will be installed. Again, for our purposes, the default folder is fine. Simply click the Yes button.

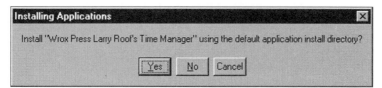

The installation process will begin. A progress dialog, as shown below, will be displayed:

Upon completion of the installation, the following dialog will be displayed. It reminds you to check on the targeted handheld device for any additional steps that may need to be performed:

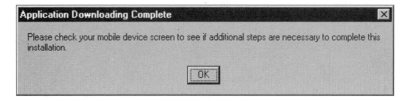

What you most typically will encounter on the handheld device is confirmation to overwrite files that already are resident on that device.

Next you will confirm the successful installation of the Time Manager program. The first step is to check if Time Manager has been added to the Start menu as shown in the screenshot below:

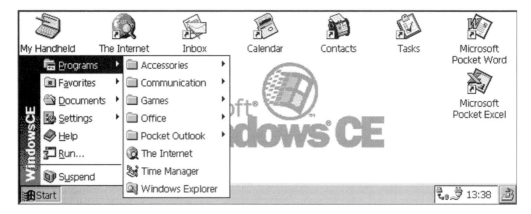

Next open up Windows Explorer on your handheld computer and navigate to the folder where you specified the installation to be placed. You should find the file **TimeManager.pvb** located in this folder as shown in the screenshot below:

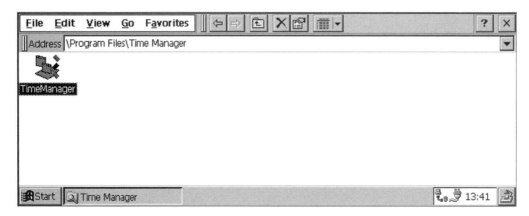

Start the application to confirm a successful installation. Try out its features. Close the application after you have finished.

The last step of this confirmation process is to verify that the uninstall process will work with our application. Under the Start menu select Settings, then Control Panel. From the Control Panel interface start Remove Programs. An example of the Remove Program interface is shown in the screenshot below.

Select your program and then click on the Remove button. The application will be removed from your handheld device.

> **This procedure does not remove any runtime files that were downloaded onto your system.**

If you are developing CE applications that will be deployed on a variety of platforms make sure to test the installation and the performance, on all of the targeted platforms.

Summary

That's it – the complete creation process, from conception to installation. I have just walked you through the creation, construction, coding, testing and deployment of a CE application. As I showed you, there are many similarities between developing an application using the Visual Basic for Windows CE Toolkit and straight Visual Basic. At the same time, VBCE contains some unique steps, such as the testing in the CE emulator and on the handheld computer.

Hopefully, at this point you are comfortable with the process of creating CE applications and we can turn our attention to common techniques that you will use to construct your own CE apps. That is the focus of the chapters to follow.

Designing Applications for Windows CE

CHAPTER 3

In Chapter 2 you were shown how to create applications using the VBCE Toolkit. However, the physical process is only part of the procedure. You also need to learn how to design applications for use on a handheld computer.

I know, you're saying to yourself, "Hey Larry, I already know how to design apps! I've been building applications for years with VB". Well this is a whole different ballgame. While some design techniques carry over from the desktop to the handheld there is a whole new set of criteria you need to consider as well. That's the focus of this chapter.

I will lead you through an examination of some of the key areas of design for CE applications. This not only includes sections on effective user interfaces but also how to cope with the restricted input capabilities found in handheld computers. I will also provide key points to consider during your design process to improve the functionality of your CE applications.

The key point to garnish from this chapter is that while the process for developing VBCE applications is similar to that used for developing desktop applications, the design of these applications can in reality be vastly different. Don't let his alarm you too much. It doesn't mean that you'll have to abandon the skills that you used to create ripping desktop apps. You will still keep your solid programming skills and still write tight, clean code. You just need to look at designing CE apps in a different way than you would desktop apps, and in this chapter I will show you how.

How to Design an Effective CE Application

As I stated in the introduction, the focus of this chapter is to show you how to design applications that will be both effective and easy to use on a handheld computer. Much of what will be presented in this chapter will address these two issues:

- Restrictions imposed by the handheld computer
- Differences in where an application may be used

It would be a mistake on your part to assume that since you are using Visual Basic to create applications for both the desktop and the handheld computer that the design process is the same. It isn't. What works well for a desktop application may not work at all for a handheld application. How a user interfaces with one of your desktop apps may be, and probably will be, different than how they work with your handheld applications.

In the following sections you will be shown three **key areas** to consider when designing handheld applications:

▲ The **display**

▲ The **method of input**

▲ The **location** of the user

Designing for the Handheld Display

I would expect by now that all of you have experienced the limitations imposed by the display on handheld devices. For those that haven't noticed let me point out the obvious. They are small and often hard to read. With that said, let me state something even more obvious. You must adjust your design techniques to accommodate for this shortcoming.

To make matters worse, the displays used on a handheld can differ substantially from one unit to the next. While the most popular units have displays that are 640 x 240, some of the older units have displays of 480 x 240. In addition, most of the handheld computers sport gray scale displays while some now feature color displays. Throw in backlighting and you have a soon difficult and complicated problem to deal with.

> *Want to create great handheld applications? Here is one simple way to improve your chances. Use your handheld computer everywhere and for everything.*
>
> > *Use it on the plane. Use it on the train.*
> > *Use it in your car. Use it at the bar.*
> > *Use it while you play. Use it every day!*
>
> *You get the point. The more that you use your computer, the better you will be at understanding what works and what doesn't work.*

Larry Roof's Display Rule Number One – Bigger is Better

What I mean is the **bigger** that you can make the objects that are part of your CE application interface, the better, or greater chance of success your apps will have.

For an example of this take a look at the first screenshot below. It's comprised of small controls with small text. It is hard to read and accordingly hard to use:

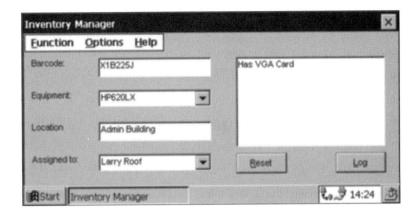

This may seem alright to read in this screenshot but try imagining it on your handheld.

Now look at the improved version. It makes use of the same basic controls, but this time the controls are larger and so is the font:

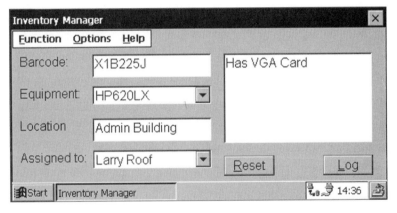

As you can see by the above example, simply by making use of larger controls and larger fonts you can dramatically improve the appearance, and usefulness of your applications.

> **The first mistake developers make when they start creating applications for the handheld computer is they think that since the physical display is smaller then the appearance of their interface should be smaller. Just the opposite applies. Make your interface *bigger* to accommodate for the shortcomings of the handheld display.**

Here's an exercise that may help you understand this rule. Go to your nearest appliance store. In the TV section of that store find the small handheld TVs. Turn on a sporting event on one of those TVs. Baseball, basketball, football, hockey – it doesn't matter. What I want you to notice is how hard it is to figure out what's going on when they show those full view shots where you are looking at the whole playing field. It simply is just too small to comprehend the detail being shown.

That is exactly the same problem that you face with handheld computers. Their displays are too small to show the same level of detail as you would on a desktop computer. So how do you make your displays bigger? Simple, make use of larger fonts and larger controls whenever possible. I typically will use font sizes in the range of 10 to 12 points. They are far easier to read yet not so large that they dominate the user interface.

Larry Roof's Display Rule Number Two – Less is More

If you are still standing in the appliance store switch the handheld TV over to a news broadcast. Wait until they go to one of those close-ups where all they show is the torso of a single newscaster. Do you notice how this is easier to view than the sporting event you just turned from? The reason? **Less is more**. What I mean by this is the less that is shown on a small display, the more successful, or easier to view, it will be.

Take for example the following screenshots. This first screenshot offers a cluttered display with too many controls packed together:

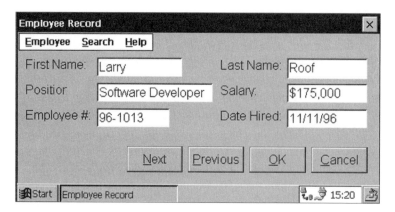

A cleaner version of this application is shown below. This revised edition has half the number of controls, they are spaced further apart, a larger font is used and as a result the screen is much simpler:

How this technique applies to your CE application design is as follows: the fewer objects that you include in an interface, the cleaner, and easier it will be to use. Don't try to fit everything onto a single screen. If you can't fit it easily onto one screen, with plenty of visual 'room to breathe', design your application so that it makes use of several, less cluttered screens.

> *If you have an application with a very complicated interface try simplifying it by dividing up the controls into different pages of a wizard. What you will find is that you can present everything that you need but in a much more workable fashion.*

Larry Roof's Display Rule Number Three – The Snapshot Test

This one is a bit trickier and requires an assistant that *has not seen your application*. The assistant can be anyone, your spouse, a co-worker or if you're really lucky, one of those magician assistant-types all done up in a sparkly outfit. Have the assistant close their eyes and then hand them your handheld computer with your application running. Now is where the snapshot part comes in. One time only, have the assistant open their eyes and examine the interface for 10 seconds. They are to build in their mind a mental 'picture' of your application. The test part of this rule is to then have the assistant explain the interface from their mental picture.

You are going to have to trust me on this one. The more of your interface the assistant can explain from their brief exposure to your application, the easier your interface is to understand.

Designing for Handheld Input

Okay, let's have a show of hands. Who among you thinks that the keyboards on handheld computers are big enough to use effectively? Well, if no one raises his or her hand it does make it easier to count. This is not a secret. The keyboards on handheld devices are too small to type on *in a normal fashion*. What does this mean to you, the designer of a handheld application? Well for starters, don't design applications that require lots of input as you might with a desktop application.

At the same time, unless you have created some type of Vulcan mind-meld ActiveX control, you have to assume that the user is going to have to use the keyboard and stylus to enter information. That is where your challenge comes in. To create truly great CE apps you must find a way to work within the limitations of a handheld computer to allow the user to easily input information.

Larry Roof's Input Rule Number One – Bigger is Better

Wait. Wasn't that display rule number one? Yes it was. And it's not by coincidence that it's the first rule of input as well. If the user is going to have to use the stylus to click on, or select controls, why not make them as **big** as you possibly can? After all, you don't want your applications to turn into some sort of a dexterity test.

Look again at the example shown earlier in this chapter. In the first screenshot the controls are small, some because of how we drew the controls and others as a result of the font that was used:

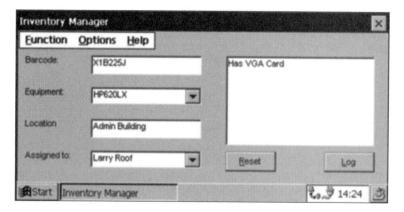

Now look at the improved version. Simply by drawing the controls bigger and using a larger font we have improved the usability of the application:

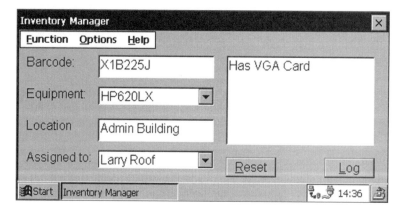

Larry Roof's Input Rule Number Two – To Each Their Own

In case you haven't noticed users like to do things their own way. That trait holds true for users of handheld computers where the input tools are limited. You will find that some users want to be able to do everything from keyboard commands. They make use of every key combination that exists to expedite the task at hand. Others will want to do as much as possible with their stylus and will only resort to the keyboard when they are forced to.

Your challenge is to design your applications to offer as many methods to perform the same input as possible. Try to incorporate the following features into all of your applications:

- Menus
- Shortcut keys
- Dropdown lists

Test your application out on a variety of handheld computers. What is a simple input process on your handheld might be difficult on another brand of computer.

The use of shortcut keys is not supported within the CE emulator. As a result you are forced to test this functionality out on your handheld computer.

Larry Roof's Input Rule Number Three – Do it for Them

You may find that this third rule is a bit harder to implement then the previous two. What **doing it for them** means is that whenever possible, have your application try to help the user with their input. Some features you may want to use are:

- Offer default values for fields whenever possible
- Auto-fill fields based upon the value of other fields
- Select existing text when moving to a field so that the user doesn't need to erase characters in addition to entering data

Designing for Handheld Usage

Handheld computers, by design, are intended to be used nearly anywhere. This is a critical point to remember while you are developing your CE applications. During the design process you must anticipate your application being used in different environments and conditions. Some items to consider are:

- **How** will your application be used? Will the user of your application be focusing intently on their handheld or merely glancing at it for information?
- **Where** will your application be used? Interface needs in a moving car differ substantially from those needed for an office.
- **When** will your application be used? Using a handheld computer in the bright light of a sunny day or the limited light of a rainy day may reduce the effectiveness of your interface design.

The key method to determine how well your application will perform under a variety of conditions is to test under a variety of conditions. I know what you are thinking, "Hey Larry, could you state something a bit more obvious?" Surprisingly, many developers never test their application anywhere but on their desktop.

Larry Roof's Usage Rule Number One – Does it Work There?

Good developers should carry their handheld computer with them at all times. No, this isn't some type of geek identification method that I'm proposing. What it does allow you to do is to test your application under a variety of situations and conditions. For instance:

- While you are standing in a local bookstore waiting patiently for the latest book from Larry Roof to arrive try running your application. Does your interface lend itself to easy usage while standing?

- Can you easily use your app while standing at a public phone booth with a phone in one hand or the phone cradled against your shoulder?

- When you are in your car at a stoplight can you make use of your app while glancing back and forth between your handheld display and the traffic light?

Larry Roof's Usage Rule Number Two – It Has to Work There

This is more of a sin than a rule. If you know that your application has to work in a particular condition or situation, then you had better test it there. If you know an app is going to be used in the field, say for cataloguing species of plants, then don't get caught designing for use in the office when that's not where it will be used.

Larry Roof's Usage Rule Number Three – The Hardware Blues

This rule is applicable to any environment, not just handheld computers. Remember this warning: Be careful not to develop your application on a top of the line computer only to have it be used on a system with fewer capabilities.

Handheld computers, like desktop computers, are offered in a variety of configurations. You will find that units have different processors and amounts of memory. As such, the performance, and usefulness of your application may vary considerably from one brand of computer to the next.

Larry Roof's Usage Rule Number Four – Right Here, Right Now

Remember when designing your application that H/PC users will often flip open their handheld computer, turn it on, use an application to get a single piece of information and then put their computer away. The fewer steps that a user has to take to access the desired information from your application the better.

Enhancing Time Manager

In this section we are going to take the design principles that we just covered and apply them to my Time Manager application that was introduced in Chapter 2. You will see how even a simple application like the Time Manager can be improved dramatically by adhering to these few rules.

What is Wrong with Time Manager?

The answer is that many things are wrong with my Time Manager application. In fact, it has problems in each of the three areas: display, input and usage. That is where we will start our examination by listing the shortcomings in each area.

Display Problems

The Time Manager application suffers from the most common problem that I find in CE applications today – the interface is too small. Notice I didn't say the display is too small. I know that the display is small. It's a handheld computer. That doesn't mean that the interface has to be small. How do you create a workable interface on a small display? For starters don't put everything in the default font. It's just too small to work with.

To make things worse the key component of the interface, the time display, is lost amongst the rest of the controls. It simply does not stand out. What is the point of having a time management tool if you have a hard time making out the time it is tracking?

Input Problems

Second to the Time Manager's display problems is its input problems. Everything on the interface is dependent upon the stylus. There are no keyboard shortcuts offered nor are there any menu substitutes for the commonly performed actions.

In addition, there are no input aids provided. There is no selection of text when the user enters a field. There is no list of items from which to select. The user is forced to handle everything with their keyboard and stylus.

The final input problem is that the controls are just too small. Activation of each requires too high a level of concentration and dexterity.

Usage Problems

The Time Manager application, as a utility category program, should be useable in a variety of settings. But in its current form it is not. The size of fonts that are used and the placement of controls limit its effectiveness to the user's desktop. Even there, the user is required to focus on the application and not the task at hand. This is hardly a desirable feature for a time management application.

Time Manager – The Revised Project

Before we look into the details of how the Time Manager application is revised, let's take a look at the completed renovation. Again, this approach is used so that you can better understand the discussions on its development.

To install the revised version of Time Manager on your handheld computer follow these steps:

- ▲ Establish a connection between your desktop and handheld computer
- ▲ Using the instructions laid out in Appendix A, find the version of Larry Roof's Time Manager for Chapter 3
- ▲ Follow the installation directions

Using the Revised Time Manager

Once you've completed the installation of this example, run it on your handheld computer. The Time Manager interface should be displayed as shown in the screenshot below:

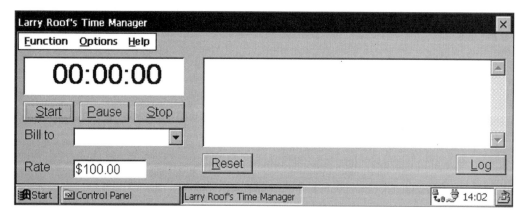

Test out the features of this application. Like the previous version of Time Manager it provides the minimal timing functionality. Some of the new features incorporated into this version are the menu control of timer functions (see items under the Eunction menu) and the access key capabilities that have been added to the command buttons.

Time Manager – The Requirements

This revised version of Larry Roof's Time Manager application is a simple rework of the version presented in Chapter 2. Its primary purpose is to demonstrate design techniques that can be applied to improve your applications. The only requirements for this version are to provide:

- A working timer that can be started, paused, stopped and reset
- Ability to specify a client to bill for this time
- Ability to specify an hourly rate at which to bill
- Simple note-taking capability

Time Manager – The Design

This second version of Larry Roof's Time Manager application, like the first, has a fairly simple design. Much of the renovation has to do with placement and sizing of the controls. The most notable addition we have made is a menu structure.

As was found in the initial version of Time Manager, this version provides minimal functionality. All that it will do is allow the user to time a session. It will not calculate or store billing information. Subsequent versions of the Time Manager will incorporate a CE database and a help file. The design of this version will be limited to these original features:

- A single form
- Five command buttons for starting, pausing, stopping, resetting and logging time
- A combo box from which client names can be selected (in this second version there are no names provided)
- A text box in which an hourly rate can be entered
- A multi-line text box for notes

Plus these new features which incorporate some of the design principles we discussed earlier in the chapter:

- A larger time display
- An improved interface for ease of use including larger controls and larger fonts
- Menu structures for easier keyboard access during operation
- Additional access keys to improve the keyboard interface
- Auto-formatting of the rate field to currency to improve data entry
- Auto-select of existing text when returning to the rate field to improve data entry
- A more logical layout of the timer control buttons
- The ability to specify a default rate

With the requirements laid out, we can turn our attention to the process of renovating the Time Manager application.

You may want to remove the revised version of Larry Roof's Time Manager program from your handheld computer at this time. The easiest way to accomplish this is through the Start menu, then Settings, Control Panel and finally Remove Programs.

Time Manager – The Construction

In the pages that follow you will be led through the nine step creation process to modify the previous version of the Time Manager application. As I mentioned in the previous chapter, I would suggest that you work along with the instructions to create your own copy of the Time Manager.

The Chapter 3 version of `TimeManager.vbp` in the source code contains a completed version of this project. Refer to Appendix A for instructions on downloading and installing the examples included in this book.

Step 1 - Starting a New Project

Since we will be using the previous version of Time Manager as a starting point this step is unneeded. Instead simply load the project you created in Chapter 2 or the finished solution from **Chapter 2\TimeManager.vbp**. See the note above for instructions on accessing example applications.

Step 2 - Setting the Project Properties

As was the case with Step 1, this step is unneeded since we are making use of an existing project.

Step 3 - Constructing the User Interface

Well technically this should read 'Reworking the user interface'. You are going to create a more useable interface for Time Manager by modifying the interface from the previous version following the instructions below:

Open the **frmTimeManager** form.

Modify and reposition the existing controls on this form to construct the interface shown in the screenshot below. The font size for all of the objects except the time display has been set to MS Sans Serif 12 point. The font used for the time display is Verdana 26 point that has been set to bold.

You don't need to use the same fonts as me. The basic idea is simply to make the text larger and clearer to read.

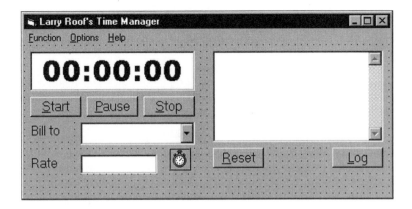

The keys to this renovation of the Time Manager interface are:

▲ The size of font that is used

▲ The placement of the controls

The larger fonts simply make it far easier to read the interface without limiting the applications functionality.

The placement of the controls lends itself to the logical use of the program. Take for instance how the Start, Pause and Stop buttons are arranged right under the timer that they control. Or how the Reset and Log buttons have been separated from the other buttons and placed in an area where they are more functionally effective.

Change the WindowState property of the Time Manager form to 2 – Maximized. This will cause the form to fill up the complete display of a handheld regardless of whether it's running a 640 x 240 or 480 x 240 resolution.

Construct the following menu structure using the Visual Basic Menu Editor:

Menu Caption	Object Name	Enabled
&Function	mnuFunction	True
&Start Timer	mnuFunctionStart	True
&Pause Timer	mnuFunctionPause	False
S&top Timer	mnuFunctionStop	False
-	mnuFunctionBar1	n/a
&Reset Timer	mnuFunctionReset	False
&Log Record	mnuFunctionLog	False
-	mnuFunctionBar2	n/a

Menu Caption	Object Name	Enabled
E&xit	mnuFunctionExit	True
&Options	mnuOptions	True
&Round Billing To Next	mnuOptionsBilling	True
&Hour	mnuOptionsHour	True
H&alf hour	mnuOptionsHalf	True
&Quarter hour	mnuOptionsQuarter	True
&Minute	mnuOptionsMinute	True
&Set Default Rate...	mnuOptionsDefault	True
&Help	mnuHelp	True
&Using Time Manager	mnuHelpUsing	True
&About Time Manager	mnuHelpAbout	True
-	mnuHelpBar1	n/a
&Error	mnuHelpError	True

Finish this step by saving your project.

Step 4 - Setting the Form and Control Properties

The only properties that we needed to set were handled in the previous step.

Step 5 - Adding your Coding

Although relatively little code has been added to this revised version of the Time Manager, there is some extra coding required for the menu structure. We will also build in some support for future features.

Our examination of the revised code will start with the click event procedures for the five command buttons. To each of these procedures you will need to add a call to the **SetMenuItems** procedure that configures the availability of menu items to match the availability of the buttons. An example of this modification is shown in the code below:

```
    Private Sub cmdStart_Click()

  ' Adjust the time as needed to take care of the differences between
  ' "paused" and "stopped" modes.
    If (cmdStop.Enabled = False) Then
      ElapsedTime = 0
    End If
    mdtmStartTime = Now
```

```
' Set the availability of buttons.
  cmdStart.Enabled = False
  cmdPause.Enabled = True
  cmdStop.Enabled = True
  cmdReset.Enabled = False
  cmdLog.Enabled = False

' Set the availability of menu items.
  SetMenuItems

' Turn on the clock.
  tmrClock.Enabled = True

End Sub
```

Add the code for the **SetMenuItems** routine to the form module as shown below. As stated earlier, this procedure configures the availability of menu items to match the corresponding command buttons:

```
Sub SetMenuItems()

' Set the menu items to match the corresponding command buttons.
  mnuFunctionStart.Enabled = cmdStart.Enabled
  mnuFunctionPause.Enabled = cmdPause.Enabled
  mnuFunctionStop.Enabled = cmdStop.Enabled
  mnuFunctionReset.Enabled = cmdReset.Enabled
  mnuFunctionLog.Enabled = cmdLog.Enabled

End Sub
```

The constant value **DEFAULTRATE** needs to be converted to a variable so that the user, through the Options menu item, can modify it. This impacts the code in several places. First the declaration must be modified in the General Declarations section of the form module:

```
Option Explicit

Dim msngDefaultRate    ' The standard rate to charge clients.
Dim mdtmElapsedTime    ' Used to track the time that has elapsed.
Dim mdtmStartTime      ' Holds the time that the timer was started.
```

Then the **Form_Load** procedure is modified to define a default rate when the application is started. It also needs to include calling a routine that will adjust the interface of the Time Manager application to match the size of the user's display:

```
Private Sub Form_Load()

' Fit the interface to the palmtop.
  AdjustControls

' Initialize the controls on the form.
  msngDefaultRate = 100
  txtRate.Text = FormatCurrency(msngDefaultRate)

End Sub
```

Finally we need to modify the cmdReset_Click procedure:

```
Private Sub cmdReset_Click()

' Reset all of the controls.
  cboBillTo.ListIndex = -1
  txtRate.Text = FormatCurrency(msngDefaultRate)
  txtNotes.Text = ""
  lblTimeDisplay.Caption = "00:00:00"

' Set the availability of buttons.
  cmdStart.Enabled = True
  cmdPause.Enabled = False
  cmdStop.Enabled = False
  cmdReset.Enabled = False
  cmdLog.Enabled = False

' Set the availability of menu items.
  SetMenuItems

End Sub
```

Now that we taken care of that, we need to backtrack and insert the code to handle the adjustment of the interface, as shown in the example below. Since we have the form configured to start in a maximized state, it will fill up the screen. What we need to do is to use the resulting size of the form to resize and reposition controls:

```
Sub AdjustControls()

' Extend the size of the interface to match the size of the
' display on the palmtop.
  txtNotes.Width = frmTimeManager.Width - txtNotes.Left - 150
  cmdLog.Left = frmTimeManager.Width - 150 - cmdLog.Width

End Sub
```

> You can use this technique within your own applications to adjust your application's interface to displays of different sizes. The key to making this trick work is to design your interface in such a way that it can be stretched without losing its look. For example, I designed the Time Manager interface with a text box on the right side of the form that could be widened without distorting the 'look' of the application. The same holds true for the Log command button, which can be repositioned without ruining our application interface.

For the Exit menu item use the **End** method to the **App** object to terminate the program:

```
Private Sub mnuFunctionExit_Click()

  App.End

End Sub
```

> When working within the Visual Basic IDE, the **End** method will not appear in the popup list of properties and methods for the **App** object. That is because the **End** method is not supported in Visual Basic, only in Visual Basic for Windows CE.

Add the following code to the appropriate menu items under the Function menu. Each event procedure simply links a menu item to a command button:

```
Private Sub mnuFunctionLog_Click()

  cmdLog_Click

End Sub

Private Sub mnuFunctionPause_Click()

  cmdPause_Click

End Sub

Private Sub mnuFunctionReset_Click()

  cmdReset_Click

End Sub

Private Sub mnuFunctionStart_Click()

  cmdStart_Click

End Sub

Private Sub mnuFunctionStop_Click()

  cmdStop_Click

End Sub
```

Add the following code to the appropriate menu items under the Options | Round Billing To Next submenu. As was with the previous Options submenu, the functionality which makes use of this configuration will be added in Chapter 7. This code simply toggles menu checkmarks:

```
Private Sub mnuOptionsHour_Click()

  If Not mnuOptionsHour.Checked Then
    mnuOptionsHour.Checked = True
    mnuOptionsHalf.Checked = False
    mnuOptionsQuarter.Checked = False
    mnuOptionsMinute.Checked = False
  End If

End Sub
```

```
Private Sub mnuOptionsHalf_Click()

  If Not mnuOptionsHalf.Checked Then
    mnuOptionsHour.Checked = False
    mnuOptionsHalf.Checked = True
    mnuOptionsQuarter.Checked = False
    mnuOptionsMinute.Checked = False
  End If

End Sub
```

```
Private Sub mnuOptionsQuarter_Click()

  If Not mnuOptionsQuarter.Checked Then
    mnuOptionsHour.Checked = False
    mnuOptionsHalf.Checked = False
    mnuOptionsQuarter.Checked = True
    mnuOptionsMinute.Checked = False
  End If

End Sub
```

```
Private Sub mnuOptionsMinute_Click()

  If Not mnuOptionsMinute.Checked Then
    mnuOptionsHour.Checked = False
    mnuOptionsHalf.Checked = False
    mnuOptionsQuarter.Checked = False
    mnuOptionsMinute.Checked = True
  End If

End Sub
```

One of the new features that we added to Time Manager is the ability to set a default rate to charge clients. This falls under the design for input category, where we can minimize what the user is required to enter by providing meaningful default values.

This functionality is added with the following code. Here we use the **InputBox** function to solicit the user for a default value. In addition, this code will set the current rate to this new rate if a billing session is not already in progress.

```
Private Sub mnuOptionsDefault_Click()

  Dim strTempString
  strTempString = InputBox("Enter the default rate. This rate will
  ↳ be used whenever a new record is started.", "Set Default
  ↳ Rate", msngDefaultRate)
  If (strTempString <> "") Then
    If IsCurrency(strTempString) Then
      'A currency value specified so set the Derault rate
      msngDefaultRate = Right(strTempString, Len(strTempString) - 1)
    Else
      If IsNumeric(strTempString) Then
        msngDefaultRate = strTempString
      End If
    End If

    'Update the billing rate box if the timer is not active
    If (Not tmrClock.Enabled) Then
      txtRate.Text = FormatCurrency(msngDefaultRate)
    End If
  End If

End Sub
```

Add the **IsCurrency** function as shown below. This function is used to verify that the value entered is the appropriate data type:

```
Function IsCurrency(strExpressionToCheck)

' This routine checks to see if the specified expression is in currency format.
  If (Mid(strExpressionToCheck, 1, 1) = "$") Then
    If (IsNumeric(Right(strExpressionToCheck, _
    Len(strExpressionToCheck) - 1))) Then
      IsCurrency = True
    Else
      IsCurrency = False
    End If
  Else
    IsCurrency = False
  End If

End Function
```

You may be wondering why I have used the **Mid** *function and not* **Left** *in the above code. This is due to a bug with the SDK that prevents you from using the* **Left** *function from within a form.*

There are two new features we added associated with the rate field. The first automatically selects the existing text in this control whenever the user tabs to the rate field. The feature is implemented via the **GotFocus** event as shown in the following code:

```
Private Sub txtRate_GotFocus()

  SelectText txtRate

End Sub
```

The **SelectText** procedure is a universal procedure that you can incorporate into your own applications. Simply call the procedure passing the name of the control to select:

```
Sub SelectText(ControlToSelect)

' Select the text whenever the user moves to this control.
  ControlToSelect.SelStart = 0
  ControlToSelect.SelLength = Len(ControlToSelect.Text)

End Sub
```

Another new feature of this version of the Time Manager is the automatic formatting of the rate field. This is handled in the **LostFocus** event of the rate control. The VBCE function **FormatCurrency** is one of several functions that have been provided to take the place of VB's more universal **Format** function:

```
Private Sub txtRate_LostFocus()

' Convert the text to currency format whenever the user leaves
' this control.
  txtRate.Text = FormatCurrency(txtRate.Text)

End Sub
```

Finish this step by saving your project.

Step 6 - Testing in the CE Emulator

Next you will test your version of the Time Manager application out in the emulator. Make sure that Project Properties option for Run on Target is set to Emulator before running your project. Once the application is running in the emulator, test the functionality of the new features and judge what you think about the new appearance that was introduced with this version. Some things that you might want to try include:

- The command buttons to start, pause, stop, reset and log the time
- The menu items that correspond to the command buttons
- Setting the default value to bill clients
- The rate text being selected when you tab to its field
- Entering a rate to bill a client as just a number, and have it reformatted to a currency value when you leave the field
- Input a brief note
- Use just the keyboard to control the timer either through the command button or menu access keys

Step 7 - Testing on a Handheld Computer

In any application that you create, the testing stage has to be the most telling step in the process. Why? Because it's through testing that you validate all of your work up to this point. What you need to do here is run through all of the tests that you ran in the CE emulator. Don't assume anything is okay just because it functioned properly in the emulator.

By doing these tests you are validating all of the modifications that you made to Time Manager to improve its usefulness and functionality.

Auto-Sizing the Form

Take a look at the screenshots below to see how the revised Time Manager application automatically adjusts its interface to match the size of the user's display.

In this first example, taken from the CE emulator, you see the narrow version of Time Manager as the emulator runs a 480 x 240 display:

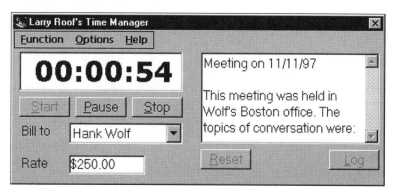

The second example, taken from a connected handheld device, displays the wide version of Time Manager on the 640 x 240 display of the handheld. Note how the note text box is widened to fill up the size of the form and also how the Log command button is moved as well. The result is a form that looks as if it were designed just with the wide display in mind when in actuality we created it for a 480 x 240 resolution display:

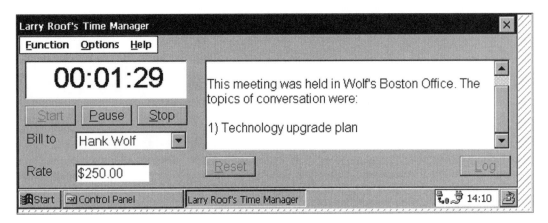

Step 8 - Creating an Installation Program

Normally you would complete the process by creating an installation program. For the purpose of this exercise you can skip this step.

Step 9 - Test the Installation Program

There is some way to go before the Time Manager is finally complete so we did not build an installation program at this stage. Consequently, testing of the installation program is not required.

Summarizing the Revised Time Manager

Hopefully, by this point you can see how the modifications that were made have improved both the functionality and usefulness of this application. What I want you to take away from this exercise is just how dramatically some simple modifications in design can improve your CE applications.

Converting Your Desktop Applications

During the beta development stage of the VBCE Toolkit, one question that seemed on everyone's mind was, "How do I convert my desktop applications written in Visual Basic to run under Windows CE?" In attempting to answer this question, many found out that the VBCE Toolkit was missing one or more key components that they had used in the construction of their desktop applications. At that point, they would get upset or disgusted with this new product and write it off. What they needed to understand was the exact purpose of the VBCE Toolkit. The Toolkit was designed to provide an easy way to create applications for *the Windows CE operating system*. Pretty tricky huh? Note, nowhere in defining the purpose of Visual Basic for Windows CE did I mention that it was intended to allow you to run applications designed for the desktop on a handheld computer.

Even if the VBCE Toolkit allowed you to use every function of Visual Basic itself, I still contend that there is little practicality to reusing desktop applications on a handheld computer. My reasoning is simple. All of the points that I covered earlier in this chapter quite clearly demonstrate the unsuitability and impracticality of running desktop apps on a handheld. The fact of the matter is that handheld computers are different from desktop computers. How they are used is different. Where they are used is different.

> *In case you haven't guessed by this point, I'm not a strong supporter of converting desktop applications for use on handheld computers. What I do support is the development of complementary applications; a version that runs on the desktop and another that runs on the handheld. They can share the same backend systems, making use of the same relational databases and servers. But their interfaces and their features will typically need to be adjusted to provide the maximum functionality given the environment in which they run.*

I have found it useful to develop subroutines and functions that can be used for both environments, the desktop and the handheld. In doing so you can encapsulate key components of an application for shared use. The best approach that I have found is to write these common routines using the subset of commands that are supported by both Visual Basic and the VBCE Toolkit.

For variables I will have two statements for the declaration of each variable, using the more descriptive version in VB where it is supported. An example of this technique is shown below. Simply comment out the version you are not using:

```
Dim curTotalWages As Currency       ' VB
'Dim curTotalWages            ' VB for CE
```

Handling Errors in Your Apps

No discussion on design would be complete without considering error handling. The reason for this is that in most applications there is some chance of encountering an error. Therefore you had better plan for it in your application design.

Now there is nothing I would like to say more than, "Just do it the same way as you would in VB". The fact of the matter is though that like everything else we have been looking at, error handling in Visual Basic for Win CE has to be approached differently than error handling in VB.

The On Error Resume Next Statement

The VBCE Toolkit provides only a single method for error handling, the **On Error Resume Next** statement. The more commonly used VB statement, **On Error GoTo,** is not provided in VBCE.

Because of this exclusion you are forced to use what is commonly referred to as "inline error handling". This term simply means that you have to check for errors within the normal flow of your program rather than in special error handling sections of your routines.

An example of this is shown in the code fragment below. Here we use the **On Error Resume Next** statement to instruct our procedure to continue processing *even in the event that a runtime error is encountered.* What we then do is check the value of the **Number** property of the **Err** object to see if an error has occurred. It will have a value of zero (0) if no error was encountered. The other popular property of the **Err** object is the **Description** property, which provides a brief description of the error.

```
Sub ExampleRoutine ()
  On Error Resume Next            'Continue after error.

' Some operation is performed that may generate an error.

  If Err.Number <> 0 Then
    MsgBox "An error has occurred." & vbCrLf _
      & "The error number was " & Err.Number _
      & "The error description was " & Err.Description
  End If

' Some other operations are performed that would not generate an error.
End Sub
```

Using inline error handling offers one serious pitfall. It assumes that you are going to handle all of the errors that are encountered. After all, the purpose of the **On Error Resume Next** statement is to say to the VBCE runtime, "Hey, don't worry about it. I'm taking care of it." To which the runtime responds "Cool!" Therefore don't take the use of this statement lightly. It can cause you many problems if you do not correctly anticipate every situation where your program may encounter a runtime error.

The Err.Number Property

At the heart of this form of error handling is the **Number** property of the **Err** object. Understanding how this property is set is critical to writing effective error handling code.

Let's take a look at several examples to further examine just how and when the **Err.Number** property is set.

The First Err.Number Example

In our first example we set the error handler right at the top of the routine. Later, immediately after processing a statement that could generate an error, we check the value of the **Err.Number** property. If it is anything other than 0, we know that the operation failed.

```
Sub ExampleRoutine ()
  On Error Resume Next            'Continue after error.

' Some operation is performed that may generate an error.

  If Err.Number <> 0 Then
    MsgBox "An error has occurred." & vbCrLf _
      & "The error number was " & Err.Number _
      & "The error description was " & Err.Description
  End If

' Some other operations are performed that would not generate an error.
End Sub
```

The Second Err.Number Example

The approach used in the first example is fairly straightforward. Now let's take a look at a slightly more complex example:

```
Sub ExampleRoutine ()
  On Error Resume Next            'Continue after error.

' Some operation is performed that may generate an error.

' Some operation is performed that WILL NEVER generate an error.

  If Err.Number <> 0 Then
    MsgBox "An error has occurred." & vbCrLf _
      & "The error number was " & Err.Number _
      & "The error description was " & Err.Description
  End If

' Some other operations are performed that would not generate an error.
End Sub
```

In this example, we setup an error handler at the start of the routine, just as we did in the previous example. Then we process two statements. The first may cause a runtime error; the second will never cause a runtime error. The question is what is the value of the **Err.Number** property when we get to the **If** statement? If you guessed that it will always be zero (since the second operation is always successful) you are wrong. If you said that it depends on whether or not the first statement completed without error, you are right.

> The value of the **Err.Number** property will always contain the *last* runtime error encountered. If you handle an error within your code, make sure that you clear the **Err.Number** property before resuming the normal functions of your program. This can be accomplished using the **Clear** method of the **Err** object.

The **Err.Number** property is not the same thing as a return status from a subroutine. It only gets set when an error occurs. It does not get set to 0 when an operation completes successfully. Therefore it will always contain the value for the last error encountered by your program. It is this 'feature' of the **Err** object that we will be examining in the following section.

Runtime Errors in Visual Basic for Windows CE

One of the many differences between VB and VBCE is the way that they handle runtime errors. Visual Basic, upon encountering an unhandled runtime error will:

- Display a message stating what error has occurred

- Terminate the application

Visual Basic for CE on the other hand, upon encountering an unhandled runtime error will:

- Display a generic error message, as shown in the screenshot below
- Continue with the application

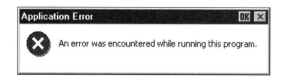

> Often, the runtime error that is encountered is simply caused by the use of a Visual Basic statement that is not supported by Visual Basic for CE. Before tearing your program apart, first check to make sure that the statements you are using are part of VBCE.

Adding Error Handling to Time Manager

We will wrap up our discussion on error handling by incorporating two simple examples of error handling techniques into the Time Manager application.

The Programmer's 'Safety Chute'

The fact that VBCE does not support the complete Visual Basic language, permits you to include unsupported statements in your CE programs and reports processing unsupported statements as generic errors, can drive someone crazy when they are just starting out creating CE apps. One aid, or 'safety chute', that you can incorporate into your applications is to use an object that has the sole purpose of displaying the last error that was encountered. Take for example the modified version of Time Manager shown in the screenshot below:

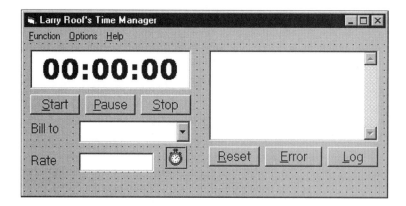

An Error command button has been added to the interface. In the **click** event for this control we place the following code:

```
Private Sub cmdError_Click()

  MsgBox "Error number " & Err.Number & vbCrLf & Err.Description

End Sub
```

We also added a menu item for Error so place the same line of code under the **click** event for that menu item:

```
Private Sub mnuHelpError_Click()

  MsgBox "Error number " & Err.Number & vbCrLf & Err.Description

End Sub
```

While testing this allows us to display a more detailed message of any unexpected errors. What will happen is an error will occur, VBCE will display a generic error message and then we can click the command button to get a more detailed message. When your application is ready to distribute simply either delete the command button or set its Visible property to False.

While displaying the raw error number and message is fine for you as the developer, you do not want to use this technique with your end users. Instead, use the value of the error number to display more meaningful messages. An example of this is shown in the code below.

Note the **Case Else** branch of the **Select Case** statement. It should always be included to handle errors that you may not have anticipated:

```
Sub ExampleRoutine ()
  On Error Resume Next              'Continue after error.

' Some operation is performed that may generate an error.

  If Err.Number <> 0 Then
    Select Case Err.Number
      Case 50:
' Use the MsgBox function to display a message for this error.


      Case 65:
' Use the MsgBox function to display a message for this error.


      Case Else:
' Display a generic message that will provide you with the info you
' need.

    End Select
  End If

End Sub
```

A method that I prefer to adding a command button control for reporting error messages is to add a menu item instead. This method doesn't interfere with the interface design. As with the command button, simply set the Visible *property of the menu item to* False, *before distributing your application. The Time Manager example for Chapter 3 includes both of these methods.*

Handling Formatting Errors

In this revised version of Time Manager we added the feature to auto-format the Rate field as currency as the user leaves the field. A problem with this approach is that the VBCE function **FormatCurrency** will generate a runtime error if you pass it a string that is already formatted as currency. To address this situation the **Lost_Focus** event procedure of the Rate field has been supplemented with the following code for error handling:

```
Private Sub txtRate_LostFocus()

' Convert the text to currency format whenever the user leaves
' this control.
  On Error Resume Next
  txtRate.Text = FormatCurrency(txtRate.Text)
  If (Err.Number <> 0) Then
    If Not IsCurrency(txtRate.Text) Then
      txtRate.SetFocus
    End If
    Err.Clear
  End If

End Sub
```

Walking through this code we can see that an error handler is set at the beginning of this routine. After formatting the value that the user enters as currency the **Err.Number** property is checked to determine if the conversion was successful. If the conversion failed, a simple check, using the **IsCurrency** function, is performed to see if the value of the Rate field is already formatted as currency. If it's not then the user is returned to the Rate field so that they may re-enter the value.

Summary

This completes our examination of how to design effective applications for Windows CE. What you need to keep in mind is that creating applications for use under Windows CE requires a different set of design criteria. Don't get lured into the misconception that since handhelds are just small computers you can create applications for them in the same fashion as you would build desktop applications. Remember that they:

- ▲ Have hardware limitations that don't exist in desktop systems
- ▲ Are used in different locations than desktop systems
- ▲ Are used for different purposes than desktop systems

The best way for you to acquire the skills necessary for designing solid, workable handheld applications is to use as many different CE applications as you can, in as many situations as possible. It's only then that you will be able to develop an understanding of just how drastically the handheld environment differs from the desktop environment.

ActiveX Controls for Windows CE – Interface Tools

When I first started working with Visual Basic, back in the days of version 1, I can remember thinking, "Gee, this would be a great tool if it only offered some functionality". Well, low and behold, out came a boatload of custom controls, the popularity of Visual Basic took off and well, the rest is, as they say, history.

When the VBCE Toolkit came out I had the same feelings working with it as I did with the initial release of VB. I thought that the Toolkit was cool but lacked the necessary functionality to make it an effective development tool. As before, Microsoft must have saw this same shortcoming because shortly after the release of the VBCE Toolkit a free upgrade was released that provided a set of tools aimed at bolstering the Toolkit's functionality.

In this chapter, I'll show you some of the components that make up the Microsoft Windows CE ActiveX Control Pack 1.0. Included in this pack is a set of new controls plus updates that fix problems with the existing controls. I've split what is essentially one topic into two chapters dealing with the interface controls and what I term data controls respectively. By interface controls I mean those controls which you incorporate to create the user interface for you applications. By data controls I don't mean database controls as in the desktop VB environment but rather I use the term as a generic phrase for those controls that add much of the functionality to your apps by manipulating and managing data. In this chapter, I will primarily be focusing on what I've termed the interface controls.

What I won't give you in these two chapters is the standard listing of properties, methods and events for the controls. You can get all of that from the documentation that is provided with the Control Pack. What I'll give you instead is a half dozen applications, spread between the two chapters, which demonstrate ways to use these controls to create fully functional CE applications.

As if that wasn't enough, tucked into these chapters is a freeware Utility control which fills in some of the gaps left between the VBCE Toolkit and the Control Pack.

So let's get right at it, for these are the chapters that take the VBCE Toolkit from just being cool, to a functional development tool.

ActiveX Controls for Windows CE

What would Visual Basic be without custom, or ActiveX controls? The answer is not much. The same holds true for the VBCE Toolkit only to a greater extent. Without the aid of ActiveX controls I expect that you would find the Toolkit only minimally useful. The language by itself simply isn't powerful enough.

With the addition of ActiveX controls the Toolkit suddenly goes from being a cute application to a serious tool that can be used to develop business quality software. And this is just the start. While presently Microsoft provides the only ActiveX controls available, expect to see a rush of third-party controls as the popularity of Windows CE increases. What does this mean to you? Simply that the VBCE Toolkit is only going to get better as time goes by.

> **What controls can you use on your H/PC? Not the controls developed for Visual Basic. You can only use controls that were created specifically for the Windows CE environment with the VBCE Toolkit.**
>
> **Want to develop your own controls? I'm afraid you can't use Visual Basic as it doesn't produce CE controls. Instead you'll have to roll up your sleeves and fire up Visual C++.**

Controls Included With the Toolkit

When the VBCE Toolkit was first released it contained only a minimal set of ActiveX controls. Accordingly, this initial release was severely limited in what it could accomplish. As you would expect, the reaction from the development community was less than favorable. After being spoiled by the abundance of controls that are available for use with Visual Basic, the sparse set of controls that was delivered with the Toolkit was a shock. Add to this the fact that you couldn't perform the simple task of saving data from a program and you could be forgiven for thinking that no one gave the VBCE Toolkit another look.

This deficiency was short lived. Microsoft immediately began work on a set of ActiveX controls that would provide enhancements to the Toolkit. After a few months they released the **Windows CE ActiveX Control Pack 1.0**. This pack contained a set of new controls as well as enhancements to the original controls that were included with the Toolkit.

What is in the Control Pack

With the release of the ActiveX Control Pack 1.0, the set of controls available to the CE developer was greatly enhanced. While not large in number, these new controls supplemented the VBCE Toolkit, providing much needed data storage, communication and interface enhancements.

> **You can get the Windows CE ActiveX Control Pack from the Microsoft web site. It's a free download.**

The Windows CE ActiveX Interface Controls

In these following sections, I'll be giving you a little guided tour of the interface enhancing components that were included with the VBCE Toolkit as well as those that make up the ActiveX Control Pack 1.0. I'll start by examining each control and looking at what it has to offer to the developer of CE applications. Then I'll take you through a set of examples that demonstrates how some of these controls can be used to enhance your applications.

The Grid Control

The **Grid** control provides a spreadsheet-like interface that can used to display large amounts of data. Its contents can be sorted and formatted to meet your needs. Unfortunately, what this control lacks is editing capabilities. You can work around this shortcoming by placing a text box directly over the cell that is to be edited to fool the user, although this doesn't really count as a quick fix as it requires substantial coding. Instead, I recommend including a text box elsewhere on the form for data editing. Hopefully this drawback will be corrected in a future version of this control.

The Grid control is a perfect match for the limited screen provided by the CE machine. It allows you to display a large amount of data in a minimal amount of space. I've included an example in this chapter called DataDisplay that demonstrates how to load and display data from a sequential file in the Grid control. In Chapter 7 I also demonstrate how the Grid control can be implemented to display data from a database.

The File System Control

No one would ever think of a version of BASIC without file I/O. However, that was exactly what the original version of the VBCE Toolkit did. It lacked even the most simple of data storage capabilities. The **File System** control fills this void. It provides access to both the **File** and **FileSystem** object. The File object allows you to read and write data from sequential, random access and binary files whilst the FileSystem object can be used to query and manipulate the directory structures on an H/PC. It allows you to copy, move, delete and obtain information on files and directories.

> Although this control really belongs to the next chapter I have included it here as well because the two sample apps that I use to demonstrate this control are in this chapter.

The use of this control is included in two examples in this chapter, Explorer and DataDisplay, as well as other examples throughout the book. I talk in great detail about this control in Chapter 6.

The Image Control

The **Image** control offers the functionality to display bitmap images. It can display images of various color depths and adjusts its resolution depending upon the capabilities of the host H/PC. How much easier can it get.

Use of the Image control is straightforward. It's pretty similar to the Image control that you're already used to except it's cut down a bit so that, for example, it doesn't support any events. Review the example program that was included with the Toolkit and the Books Online reference if you want further details.

The ImageList Control

The **ImageList** control offers exactly what its name says – a way to build a list of images. By itself it's a worthless control as it's designed to be used in conjunction with other controls, providing them with access to the images that it contains.

You will find an example of how to use the ImageList control in the Explorer application later in this chapter and also in the Note Manager case study.

The ListView Control

The **ListView** control allows you to display data in one of these four views: Icon, Small Icon, List and Report. It provides the same interface functionality as you see in the right-hand pane of the Windows 95 or NT Explorer.

It's a good control to add to your programming repertoire as it allows you to create applications sporting an interface that is familiar to the typical Windows user. The Explorer example later in this chapter demonstrates how you can use the ListView control to just such a purpose.

The PictureBox Control

The **PictureBox** control, like the Image control can be used to display bitmaps. It also provides additional functionality in the form of a set of graphical methods for drawing and printing text on this control.

I chose not to include a PictureBox example in this chapter because it's fairly easy to use and the sample application that is provided with the Control Pack does an adequate job of demonstrating how to use this control. I anticipate that as the storage resources found on the H/PC increase there will be an increase in the use of bitmaps in CE applications. Right now it is a fairly resource-expensive option.

The TabStrip Control

Along with the Grid control, the **TabStrip** control is one of the most useful additions to the VBCE Toolkit. Its interface appears as a set of notebook dividers. What it enables you to do is to divide up user input between a series of tabs. This allows you to improve the appearance of an application while at the same time simplifying the user interaction.

This is another of those 'must have' skills of a CE developer. You will want to be intimately familiar with what the TabStrip control has to offer and how it's used. What you'll find is that in many cases where you might think that you need additional forms, you can instead get away with a single form and the TabStrip control. I've included a demonstration of the use of this control in the CEWizard example later in this chapter.

The TreeView Control

The **TreeView** control provides an interface that presents data using a hierarchical view much like that found in the left-hand pane of the Windows 95 or NT Explorer. Because of the familiar interface that it offers it is easily understood and accepted by the common Windows user.

It can be a bit tricky to work with at first, with its object structure comprised of various methods and events. I've included two examples in this book that demonstrate its use. The first is the Explorer example that can be found later in this chapter. The second is the Note Manager application that can be found in the case studies.

The VBCE.com Utility Control

Although this freeware control fits more into the data control category it does have several features which are interface based:

▲ A feature that allows you to play wave files from within your applications. This provides a much needed work-around for the absence of the **Beep** function in the VBCE Toolkit.

▲ A way to display an hourglass icon while your application is busy.

▲ It also provides a method which can be used, with the addition of a few subroutines, to get around the text box bugs.

> **The VBCE.com Utility control is provided by those fine folks out at www.vbce.com the web site. There you will find code examples, news updates and bug fixes along with a wide variety of other selections. You will want to check their site for updates to the Utility control and other items.**

For more details on using the VBCE.com Utility control I suggest you refer to the next chapter where there is more detailed discussion plus an entire sample application which demonstrates the full range of the its features.

Working with ActiveX Controls

If you are an experienced Visual Basic developer you may be thinking, "I don't need any help working with ActiveX controls. Been there. Done that." However, you may still want to read the following section through as the VBCE Toolkit throws in a few twists of its own regarding the use of ActiveX controls. It may just save you a couple of headaches.

Adding Them to Your Project

The first step in using ActiveX controls is to add them to your project. This is accomplished in exactly the same way as in VB:

▲ Use the Components dialog to select the controls you want to add to your project, they will be added to your toolbox

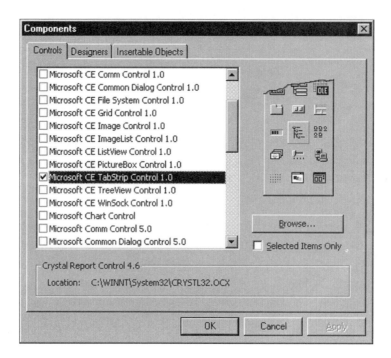

The Control Manager

This step on the other hand is unique to CE projects. Before you can test any CE application that includes an ActiveX control you must first copy that control to the target environment where the application will run. What this means is that even though the VBCE Toolkit handles that copying and running of your application it doesn't go so far as to copy the controls that an application uses. The result of this shortcoming is that you get the infamous An error occurred during startup message, which more times than not simply means that you forgot to copy one or more controls to either the emulator or your H/PC.

The tool that is provided for copying controls is the **Control Manager**. This utility can be used to query, update and delete controls from the desktop, emulator and H/PC environments. It's found under the Windows CE menu item in the Visual Basic IDE. Once selected, it will firstly query the various environments to determine what controls are present. During this time the following dialog will be displayed:

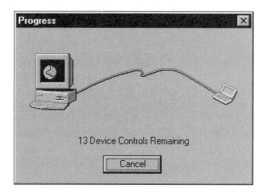

After it completes its surveying process it will display the following form:

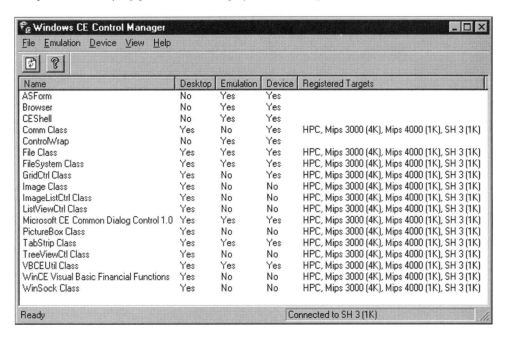

Note your display will most likely differ depending upon the controls that are present on your desktop PC, emulator and H/PC.

The layout of this display is as follows:

- ▲ The Name column contains the control name.

- ▲ The Desktop column shows whether a control is installed on your desktop PC.

- ▲ The Emulation shows whether a control is installed on your emulator.

- ▲ The Device shows whether each control is installed on your H/PC. Obviously your H/PC must be connected to your desktop for this to work.

- ▲ The final Registered Targets column displays what platforms the control can be used with.

Installing a Control on the Emulator

To install a control on the emulator perform the following steps:

- ▲ Select the control that you want to install from the body of the Control Manager interface.

- ▲ From the Emulation menu select Install. The Windows CE emulator will be started if it's not already running. A dialog similar to the following will be displayed:

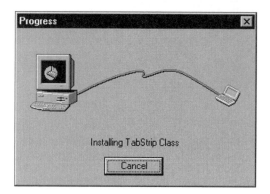

▲ After the transfer has completed the following dialog will be displayed on the emulator:

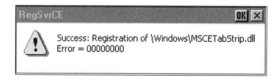

Installing a Control on Your H/PC

To install a control on an H/PC, the steps are almost identical - except that you use the Device menu, and you obviously use this while the H/PC is connected to the desktop computer:

▲ Select the control that you want to install from the body of the Control Manager interface

▲ From the Device menu select Install; a dialog similar to that shown for the emulator will be displayed

▲ After the transfer has completed the following dialog will be displayed on the hand-held:

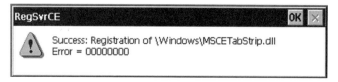

Removing Controls

The process of removing controls is nearly identical to adding controls but instead of selecting Install from either the Emulation or Device menus you use the Uninstall menu item. This is useful to do after you have been testing out new applications to clean up your H/PC.

Distributing Controls with Your CE Apps

When you create a CE application that makes use of ActiveX controls you must include those controls in your distribution of the application. The easiest way to accomplish this is by using the CE Application Installation Wizard. As part of the process your project will be queried to determine what ActiveX controls it uses. An example of this part of the wizard is shown in the screenshot below:

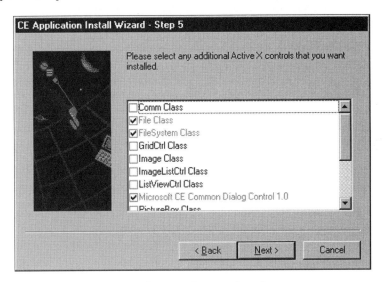

All you need to do is to confirm that the right controls are selected.

The Sample Applications

Now that we have covered the basics of some of the controls that are available, and how ActiveX controls can be incorporated into your programs, let's turn our attention to the first set of example applications. These programs demonstrate how to use various ActiveX controls in your applications. In this chapter the apps will primarily be demonstrating the use of the interface controls, although, also incorporated into the apps of this chapter is the demonstration of the File System control.

Unlike other examples from this book I will not be discussing these applications line-by-line but instead will focus on the most important facets of each example. I will also not be using the 9 step process that I have used previously as these apps are only intended to give you a quick introduction to the controls they utilize.

Application One – The CEWizard

I created the **CEWizard** application to show you two things. First, to demonstrate how to use the TabStrip control and secondly to show how you can simplify and improve the interface of complex CE applications through the use of the TabStrip control.

The CEWizard application is a mock-up of a surveying program. You can imagine it being used in a mall, or door-to-door to record information. It guides the surveyor through a series of tabs, each of which requests different types of information. The 'smarts' in the program determine how to move the surveyor through the application, making sure that each appropriate tab is visited and making sure that all mandatory data is provided.

> *The Chapter 4 version of* **CEWizard.vbp** *contains a completed version of this project. Refer to Appendix A for instructions on downloading and installing the examples included in this book.*

Features Found in the CEWizard Application

This application demonstrates the use of the following ActiveX controls:

- The TabStrip control
- The Utility control (only the playing wave files feature)

It also demonstrates the following techniques:

- How to limit access to individual tabs
- How to control movement between tabs
- How to ensure that all mandatory data is provided

Using the CEWizard

The interface of this application is dominated by the TabStrip control as shown in the figure below. It offers four tabs: General, Sleeping, Exercise and Eating. The only tab that has to be filled out is the General tab. The other tabs come into play when any of the three check boxes, Sleeping, Exercise, or Eating are selected from the first tab:

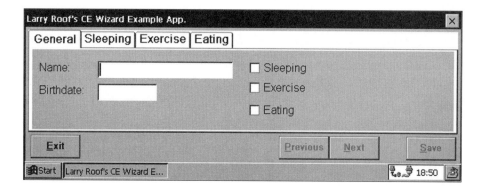

The navigational buttons located at the bottom of the interface are controlled based upon the check boxes that are selected on the first tab. The Save button is enabled when all of the active tabs have their mandatory data entered. In the case of the General tab, the Name: is mandatory. Note how the Save button becomes available when this is present. An example of this can be seen below:

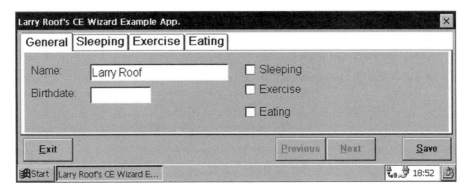

Now try selecting both the Sleeping and Eating check boxes. Note how the Save button is again disabled but now the Next button is available. Move to the next page. Select a time from the Avg. hours of sleep combo box and move to the next field. Now both the Previous and Next buttons should be available. An example of this can be seen in the following screenshot:

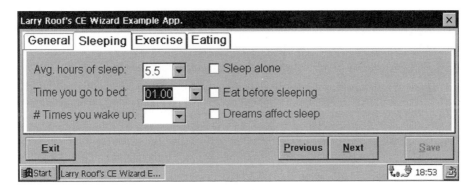

Try clicking on the Exercise tab. You should here an alarm that is informing you that you can't switch to that tab. Finally fill in all of the mandatory fields from each tab and tap the Save button. You will be informed that the data is being saved and the application will be reset back to its starting point:

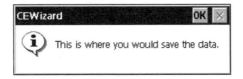

Building the CEWizard

The key to this application is the TabStrip control. It provides the foundation on which everything else is built. What you will find out about the TabStrip control, after working with it for a while, is that it's fairly limited. If you want it to do anything, say something as simple as switching the interface that is displayed for each tab, you have to write code to make it happen. Don't get discouraged before we get started though. I'll walk you through the key points in making this control work.

The Basics of the TabStrip Control

The TabStrip control offers two features for a software developer to use. The first is that it automatically updates the **Tab**, or top part of the display so that the appropriate tab is brought to the front as it's tapped. Second, as a tab is clicked the TabStrip **Click** event is fired. It's in this event that you will place your code to update the body of the TabStrip display.

Why do you have to update the body of the TabStrip control? Simply because if you don't, no one else will. That's right, the way the TabStrip control works is that when the user taps a tab, that is they tap on the descriptive part of the tab where the titles are displayed, all the TabStrip control does is bring the appropriate tab, the title area, to the front. It does not update the body of the control. In fact it doesn't have any idea of what the pages for its tabs should look like. That is up to you to handle from code. The TabStrip just gives you a graphical client area in which to position your user interface controls.

So just how do you make it look as it there are controls on each tab of a TabStrip control? By enabling and hiding sets of controls contained within Frame controls. The process that occurs is:

- ▲ User taps tab. The title for the tab that they have selected is brought to front.
- ▲ The TabStrip **Click** event is fired.
- ▲ In the **Click** event procedure your code determines which page was selected.
- ▲ Your code disables and hides the frame (and its controls) from the previous page.
- ▲ Your code enables and brings to the front the frame (and its controls) for the new page.

So, in a nutshell what you have is a series of frames containing controls that you hide and show on the interface as the various tabs of the TabStrip control are selected.

The CEWizard Form

Let's take a look at the form used by CEWizard (**frmCEWizard**) as shown in the screenshot below. Its WindowState property is set to 2 - Maximized:

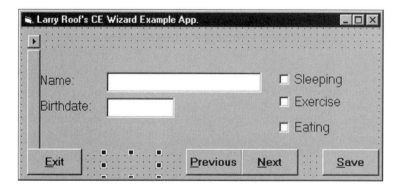

At the far left, that thin raised bar with the arrow at the top is the TabStrip control (**ceTabStrip**). I set it to this small width at design time to get it out of the way. At runtime it is resized to the appropriate proportions. In the middle of the form (shown by the area without the grid) is the frame (**fraGeneral**) for the first, or General tab. Inside this frame are the controls that will be displayed for this tab. There are two text boxes (**txtName** and **txtBirthdate**) for the pertinent information as described by two labels. Then there are the three check boxes (**chkSleeping**, **chkExercise** and **chkEating**) that govern which of the subsequent tabs are available. At the bottom of the form is a set of command buttons (**cmdExit**, **cmdPrevious**, **cmdNext** and **cmdSave**), which, like the TabStrip control, will be repositioned when the application is started. The control outline that you can see is the VBCE.com Utility control (**ceUtility**) which will be used to play a warning wave file.

The frames for the other three tabs look like this:

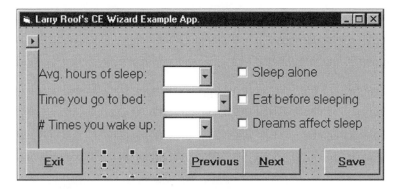

The Sleeping frame (**fraSleeping**) has 3 check boxes (**chkSleepAlone**, **chkEatSleep** and **chkDream**) and 3 combo boxes for describing sleeping habits and their accompanying descriptive labels. The Avg. hours of sleep combo box (**cboAvgSleep**) is filled with List entries ranging from < 2 to 4.5 increasing in 0.5 hour intervals. The Time you go to bed combo box (**cboTimesBed**) has entries for the full 24 hours increasing in 30 minute intervals. The # Times you wake up combo box (**cboTimesAwake**) has entries ranging from 1 to > 4.

The Exercise frame (**fraExercise**) simply has two combo boxes in it and two descriptive labels for them. The # Times you exercise per week combo box (**cboTimesExercise**) has entries ranging from 0 to 6 and the Where you exercise combo box (**cboWhereExercise**) has entries: Home; Gym; Office; Home & Gym; Home & Office; and Gym & Office.

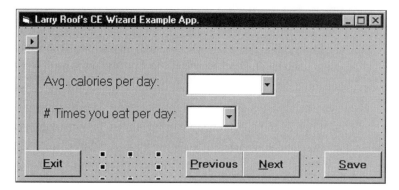

The Eating frame (**fraEating**) similarly has only two combo boxes and their descriptive labels. The Avg. calories per day combo box (**cboCalories**) has entries ranging from < 1000 to 3500 - 3999 and the # Times you eat per day combo box (**cboTimesEat**) has entries ranging from 1 to > 5.

You need not set the frames be identical in size because they get resized in the code according to the size of the handheld's display.

In order to set the tabs of the TabStrip control you need to access the Property Pages for the control by double-clicking on the (Custom) property:

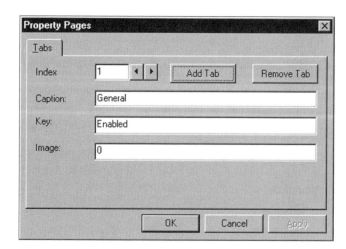

Add a tab for each of the four tabs in the Index order General, Sleeping, Exercise and Eating. Also set the **Key** of the General tab to **Enabled** and the **Key** of the other three tabs to **Disabled**.

Next we will look at some of the key code that is behind the CEWizard application.

Starting the Application

When the CEWizard application starts, the **Form_Load** procedure is executed. In this procedure, the **AdjustControls** procedure is called which will handle the resizing of positioning of the controls that comprise the interface.

Also the **mintPreviousTab** flag is initialized to the first tab. This flag is used to limit access to tabs. It's used when the user tries to select a tab that is disabled, the application sets focus back to the tab as defined by **mintPreviousTab**. Finally, I set the focus to the Name text entry control. This is what we would expect the surveyor to ask first:

```
Private Sub Form_Load()

' Setup the tabstrip interface.
  AdjustControls

' Initialize the variable used to control tab access.
  mintPreviousTab = 1

' Start with the Name Entry
  txtName.SetFocus

End Sub
```

Adjusting CEWizard's Interface

The **AdjustControls** procedure handles the adjustment of the CEWizard interface. It starts by declaring some variables we use later in the routine to position the frame controls and then sets the TabStrip controls positional properties:

```
Private Sub AdjustControls()

' Extend the size of the interface to match the size of the
' display on the palmtop.
  Dim intButtonHeight
  Dim intButtonWidth
  Dim intFrameWidth
  Dim intFrameHeight
  Dim intFrameTop
  Dim intFrameLeft

  'Form Width to screen
  frmCEWizard.Width = Screen.Width

  'Set up Tabstip dimensions with a 60 border each side
  ceTabStrip.Left = 60
  ceTabStrip.Top = 60
  ceTabStrip.Width = frmCEWizard.ScaleWidth - 120
  ceTabStrip.Height = frmCEWizard.ScaleHeight - (180 + cmdNext.Height)
```

Throughout the example apps in this chapter I will be resizing controls at runtime to make better use of the handheld display's dimensions. Depending on how you construct the forms you may want to change the twip dimensions.

Next we calculate the sizes for the frames. Notice that here I have used several **ClientX** properties of the TabStrip control. These give the size and co-ordinates for the area of the tab strip that the frames should be placed in:

```
intFrameWidth = ceTabStrip.ClientWidth - 60
intFrameHeight = ceTabStrip.ClientHeight - 120
intFrameLeft = ceTabStrip.Clientleft + 30
intFrameTop = ceTabStrip.ClientTop + 120
```

Having calculated the correct dimensions for the display the dimensions of each frame needs to be set:

```
' Size the tab "frames"
fraGeneral.Width = intFrameWidth
fraSleeping.Width = intFrameWidth
fraExercise.Width = intFrameWidth
fraEating.Width = intFrameWidth

fraGeneral.Height = intFrameHeight
fraSleeping.Height = intFrameHeight
fraExercise.Height = intFrameHeight
fraEating.Height = intFrameHeight

fraGeneral.Top = intFrameTop
fraSleeping.Top = intFrameTop
fraExercise.Top = intFrameTop
fraEating.Top = intFrameTop

fraGeneral.Left = intFrameLeft
fraSleeping.Left = intFrameLeft
fraEating.Left = intFrameLeft
fraExercise.Left = intFrameLeft
```

Next it repositions the <u>E</u>xit, <u>P</u>revious, <u>N</u>ext and <u>S</u>ave command buttons. The **ScaleHeight** property is used in this case because it gives a value for the client area of the form, that is the part that controls are added to without taking the height of the title bar into account.

```
' Position the buttons (all the same height)
intButtonHeight = frmCEWizard.ScaleHeight - cmdNext.Height - 60
intButtonWidth = cmdNext.Width
cmdExit.Top = intButtonHeight
cmdPrevious.Top = intButtonHeight
cmdNext.Top = intButtonHeight
cmdSave.Top = intButtonHeight

cmdNext.Left = frmCEWizard.Width - intButtonWidth - 1800
cmdPrevious.Left = cmdNext.Left - intButtonWidth
cmdSave.Left = frmCEWizard.Width - intButtonWidth - 120
```

The **Font** settings for the TabStrip control are then configured. This is handled here because there is no design time access to these properties:

```
' Configure other settings for the tab stripe.
ceTabStrip.FontSize = 12
ceTabStrip.FontBold = True
```

Finally the first frame, that contains the controls for the General tab, is brought to the front of all the other controls. This gives the appearance that the controls within this frame are sitting on top of the TabStrip control. The other controls are disabled and hidden:

```
' Finally make sure that the "General" tab is showing.
  fraGeneral.ZOrder 0
  fraSleeping.Visible = False
  fraExercise.Visible = False
  fraEating.Visible = False
  fraSleeping.Enabled = False
  fraExercise.Enabled = False
  fraEating.Enabled = False

End Sub
```

Updating the Display when the User Selects a Tab

This is the most important procedure in the CEWizard application for it's responsible for giving the appearance of moving between tabs. It starts by checking to make sure that the tab that the user selected is available. The way that I handle disabling particular tabs is by setting their **Key** property to either **Enabled** or **Disabled**. Then when the user selects a tab I simply check the value of its **Key** property. If it's disabled I play a wave file to let the user know of their error and exit.

> *Unlike the **Key** property of a tab control in the desktop VB environment we do not have to use a unique value. In fact, the **Key** here is more akin to the **Tag** property found in the desktop equivalent.*

If the tab is enabled the **mintPreviousTab** flag is used to remove the previous page and the flag value is set to that of the new page ready for the next tab click:

```
Private Sub ceTabStrip_Click()

' Don't let the user go to a tab that is not enabled.
  Dim objFrame

  If (ceTabStrip.SelectedItem.Key = "Disabled") Then
    Set ceTabStrip.SelectedItem = ceTabStrip.Tabs(mintPreviousTab)
    ceUtility.PlayWaveFile "\windows\alarm1.wav"
    Exit Sub

  Else
    'Need to disable Previous page's frame
    Set objFrame = GetPageFrame(mintPreviousTab)
    objFrame.Enabled = False
    objFrame.Visible = False
    mintPreviousTab = ceTabStrip.SelectedItem.Index

  End If
```

The old page is removed by hiding and disabling the frame control. The variable **objFrame** is set to reference the appropriate frame control by the **GetPageFrame** function. This function simply uses a **Select Case** block of code to return a reference to one of the four frames used with the tabs.

If I get to this point then the clicked tab must have been enabled. **GetPageFrame** is again used to set a reference to a frame, but this time the value of **mintPreviousTab** is for the new tab:

```
' Get a reference to the new frame
  Set objFrame = GetPageFrame(mintPreviousTab)
  objFrame.Enabled = True
  objFrame.Visible = True
  objFrame.Zorder
```

The frame for the new tab is made **Visible**, **Enabled** and brought to the front of the display with the **ZOrder** method for the frame.

In the interest of user friendliness, the focus is set to the mandatory field control for the selected page. In this the TabStrips **SelectedItem** property is used to determine which page is being used. I could have used the **mintPreviousTab** to control the select block of code, but this is more readable:

```
' Set focus to the mandatory contol to be helpful
  Select Case ceTabStrip.SelectedItem.Caption
    Case "General"
      txtName.SetFocus
      txtName.SelStart = 0
      txtName.SelLength = Len(txtName.Text)

    Case "Sleeping"
      cboAvgSleep.SetFocus

    Case "Exercise"
      cboTimesExercise.SetFocus

    Case "Eating"
      cboCalories.SetFocus

  End Select
```

The final step in displaying this new page is to update the command buttons so that only the appropriate buttons are enabled. We will look the **SetButtons** procedure in greater detail shortly:

```
' Configure the appropriate buttons for the conditions.
  SetButtons

End Sub
```

Getting a Frame Control Reference

The important act in the code above was to manipulate a pair of frame controls. First to hide a page, then to show a page. This is done with the **GetPageFrame** function:

```
Private Function GetPageFrame(intTabNum)

' To effectively control the display we will often have
' to use a reference to a Frame control
    Select Case intTabNum
```

```
        Case 1
          Set GetPageFrame = fraGeneral

        Case 2
          Set GetPageFrame = fraSleeping

        Case 3
          Set GetPageFrame = fraExercise

        Case 4
          Set GetPageFrame = fraEating

      End Select

  End Function
```

There is nothing special about this function; it just leaves the tab **Click** code in a more readable form.

Enabling the Appropriate Command Buttons

As the user works with the interface, by entering values and moving between tabs, the command buttons need to be updated so that only the appropriate buttons are enabled. That is the purpose of the **SetButtons** procedure. It checks which tab is currently displayed and which mandatory controls have been filled to determine the setting for each command button.

It starts by setting the Previous button. The previous button is enabled anytime the current tab is anything other than the General tab:

```
  Sub SetButtons()

  ' This routine handles the setting of the command buttons. It is
  ' called from mandatory fields and the tabstrip click event.
    Dim intLoop
    Dim blnNextOK

  ' Configure the Previous button. For the Previous button to be enabled
  ' any page other than the "General" page must be selected.
    If ceTabStrip.SelectedItem.Caption = "General" Then
      cmdPrevious.Enabled = False

    Else
      cmdPrevious.Enabled = True

    End If
```

The Next button is configured based upon whether there is a tab after the current tab that is enabled. This is done in a two-part process. First, I make a check to see if there are any tabs following the current one:

```
  ' Configure the Next button.
  ' For the Next button to be enabled there must be a
  ' subsequent page that is enabled.
    For intLoop = ceTabStrip.SelectedItem.Index + 1 To 4
```

```
        If ceTabStrip.Tabs(intLoop).Key = "Enabled" Then
            blnNextOK = True

            'No need to check for nore than later pagge!
            Exit For

        End If

    Next 'intLoop
```

The loop is used to examine each tab later in the sequence and compare the **Key** property to **Enabled**. As soon as an enabled tab is found I set a flag and exit the loop. I now use the **blnNextOK** flag to determine if there is a need to check the mandatory fields on the current page:

```
If blnNextOK Then

    'Check if mandatory data has been filled
    Select Case ceTabStrip.SelectedItem.Caption

        Case "General"
            If txtName.Text = "" Then
                blnNextOK = False
            End If

        Case "Sleeping"
            If cboAvgSleep.ListIndex = -1 Then
                blnNextOK = False
            End If

        Case "Exercise"
            If cboTimesExercise.ListIndex = -1 Then
                blnNextOK = False
            End If

        Case "Eating"
            'Last tab any way. Can never get here!
            blnNextOK = False

    End Select

End If

'Set Next button based on flag
cmdNext.Enabled = blnNextOK
```

At this point all that is necessary is to set the <u>N</u>ext buttons enabled property to the flag. The last thing to do is set the state of the <u>S</u>ave button:

```
' Configure the Save button. This is done by checking the mandatory
' fields of each page that is enabled.
    cmdSave.Enabled = CanSave

End Sub
```

The **CanSave** function returns **True** if all the mandatory fields on the enabled pages have been set. As soon as any one piece of data is missing the rest of the checks can be ignored:

```
Private Function CanSave()

' Return True if all the enabled tabs have their mandatory fields
' filled

  'Assume OK To Save
  CanSave = True

  'The General tab is always enabled
  If Trim(txtName.Text) = "" Then
    'Need a name to Save
    CanSave = False
    Exit Function

  End If

  'Sleeping Tab - Average Sleep mandatory
  If ceTabStrip.Tabs(2).Key = "Enabled" Then

    If (cboAvgSleep.ListIndex = -1) Then
      CanSave = False
      Exit Function

    End If

  End If

  'Excercise Tab - No. of times  Mandatory
  If ceTabStrip.Tabs(3).Key = "Enabled" Then

    If (cboTimesExercise.ListIndex = -1) Then
      CanSave = False
      Exit Function

    End If

  End If

  'Eating Tab - Calories Mandatory
  If ceTabStrip.Tabs(4).Key = "Enabled" Then

    If (cboCalories.ListIndex = -1) Then
      CanSave = False
      Exit Function

    End If

  End If

End Function
```

Updating the Display as the User Enters Data

We looked at how the interface is updated as the user moves between tabs but how about when they enter data into mandatory controls? This feature is handled in the events of that particular control.

For instance, take a look at the **KeyUp** event procedure for the text box **txtName**. Whenever a key is typed the **SetButtons** procedure is called to update the display:

```
Private Sub txtName_KeyUp(KeyCode, Shift)

  SetButtons

End Sub
```

> This is not the most efficient method to perform this task. In fact it is pretty darn slow. I used this method for ease of understanding and clarity. In actuality I would separate each of the checks made by the SetButtons routine into their own procedures and only call those routines that are needed.

In a similar manner you should attach event handlers which call **SetButtons** to the combo box controls on the other frames for their mandatory controls. However, there is a bug that prevents the **Change** event of a combo box firing when it is placed within a frame. Therefore you need to use the **Lost Focus** event instead:

```
Private Sub cboAvgSleep_LostFocus()

' Configure the appropriate buttons for the conditions
  SetButtons

End Sub
```

```
Private Sub cboCalories_LostFocus()

' Configure the appropriate buttons for the conditions
  SetButtons

End Sub
```

```
Private Sub cboTimesExercise_LostFocus()

' Configure the appropriate buttons for the conditions
  SetButtons

End Sub
```

Enabling the Other Tabs

The second, third and fourth tabs of the CEWizard application are enabled by selecting the three check box controls on the first, or General tab. How this is accomplished is demonstrated in the **Click** event procedure for the **chkSleeping** control as shown below.

Based upon the current value of the control the corresponding page is either enabled or disabled. This is accomplished by setting the **Key** property of that page. The procedure completes by making a call to the **SetButtons** routine to update the display:

```
Private Sub chkSleeping_Click()

' Set the status of the "Sleeping" tab.
  If (ceTabStrip.Tabs(2).Key = "Disabled") Then
    ceTabStrip.Tabs(2).Key = "Enabled"

  Else
    ceTabStrip.Tabs(2).Key = "Disabled"

  End If

' Configure the appropriate buttons for the conditions.
  SetButtons

End Sub
```

```
Private Sub chkExercise_Click()

' Set the status of the "Exercise" tab.
  If (ceTabStrip.Tabs(3).Key = "Disabled") Then
    ceTabStrip.Tabs(3).Key = "Enabled"

  Else
    ceTabStrip.Tabs(3).Key = "Disabled"

  End If

' Configure the appropriate buttons for the conditions.
  SetButtons

End Sub
```

```
Private Sub chkEating_Click()

' Set the status of the "Eating" tab.
  If (ceTabStrip.Tabs(4).Key = "Disabled") Then
    ceTabStrip.Tabs(4).Key = "Enabled"

  Else
    ceTabStrip.Tabs(4).Key = "Disabled"

  End If

' Configure the appropriate buttons for the conditions.
  SetButtons

End Sub
```

Using the Command Buttons to Move between Pages

The **Click** event procedure for the Next command button is smart enough to determine which tab to go to next. It does this by checking the **Key** property of each tab until it finds a tab that is enabled. If finishes by calling the **Click** event procedure for the TabStrip control so that the tab's interface can be updated:

```
Private Sub cmdNext_Click()

  Dim intCounter

' Move to the next enabled tab.
  For intCounter = ceTabStrip.SelectedItem.Index + 1 To 4

    If (ceTabStrip.Tabs(intCounter).Key = "Enabled") Then
      Set ceTabStrip.SelectedItem = ceTabStrip.Tabs(intCounter)
      Exit For

    End If

  Next

' Update the tab display.
  ceTabStrip_Click

End Sub
```

The event procedure for the Previous command button is similar to that used by the Next command button, but the checking of tabs is done before the current tab:

```
Private Sub cmdPrevious_Click()

  Dim intCounter

' Move to the previous enabled tab.
  For intCounter = ceTabStrip.SelectedItem.Index - 1 To 1 Step -1

    If (ceTabStrip.Tabs(intCounter).Key = "Enabled") Then
      Set ceTabStrip.SelectedItem = ceTabStrip.Tabs(intCounter)
      Exit For

    End If

  Next

' Update the tab display.
  ceTabStrip_Click

End Sub
```

Saving the Data

Since this is just an example application there is nothing to do with the data that has been entered. Instead, what the **Click** event procedure for the <u>S</u>ave button does is to reset the application back to the state where it began:

```
Private Sub cmdSave_Click()

' In a real life application this event would handle saving the data
' from the various tabs to either a database or file. Here we simply
' reset the display.
  MsgBox "This is where you would save the data.", vbInformation + _
    vbOKOnly, "CEWizard"
  ResetDisplay

End Sub
```

The **ResetDisplay** procedure handles the restoring of the CEWizard interface. Using a series of property sets it clears the user input:

```
Private Sub ResetDisplay()

' This routine sets the application back to its original state.
  Set ceTabStrip.SelectedItem = ceTabStrip.Tabs(1)
  chkDream.Value = False
  chkEating.Value = False
  chkEatSleep.Value = False
  chkExercise.Value = False
  chkSleepAlone.Value = False
  chkSleeping.Value = False
  cboAvgSleep.ListIndex = -1
  cboCalories.ListIndex = -1
  cboTimesAwake.ListIndex = -1
  cboTimesBed.ListIndex = -1
  cboTimesEat.ListIndex = -1
  cboTimesExercise.ListIndex = -1
  cboWhereExercise.ListIndex = -1
  txtBirthdate.Text = ""
  txtName.Text = ""
```

And finishes up by a call to the **Click** event procedure of the TabStrip control so that the first tab, the General tab, is displayed:

```
' Update the tab display.
  ceTabStrip_Click

End Sub
```

All that remains to be done is some housekeeping code.

Housekeeping Code

We still need to declare the form level variable **mintPreviousTab** and code the Exit command button:

```
Option Explicit

Private mintPreviousTab  'Used to control the switching between tabs

Private Sub cmdExit_Click()

' Exit the application
  App.End

End Sub
```

Closing Thoughts on the CEWizard

Hopefully what you gathered from the CEWizard application is that the TabStrip control can be used to greatly simplify the interface of CE programs. It's because of this that I'm such a strong supporter of the TabStrip control.

On the downside much of the functionality of the TabStrip control has to offer must be provided by code. You can use the examples from this section to aid you in this process though.

The DataDisplay Example Application

The purpose behind the **DataDisplay** application is primarily to show you how the Grid control can be used to display data. I built this application to show you how to fill a grid from a sequential file, a common function that you will most likely encounter in your applications. In Chapter 7 I will also demonstrate how you can use a Grid to display data from a database. This app also briefly demonstrates the File control from the File System control class. Chapter 6 contains a significantly more detailed demonstration of this control in action. It is used to open the sequential files, which store the data to populate the Grid control. The DataDisplay application has no other purpose other than that. It doesn't allow you to edit or add data – just display it.

> The Chapter 4 version of **DataDisplay.vbp** contains the completed version of the DataDisplay application. Refer to Appendix A for instructions on downloading and installing the examples included in this book.

Features Found in the DataDisplay Application

This application demonstrates the use of the following ActiveX controls:

- The Grid control
- The File control

It also demonstrates the following techniques:

- How to fill a grid with data from a sequential file
- How to add and remove rows from a grid control
- How to configure the appearance of the grid control
- How to use the **ItemData** property to store IDs which will be used to retrieve records

Using DataDisplay

DataDisplay is a very easy application to use. When you start this program it comes up with the data displayed in the grid from a sequential file. An example of this is displayed in the screenshot below:

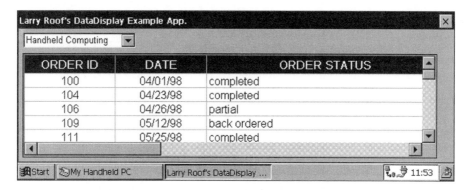

> Before you can use the DataDisplay example make sure that the files
> ddCustomers.txt and ddOrders.txt are present in the same folder as the
> DataDisplay application on the H/PC or emulator.

Selecting companies from the combo box in the upper left of the interface will cause the grid display to be updated with the orders for the selected company:

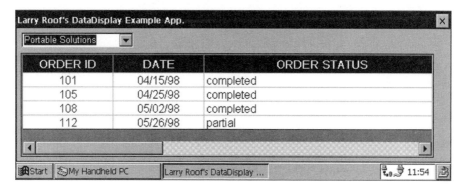

Building DataDisplay

The DataDisplay application is built to demonstrate how to work with the grid control. More specifically how to load and reconfigure the control. I'm not going to discuss the workings of retrieving data from the sequential file as I provide a more in depth look at this in Chapter 6.

The Basics of the Grid Control

The Grid control provides you with a spreadsheet type interface that is best suited for displaying multiple data records. Data can be added and removed from the control at runtime. The appearance of the control can be adjusted from code.

> The downside of the Grid control is that it doesn't allow the user to edit its contents. Instead you have to trick the user by trapping the KeyUp event of the grid control and placing a text box control over the grid so that it 'appears' that the user is typing into the grid control. Although this method can be implemented it requires substantial coding and the handheld really isn't up to it. If you look at Pocket Excel you will find it doesn't even implement this functionality but rather uses a distinct text box for data entry. This is the method I suggest you implement as well.

The DataDisplay Form

Let's take a look at the form (**frmDataDisplay**) used by DataDisplay as shown in the screenshot below. Its WindowState property has been set to 2 - Maximized:

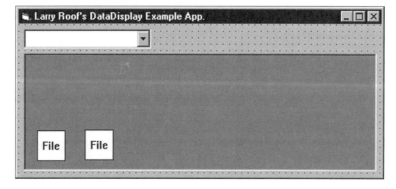

In the upper left corner is a combo box control (**cboCustomers**) that will be used to display the customers for which there are orders.

The majority of the interface is comprised of the grid control (**grdData**). At design time it is a gray mass as it has been configured to have no rows and 3 columns.

Finally, in the lower left of the form are two file controls (**ceFile** and **ceOrderFile**). One control will be used to access customer information, the other for order data.

Next we will look at some of the key code that is behind the DataDisplay application.

Starting the Application

The **Form_Load** event procedure is first used to call the **AdjustControls** procedure which simply widens the Grid to fill the handhelds display. It then calls the **FormatGrid** procedure which adjusts the Grid control's configuration and loads the data from the sequential file into the Grid's cells:

```
Private Sub Form_Load()

' Set the Grid's width
  AdjustControls

' Initialize the display using the file as the source.
  FormatGrid

End Sub
```

The **AdjustControls** is a very simple one line procedure:

```
Private Sub AdjustControls()

  grdData.Width = frmDataDisplay.Width - 500

End Sub
```

Formatting the Grid and Loading Customer Data from a Sequential File

The formatting of the Grid control and the loading of data from a sequential file is handled by the **FormatGrid** routine. This routine starts by checking the contents of the Customer combo box control. If there are customers already in this control, then no loading needs to occur. A call is made to the **Click** event procedure of the combo box to reload the grid control and the routine exits:

```
Private Sub FormatGrid()

  Dim avntCustomerRecord

' There is no sense reloading all of this if the combo box already
' has the customers info.
  If (cboCustomers.ListCount > 0) Then
    cboCustomers.ListIndex = 0
    cboCustomers_Click
    Exit Sub

  End If
```

If the customer data has not already been opened it will be loaded from file. First the file is opened:

```
' Open the file containing the customer data for this example.
  On Error Resume Next
  ceFile.Open App.Path & "\ddCustomers.txt", 1

  If Err <> 0 Then
    MsgBox "Error opening customer data file." & vbCrLf & _
    Err.Description, vbCritical, "Larry Roof's DataDisplay"
    Err.Clear
    Exit Sub

  End If
```

115

Don't concern yourself to much with the syntax for the **Open** method of the File control at the present as I'll explain all its gory details in Chapter 6. For now all you need know is the **1** parameter indicates the file is to be used for Input.

Then the first line from the file is read:

```
' Read in the file. Start by reading in the first record.
  avntCustomerRecord = ceFile.InputFields(2)
```

Next a loop is used to process the contents of the file:

```
' Now loop and read the rest of the records.
  Do While Not ceFile.EOF

    If Err <> 0 Then
      MsgBox "Error reading from customers file." & vbCrLf & _
                Err.Number & " - " & Err.Description, vbCritical, _
                "Larry Roof's DataDisplay"
      Err.Clear
      Exit Sub

    End If
```

Each customer is added into the combo box and their customer ID is in turn stored in the **ItemData** property of the control. If you haven't worked with this property before it's a pretty cool feature. It can be used to store a numeric value that is associated with each item in the control. This value will be used later in the **Click** event procedure for the combo box control to locate orders for a specific customer:

```
' Add this customer into the list.
  cboCustomers.AddItem avntCustomerRecord(1)
  cboCustomers.ItemData(cboCustomers.NewIndex) = _
    avntCustomerRecord(0)

' Read the next record.
  avntCustomerRecord = ceFile.InputFields(2)

  Loop

' All of the customers have been loaded so close the file.
  ceFile.Close
```

Finally the first customer is selected from the combo box control and the orders for that customer are displayed by calling the **Click** event procedure of the combo box control:

```
' Display data for the first customer.
  cboCustomers.ListIndex = 0
  cboCustomers_Click

End Sub
```

Displaying a Customer's Orders

When a customer is selected from the combo box control, the orders for that customer are displayed in the Grid control. This process starts by clearing out anything that is currently in the grid using the **RemoveItem** method:

```
Private Sub cboCustomers_Click()

  Dim intCounter

' Empty out the existing contents of the grid.
  Do While grdData.Rows > 0
    grdData.RemoveItem grdData.Rows - 1
  Loop
```

Then column headers are added using the **AddItem** method. This method adds a single row to the grid control. The syntax of this method allows for the passing of the column data separating each piece of data with the tab character:

```
' Add the headers for the grid.
  grdData.AddItem "ORDER ID" & Chr(9) & "DATE" & Chr(9) & _
    "ORDER STATUS"
```

The column headers are then formatted changing the **Font**, **Color** and **Height** of the row:

```
' Format the headers.
  grdData.FillStyle = 1
  grdData.Row = 0
  grdData.Col = 0
  grdData.ColSel = 2
  grdData.RowSel = 0
  grdData.CellFontSize = 16
  grdData.CellFontBold = True
  grdData.CellBackColor = &H800000
  grdData.CellForeColor = &HFFFFFF
  grdData.CellAlignment = 4
  grdData.RowHeight(0) = 400
```

Next the data is loaded by calling the **LoadOrdersFromFile** procedure:

```
' Get the data if it has not already been loaded.
  If (mintNumberOfOrders = 0) Then
    LoadOrdersFromFile
  End If
```

The order data is then loaded into the grid a record at a time. Again the **AddItem** method is used. The height of the new row is set at the same time:

```
' Load the data into the display grid.
  For intCounter = 1 To mintNumberOfOrders

    If (CInt(mavntOrderInformation(1, intCounter)) = _
        cboCustomers.ItemData(cboCustomers.ListIndex)) Then
```

```
        grdData.AddItem mavntOrderInformation(0, intCounter) & _
                Chr(9) & mavntOrderInformation(2, intCounter) & _
                Chr(9) & mavntOrderInformation(3, intCounter)
        grdData.RowHeight(grdData.Rows - 1) = 300

    End If
Next
```

> The `mavntOrderInformation` array is built by the `LoadOrdersFromFile`
> procedure. It's a two dimensional array that is used to store data on orders:

Finally the data portion of the grid control is formatted to specify **Font Size**, **Column Alignment** and
Column Widths:

```
' Format the grid.
  grdData.FillStyle = 1
  grdData.Row = 0
  grdData.Col = 0
  grdData.ColSel = 2
  grdData.RowSel = grdData.Rows - 1
  grdData.CellFontSize = 12
  grdData.ColSel = 1
  grdData.CellAlignment = 4
  grdData.ColSel = 0
  grdData.RowSel = 0
  grdData.Row = 0
  grdData.Col = 0
  grdData.ColWidth(0) = 2000 ' Order ID
  grdData.ColWidth(1) = 2000 ' Date
  grdData.ColWidth(2) = 5185 ' Status

End Sub
```

Loading Orders from a Sequential File

The **LoadOrdersFromFile** procedure handles the loading of data from the sequential file to a two-
dimensional array. It begins by opening the **ddOrders.txt** file:

```
Private Sub LoadOrdersFromFile()

  Dim avntOrderRecord

  On Error Resume Next

' Open the file containing the order data for this example.
  ceOrderFile.Open App.Path & "\ddOrders.txt", 1

  If Err <> 0 Then
    MsgBox "Error opening order data file." & vbCrLf & _
              Err.Description, vbCritical, "Larry Roof's DataDisplay"
    Err.Clear
    Exit Sub

  End If
```

Then it reads in the first record from the file:

```
' Read in the file. Start by reading in the first record.
avntOrderRecord = ceOrderFile.InputFields(4)
```

It then enters a loop that will be used to process all of the records in the orders file:

```
' Now loop and read the rest of the records.
Do While Not ceOrderFile.EOF

  If Err <> 0 Then
    MsgBox "Error reading from orders file." & vbCrLf & _
           Err.Number " - " & Err.Description, vbCritical, _
           "Larry Roof's DataDisplay"
    Err.Clear
    ceOrderFile.Close
    Exit Sub

  End If
```

As each order is read, it's added into the array that has been resized to accommodate this additional data:

```
' Add this order into the order array.
  mintNumberOfOrders = mintNumberOfOrders + 1
  ReDim Preserve mavntOrderInformation(3, mintNumberOfOrders)

  ' Order ID
  mavntOrderInformation(0, mintNumberOfOrders) = avntOrderRecord(0)

  ' Customer ID
  mavntOrderInformation(1, mintNumberOfOrders) = avntOrderRecord(1)

  ' Date
  mavntOrderInformation(2, mintNumberOfOrders) = avntOrderRecord(2)

  ' Status
  mavntOrderInformation(3, mintNumberOfOrders) = avntOrderRecord(3)

' Read the next record.
  avntOrderRecord = ceOrderFile.InputFields(4)

Loop
```

After all of the records have been processed the file is closed:

```
' All of the customers have been loaded so close the file.
ceOrderFile.Close

End Sub
```

All that remains is the declaration of two form level variables if you haven't already done so:

```
Option Explicit

Private mintNumberOfOrders
Private mavntOrderInformation()
```

Closing Thoughts on DisplayData

The Grid control like the TabStrip control is powerful, yet much of its functionality is dependent upon supporting code. As you can see from this example, it's not a difficult control to work with; nor are the commands required to manipulate this control complex.

The hardest part about working with the Grid control is trying to get its interface to appear as you desire. Making adjustments to the interface from code requires a series of tests to view and modify the look of the control. This can be a slow process until you become familiar with what works well for this control.

The Explorer Example Application

The **Explorer** application is really more of a shell then an application as it doesn't do anything more than put up its display. I chose this example though because it offers a good demonstration of how to work with the TreeView, ListView and ImageList controls.

The folder and file details that are displayed by the Explorer application are gathered with the File System control. I'll point out how this is accomplished when we get to that section of the code. Again the File System gets a more thorough workout in Chapter 6.

The Chapter 4 version of **Explorer.vbp** *contains the completed version of the Explorer application. Refer to Appendix A for instructions on downloading and installing the examples included in this book.*

Features Found In The Explorer Application

This application demonstrates the use of the following ActiveX controls:

- The TreeView control
- The ListView control
- The ImageList control
- The File System control

It also demonstrates the following techniques:

- How to retrieve folder and file details
- How to load images into the ImageList control
- How to configure the TreeView and ListView controls
- How to switch views with the ListView control

Using Explorer

There is nothing to using Explorer. After all it doesn't do anything. The only item that the user can play with is the View menu from which they can select the view to use with the ListBox control. The Explorer application does not allow you to switch directories nor does it allow you to rename, copy, move or delete folders or files.

When the application first runs it displays an Explorer-like interface as shown in the screenshot below. On the left-hand side of the interface is a listing of the folders that are found on the H/PC. While the right-hand side of the interface presents folders and files that are found in the present directory. The default view that is presented is the ListBox icon view.

> Note that for this application to run there must be the five image files:
> `application - small.bmp, application - big.bmp, closed folder - big.bmp, closed folder - small.bmp and open folder - small.bmp,` in the same folder as the Explorer application.

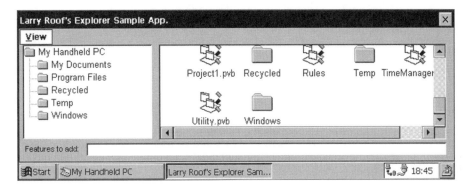

Use the View menu to select the Small Icon item. The Explorer interface will be updated and appear as shown below:

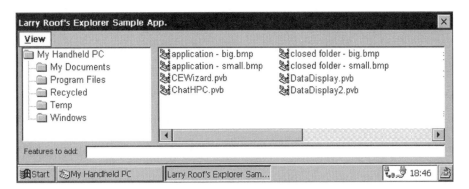

Select the List item from the View menu and once again the interface is updated. It should now appear similar to this screenshot:

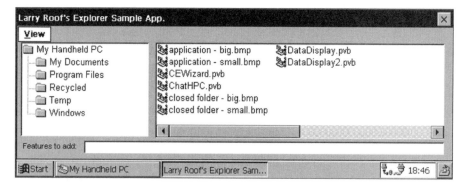

Finally select the Report item from the View menu. The Explorer interface will be updated to include this multiple column presentation of folder and file details:

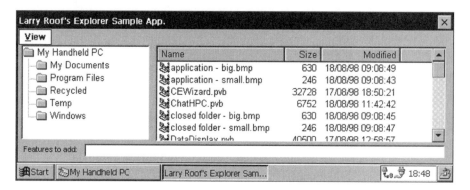

Building Explorer

The Explorer application was designed to demonstrate how to work with the TreeView, ListView and ImageList controls. Other than that there is minimal functionality provided by this program. It also makes use of the File System control, which I discuss in greater detail in Chapter 6.

The Basics of the TreeView Control

The TreeView control provides a way to display data in a tree-like hierarchical structure. It can be configured to use one of a handful of displays that can include text, lines and images. The control handles the expansion and contraction of the nodes that it contains. It also allows the user to rename nodes.

The TreeView control does not have any capabilities to store the images it uses. Instead it depends upon the ImageList control for this.

The Basics of the ListView Control

The ListView control provides a way to display data in one of four ways – **Icon**, **Small Icon**, **List** and **Report**. This view can be changed without having to reload the contents of the control. The ListView control also allows the user to rename the nodes. Like the TreeView control, the ListView control must depend upon ImageList controls for the images it uses.

The Basics of the ImageList Control

The ImageList control is an image container. As a control it has no purpose by itself, only in combination with other controls, like the TreeView and ListView controls, can it serve a purpose. Unlike the desktop version of this control, the ImageList control for CE must be loaded with images at runtime. This means that you must ship all of your images along with your CE applications.

> When creating images to use with the ImageList control keep in mind the size of the images that you are creating and the number of colors that the image should use. Typically, you'll want to create images that make use of only 16 colors. This provides an optimal appearance for all levels of H/PCs.

The Explorer Form

Let's take a look at the form (**frmExplorer**) used by Explorer as shown in the screenshot below. As usual its WindowState property has been set to Maximized:

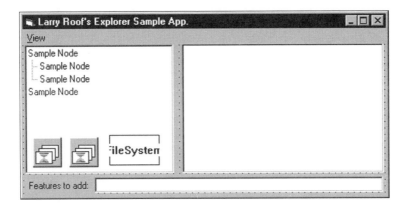

At the top is a single menu containing four items, one for each view provided by the ListView control.

The left-hand side of the form contains a TreeView control (**ceTreeView**) and the right-hand side a ListView control (**ceListView**).

At the bottom of the form are two labels (**lblStatus** and **lblFeatures**) that are used to show the user where to modify the program to add functionality.

Finally there are two ImageList controls (**ceImageListSmall** and **ceImageListBig**) and a File System (**ceFileSystem**) control. Two ImageLists are needed because the ListView control uses one set of images for its Icon view and another for its other views.

Next we will look at some of the key code that is behind the Explorer application.

Starting the Application

The **Form_Load** event procedure begins by calling the **ConfigureControls** routine. This routine handles the configuration of the TreeView, ListView and ImageList controls.

It then calls the **LoadDirectoryStructure** procedure that uses the File System control to retrieve folder and file information:

```
Private Sub Form_Load()

' Configure the TreeView and ListView controls
  ConfigureControls

' Retrieve the directory structure.
  LoadDirectoryStructure

End Sub
```

Configuring the Controls

This procedure begins by adjusting the width of the ListView and text box according to the display's dimensions. It then sets the **Font Size** used by both the TreeView and ListView controls. I happen to think that the default fonts used by both of these controls is way too small (see Chapter 3 for more details on design considerations for H/PCs):

```
Private Sub ConfigureControls()

   Dim objColumnHeader

   On Error Resume Next

' Adjust size of text box and List View
   ceListView.Width = frmExplorer.Width - 200
   lblStatus.Width = frmExplorer.Width - lblFeatures.Width - 200

' Set some default control configurations.
' First the font to use (the default font is way small).
   ceTreeView.FontSize = 10
   ceListView.FontSize = 10
```

The ImageList controls are then configured so that they can accommodate the appropriate size images. In this case one control is set up to hold small images (16 x 16) and the other big images (32 x 32):

```
' Set the size of images that each image control will store.
   ceImageListSmall.ImageHeight = 16
   ceImageListSmall.ImageWidth = 16
   ceImageListBig.ImageHeight = 32
   ceImageListBig.ImageWidth = 32
```

Next the small images are loaded into the first ImageList control using the **Add** method:

```
' Load the small images.
   ceImageListSmall.Add App.Path & "\closed folder - small.bmp"
   ceImageListSmall.Add App.Path & "\open folder - small.bmp"
   ceImageListSmall.Add App.Path & "\application - small.bmp"
```

124

The big images are loaded into the second ImageList control:

```
' Load the large images.
  ceImageListBig.Add App.Path & "\closed folder - big.bmp"
  ceImageListBig.Add App.Path & "\application - big.bmp"
```

The ImageList controls are then associated with the TreeView and ListView controls. Note the use of two ImageLists with the ListView control, one for the Small Icon views (Small Icon, List and Report) and the other for the large icon view (Icon).

```
' Associate the image controls with the TreeView and ListView
' controls.
  ceTreeView.ImageList = ceImageListSmall.hImageList
  ceListView.Icons = ceImageListBig.hImageList
  ceListView.SmallIcons = ceImageListSmall.hImageList
```

Column Headers, **Column Widths** and **Column Alignments** are then defined for the ListView control. These configurations will only appear when the Report view is selected:

```
' Set the column headers for the ListView control.
  Set objColumnHeader = ceListView.ColumnHeaders.Add(, , "Name", _
    2800, lrLeftAlignment)
  Set objColumnHeader = ceListView.ColumnHeaders.Add(, , "Size", _
    800, lrRightAlignment)
  Set objColumnHeader = ceListView.ColumnHeaders.Add(, , "Modified", _
    , lrRightAlignment)

  If (Err.Number <> 0) Then MsgBox Err.Number & " - " & _
    Err.Description

End Sub
```

I have used two user-defined constants here to make the code a little more readable. I prefix these constants with **lr** for Larry Roof so they can be easily recognized for what they are. The constants need to be declared as:

```
Option Explicit

Const lrLeftAlignment = 0
Const lrRightAlignment = 1
```

Gathering the Folder and File Details

At the heart of the Explorer application is the **LoadDirectoryStructure** procedure. This procedure is responsible for retrieving and loading folder and file details into the TreeView and ListView controls.

It starts by adding **My Handheld PC** to the TreeView control. This item can be added because we know that it's always going to be there. We store a reference to the new **Node** in the **objTop** variable, we'll use that later. The syntax of the **Add** method is:

```
ceTreeView.Nodes.Add (Relative, Relationship, Key, Text, Image, Selected Image)
```

Where:

Relative	The index number of key of a pre-existing Node object.
Relationship	Specifies the relative placement of this Node object in relationship to the relative. Acceptable values are 0 – first, 1 – last, 2 – next, 3 – previous, 4 – child.
Key	A unique string that can be used to retrieve this Node.
Text	The string that will be displayed for this Node.
Image	The index of an image that is stored in an associated ImageList control.
Selected Image	The index of an image that is stored in an associated ImageList control. This image will be displayed when this Node is selected.

So for the **My Handheld PC** entry we are using:

- ▲ No **Relative**

- ▲ No **Relationship**

- ▲ The **Key** of **"My Handheld PC"**

- ▲ The **Text** of **"My Handheld PC"**

- ▲ The first image (a closed folder) from the associated ImageList control for the standard display of this node

- ▲ The second image (an open folder) from the associated ImageList control for when this Node is selected

```
Private Sub LoadDirectoryStructure()

  Dim objDirectory
  Dim objFile
  Dim intFileAttributes
  Dim strFilesReturned
  Dim objTop

' Add "My Handheld PC" to the list.
  Set objTop = ceTreeView.Nodes.Add(, , "My Handheld PC", "My Handheld PC", 1, 2)
```

Next we begin the process of retrieving the directory structure. The **Dir** method of the File System control is used to retrieve the first item in the directory:

```
' Get the top level.
  If (mstrPath = "") Then
    strFilesReturned = ceFileSystem.Dir("*.*")

  Else
    strFilesReturned = ceFileSystem.Dir(mstrPath & "\*.*")

  End If
```

Note the form level variable **mstrPath** which needs to be declared.

A loop is used to process the complete structure. This loop will continue until the string returned from the **Dir** method is empty. It starts by using the **GetAttr** method of the File System control to retrieve the attributes for this file:

```
' Make subsequent calls until the complete list has been returned.
While (strFilesReturned <> "")
   intFileAttributes = ceFileSystem.GetAttr(strFilesReturned)
```

Each item that is returned will be added into the ListView control and also the TreeView if the item is a folder object. For each folder item that needs to be displayed in the TreeView control entry we need to use the following information:

My Handheld PC for the Relative. This string value is the **Key** property identifying the root node of the tree.

- The **Relationship** value of **4** (child). This means that this folder Node will be displayed as a subitem of My Handheld PC.

- The **Key** to identify the folder in the TreeView's collection of folder nodes is set to the filename of the folder. In a more complete example we would to use the full path name to the folder to prevent clashes with similarly named folders elsewhere in the directory structure.

- The **Text** is taken from the last part of the filename.

- The first image (a closed folder) from the associated ImageList control for the standard display of this node.

- The second image (an open folder) from the associated ImageList control for when this Node is selected.

The syntax for the add method of the ListView control is:

ceListView.ListItem.Add (Index, Key, Text, Icon, Small Icon)

Where:

Index	An integer specifying the position where you want to insert this item.
Key	A unique string that can be used to retrieve this item from the TreeViews nodes collection.
Text	A string to be displayed for this item.
Icon	The image to display for this item when the ListView control is in icon view.
Small Icon	The image to display for this item when the ListView control is in small icon, list or report view.

For the ListView control entry we are using:

- No **Index**

- An item **Key** taken from the filename

- The **Text** to display, again we use the filename

- The first image from the associated ImageList control holding large images for the icon image

- The first image from the associated ImageList control holding small images for the Small Icon image

127

The file attributes are used to determine whether this is a directory or file. Directories are added into the ListView with folder images for the icons, other file types are added with application icons:

```
' Directories get loaded into both lists.
   If (intFileAttributes = lrDirectory) Then
      Set objDirectory = ceTreeView.Nodes.Add("My Handheld PC", _
            4, strFilesReturned, strFilesReturned, 1, 2)
      Set objFile = ceListView.ListItems.Add(, strFilesReturned, _
            strFilesReturned, 1, 1)

' Files only are loaded into the ListView.
   Else
      Set objFile = ceListView.ListItems.Add(, strFilesReturned, _
            strFilesReturned, 2, 3)

   End If
```

There is another of my constants, **lrDirectory**, used here which needs to be declared:

```
   Const lrDirectory = 16
```

File details (Size, Date Modified) are stored in the ListView control. This information will only appear when the ListView control is in report view from the menu:

```
' Add file details.
  objFile.SubItems(1) = CStr(ceFileSystem.FileLen(strFilesReturned))
  objFile.SubItems(2) = _
    CStr(ceFileSystem.FileDateTime(strFilesReturned))

' Sort the ListView control.
   ceListView.Sorted = True

' Get the next entry in this directory.
   strFilesReturned = ceFileSystem.Dir()
   Wend
```

At this point all of the folders and files have been added to the controls. The TreeView control has its **Sorted** property set to **True** so that the directories will appear in order. Next, the node that represents the root of our tree, **My Handheld PC** has its **Expanded** property set to **True** so that the control displays its children. If we didn't do this all you would see is the My Handheld Computer entry. It's now apparent why we stored a reference to this particular node item when it was created:

```
' Sort and expand the contents of the TreeView control. If you didn't
' set the expanded property here all you would see would be "My
' Handheld PC".
  objTop.Sorted = True
  objTop.Expanded = True

End Sub
```

Displaying a Directory

To extend the functionality of the Explorer application by adding the ability to display other directories you would place code inside the **NodeClick** event procedure of the TreeView control. You could use the **Dir** method of the File System control just as was shown to load to initial interface. This time though start with the directory path as the first request:

```
Private Sub ceTreeView_NodeClick(ByVal Index)

  lblStatus.Caption = "You would need to add code to display the " _
    & "directory contents here."

End Sub
```

Renaming a Directory

To extend the functionality of the Explorer application by adding the ability to rename a directory you would place code inside the **AfterLabelEdit** event procedure of the TreeView control:

```
Private Sub ceTreeView_AfterLabelEdit(ByVal NewString)

  lblStatus.Caption = "You would need to add code for renaming the" _
    & " directory here."

End Sub
```

Processing a Directory Entry

To extend the functionality of the Explorer application by adding the ability to navigate directories or launch applications you would place code inside the **ItemClick** event procedure of the ListView control. You can use the **Shell** method of the VBCE.com Utility control to launch the applications:

```
Private Sub ceListView_ItemClick(ByVal Index)

  lblStatus.Caption = "You would need to add code to process the " _
    & "item that was tapped here."

End Sub
```

Renaming a Directory or File

To extend the functionality of the Explorer application by adding the ability to rename a directory or file you would place code inside the **AfterLabelEdit** event procedure of the ListView control:

```
Private Sub ceListView_AfterLabelEdit(ByVal NewString)

  lblStatus.Caption = "You would need to add code to rename the item here."

End Sub
```

Changing Views

The changing of ListView control views is easy. All you have to do is to change the **View** property of the control to **0** for large Icon, **1** for Small Icon, **2** for a List of small icons or **3** for Report of the items with extra information. Again, I have used a series of user defined constants to make the code a bit more readable. This needs to be declared as:

```
Option Explicit

Private mstrPath

Const lrLeftALignment = 0
Const lrRightAlignment = 1
Const lrDirectory = 16
Const lrIconView = 0
Const lrSmallIconView = 1
Const lrListView = 2
Const lrReportView = 3
```

The **Click** event procedure for the <u>I</u>con menu item of the <u>V</u>iew menu sets the ListView control to icon view. It also configures each of the other menu items:

```
Private Sub mnuViewIcon_Click()

' Set the view in the ListView control to Icon.
  If (mnuViewIcon.Checked = False) Then
    mnuViewIcon.Checked = True
    mnuViewSmallIcon.Checked = False
    mnuViewList.Checked = False
    mnuViewReport.Checked = False
    ceListView.View = lrIconView

  End If

End Sub
```

A similar menu **Click** event procedure is used to implement the <u>S</u>mall Icon, <u>L</u>ist and <u>R</u>eport views:

```
Private Sub mnuViewSmallIcon_Click()

' Set the view in the ListView control to Small Icon.
  If (mnuViewSmallIcon.Checked = False) Then
    mnuViewIcon.Checked = False
    mnuViewSmallIcon.Checked = True
    mnuViewList.Checked = False
    mnuViewReport.Checked = False
    ceListView.View = lrSmallIconView

  End If

End Sub
```

```
Private Sub mnuViewList_Click()

' Set the view in the ListView control to List.
  If (mnuViewList.Checked = False) Then
    mnuViewIcon.Checked = False
    mnuViewSmallIcon.Checked = False
    mnuViewList.Checked = True
    mnuViewReport.Checked = False
    ceListView.View = lrListView

  End If

End Sub
```

```
Private Sub mnuViewReport_Click()

' Set the view in the ListView control to Report.
  If (mnuViewReport.Checked = False) Then
    mnuViewIcon.Checked = False
    mnuViewSmallIcon.Checked = False
    mnuViewList.Checked = False
    mnuViewReport.Checked = True
    ceListView.View = lrReportView

  End If

End Sub
```

Closing Thoughts On Explorer

I really like the TreeView and ListView controls. They offer a familiar interface that you can use to your advantage in your CE applications. They do have a bit of a learning curve though. Getting the syntax down for adding, navigating and manipulating these controls can be a bit tricky. You may find it beneficial to reference the Visual Basic version of Books Online as it offers a far more detailed description on both of these controls than does the version that came with the VBCE Toolkit.

If you noticed, I've given you a number of hooks that you can use to build additional capabilities into the Explorer application. The File System control can be used to move, copy, delete and rename folders and files. The **Shell** method of the VBCE.com Utility control will allow you to launch files. You are on your own for any other features that you may want to add.

Summary

As this chapter began to hint the addition of a few controls turned a minimally functional development tool into a package that allows you to develop full-featured CE applications. These new controls fall into two categories – first, tools that enhance the user interface; second, tools for managing data.

This chapter concentrated primarily on the Interface controls like the TreeView, ListView, TabStrip and Grid controls which allow you to construct CE applications that present a useful, easy to read screen. In the next chapter, I'll be focusing on the second type of ActiveX control, those that are used to manipulate and manage data.

ActiveX Controls for Windows CE – Data Tools

In the previous chapter I concentrated primarily on controls used to create the user interface for CE apps. In this chapter I'll be concentrating on those controls that are used to manipulate and manage your data.

Although the interface controls that I discussed in the previous chapter can significantly improve the way your CE apps can interact with the user, it is really what I have termed the 'data controls' that add powerful functionality to your apps. These controls are what really make VBCE a serious development tool.

> *All the controls (with the exception of the Utility control) are included in the Windows CE ActiveX Control Pack, which you downloaded for the previous chapter.*

The Windows CE ActiveX Data Tool Controls

In these following sections, I'll be giving you a guided tour of the data management components that were included with the VBCE Toolkit - as well as those that make up the ActiveX Control Pack 1.0. I'll start by examining each control and looking at what it has to offer to the developer of CE applications. Then I'll take you through a set of examples that demonstrates how some of these controls can be used to enhance your applications.

The Comm Control

The **Comm**, or communication control provides access to the serial port(s) on your H/PC for the purpose of communicating with other PCs, H/PCs or external devices. Basically, it allows you to develop applications that transmit and received data through a serial port.

This is a seriously cool control. It can be used to send and receive data to a desktop PC, talk to barcode scanners, GPS units and anything else that transmits via a serial connection. It's very similar to the desktop version of the Comm control. I have written an example program, Chat, that demonstrates the use of this control. This is a simple chat program that shows how a desktop and H/PC app can talk to each other.

The Common Dialog Control

The **Common Dialog** control provides access to the CE dialogs that are used for opening and saving files, selecting colors and defining font configurations. It also provides the means for running the CE help engine.

This is a 'must' use control if you are developing any application that includes one or more of these features. It's also one of the easiest ActiveX controls to use. The sample program that is shipped with the Control Pack does a sufficient job of demonstrating the use of the Common Dialog control. In addition, I have used this control in many of the examples throughout this book including Inventory Manager (which you'll see later), Time Manager and EasyEdit.

The File System Control

No one would ever think of a version of BASIC without file I/O. However, that was exactly what the original version of the VBCE Toolkit did. It lacked even the most simple of data storage capabilities. The **File System** control fills this void. It provides access to both the **File** and **File System** object. The File object allows you to read and write data from sequential, random access and binary files whilst the File System object can be used to query and manipulate the directory structures on an H/PC. It allows you to copy, move, delete and obtain information on files and directories.

The use of this control was demonstrated in two of the example apps in the previous chapter: Explorer and DataDisplay. However, for a considerably more detailed discussion, I suggest you turn to Chapter 6.

The Finance Control

The **Finance** control provides access to the **Financial** object. This object provides a comprehensive set of financial functions that can be used to create loan, mortgage and other types of financial-based programs.

While there is no example in this book that demonstrates the use of this function, there is an example included with the VBCE Toolkit. It shows the basics which when combined with the additional documentation found in Books Online should provide you with all that you need to know on using this control.

The Winsock Control

I've got to tell you that the **Winsock** control is my favorite ActiveX control. There are just so many cool things that you can do with it. Basically, it enables you to create CE applications containing communication capabilities. This could be in the form of infrared communications between two H/PCs or an H/PC and a desktop. Or it could be in the form of a venture out onto the Internet to talk with web sites, FTP servers, newsgroups, or some other custom applications that you write. Any control that will allow you to do all of that just seriously rules.

As controls go it can be a bit tricky to start with unless you have some solid sample programs at hand. But not to worry, you'll find the HTML Viewer, later in this chapter, and the ASP Interface in Chapter 8, will get your feet wet working with the Winsock control.

The VBCE.com Utility Control

This control is the Swiss army knife of tools combining a number of different functions into a single control. If provides the following:

- The ability to set and remove a window from being the 'top most' window. This is particularly useful in the construction of toolbar components that you want to always be visible.

- An enhanced version of the **MsgBox** function providing the ability to stay on top of other windows - a feature that is missing from the version included with the VBCE Toolkit.

- A feature that allows you to play wave files from within your applications. This provides a much needed work around for the absence of the **Beep** function in the VBCE Toolkit.

- Two methods that allow you to communicate with windows directly. As you'll see in the example later in this chapter, they can be used to build searching combo boxes and to work around the arrow key navigational bug found in the text box control (more on this later).

- The ability to start another application from within your CE programs.

- A way to display an hourglass icon while your application is busy.

> The VBCE.com Utility control is provided by the fine folks at the www.vbce.com web site. At that site, you'll find code examples, news updates and bug fixes along with a wide variety of other selections. You'll probably want to check their site for updates to the Utility control and other items.

For more details on using the VBCE.com Utility control see the Utility application later in this chapter and the documentation that is provided with the control.

Working with ActiveX Controls

For a detailed discussion on adding ActiveX controls to your projects and using Control Manager refer to this section in the previous chapter.

The Sample Applications

Now that we have covered the basics of the rest of controls, let's turn our attention to the second set of example applications. In this chapter the apps will primarily be demonstrating the use of the data controls, although, except the File System control which has already been demonstrated in the previous chapter.

Unlike other examples from this book, I won't be discussing these applications line-by-line – instead, I'll focus on the most important facets of each example. Neither will we be using the 9 step process that we've seen in the previous chapters, as these apps are only intended to give you a quick introduction to the controls they utilize.

The Chat Example Application

I created the **Chat** application not so much as a functional application - but more to show you how you can use the Comm control to transfer data between a desktop PC and an H/PC.

The Chat application has two components: the desktop version, and H/PC version of Chat. Each of these programs uses a serial port on their respective systems to establish a connection with the other computer. This connection is then used to transfer data that is typed in on one system to the other system.

> *The Chapter 5 versions of* `\Chat Desktop\Chat.vbp` *and* `\Chat HPC\Chat.vbp` *contain the completed versions of the desktop and H/PC versions of Chat. Please refer to Appendix A for instructions on downloading and installing the examples included in this book.*

Features Found in the Chat Application

This application demonstrates the use of the following ActiveX controls:

▲   The Comm control

It also demonstrates the following techniques:

▲   How to establish a communication channel between a desktop PC and an H/PC

▲   How to transfer data between the two systems

Using Chat

The hardest part about using the Chat application is that you need to get the H/PC version of the program onto your hand-held computer and then turn off the Mobile Devices services so that the communication port (and the cable it uses) is free. Once this is done run the Chat program on both your desktop and H/PC.

The easiest way I have found to do this is to access the Communications tab of Windows CE Services Properties dialog (it can be easily accessed by right-clicking on the icon in the taskbar if you have this option set up). From there simply uncheck the Enabled checkbox under Device Connections via Serial Port:

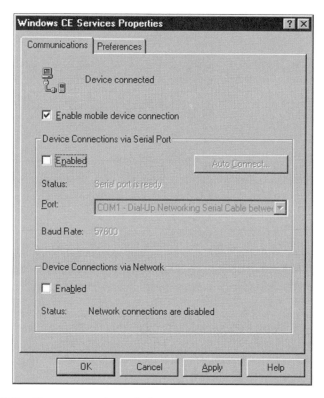

The display on the H/PC will appear as shown below:

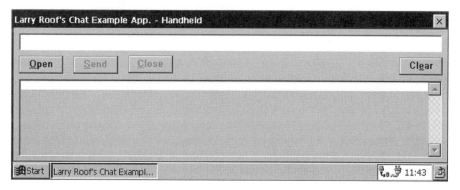

A nearly identical display will be shown on your desktop PC:

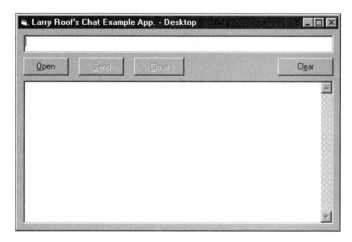

Both of these displays are identical in their layout. At the top of each is a single line text box in which you can enter messages to send to the other Chat application. Clicking on the Open button enables this text box. At the bottom of each is a multi-line text box that is used to display messages received from the other Chat application.

The purpose of the command buttons is as follows:

- ▲ Open – opens the serial communications port
- ▲ Send – sends the contents of the top-most text box to the communications port
- ▲ Close – closes the serial communications port.
- ▲ Clear – clears the lower text box of messages received from the other Chat application

Opening a Communication Port

On each system tap or click the Open button to open serial communication ports that will be used to transfer messages between the two Chat applications. The Send and Close buttons will be enabled while the Open button will be disabled.

Sending Messages

Enter a message into the top text box control on the H/PC and tap the Send button. The message will be displayed in the desktop Chat application. Enter a message on the desktop PC and click the Send button. The message will be transferred to the H/PC and be displayed.

An example of how the H/PC display should appear at this point is shown below. Obviously, the text of the message *you* sent may be different.

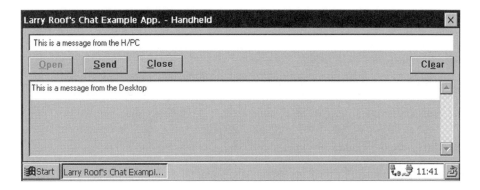

The desktop PC display at this point should appear like this:

Building Chat

At the heart of this application is the Comm, or communication, control. It provides the conduit for transferring the messages between the desktop and H/PC. The techniques demonsrated in this chapter can be used in your own CE applications to transfer data to and from desktop systems. These will work with either a direct connection using a cable or over a phone connection by using a modem.

The Basics of the Comm Control

The Comm control allows you to send and receive data over serial communication ports. This can be a useful tool in any CE applications that require transferal of data to or from a desktop computer. It gives you a significant level of control as to how the data is transferred, much more than is provided by the automatic synchronization feature built into the Windows CE Services.

Working with the Comm control involves two steps:

- Step One is the configuration and opening of a serial port
- Step Two is the transfer and receipt of data via the serial port

In the following section, you'll see how these two steps are implemented in the Chat program.

The Chat Form

Let's take a look at the form (**frmChat**) used by Chat as shown in the screenshot below. This is the H/PC version - but as you'll see shortly, it's virtually identical in design to the desktop version:

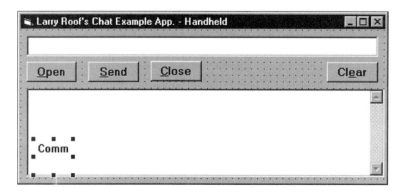

At the top is a single-line text box (**txtSend**) that's been disabled. This control is used to enter messages that will be sent to the other computer. It's enabled in the **Click** event of the Open command button (**cmdOpen**).

Below that are four command buttons. Two of the buttons (Open and Clear) are enabled. The other two (Send (**cmdSend**) and Close (**cmdClose**)) are disabled. The buttons will be enabled and disabled depending upon the current status of the application.

At the bottom of the interface is a multi-line text box (**txtReceive**). It's used to display messages as they are received. This text box is locked and can only be cleared by using the Clear command button (**cmdClear**).

The control outline that you see at the bottom of this screenshot is the Comm control (**ceComm**).

The screenshot below shows the interface to the desktop version. The only noticeable difference between the H/PC and desktop versions is that the MSComm control sports an icon in design mode on the desktop:

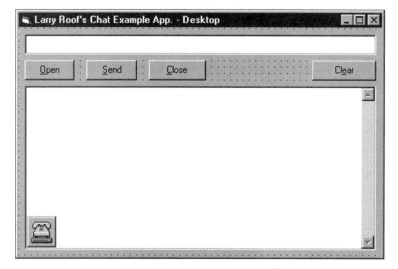

The only other real difference is that the handheld's form has its WindowState property set to 2 - Maximized.

> **There is a problem working with the Comm control on the H/PC. It stems from the fact that every time that you want to test out a program you have to first transfer the program to the H/PC, then stop and disconnect the services between the two computers to free up the Comm port.**

Basically you need to get the **.pvb** file onto the handheld and then you can simply run the app. using the Run dialog under the Start menu. There are two simple methods to do this:

▲ Make the H/PC program using the File | Make menu item. This will create your H/PC program on your desktop PC

▲ Use NT Explorer to copy the **.pvb** file onto the handheld

▲ Disconnect Windows Services as described above

or you can:

Run the program from VB with the Target set at Remote Device, this will copy the **.pvb** onto the handheld

▲ Close the app. and then run it using the Start menu's Run option

▲ Disconnect Windows Services as described above

Next we will look at some of the key code that is behind the Chat application.

The code for the desktop and handheld versions of the Chat application is identical, although you may want to name the projects and forms differently so that there is less confusion over which version is run where. You can also miss out the lines that deal with resizing the controls to fit the display.

Starting the Application

When this application begins it starts by adjusting the controls that comprise the interface. There is nothing tricky here; it simply stretches and repositions controls as is appropriate for the H/PC.

It then sets the **Rthreshold** property to **1**. This property is used to specify how many characters this control receives before firing an **OnComm** event:

> **The reason that I set this property in code was to make sure that you were aware of this configuration. The Rthreshold property must be set to a value other than zero for the OnComm event to fire.**

```
Private Sub Form_Load()

' Fit the interface to the palmtop.
  AdjustControls

' Set the threshold property to a single character.
' You could just as well set this property from code but I wanted to
' make sure that you saw them being configured.
  ceComm.Rthreshold = 1

End Sub
```

```
Sub AdjustControls()

' Extend the size of the interface to match the size of the display
' on the palmtop.
  txtSend.Width = frmChat.Width - txtSend.Left - 150
  txtReceive.Width = frmChat.Width - txtReceive.Left - 150
  txtReceive.Height = frmChat.Height - 1550
  cmdClear.Left = frmChat.Width - cmdClear.Width - 150

End Sub
```

Opening the Communications Port

The click event procedure for the <u>O</u>pen button contains the code used to open the serial communications port. The procedure begins by setting up an error handler. This is probably unnecessary in an example program. I included it so that you would remember the importance of its use in your communication applications:

```
Private Sub cmdOpen_Click()

  On Error Resume Next
```

Next the settings for the Comm control are defined. I did this from code so that you could see the formation of this property setting. If you wanted you could add functionality into your programs so that the user could configure these settings:

```
' Configure the settings of 19200 bps, no parity, 8 data bits, and
' 1 stop bit.
  ceComm.Settings = "19200,n,8,1"

  If Err.Number <> 0 Then
    MsgBox "Error setting properties." & vbCrLf & Err.Number & _
           " - " & Err.Description
    Err.Clear
    Exit Sub

  End If
```

Then set the **CommPort** property to the port that we will be using.

```
' Configure it to use Comm port 1.
ceComm.CommPort = 1

If Err.Number <> 0 Then
  MsgBox "Error setting Comm port number." & vbCrLf & Err.Number _
         & " - " & Err.Description
  Err.Clear
  Exit Sub

End If
```

Finally, the communications port is opened by setting the **PortOpen** property to **True**:

```
' Open the Comm port.
ceComm.PortOpen = True

If Err.Number <> 0 Then
  MsgBox "Error opening the Comm port." & vbCrLf & Err.Number & _
         " - " & Err.Description
  Err.Clear
  Exit Sub

End If
```

This procedure concludes by configuring the interface accordingly:

```
' Set the controls according to the current status.
cmdOpen.Enabled = False
cmdSend.Enabled = True
cmdClose.Enabled = True
txtSend.Enabled = True
txtSend.SetFocus

End Sub
```

Sending a Message

The **Click** event procedure for the <u>S</u>end button handles the transferal of data via the communication port to the other system. This is accomplished by setting the **Output** property of the Comm control to the contents of the top-most text box with the addition of a carriage return - line feed combination. Adding the carriage return – line feed characters will help format the messages as they are displayed by the receiving application:

```
Private Sub cmdSend_Click()

  On Error Resume Next

' Send the message via the Comm port.
  ceComm.Output = txtSend.Text & vbCrLf

  If Err.Number <> 0 Then
    MsgBox "Error sending message." & vbCrLf & Err.Number & _
           " - " & Err.Description
```

```
            Err.Clear

      End If

End Sub
```

Closing the Communication Port

The closing of the serial communication port is handled in the **Click** event procedure for the <u>C</u>lose button. This is accomplished by setting the **PortOpen** property to **False**:

```
Private Sub cmdClose_Click()

  On Error Resume Next

' Close the Comm port.
  ceComm.PortOpen = False

  If Err.Number <> 0 Then
    MsgBox "Error closing the Comm port." & vbCrLf & Err.Number & _
           " - " & Err.Description
    Err.Clear

  End If
```

The command buttons are then reconfigured to represent this new state:

```
' Set the controls according to the current status.
  cmdOpen.Enabled = True
  cmdSend.Enabled = False
  cmdClose.Enabled = False
  txtSend.Enabled = False

End Sub
```

Receiving a Message

The Comm control offers two ways to determine if any data has been received:

▲ To continuously poll the control checking to see

▲ To configure the **Rthreshold** property to a value greater than **1** and use the **OnComm** event

I prefer the second method; it's much cleaner and doesn't sit and consume processor cycles as it repetitively polls the Comm control. An example of this second method is shown in the code fragment below. By checking the **CommEvent** property you can determine why this event was fired. A value of **2** means that data has been received.

```
Private Sub ceComm_OnComm()

  Select Case ceComm.CommEvent

    Case 2 ' Data received.
      txtReceive.Text = txtReceive.Text & ceComm.Input
```

```
        End Select

    End Sub
```

Clearing the Receive Text Box

Finally we just need to allow the large text box to be cleared when the Clear button is pressed:

```
    Private Sub cmdClear_Click()

      txtReceive.Text = ""

    End Sub
```

Closing Thoughts on Chat

As you can see from this example using the serial communications port to transfer data between a desktop PC and an H/PC is not that difficult. A more detailed discussion on the use of the serial port to transfer data can be found in Chapter 8.

> *If you want to see another example app using the Comm control then take a look at the GPS example in the source code. Refer to Appendix A for more information.*

The Utility Example Application

The **Utility** program is included to demonstrate how to use the various functions of the VBCE.com Utility control that is used with this book. Instructions on how to obtain this control can be found in Appendix A. Included in this application are examples of nearly all of the methods that are provided by this control.

> *The Chapter 5 version of* **Utility.vbp** *contains the completed version of the Utility example program. Refer to Appendix A for instructions on downloading the examples in this book.*

Features Found in the Utility Program

This application demonstrates the use of the following ActiveX control:

▲   The VBCE.com Utility control

It also demonstrates the following techniques:

▲   How to use the **MsgBox** method
▲   How to use the **OnTop** method
▲   How to use the **PlayWaveFile** method
▲   How to use the **SendMessageLong** method
▲   How to use the **SendMessageString** method
▲   How to use the **Shell** method
▲   How to use the **WaitCursor** method

Using the Utility Program

The Utility program is designed to demonstrate the various methods provided by the VBCE.com Utility control. A single form application is used for this purpose. When the application runs it displays the interface as you can see here:

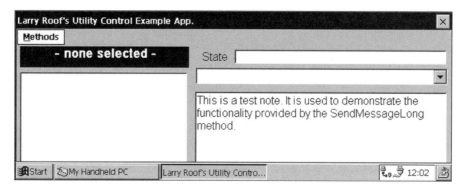

The Methods menu provides access to a set of demonstrate the methods. Selecting the menu item AlwaysOnTopOn will cause a small form (see below) to be displayed over the form of the Utility program. This form has been configured so that it will always stay on top of the other forms. To see this try tapping on the Utility program. Even though the Utility program now has the focus the On Top form remains in the display. Close the On Top form by tapping the X.

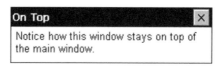

Selecting the MsgBox menu item from the Methods menu will cause the following dialog to be displayed:

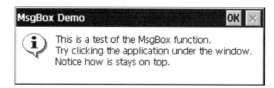

Unlike the dialog display by the **MsgBox** function included with the VBCE Toolkit, this dialog will remain on top of other forms. Close the MsgBox dialog by tapping the OK button.

Next, select the PlayWaveFile menu item. If the audio is enabled on your H/PC you will hear an alarm played.

To test the SendMessageLong method, select it from the Methods menu. This method allows you to send messages to the components of your applications, extending the functionality provided by the VBCE Toolkit. In this example the **SendMessageLong** method is being used to correct a bug in the text box control.

> One of the biggest bugs in the VBCE Toolkit is the way that the arrow keys do not function in a text box. Fortunately, using the Utility control plus a bit of coding allows you to get around this problem!

Now select SendMessageString from the Methods menu. This method, like the **SendMessageLong** method is used to send messages to the form and controls that make up your application. The example that demonstrates the uses for this method shows a searching combo box. As you type in the name of a state in a text box the state is found in a combo box.

The demonstration for the Shell method launches the CE calculator application:

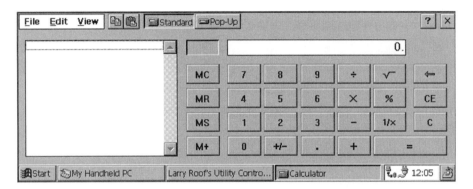

Finally selecting WaitCursor from the Methods menu will cause the hourglass cursor to be displayed for three seconds. You can use this feature to inform your user that a process is occurring and that they should wait:

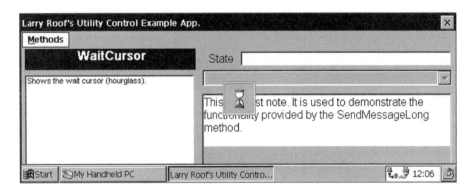

Building the Utility Program

The Utility program is a sampler plate of the VBCE.com Utility control methods. It has no purpose other than to show what the control can do.

The Utility Program Forms

Let's take a look at the forms used by the VBCE.com Utility program. There are two forms - the primary form (**frmUtiltiy**) and a secondary form (**frmOnTop**) that is used to demonstrate the **AlwaysOnTopOn** method. The primary form is set to run in a Maximized state. An example of the primary form is shown in the screenshot below.

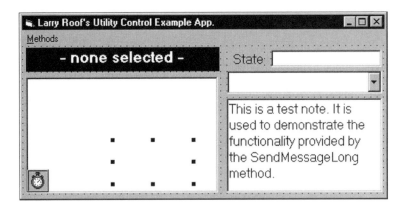

At the top of the primary form is a single menu titled <u>M</u>ethods. This menu contains items for each of the methods provided by the VBCE.com Utility control.

Positioned under the menu is a label (**lblMethod**) used to display the name of the method that is currently selected. Underneath the **lblMethod** label is another label (**lblDescription**) used to display a description of the method that is currently selected.

At the top of the right-hand side of the display are a label (**lblState**) and a text box (**txtState**). The text box is used to demonstrate the **SendMessageString** method.

Below the text box is a combo box control (**cboStates**) that contains the names of the 50 states in the United States in its List property. This control is used in conjunction with the text box to build a 'searching' combo box.

At the lower right of the display is a multi-line text box (**txtNote**). This control is used to demonstrate the **SendMessageLong** method.

Also, at the lower left of the display is a timer control (**ceTimer**) that is used to remove the hourglass cursor that is displayed by the **WaitCursor** method.

Finally, the control outline that you can see is the VBCE.com Utility control (**ceUtility**) which provides all the functionality for this application.

The secondary form is simple. It has a single label control and a VBCE.com Utility control on its interface:

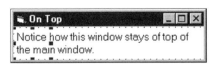

Next we will look at some of the key code that is behind the Utility program.

Starting the Application

In this instance the **Form_Load** event procedure does little more than resize several of the controls:

```
Private Sub Form_Load()

' Adjust the controls
  txtNote.Width = frmUtility.Width - lblDescription.Width - 350
  cboStates.Width = frmUtility.Width - lblDescription.Width - 350
  txtState.Width = frmUtility.Width - lblMethod.Width - lblState.Width - 600

End Sub
```

The MsgBox Method

The **MsgBox** method of the VBCE.com Utility control operates identical to the **MsgBox** function supplied with the VBCE Toolkit. The **Click** event procedure for the M̲sgbox menu item begins by configuring the interface of the Utility program. It displays the name of the method and its description:

```
Private Sub mnuMsgbox_Click()

  Dim intUserSelection

' Update the informational part of the display.
  lblMethod.Caption = "MsgBox"
  lblDescription.Caption = "Displays a message in a dialog box, " _
    & "waits for the user to click a button, and returns an " _
    & "Integer indicating which button the user clicked." _
    & vbCrLf & vbCrLf & "The MsgBox function is identical to that " _
    & "of the standard VBCE MsgBox function, except that the " _
    & "message box displayed will be modal to the application " _
    & "unlike the VBCE function."
```

It then disables all of the controls on the right-hand side of the interface, as they have nothing to do with this method:

```
  txtState.Enabled = False
  cboStates.Enabled = False
  txtNote.Enabled = False
```

Finally the message box is displayed. Note the use of the Visual Basic constants here. The **MsgBox** method can use all of the constants that you would use with the Visual Basic **MsgBox** function:

```
' Display a message box.
  intUserSelection = ceUtility.MsgBox("This is a test of the " _
    & "MsgBox function." & vbCrLf & "Try clicking the " _
    & "application under the window." & vbCrLf & "Notice how is " _
    & "stays on top.", vbInformation, "MsgBox Demo")

End Sub
```

The AlwaysOnTopOn Method

The **Click** event procedure for the **AlwaysOnTopOn** method begins by displaying the name and description of the method:

```
Private Sub mnuAlwaysOnTopOn_Click()

' Update the informational part of the display.
  lblMethod.Caption = "AlwaysOnTopOn"
  lblDescription.Caption = "The AlwaysOnTopOn method places a " _
    & "window on top of all other windows. When the window is " _
    & "no longer needed to be on top, use the AlwaysOnTopOff " _
    & "method to turn it off." & vbCrLf & vbCrLf & "This " _
    & "functionality could be used to create toolbar or control " _
    & "windows that sit on top of your applications interface."
```

It then disables all of the controls on the right-hand side of the interface, as they have nothing to do with this method:

```
  txtState.Enabled = False
  cboStates.Enabled = False
  txtNote.Enabled = False
```

Finally it displays the secondary form that will be used to demonstrate the On Top functionality. The configuration of that form is handled in the **Form_Load** event procedure for the form:

```
' Display the form used to demonstrate the on top functionality.
  frmOnTop.Show

End Sub
```

Setting the Form to be on Top

When the secondary form is shown, its **Form_Load** event procedure is executed. In this procedure the **AlwaysOnTopOn** method is demonstrated. This method accepts a single argument that is the **hWnd** property of the form to be set on top. **hWnd** is the windows handle, which is nothing more than an identification number that the operating system assigns to windows (forms) as they are created:

```
Private Sub Form_Load()

' Set this form to stay on top.
  ceUtility.AlwaysOnTopOn frmOnTop.hWnd

End Sub
```

> There is a complementary method called **AlwaysOnTopOff** - but I'll leave to you to figure out what it does.

The PlayWaveFile Method

Another feature left out of the VBCE Toolkit is the **Beep** function. The **PlayWaveFile** method provides a substitute for this. This method can be used to play any wave file that is resident on the H/PC.

The **Click** event procedure for this menu item begins just as the previous examples have by displaying the name of the method and its description. It then disables all of the controls on the right-hand side of the interface.

```
Private Sub mnuPlayWave_Click()

' Update the informational part of the display.
    lblMethod.Caption = "PlayWave"
    lblDescription.Caption = "Plays a *.wav file."

    txtState.Enabled = False
    cboStates.Enabled = False
    txtNote.Enabled = False
```

Using the **PlayWaveFile** method is simple. It has a single argument that is the path to a wave file:

```
' Play a wave file.
    ceUtility.PlayWaveFile "\windows\alarm1.wav"

End Sub
```

The SendMessageLong Method

The **Click** event procedure for the **SendMessageLong** method begins like all of the others by displaying the name and description of this function:

```
Private Sub mnuSendMessageLong_Click()

' Update the informational part of the display.
    lblMethod.Caption = "SendMessageLong"
    lblDescription.Caption = "Sends a message to a window. This can " _
        & "be used for multiple purposes." & vbCrLf & vbCrLf _
        & "In this example it is used to fix the arrow key " _
        & "navigational bug in the textbox control. Try using the " _
        & "arrow keys to move about the textbox in the lower right " _
        & "of this interface."
```

The controls on the right-hand side of the interface are configured so that only the bottom multi-line text box is accessible. The focus is moved to that control as well so that the user can test out the bug fix for the text box navigational keys:

```
    txtState.Enabled = False
    cboStates.Enabled = False
    txtNote.Enabled = True
    txtNote.SetFocus

End Sub
```

Processing Arrow Keys in a Text Box Control

The **KeyUp** event of the multi-line text box is used to trap arrow keys as they are entered.

> Normally you would expect to see this code in the KeyDown event, but there is yet
> another bug in the VBCE Toolkit – one that prohibits the KeyDown event from
> firing!

The **KeyCode** argument is examined to determine if the key pressed was one of the arrow keys. If it was, then the appropriate navigational procedure is called:

```
Private Sub txtNote_KeyUp(KeyCode, Shift)

' If an arrow key was pressed process it.
  If (Shift = 0) Then

    Select Case KeyCode

      Case 37: ArrowLeft txtNote, ceUtility

      Case 38: ArrowUp txtNote, ceUtility

      Case 39: ArrowRight txtNote, ceUtility

      Case 40: ArrowDown txtNote, ceUtility

    End Select

  End If

End Sub
```

All of the navigational procedures accept two arguments. The first argument is the text box control to navigate. The second argument is the VBCE.com Utility control that will be used to control movement about the text box. These procedures are written so that you can easily incorporate them into your applications.

The **ArrowDown** procedure begins by using the **SendMessageLong** method to determine where the cursor is presently located at in the text box control. There are a wide variety of messages that this method can be used for. Some are demonstrated in this procedure to query and manipulate text box controls:

```
Private Sub ArrowDown(TextBox, Utility)

  Dim intCharPos
  Dim intCharsPriorToLine
  Dim intCurLine
  Dim intCursorPosOnLine
  Dim intNextLineLen
  Dim intTotalLines


  On Error Resume Next
```

```
' Find out where the cursor is presently at in the textbox.
intTotalLines = Utility.SendMessageLong(TextBox.hWnd, _
            EM_GETLINECOUNT, 0, 0)
intCharPos = Utility.SendMessageLong(TextBox.hWnd, _
            EM_LINEINDEX, -1, 0)
intCurLine = Utility.SendMessageLong(TextBox.hWnd, _
            EM_LINEFROMCHAR, intCharPos, 0)
```

Since this is a down arrow operation, if the cursor is already at the last line it cannot move any lower:

```
' The cursor is already at the last line. It can't move down.
If intCurLine = (intTotalLines - 1) Then Exit Sub
```

If this is not the last line then we need to gather some more information. Particularly we are interested in where the cursor is in the current line, how many characters there are prior to the current line and how long the next line is:

```
' Get more information on the cursor position.
intCharsPriorToLine = Utility.SendMessageLong(TextBox.hWnd, _
            EM_LINEINDEX, intCurLine, 0)
intCursorPosOnLine = TextBox.SelStart - intCharsPriorToLine
intCharsPriorToLine = Utility.SendMessageLong(TextBox.hWnd, _
            EM_LINEINDEX, intCurLine + 1, 0)
intNextLineLen = Utility.SendMessageLong(TextBox.hWnd, _
            EM_LINELENGTH, intCharsPriorToLine, 0)
```

All of this information is used to determine where to position the cursor in the next line:

```
' Set the new cursor position.
If (intCursorPosOnLine <= intNextLineLen) Then
  TextBox.SelStart = intCharsPriorToLine + intCursorPosOnLine

Else
  TextBox.SelStart = intCharsPriorToLine + intNextLineLen

End If
```

Finally we want to be sure that the cursor is visible in the text box control window. The **ScrollTextBox** procedure verifies this. It makes use of the **SendMessageLong** function as well:

```
' Make sure that the cursor is visible.
ScrollTextBox TextBox, Utility

End Sub
```

The **ScrollTextBox** procedure...

```
Public Sub ScrollTextBox(TextBox, Utility)

' This routine works around the textbox scrolling bug by manually
' scrolling the text box so that the caret (cursor) is in view.
  Call Utility.SendMessageLong(TextBox.hWnd, EM_SCROLLCARET, 0, 0)

End Sub
```

I'm not going to go into the discussion of the other Arrow procedures here – **ArrowLeft**, **ArrowRight** and **ArrowUp**. They all perform similar functions to this procedure by querying and manipulating the text box control using the **SendMessageLong** method:

```vb
Private Sub ArrowUp(TextBox, Utility)

    Dim intCharPos
    Dim intCRLFOffset
    Dim intCurLine
    Dim intCharsPriorToLine
    Dim intCursorPosOnLine
    Dim intPrevLineLen

    On Error Resume Next

' Find out where the cursor is presently at in the textbox.
    intCharPos = Utility.SendMessageLong(TextBox.hWnd, EM_LINEINDEX, -1, 0)
    intCurLine = Utility.SendMessageLong(TextBox.hWnd, _
                    EM_LINEFROMCHAR, intCharPos, 0)

' The cursor is already at the first line. It can't move up.
    If (intCurLine = 0) Then Exit Sub

' Get more information on the cursor position.
    intCharsPriorToLine = Utility.SendMessageLong(TextBox.hWnd, _
                    EM_LINEINDEX, intCurLine, 0)
    intCursorPosOnLine = TextBox.SelStart - intCharsPriorToLine
    intPrevLineLen = Utility.SendMessageLong(TextBox.hWnd, _
                    EM_LINELENGTH, TextBox.SelStart - intCursorPosOnLine - 2, 0)

' Handle carriage return / line feed combinations that are
' encountered.
    If (Mid(TextBox.Text, intCharsPriorToLine - 1, 2) = vbCrLf) Then _
                                                intCRLFOffset = 2

' Set the new cursor position.
    If (intPrevLineLen < intCursorPosOnLine) Then
      TextBox.SelStart = intCharsPriorToLine - intCRLFOffset

    Else
      TextBox.SelStart = intCharsPriorToLine - (intPrevLineLen - _
                    intCursorPosOnLine) - intCRLFOffset

    End If

' Make sure that the cursor is visible.
    ScrollTextBox TextBox, Utility

End Sub

Private Sub ArrowLeft(TextBox, Utility)

    Dim intCharPos
    Dim intCharsPriorToLine
    Dim intCurLine
```

```
    On Error Resume Next

' The cursor is already at the first character. It can't move left.
    If (TextBox.SelStart = 0) Then Exit Sub

' Get move information on the cursor position.
    intCharPos = Utility.SendMessageLong(TextBox.hWnd, EM_LINEINDEX, -1, 0)
    intCurLine = Utility.SendMessageLong(TextBox.hWnd, _
                        EM_LINEFROMCHAR, intCharPos, 0)
    intCharsPriorToLine = Utility.SendMessageLong(TextBox.hWnd, _
                        EM_LINEINDEX, intCurLine, 0)

' Set the new cursor position.
    If TextBox.SelStart - intCharsPriorToLine = 0 Then
      TextBox.SelStart = intCharsPriorToLine - 2

    Else
      TextBox.SelStart = TextBox.SelStart - 1

    End If

' Make sure that the cursor is visible.
    ScrollTextBox TextBox, Utility

End Sub


Private Sub ArrowRight(TextBox, Utility)

    Dim intCharPos
    Dim intCharsPriorToLine
    Dim intCurLine
    Dim intCursorPosOnLine
    Dim intLineLen
    Dim intTotalLines

    On Error Resume Next

' Find out where the cursor is presently at in the textbox.
    intTotalLines = Utility.SendMessageLong(TextBox.hWnd, _
                EM_GETLINECOUNT, 0, 0)
    intCharPos = Utility.SendMessageLong(TextBox.hWnd, EM_LINEINDEX, -1, 0)
    intCurLine = Utility.SendMessageLong(TextBox.hWnd, _
                EM_LINEFROMCHAR, intCharPos, 0)

' The cursor is already at the last line. It can't move down.
    If intCurLine = (intTotalLines - 1) Then

      If (TextBox.SelStart < Len(TextBox.Text)) Then
            TextBox.SelStart = TextBox.SelStart + 1
      End If
      Exit Sub

    End If
```

```
' Get more information on the cursor position.
  intCharsPriorToLine = Utility.SendMessageLong(TextBox.hWnd, _
                        EM_LINEINDEX, intCurLine, 0)
  intCursorPosOnLine = TextBox.SelStart - intCharsPriorToLine

  If (intCurLine = 0) Then
    intLineLen = Utility.SendMessageLong(TextBox.hWnd, _
               EM_LINELENGTH, 0, 0)

  Else
    intLineLen = Utility.SendMessageLong(TextBox.hWnd, _
               EM_LINELENGTH, intCharsPriorToLine + 2, 0)

  End If

' Set the new cursor position.

  If intCursorPosOnLine < intLineLen Then
    TextBox.SelStart = TextBox.SelStart + 1

  Else
    TextBox.SelStart = TextBox.SelStart + 2

  End If

' Make sure that the cursor is visible.
  ScrollTextBox TextBox, Utility

End Sub
```

In order for these procedures to work you need to declare some constants:

```
Option Explicit

Const EM_LINEFROMCHAR = &HC9
Const EM_LINEINDEX = &HBB
Const EM_LINELENGTH = &HC1
Const EM_SCROLLCARET = &HB7
Const EM_GETLINECOUNT = &HBA
```

> *This code isn't a perfect solution, as it uses the number of characters in a line to track the cursor position rather than the relative position in the text box itself. This can make the up and down arrow keys seem like they are acting a little erratically if the font used doesn't have proportional characters.*

The SendMessageString Method

Like the **SendMessageLong** method, the **SendMessageString** method can be used to query and manipulate the controls that are used by an application. In this example the control that is being manipulated is a combo box.

This procedure starts like all the others – by displaying the name and description of this method:

```
Private Sub mnuSendMessageString_Click()

' Update the informational part of the display.
   lblMethod.Caption = "SendMessageString"
   lblDescription.Caption = "Sends a message to a window. This can " _
             & "be used for multiple purposes." & vbCrLf & vbCrLf _
             & "In this example it is used to auto-locate an entry in a " _
             & "combo box."
```

It then enables two of the controls on the right-hand side of the interface – the text box control that will be used to type in the name of the states and the combo box control that will be augmented with the search capabilities.

Finally the focus is set to the text box where the state will be typed:

```
   txtState.Enabled = True
   cboStates.Enabled = True
   txtNote.Enabled = False
   txtState.SetFocus

End Sub
```

Adding the Search Capability

It's in the **Change** event procedure of the text box that the 'search' feature is implemented. The **SendMessageString** method of the VBCE.com Utility control is used to send a message to the combo box asking it if it contains a string that matches what has been typed into the text box. The combo box will respond with an index into its contents referencing where the matching string is located. If no match is found the combo box returns a value of –**1**.

What happens is that as every character is typed into the text box, the first occurrence of the matching string is located in the combo box. This will give the combo box the appearance of searching out items in a more restrictive fashion as each additional character is typed into the text box:

```
Private Sub txtState_Change()

   Dim intMatchIndex

' Locate the state in the list. If a match is not found the index will
' contain the value of -1.
   intMatchIndex = ceUtility.SendMessageString(cboStates.hWnd, _
               CB_FINDSTRING, -1, txtState.Text)
```

Setting the **ListIndex** property of the combo box to the value returned from the **SendMessageString** method will position the combo box to display the matching entry:

```
' Set the index for the control.
   cboStates.ListIndex = intMatchIndex

End Sub
```

Again there's a constant to declare:

```
Const CB_FINDSTRING = &H14C
```

The Shell Method

The **Shell** method provides the same functionality as the **Shell** function that is part of Visual Basic but missing from the VBCE Toolkit.

The **Click** event procedure for this method starts like all of the other method procedures by displaying the name and description of the method:

```
Private Sub mnuShell_Click()

' Update the informational part of the display.
  lblMethod.Caption = "Shell"
  lblDescription.Caption = "Runs an executable program."
```

It then disables all of the controls on the right-hand side of the interface, as they are not used in this example:

```
  txtState.Enabled = False
  cboStates.Enabled = False
  txtNote.Enabled = False
```

Finally the **Shell** method is used passing as its single argument the name of the program to execute. In the case of this demonstration that program is the CE calculator program:

```
' Launch the calculator.
  ceUtility.Shell "\windows\calc.exe"

End Sub
```

The WaitCursor Method

The final method is the **WaitCursor** method. The purpose of this method is to display the hourglass cursor on the H/PC to inform the user that something is being processed and that they should wait.

This procedure, like all the rest, starts with a description of the method and configurations of the interface:

```
Private Sub mnuWaitCursor_Click()

' Update the informational part of the display.
  lblMethod.Caption = "WaitCursor"
  lblDescription.Caption = "Shows the wait cursor (hourglass)."

  txtState.Enabled = False
  cboStates.Enabled = False
  txtNote.Enabled = False
```

This demonstration of the **WaitCursor** method involves two steps. The first step configures and starts a Timer control to go off in 3 seconds. The second step uses the **WaitCursor** method to display the hourglass. This is accomplished by passing the value **True** as the only argument to this method:

```
' Display the wait cursor. It will be displayed for 3 seconds after
' which the timer event will clear it.
  ceTimer.Interval = 3000
  ceTimer.Enabled = True
  ceUtility.WaitCursor True

End Sub
```

In the **Timer** event of the Timer control is the code to turn the hourglass off. Again the **WaitCursor** method is called but this time with the argument of **False**:

```
Private Sub ceTimer_Timer()

' The purpose of this procedure is to clear the wait cursor after 3
' seconds.
  ceTimer.Enabled = False
  ceUtility.WaitCursor False

End Sub
```

Closing Thoughts on the Utility Program

As you have seen in this section the VBCE.com Utility control offers a wide variety of functionality and complexity. Some of its methods, like **WaitCursor** and **PlayWaveFile** provide a specific feature and are very easy to use. Others, like the **SendMessageLong** and **SendMessageString** methods, will require you to use a Windows API reference to utilize all that they have to offer. Overall this control provides many of the features and functions that are lacking from the VBCE Toolkit.

Don't forget to check the VBCE.com web site at **www.vbce.com** for updates on this control.

The HTML Viewer Example Application

The **HTML Viewer** demonstrates how to extend the communication capabilities of your applications through the use of the Winsock control. In this example application, you'll see how to request and receive documents from a web server. This is a powerful tool that can be used to enable your applications to send and receive data wherever they may be used – just as long as there is a phone line and modem to establish an Internet connection.

> The Chapter 5 version of **HTML Viewer.vbp** *contains the completed version of the HTML Viewer example program. Refer to Appendix A for instructions on downloading and installing the examples included in this book.*

> **There are numerous bugs with the Winsock control, which means that you may experience some problems running this app. For example, it tends to only work with a dial-up connection not a network connection. See Appendix B for more details on bugs.**

Features Found in HTML Viewer

This application demonstrates the use of the following ActiveX control:

- The Winsock control

It also demonstrates the following techniques:

- How to connect to a web server
- How to request a document from a web server
- How to access a document once it has been received

Using the HTML Viewer

The HTML Viewer can be used to request a document from a web server and then display the HTML code that is returned. It doesn't do anything fancy with the code that is returned. It simply loads the raw HTML into a text box control.

> **To use this application you must first establish an Internet connection from your H/PC.**

When this application runs it displays the interface as shown below:

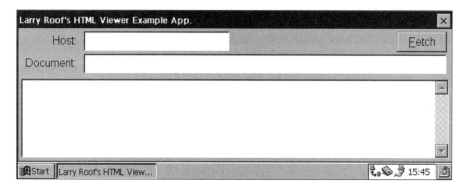

To use HTML Viewer, enter the host and the document that you want delivered and tap the Fetch button. The message - Fetching page... will be displayed informing you that the retrieval process has begun. Assuming that you requested a valid page from a valid server, and that the server is accessible, and not to busy, well you get the point, the document will be displayed in the multi-line text box control at the bottom of the form. An example of this is shown in the screenshot below:

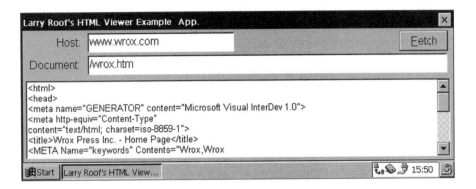

Building the HTML Viewer

The HTML Viewer application is not intended to show you everything that you can do with the Winsock control. The fact of the matter is that it barely scrapes the surface. I created this application to introduce you to some of the possibilities that are available to you as the developer of CE applications.

The Basics of the Winsock Control

The Winsock control is not difficult to use but certainly is difficult to master. That is because much of what you do with this control is dependent upon understanding another protocol such as the HTTP protocol used by web servers, or another language such as the HTML documents returned by web servers. The fact of the matter is that there are whole books that deal with using the Winsock control.

What I'm going to show you in this example are the basic steps that you need to use the Winsock control to access web servers to retrieve HTML documents. In a real application you could then parse the HTML to extract information or even send data to the server to be processed as part of an Active Server Page (you will see an example of this in Chapter 8).

The HTML Viewer Form

Let's take a look at the form (**frmHTMLViewer**) used by the HTML Viewer, as shown in the following screenshot. As usual, it's set to run Maximized:

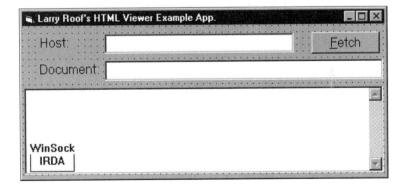

At the top of the form is a label and text box (**txtHost**) used to enter the name of the host to access. Next to that is a command button (**cmdFetch**) that triggers the retrieval process.

Immediately below that is another label and text box (**txtDocument**) combination that is used to enter the name and path of the document to retrieve.

The majority of the HTML Viewer interface is made up of a multi-line text box control (**txtHTML**) that is used to display the documents as they are received.

Finally, at the bottom of the form is the Winsock control (**ceWinsock**). It does not have a runtime interface so it can be placed anywhere on a form.

Next we will look at some of the key code that is behind the HTML Viewer program.

> Developing a Winsock application can be a pain because you need a connection to your desktop computer to transfer the program and another connection to the Internet for testing. Something that I have found which works as well is the Ethernet / Serial Combo PC card from Socket Communications. This card is a combination of a Ethernet card and a serial communications port. With this card you can use an Ethernet connection for transferring your program and the serial port to access a modem so that you can load and test without having to change connections. The card is designed to use minimal power. Hey what more could you ask for? For more information on this product visit Socket's site at www.socketcom.com.

Starting the Application- The Form_Load Event

All that happens in the **Form_Load** event is that the controls are resized and the focus is set:

```
Private Sub Form_Load()

' Adjust the control's sizes
  txtDocument.Width = frmHTMLViewer.Width - txtDocument.Left - 150
  txtHTML.Width = frmHTMLViewer.Width - 150
  cmdFetch.Left = frmHTMLViewer.Width - cmdFetch.Width - 150

' Set the focus
  txtHost.SetFocus

End Sub
```

Requesting the Document

The process of getting a document from a web server is a two step process:

- First you request a document
- Second it is returned

The code behind the **Click** event of the Fetch command button is responsible for requesting the document. It begins by clearing out the text box used to display HTML documents as they are received. It then places the Fetching page... message in the text box just to let the user know what is going on:

```
Private Sub cmdFetch_Click()

' Clear out the text box used to display the document, putting up a
' message so that the user knows what is going on.
   txtHTML.Text = "Fetching page..."
```

> This is an important point in developing Winsock-enabled applications. The
> Internet is fraught with all kinds of communication problems that can delay or
> hinder the receipt of requested documents. You need to include interface aids in
> your applications that will keep the user informed as a process proceeds.

Next we set the **RemoteHost** property of the Winsock control to the value provided by the user. The
RemotePort property is set to **80**, the default port number for communicating to a web server:

```
' Configure the winsock control.
ceWinsock.RemoteHost = txtHost.Text
ceWinsock.RemotePort = 80
```

Now we are ready to establish the connection to the desired host. It's the client's responsibility to perform
this function. The host will then close the connection after they have delivered the document that you
requested:

```
' Establish a connection to the host.
ceWinsock.Connect
```

Finally the request is set for the document that the user entered. This is accomplished by sending the **GET**
command to the web server followed by the document path:

```
' Send a request for the selected page.
ceWinsock.SendData "GET " & txtDocument.Text & vbCrLf & vbCrLf

End Sub
```

That is all that you need to do to request a document from a web server. You could use this code with
minimal modifications in your own applications to retrieve web documents of your choice.

Coding for Errors with the Winsock Control

If the Winsock control runs into an error in its background processing it will not set the **Err** object.
Fortunately the Winsock control features an **Error** event which we can code to display any error
messages:

```
Private Sub ceWinsock_Error(ByVal number, ByVal description)

' Display that an error has occured
   MsgBox description

End Sub
```

Receiving the Document

As I stated earlier in this section the second part of getting a document from a web server involves the
receipt of the document. This process occurs in the **DataArrival** event of the Winsock control. The

DataArrival event is fired after a document has been received. Normally when this occurs all that you would need to do is use the Winsock's **GetData** method to get the document. However, the current version of the CE Winsock control has a bug that requires you to close and reopen the connection before you can get the data:

```
Private Sub ceWinsock_DataArrival(ByVal bytesTotal)

  Dim strHTML

' There is a bug in the winsock control where in it
' doesn't tell you that data has arrived until after the connection
' has begun to be closed. In this state the data can not be read from
' the winsock control. The work around to this bug is to close the
' control and then reconnect the control so that you can get access
' to the data that was returned.

  On Error Resume Next

  ceWinsock.Close

  If (Err.Number <> 0) Then
     MsgBox "Error closing the first time, Err #" & Err.Number & " - " _
         & Err.Description
     Err.Clear

  End If

  ceWinsock.Connect

  If (Err.Number <> 0) Then
    MsgBox "Error reconnecting, Err #" & Err.Number & " - " _
          & Err.Description
    Err.Clear

  End If

  ceWinsock.GetData strHTML
```

Once we have the data it is loaded into the multi-line text box control for displaying. If you were using the web documents as a source of input for your CE application this is where you would call a routine to parse the document that was returned:

```
  txtHTML.Text = strHTML

  If (Err.Number <> 0) Then
    MsgBox "Error retrieving data, Err #" & Err.Number & " - " _
          & Err.Description
    Err.Clear

  End If
```

Finally we close the connection that we reopened:

```
    ceWinsock.Close

  If (Err.Number <> 0) Then
    MsgBox "Error closing the second time, Err #" & Err.Number _
          & " - " & Err.Description
    Err.Clear

  End If

End Sub
```

As I said earlier, much of the code in this procedure is required to work around a bug in the CE Winsock control. Once this control is fixed, all you will need is the **GetData** statement to load data into and transfer data from your CE applications, a modem and a phone line, and you'll be successful.

> If you're serious about working with this control, then I'd recommend that you purchase a book that focuses on using the Winsock control with Visual Basic. It will be well worth your investment.

Summary

This chapter completed the demonstration of how the addition of a few controls can turn a minimally functional development tool into a package that allows you to develop full-featured CE applications.

This chapter concentrated on the controls that are used for the manipulation and management of data. These tools provide a powerful base on which to gather, modify and store data. The combination of these data management tools, and the interface tools from the previous chapter, allows you to use the VBCE Toolkit to create a wide variety of business-quality applications. And this is just the start. As the popularity of Windows CE-based handheld and palmtop computers increase, you can expect to see more third-party ActiveX controls becoming available.

Working with Files

Mention creating an application to receive and store information and most people will immediately think of a database. Developers of desktop apps created with Visual Basic have come to depend upon using products such as SQL Server, Oracle and Access to store, manipulate and retrieve data. However, you may find that you need to use some different techniques in building similar applications for Windows CE. As you will see in Chapter 7, Windows CE offers only limited database functionality.

Don't be too concerned by the absence of a robust database for the handheld computer. It doesn't mean that you cannot develop applications to accept, store and display data. It simply means that you might need to use the other file tools that are provided with the VBCE Toolkit. Specifically, the **File** and **File System** controls. These two controls provide access to the File and File System objects that in turn offer a comprehensive set of tools for working with sequential, random access and binary files.

In this chapter I will teach you how, and where, you can use the File and File System controls to create effective CE applications. I will show you how these tools can not only aid development on the handheld computer but can also be used to simplify the task of transferring data to desktop computers.

Bundled into this chapter is the EasyEdit application, a simple text editor that is similar to Notepad. It uses the File and File System controls to store and retrieve sequential text files. I will lead you through the process I use to construct EasyEdit and show you how various file I/O techniques can be used to address application needs.

Using Files with Your Applications

The file I/O capabilities that are found in the VBCE Toolkit provide you with a set of tools to incorporate sequential, random access and binary files into your applications. You will most certainly want to be familiar with what these tools are, what they have to offer and how they are used. Why? Because of these two reasons:

- The database capabilities provided within the Windows CE environment are not as robust as those found on desktop PC or database servers

- The complexity of data being used by CE applications is typically far simpler than found on desktop PCs or database servers. Which lends itself for use with standard file I/O.

As you build your understanding of the VBCE file I/O capabilities you'll find that they can provide simple and efficient alternatives to CE databases. If you have worked with file I/O in Visual Basic, you should be comfortable with much of what is presented in this chapter. On the other hand if you never used VB's file I/O features you will want to take your time to work through this chapter. Make sure that you understand both how to use file I/O in VBCE and where it can be used to improve the performance and usability of your applications.

Doubtful about the performance of standard file I/O in your CE applications? Remember that everything on your handheld computer is in memory. As such, standard file I/O will be faster than you might expect to find on a desktop system.

In the following sections, I'm going to show you how to use the file I/O capabilities that are provided with VBCE. I will start by teaching you how the File control provides access to sequential, random access and binary files. After that, I'll show you how the File System control is used to manage files and folders. These sections are laid out in such a way so that they can be easily referenced for when you incorporate standard file I/O into your own applications.

Working with the File Control

The VB CE File control can be used to incorporate sequential, random access and binary files into your applications. It provides a set of methods and properties that allow you to create, update and save data much like you would using Visual Basic's **Open**, **Input**, **Print**, **Get**, **Put** and **Close** statements.

In these following sections, you'll learn how to work with sequential, random access and binary files. The discussion of each file type includes how to open, write to, read from and close files of the appropriate type.

Working with Sequential Files

Sequential files offer a simplistic form of data storage. They are typically used to store data either in the form of straight text or as a series of comma-delimited data items. Sequential files can be used in your CE application for storing:

- Documents, notes and memos. The EasyEdit application found later in this chapter demonstrates this use.

- Initialization and configuration of data for your applications. You can save items such as font sizes and selection of features when exiting your application and then reload the configurations when the application is restarted.

- Data that will later be sent onto a desktop system for processing. Comma-delimited data can be easily processed by desktop applications. An example of this technique is presented in Chapter 8.

- Reports that can be later viewed using a text editor or Pocket IE.

> Remember to add the Microsoft CE File System Control to your project. It provides both the File and File System controls. An example of adding controls to VBCE projects can be found in Chapter 4.

Opening Sequential Files

Before you can use a sequential file within your program you must first open the file. The syntax for the **Open** method is:

```
file.Open PathName, Mode, [Access], [Lock], [RecLength]
```

In this case, **file** refers to the File control.

PathName is a string expression that specifies the path and filename of the file.

Mode specifies the file mode or how the file will be used. Valid values for this argument are **Input** (**1**), **Output** (**2**), **Random** (**4**), **Append** (**8**) or **Binary** (**32**). For the purpose of sequential files you will be using **Input**, **Output** or **Append**.

Access specifies what operations are permitted on the file being opened. Valid values are **Read** (**1**), **Write** (**2**) and **ReadWrite** (**3**). **ReadWrite** is the default value for this argument.

Lock defines what operations are allowed on this file by other processes. Valid arguments are **Shared** (**1**), **LockRead** (**2**), **LockWrite** (**3**) and **LockReadWrite** (**5**). The default value for this argument is **LockWrite**.

RecLength specifies the number of characters buffered for sequential files and the length of a record for random access files. This argument is ignored for files opened in binary mode.

To get a better understanding of the **Open** method lets take a look at a few examples.

Opening a Text File for Input

This technique is used when all you need to do is read in the contents of a sequential file. For example, let's say your application makes use of the text file **settings.ini** to store initialization configurations. This text file is located in the root folder of your handheld. You have added a File control to your project and have named the control **ceFile**. To open this file you use the following:

```
Const lrFileModeInput = 1

ceFile.Open "settings.ini", lrFileModeInput
```

First you should note that this code fragment will only work if you have a file named **setting.ini** present. Also note my use of the constant **lrFileModeInput**. Since there are no constant values provided for the file Input modes, I created my own constant. When I create my own constants I add the prefix of **lr**, for Larry Roof, so that from within my code it's clear which constants I have defined.

What if you want the configuration file to reside in the same directory as your application? In that case use the following approach with the **Open** method:

```
Const lrFileModeInput = 1

Dim strDataFile

If (Len(App.Path) > 0) Then
   strDataFile = Right(App.Path, Len(App.Path) -1) & "\" & "settings.ini"
```

```
    Else
        strDataFile = "settings.ini"

    End If

    ceFile.Open strDataFile, lrFileModeInput
```

What this example does differently is to first check the location from where your application is being run. If it's not the root it appends the pathname to the front of the file name if needed. Basically what is happening here is a check is made of the length of the string returned by **App.Path**. Anything that is returned from **App.Path** is appended onto the front of the filename.

The other bit of manipulation that is occurring here addresses the fact that the string returned from **App.Path** contains a leading "\" which must be removed to open the file.

> CE path names differ from Windows 95 or NT path names. Under 95 or NT a path name would include the drive, directory path and filename. For example:
>
> `C:\Program Files\EasyEdit\settings.ini`
>
> That same file under Windows CE would be referred to as follows:
>
> `Program Files\EasyEdit\settings.ini`
>
> Remember, with CE there is no drive letter or leading "\".

Opening a Text File for Output

Let's take a look at another example. In this case you want to open your **settings.ini** file for output. Again assuming that the File control is named **ceFile** you can use the following to open the file **settings.ini** in the root directory of your handheld computer:

```
    Const lrFileModeOutput = 2

    ceFile.Open "settings.ini", lrFileModeOutput
```

If you wanted to open the file for output in the same directory as where your application resided use the following:

```
    Const lrFileModeOutput = 2

    Dim strDataFile

    If (Len(App.Path) > 0) Then
        strDataFile = Right(App.Path, Len(App.Path) -1) & "\" & "settings.ini"
```

```
    Else
        strDataFile = "settings.ini"

    End If

    ceFile.Open strDataFile, lrFileModeOutput
```

> Opening a file for output will overwrite an existing file with the same name. Later
> in this chapter you will see a technique that uses the File System control to first
> check to see if a file exists.

Opening a Text File for Append

Our final sequential file open example demonstrates the **Append** file mode. This would be used where you
have an existing file on which you want to add additional data. The following example would open the file
tracking.log located in the root directory of your handheld computer for **Append** mode:

```
    Const lrFileModeAppend = 8

    ceFile.Open "tracking.log", lrFileModeAppend
```

As with the earlier examples, if the log file was located in the same directory as where your application
resided use the following:

```
    Const lrFileModeAppend = 8

    Dim strDataFile

    If (Len(App.Path) > 0) Then
        strDataFile = Right(App.Path, Len(App.Path) -1) & "\" & "tracking.log"

    Else
        strDataFile = "tracking.log"

    End If

    ceFile.Open strDataFile, lrFileModeAppend
```

Writing to Sequential Files

Data is written to sequential files using either the **LinePrint** or **WriteFields** methods of the File
control. Examples of each method and how they are most commonly used are provided below.

> *In order to write to a sequential file, you must open that file using the file mode of Output or Append with
> the access mode of either Write or Read/Write.*

Writing Text, a Note or a Memo to a Sequential File

One common use for sequential files is to save text, notes and memos. In these cases you typically would be writing out the complete file with one statement, such as writing out the contents of a multiple-line text box control.

Dumping the contents of a control out to a file is a pretty easy process. Start by opening the file for output as shown earlier in this chapter. Next use the **LinePrint** method of the File control to write out the text. In this example, the contents of the text box control is written out to the file **note.txt**:

```
Const lrFileModeOutput = 2

Dim strDataFile

If (Len(App.Path) > 0) Then
    strDataFile = Right(App.Path, Len(App.Path) -1) & "\" & "note.txt"

Else
    strDataFile = "note.txt"

End If

' Start by opening the file.
ceFile.Open strDataFile, lrFileModeOutput

' The file is open so write out the note.
ceFile.LinePrint txtNote.txt
```

The drawback of using the **LinePrint** method is that it appends an ASCII carriage return and linefeed combination onto the end of the file. You need to be aware that these two characters have been added so that you can remove them when you read the data back in from the file. An example of this technique is shown in the section on 'Reading from Sequential Files'.

Writing Data Items to a Sequential File

Another use for sequential files is to store comma-delimited data. How this typically works is that every line of the data file contains a record of data with commas separating each field in the record. This form of data storage provides an easy and simple method for transferring data between applications. Commercial applications such as Excel and Access will readily import comma-delimited data. In Chapter 8 you will see how comma-delimited sequential files, the Windows CE **Synchronized Files** folder, and the Windows CE Services AutoSync feature can be used together to transfer data from the handheld to the desktop with minimal effort.

To write data taken from a set of controls out as a record you start by opening the file for either output or append. The **WriteFields** method is then used to store the individual data taken from the controls:

```
Const lrFileModeOutput = 2

Dim astrInventoryRecord(2)
Dim strDataFile

If (Len(App.Path) > 0) Then
    strDataFile = Right(App.Path, Len(App.Path) -1) & "\" & "inventory.dat"
```

```
    Else
        strDataFile = "inventory.dat"

    End If

' Start by opening the file.
  ceFile.Open strDataFile, lrFileModeOutput

' Load the data into an array.
  astrInventoryRecord(0) = txtItem.Text
  astrInventoryRecord(1) = txtDescription.Text
  astrInventoryRecord(2) = txtLocation.Text

' The file is open so write out the data.
  ceFile.WriteFields astrInventoryRecord
```

Writing a record out to the **WriteFields** method requires you to pass the individual control values in an array. In the example above each of the three values from the text box controls were first loaded into the array before they were written to the file.

Some other items to note regarding the use of the **WriteFields** method:

- The ASCII carriage return and linefeed combination will be added to the end of each record
- Quotes will be placed around text strings
- Numeric data is written using a period separator
- Boolean data is written out as either a #TRUE# or #FALSE#
- If an item contains null data it is written out as #NULL#
- Error data is written out as #ERROR error code#
- Date data is written using the universal date format

Reading from Sequential Files

Data is read from a sequential file using the **Input**, **InputB**, **InputFields**, or **LineInputString** methods of the File control. Examples of each method and how they are most commonly used are provided below.

In order to read from a sequential file it must be opened using the file mode of Input or Binary with the access mode of either Read or Read/Write.

Reading Text, a Note or a Memo From a Sequential File

Text, notes and memos that have been written out to a sequential file can be read back into your application using the **Input** method. This method returns all of the characters it reads, including any punctuation, carriage returns and linefeeds. The **Input** method is typically used to read in data that was written out with the **LinePrint** method.

> Remember to remove the trailing carriage return and linefeed characters when reading in a file using the **Input** method that was written out with the **LinePrint** method.

In an earlier example you were shown how to write the contents of a control out to disk using the **LinePrint** method. That example is included below for reference purposes:

```
Const lrFileModeOutput = 2

Dim strDataFile

If (Len(App.Path) > 0) Then
    strDataFile = Right(App.Path,Len(App.Path)-1) & "\" & "note.txt"

Else
    strDataFile = "note.txt"

End If

' Start by opening the file.
ceFile.Open strDataFile, lrFileModeOutput

' The file is open so write out the note.
ceFile.LinePrint txtNote.txt
```

To read the contents of the file back into the text box control use the following code. This example assumes that the file was closed after the previous example:

```
Const lrFileModeInput = 1

Dim strInputString
Dim strDataFile

If (Len(App.Path > 0) Then
    strDataFile = Right(App.Path, Len(App.Path) -1) & "\" & "note.txt"

Else
    strDataFile = "note.txt"

End If

' Start by opening the file.
ceFile.Open strDataFile, lrFileModeInput

' The file is open so read in the note.
strInputString = ceFile.Input(ceFile.LOF)
txtNote.txt = Mid(strInputString, 1, ceFile.LOF - 2)
```

The important points in this example are:

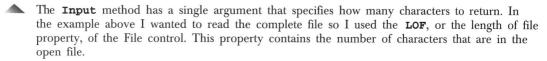

- The **Input** method has a single argument that specifies how many characters to return. In the example above I wanted to read the complete file so I used the **LOF**, or the length of file property, of the File control. This property contains the number of characters that are in the open file.

- The trailing carriage return and linefeed characters were removed from the file. As you remember **LinePrint** method adds this character combination when it writes out the data.

Optionally, you could have used the **LineInputString** method to read the file in a line at a time. This technique is useful if you have a set of statements, or records that comprise single sentences. Typically this method is used within a loop that will continue to read lines in from the file until the end of file (**EOF**) property is encountered.

Reading Data Items in from a Sequential File

Comma-delimited data is read in from a sequential file with the **InputFields** method. This method is commonly used in combination with the **WriteFields** method to read and write records. The **InputFields** method has a single argument that specifies how many fields to read.

In an earlier example you were shown how to write the contents of three controls out to disk as a single record by using the **WriteFields** method. That example is included below for reference purposes:

```
Const lrFileModeOutput = 2

Dim astrInventoryRecord(2)
Dim strDataFile

If (Len(App.Path) > 0) Then
    strDataFile = Right(App.Path, Len(App.Path) -1) & "\" & "inventory.dat"

Else
    strDataFile = "inventory.dat"

End If

' Start by opening the file.
ceFile.Open strDataFile, lrFileModeOutput

' Load the data into an array.
astrInventoryRecord(0) = txtItem.Text
astrInventoryRecord(1) = txtDescription.Text
astrInventoryRecord(2) = txtLocation.Text

' The file is open so write out the note.
ceFile.WriteFields astrInventoryRecord
```

To read a record back into the controls use the following code:

```
Const lrFileModeInput = 1

Dim astrInventoryRecord(2)
Dim strDataFile

If (Len(App.Path) > 0) Then
    strDataFile = Right(App.Path, Len(App.Path) -1) & "\" & "inventory.dat"

Else
    strDataFile = "inventory.dat"

End If

' Start by opening the file.
ceFile.Open strDataFile, lrFileModeInput

' The file is open so read in records.
astrInventoryRecord = ceFile.InputFields(3)

' Load the data into the controls.
txtItem.Text = astrInventoryRecord(0)
txtDescription.Text = astrInventoryRecord(1)
txtLocation.Text = astrInventoryRecord(2)
```

Some other items to note regarding the use of the **InputFields** method:

- String data is read in without modification
- Numeric data is read in without modification
- Date data is read in as the date and time represented by the date string stored in the file
- Boolean values of True and False are assigned to variables for #TRUE# and #FALSE# fields in the file
- Null is assigned to variables for #NULL# fields in the file
- A variant variable tagged as an error is assigned for #ERROR# fields in the file

Closing Sequential Files

The **Close** method is used to close a sequential file. An example of this is shown below:

```
' Close the file.
ceFile.Close
```

Working with Random Access Files

Random access files allow you to store data as individual records. Each record is comprised of one or more fields. They differ from sequential files in the fact that they allow you to store and retrieve specific records from a file.

The implementation of random access files in VBCE is hindered by the absence of user-defined data types. Where in VB you would define a data type representing each record in file, in VBCE you must use variant arrays. Despite this shortcoming, random access files offer plenty of functionality and are very useful.

Opening Random Access Files

Before you can use a random access file within your program it must first be opened. As was detailed as part of the discussion of sequential files, the syntax for the **Open** method is:

```
file.Open PathName, Mode, [Access], [Lock], [RecLength]
```

A key argument to the **Open** method is the **RecLength**. This argument specifies the length of the records you will be using with the file.

There is much written in the Books Online included with the VBCE Toolkit regarding the calculation of record lengths. It provides sizes and overhead values to use for calculating the storage of the different data types that you may use in your records. I have found is a far simpler approach is to:

- Set all of your string variables to a fixed length by padding them with spaces
- Open the file using a large record size
- Write a single record to the file
- Close the file
- Use the CE Explorer to see how many bytes were used to store the record

The size of your test file will be the size to use as your record length.

Opening a Random Access File for Reading and Writing

Unlike sequential files that offer **Input**, **Output** and **Append** as alternatives when opening a file, random access files instead make use of the **Access** mode argument of the File control **Open** method to define whether the file will be used for reading, writing or both reading and writing.

The following example opens a random access data file for both reading and writing using the record length of 56. As was with the examples shown for sequential files, this file will be opened in the path where the application resides:

```
Const lrFileModeRandom = 4
Const lrFileLockWrite = 2
Const lrFileReadWrite = 3

Dim strDataFile

If (Len(App.Path) > 0) Then
    strDataFile = Right(App.Path, Len(App.Path) -1) & "\" & "employee.dat"

Else
    strDataFile = "employee.dat"

End If
```

```
    ceFile.Open strDataFile, _
       lrFileModeRandom, _              ' Random access
       lrFileReadWrite, _               ' Allow both reading and writing
       lrFileLockWrite, _               ' Prohibit access while we are writing
       56                               ' Length of each record
```

If we want to allow only writing to the file change the **Access** mode argument to a value of **2**. For read only change the **Access** mode argument to **1**.

Writing to Random Access Files

Data is written to random access files using the **Put** method of the File control. The syntax of the **Put** method is:

```
file.Put Data, [RecNumber]
```

Where **Data** is an array of variants and the **RecNumber** argument specifies where in the file the record is written.

The following example demonstrates the use of this method.

> *In order to write to a random access file it must be opened using the file mode of Random with the Access mode of either Write or Read/Write.*

Working with random access files in VBCE is slightly more difficult than in Visual Basic because of the absence of the user-defined data types. What you are forced to use instead is variant arrays which offer neither the control nor definition found in user-defined data types.

To write data taken from a set of controls out as a record, you start by opening the file for random access as shown in the earlier example. The **Put** method is then used to write the record, which is comprised of an array containing the control values, to the file:

```
    Const lrFileModeRandom = 4
    Const lrFileLockWrite = 2
    Const lrFileReadWrite = 3

    Dim strDataFile
    Dim avntDataRecord
    ReDim avntDataRecord(2)

    If (Len(App.Path) > 0) Then
       strDataFile = Right(App.Path, Len(App.Path) -1) & "\" & "employee.dat"

    Else
       strDataFile = "employee.dat"

    End If

' Open the file.
    ceFile.Open strDataFile, _
       lrFileModeRandom, _     ' Random access
       lrFileReadWrite, _      ' Allow both reading and writing
```

```
      lrFileLockWrite, _              ' Prohibit access while we are writing
      56                              ' Length of each record

   ' Load the array with the control values.
     avntDataRecord(0) = txtName.Text & Space(20 - Len(txtName.Text))
     avntDataRecord(1) = CCur(txtHourlyWage.Text)
     avntDataRecord(2) = CDate(txtDateHired.Text)

   ' Write the record to the file.
     ceFile.Put avntDataRecord, 5
```

Let's examine what is happening here. This example starts by creating a variant array of three items by first declaring the variable **avntDataRecord** and then redimensioning it to have three items (0, 1 and 2).

The array that will be used to write the record to the random access file must be declared using the method below; first you declare the array and then you redimension it to the necessary size.

```
Dim avntDataRecord
ReDim avntDataRecord(2)
```

If you create the array in the size required, for example:

```
Dim avntDataRecord(2)
```

You will encounter a runtime error when you later attempt to read the data with the **Get** method.

The file **employee.dat** is opened for random access as shown in the example from the previous page.

Next the variant array **avntDataRecord** is loaded with the values of three controls. Note that two of the values are first converted from their text values to the appropriate data type. The text taken from **txtHourlyWage** is converted to currency. The text from **txtDateHired** is converted to a date. The third control value, **txtName**, is padded with spaces so that the resulting string is 20 characters long. This forces each record to be the same length.

Finally the record is written to the file with the **Put** method. The second argument of the **Put** method, the **RecNumber**, specifies that this data should be written into the fifth record in the random access file.

Reading from Random Access Files

Data is read from random access files using the **Get** method of the File control. The syntax of the **Get** method is:

file.Get Data, [RecNumber]

Where **Data** is a variant array and **RecNumber** specifies which record to read.

The following example demonstrates the use of this method:

```
Const lrFileModeRandom = 4
Const lrFileLockWrite = 2
Const lrFileReadWrite = 3
```

```
        Dim strDataFile
        Dim astrDataRecord
        ReDim astrDataRecord(2)

        If (Len(App.Path) > 0) Then
            strDataFile = Right(App.Path, Len(App.Path) -1) & "\" & "employee.dat"

        Else
            strDataFile = "employee.dat"

        End If

    ' Open the file.
        ceFile.Open strDataFile, _
            lrFileModeRandom, _           ' Random access
            lrFileReadWrite, _            ' Allow both reading and writing
            lrFileLockWrite, _            ' Prohibit access while we are writing
            56                            ' Length of each record

    ' Read the record from the file.
        ceFile.Get astrDataRecord, 5

    ' Load the array with the control values.
        txtName.Text = Trim(astrDataRecord(0))
        txtHourlyWage.Text = astrDataRecord(1)
        txtDateHired.Text = astrDataRecord(2)
```

Let's examine what is happening here. This example starts by creating a variant array of three items. The fifth record from the file is retrieved using the **Get** method. The contents of that record are returned in the variant array.

Finally, the contents of the array are used to load the three controls. Note that the **Trim** function is used to strip the name value of spaces before loading it into the appropriate text box control. This process removes the spaces that were added when the record was written to control the length of each record.

Closing Random Access Files

The **Close** method is used to close a random access file. An example of this is shown below:

```
    ' Close the file.
        ceFile.Close
```

Working with Binary Files

Of sequential, random access and binary files it is binary files that provide you with the most flexibility for data storage. Typically, a binary file will be used in situations where disk space, or in the case of handheld computers, memory space, is at a premium. The reason for this is that binary files allow you to work with variable length records. The advantage of variable length records is that no more space than necessary needs to be used.

Let's look at an example of this. Below is a 'typical' record structure for a partial employee record. Using this structure each record will consume 100 bytes regardless of the size of the actual data being stored:

Field	Type and Size
Name	30 characters
Address	50 characters
City	20 characters

Using binary files you can use variable length records, which only use the space required to store the data. An example of this is shown in the record below where the storage of a record consumes 20 bytes instead of the 100 used with fixed length records.

Field	Type and Size
Larry Roof	10 characters
123 Main St.	12 characters
New York	8 characters

As you can see, binary files can offer a dramatic saving in size. They also have their own limitations, the largest of which is the fact that they must be read in a sequential fashion. What this means is that to get to the 30th record in a binary file you must read the 29 records before it. Using a random access file you could read the 30th record directly.

> *Binary files offer a trade off. They offer a more efficient method to store data at the cost of data accessibility. They are best suited for situations where you will be processing a whole file from beginning to end rather than working with selective records from the file.*

Binary files offer superior flexibility in comparison to random files - but not without a cost. Applications that make use of binary files typically will require more complex coding to handle the navigation of the data file.

Opening Binary Files

Before you can use a binary file within your program it must first be opened. As was detailed as part of the discussion of sequential and random access files, the syntax for the **Open** method is:

```
file.Open PathName, Mode, [Access], [Lock], [RecLength]
```

The **RecLength** argument is ignored for binary files.

Opening a Binary File for Reading and Writing

Like random access files, binary files make use of the **Access** mode argument of the File control **Open** method to define whether the file will be used for reading, writing or both reading and writing.

The following example opens a binary file for both reading and writing. Note that the **RecLength** argument is not included as part of the **Open** method as it's not used when opening a binary file. As was with the examples shown for sequential and random access files, this file will be opened in the path where the application resides:

```
Const lrFileModeBinary = 32
Const lrFileLockWrite = 2
Const lrFileReadWrite = 3

Dim strDataFile

If (Len(App.Path) > 0) Then
    strDataFile = Right(App.Path, Len(App.Path) -1) & "\" & "binary.dat"

Else
    strDataFile = "binary.dat"

End If

ceFile.Open strDataFile, _
   lrFileModeBinary, _          ' Binary mode
   lrFileReadWrite, _           ' Allow both reading and writing
   lrFileLockWrite              ' Prohibit access while we are writing
```

If we want to allow only writing to the file change the **Access** mode argument to a value of **2**. For read only, change the access mode argument to **1**.

Writing to Binary Files

Data is written to a binary file using the **Put** method of the File control. As was shown in the discussion of random access files, the syntax of the **Put** method is:

```
file.Put Data, [RecNumber]
```

The following example demonstrates the use of this method.

> *In order to write to a binary file it must be opened using the file mode of Binary with the Access mode of either Write or Read/Write.*

Working with a binary file is very similar to working with a random access file. What you gain is the ability to read single characters at a time. What you lose is the ability to directly read a whole record at once.

To write data taken from a set of controls out as a record you start by opening the file for binary as shown in the earlier example. The **Put** method is then used to store the record, which is comprised of the control values, to the file:

```
Const lrFileModeBinary = 32
Const lrFileLockWrite = 2
Const lrFileReadWrite = 3

Dim strDataFile
Dim avntDataRecord
ReDim avntDataRecord(2)

If (Len(App.Path) > 0) Then
    strDataFile = Right(App.Path, Len(App.Path) -1) & "\" & "binary.dat"
```

```
       Else
          strDataFile = "binary.dat"

       End If

  ' Open the file.
     ceFile.Open strDataFile, _
        lrFileModeBinary, _          ' Binary mode
        lrFileReadWrite, _           ' Allow both reading and writing
        lrFileLockWrite              ' Prohibit access while we are writing

  ' Load the array with the control values.
     avntDataRecord(0) = txtName.Text
     avntDataRecord(1) = CCur(txtHourlyWage.Text)
     avntDataRecord(2) = CDate(txtDateHired.Text)

  ' Write the record to the file.
     ceFile.Put avntDataRecord
```

Let's examine what is happening here. This example starts by creating a variant array of three items by first declaring the variable **avntDataRecord** and then redimensioning it to have three items (0, 1 and 2).

The file **binary.dat** is opened for binary mode as shown in the earlier example.

Next the variant array **avntDataRecord** is loaded with the values of three controls. Note that two of the values are first converted from their text values to the appropriate data type. The text taken from **txtHourlyWage** is converted to currency and the text from **txtDateHired** is converted to a date.

Finally the record is written to the file with the **Put** method. Note in this situation the record is written to the end of the file. Binary access also lets you write to specific locations within the contents of a file.

Reading from Binary Files

Date is read from binary mode files using the **Get** method of the File control. As was shown in the discussion of random access files, the syntax of the **Get** method is:

```
file.Get Data, [RecNumber]
```

The following example demonstrates the use of this method:

```
     Const lrFileModeBinary = 32
     Const lrFileLockWrite = 2
     Const lrFileReadWrite = 3

     Dim strDataFile
     Dim astrDataRecord
     ReDim astrDataRecord(2)

     If (Len(App.Path > 0) Then
        strDataFile = Right(App.Path, Len(App.Path) -1) & "\" & "binary.dat"

     Else
        strDataFile = "binary.dat"
```

```
      End If

   ' Open the file.
     ceFile.Open strDataFile, _
        lrFileModeBinary, _          ' Binary mode
        lrFileReadWrite, _           ' Allow both reading and writing
        lrFileLockWrite, _           ' Prohibit access while we are writing

   ' Read the record from the file.
     ceFile.Get astrDataRecord

   ' Load the array with the control values.
     txtName.Text = astrDataRecord(0)
     txtHourlyWage.Text = astrDataRecord(1)
     txtDateHired.Text = astrDataRecord(2)
```

Let's examine what is happening here. This example starts by creating a variant array of three items.

The file **binary.dat** is opened for binary mode as shown in the earlier example.

Next a record is retrieved using the **Get** method. The contents of that record are returned in the variant array.

Finally, the contents of the array are used to load the three controls.

Closing Binary Files

The **Close** method is used to close a binary file. An example of this is shown below:

```
   ' Close the file.
     ceFile.Close
```

Working with the File System Control

The VBCE File System control allows you to add file management functionality to your applications. It provides a set of methods and properties for working with directories, files and their attributes.

> *A detailed listing of the properties and methods provided by the File System control can be found in Chapter 4.*

You can think of this following section as the VBCE file management sampler plate that covers how to:

- ◢ Obtain a directory listing
- ◢ Create a new directory
- ◢ Delete a directory
- ◢ Copy a file
- ◢ Move a file

▲ Delete a file

▲ Retrieve a file date and time stamp

▲ Determine the size of a file

▲ Retrieve file attributes

▲ Set file attributes

Obtaining a Directory Listing

Retrieving a directory listing in VBCE is identical to the process you would use with VB5 and the **Dir** function. In this case **Dir** is a method of the File System control. To generate a directory listing you must:

▲ Making an initial request for a file from the directory

▲ Make subsequent requests for files within a loop until the complete listing has been returned

The syntax for this method is:

filesystem.Dir(PathName[, Attributes])

Where **filesystem** refers to the name of the File System control, **PathName** (optional) is the path and filename that you are requesting and **Attributes** (optional) specifies attributes to match on the files returned.

The example below demonstrates this process by populating a list box control **lstFiles**. The text box control **txtPath** allows the user to specify the directory to retrieve. If no path is provided the root path will be used:

```
    Dim strFileReturned

 ' Get the initial file.
    lstFiles.Clear
    strFileReturned = ceFileSystem.Dir(txtPath.Text)

 ' Make subsequent calls until the complete list has been returned.
    While (strFileReturned <> "")
      lstFiles.AddItem sFileReturned
      strFileReturned = ceFileSystem.Dir()

    Wend
```

While the common dialog control provides a far greater amount of functionality and consistency with the Windows CE environment, don't overlook the usefulness of the **Dir** method. It provides an easy way to build a list of files that exist in a directory. I've used this technique to process data updates that have been sent to a handheld. Each update was sent in a file with the same special extension, for instance **.upd**. I would first build a list of these files using the **Dir** method and then loop through the list to process each file.

Creating a New Directory

The VBCE Toolkit provides the **MkDir** method of the File System control that allows you to create a new directory on the handheld computer. The syntax for this method is:

```
filesystem.MkDir PathName
```

Where **PathName** specifies the directory to create.

The example below demonstrates the use of the **MkDir** method to create the directory specified by the user in the text box control **txtPath**.

```
' Setup the error handler.
  On Error Resume Next

' Create the directory.
  ceFileSystem.MkDir txtPath.Text
  If (Err.Number = 0) Then
    MsgBox "Directory created."

  Else
    MsgBox "Creation of directory failed."
    Err.Clear

  End If
```

Deleting a Directory

The **RmDir** method of the File System control allows you to remove, or delete a directory on the handheld computer. The syntax for this method is:

```
filesystem.RmDir PathName
```

Where **PathName** specifies the directory to delete.

The example below demonstrates the use of the **RmDir** method to delete the directory specified by the user in the text box control **txtPath**:

```
' Setup the error handler.
  On Error Resume Next

' Delete the directory.
  ceFileSystem.RmDir txtPath.Text
  If (Err.Number = 0) Then
    MsgBox "Directory deleted."

  Else
    MsgBox "Deletion of directory failed."
    Err.Clear

  End If
```

Copying a File

The **FileCopy** method of the File System control allows you to copy an existing file to a new file. The syntax for this method is:

filesystem.FileCopy PathName, NewPathName

Where **PathName** specifies the file to copy and **NewPathName** specifies the new filename.

The example below demonstrates the use of the **FileCopy** method to copy the file specified by the user in the text box control **txtPath** to a filename that the user will be prompted for:

```
Dim strNewPathName

' Setup the error handler.
  On Error Resume Next

' Get the name of new file and perform the copy operation.
  strNewPathName = InputBox("Enter new path and filenane:", _
    "File I/O Demo", "")
  ceFileSystem.FileCopy txtPath.Text, strNewPathName

' Check to see if the copy was performed.
  If (Err.Number <> 0) Then
    MsgBox "File copy failed."
    Err.Clear

  End If
```

Moving a File

The **MoveFile** method of the File System control allows you to rename a file or directory. The syntax for this method is:

filesystem.MoveFile PathName, NewPathName

Where **PathName** specifies the file or directory to rename and **NewPathName** specifies the new filename.

The example below demonstrates the use of the **MoveFile** method to move the file specified by the user in the text box control **txtPath** to a filename that the user will be prompted for:

```
Dim strNewPathName

' Setup the error handler.
  On Error Resume Next

' Get the name of new file and perform the move operation.
  strNewPathName = InputBox("Enter new path and filenane:", _
    "File I/O Demo", "")
  ceFileSystem.MoveFile txtPath.Text, strNewPathName
```

```
' Check to see if the move was performed.
  If (Err.Number <> 0) Then
    MsgBox "Failed to move file."
    Err.Clear

  End If
```

Deleting a File

The `Kill` method of the File System control allows you to delete a file. The syntax for this method is:

`filesystem.Kill PathName`

Where `PathName` specifies the file to delete and must include a directory.

The example below demonstrates the use of the `Kill` method to delete the file specified by the user in the text box control `txtPath`:

```
' Setup the error handler.
  On Error Resume Next

' Delete the file.
  ceFileSystem.Kill txtPath.Text

' Check to see if the deletion was performed.
  If (Err.Number = 0) Then
    MsgBox "File was deleted."

  Else
    MsgBox "Failed to delete the file."
    Err.Clear

  End If
```

> The `Kill` method requires that you provide a complete path for the file that you want to delete. For files that are located in the root directory provide a leading "\".

Retrieving the File Date and Time Stamp

The `FileDateTime` method of the File System control can be used to retrieve the date and time when a file was created or last modified. The syntax for this method is:

`filesystem.FileDateTime(PathName)`

Where `PathName` specifies the file to report on.

The example below demonstrates the use of the **FileDateTime** method to return the size of the file specified in the text box control **txtPath**:

```
    Dim dtmFileTimeStamp

' Setup the error handler.
    On Error Resume Next

' Retrieve the timestamp for the file.
    dtmFileTimeStamp = ceFileSystem.FileDateTime(txtFile.Text)

' Check to see if the operation completed successfully.
    If (Err.Number <> 0) Then
      MsgBox "Error obtaining timestamp for the file."
      Err.Clear

    Else
      txtFileDate.Text = dtmFileTimeStamp

    End If
```

Determining the Size of a File

You can use the **FileLen** method of the File System control to find the size of a file in bytes. The syntax for this method is:

filesystem.FileLen(PathName)

Where **PathName** specifies the file to report on.

The example below demonstrates the use of the **FileLen** method to return the size of the file specified in the text box control **txtPath**:

```
    Dim strFileSize

' Setup the error handler.
    On Error Resume Next

' Retrieve the file size.
    strFileSize = ceFileSystem.FileLen(txtFile.Text)

' Check to see if the operation completed successfully.
    If (Err.Number <> 0) Then
      MsgBox "Error obtaining file size."
      Err.Clear

    Else
      txtFileSize.Text = strFileSize

    End If
```

Retrieving File Attributes

Determining a file's attributes is performed by the **GetAttr** method of the File System control. The syntax for this method is:

```
filesystem.GetAttr(PathName)
```

Where **PathName** specifies the file to report on.

The **GetAttr** method returns a long value that represents the attributes that are set for the specified file. The value that is returned is the sum of these attribute values:

Value	Description
0	normal
1	read-only
2	hidden
4	system
16	directory
32	archive - the file has changed since the last backup

The tricky part with using this method is that you need to perform a bitwise comparison of the value returned to determine which of the individual attributes is set.

The example below demonstrates the use of the **GetAttr** method as well as a simple bitwise comparison technique:

```
Const lrReadOnly = 1
Const lrHidden = 2
Const lrSystem = 4
Const lrDirectory = 16
Const lrArchive = 32

Dim strAttributeString
Dim intFileAttributes

' Setup the error handler.
On Error Resume Next

' Retrieve the file attributes.
intFileAttributes = ceFileSystem.GetAttr(txtFile.Text)

' Check to see if the operation completed successfully.
If (Err.Number <> 0) Then
  MsgBox "Error obtaining file attributes."
  Err.Clear
```

```
' It did complete so first convert and then display the attributes.
  Else

    If (intFileAttributes And lrReadOnly) Then
      strAttributeString = "R"
    End If

    If (intFileAttributes And lrHidden) Then
      strAttributeString = strAttributeString & "H"
    End If

    If (intFileAttributes And lrSystem) Then
      strAttributeString = strAttributeString & "S"
    End If

    If (intFileAttributes And lrDirectory) Then
      strAttributeString = strAttributeString & "D"
    End If

    If (intFileAttributes And lrArchive) Then
      strAttributeString = strAttributeString & "A"
    End If

    txtFileAttributes.Text = strAttributeString

  End If
```

Setting File Attributes

You can set the attributes on a file using the **SetAttr** method of the File System control. The syntax for this method is:

filesystem.SetAttr PathName, Attributes

Where **PathName** specifies the file to report on and **Attributes** is a sum of numeric values that specifies which attributes to set for the specified files.

The value that specifies the attributes to set should be comprised of the sum of the following values:

Value	Description
0	Normal
1	read-only
2	Hidden
4	System
16	Directory
32	Archive - the file has changed since the last backup

To build the value to pass as the **Attributes** argument simply, sum the values of the individual attributes. For example, if you wanted a file to be read-only and hidden, you would pass the value of 3 (1 for read-only plus 2 for hidden).

The example below demonstrates the use of the **SetAttr** method:

```
    Const lrReadOnly = 1
    Const lrHidden = 2
    Const lrSystem = 4
    Const lrDirectory = 16
    Const lrArchive = 32

' Setup the error handler.
  On Error Resume Next

' Set the file attributes.
  ceFileSystem.SetAttr txtFile.Text, txtFileAttributes.Text

' Check to see if the operation completed successfully.
  If (Err.Number <> 0) Then
    MsgBox "Error setting file attributes."
    Err.Clear

  End If
```

EasyEdit – A Step-By-Step Example

Now that you've seen how to use the functionality provided by the File and File System controls we will turn our attention at how these controls can be used as the foundation for an application. The application that we will be creating is called EasyEdit. It's a simple text editor, a Notepad knockoff of sorts. It provides a simple alternative for creating and modifying text files on your handheld computer. At the root of EasyEdit you will find two routines that allow you to read and write sequential files. While this is in no way a complicated application, it does demonstrate how you can create a useful utility both quickly and easily with VBCE.

EasyEdit – The Completed Project

Before we start constructing the EasyEdit application, let's take a look at the completed project. I use this approach because I believe that seeing the finished product aids in understanding discussions on its development.

To install EasyEdit on your handheld computer follow these steps:

▲ Establish a connection between your desktop and handheld computers

▲ Using the instructions laid out in Appendix A, find the version of EasyEdit for Chapter 6

▲ Follow the installation directions

Using EasyEdit

Once you have completed the installation of this example, run it on your handheld computer. The EasyEdit interface should be displayed as shown in the screenshot below:

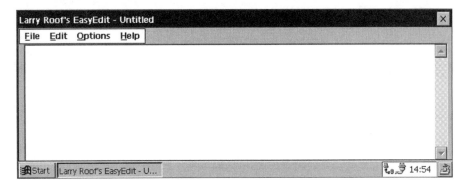

As you will note, EasyEdit looks much like any typical Windows-based text editor that you may have used. It offers a simple menu interface from which you can create, save and open files:

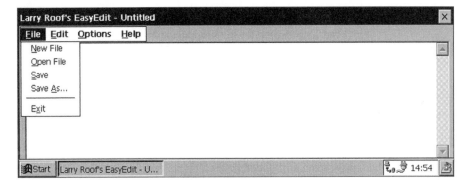

You can perform common text manipulation functions like cut, copy, paste and find:

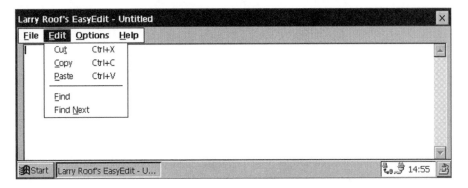

Plus you can change the size of the font in which the active file is displayed. Note that this feature does not affect the file itself: only how it is displayed:

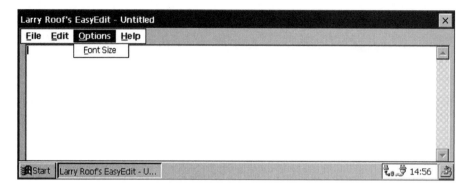

EasyEdit – The Requirements

The purpose for EasyEdit is to provide the functionality found in a simple text editor. The requirements for this application are to:

- Allow you to create new files
- Save files
- Resave files under a different name
- Open files that have been saved
- Perform the standard text manipulation techniques of cut, copy and paste
- Find a text string within the active document
- Be able to adjust the size of the font being displayed

EasyEdit – The Design

The EasyEdit application has a fairly simple design. That is because the File, File System, text box and common dialog controls provide most of its functionality. The design of EasyEdit includes the following:

- A single form that is composed of primarily a large multi-line Text Box control
- A simple menu structure including File, Edit, Options and Help menus
- A File control for reading and writing sequential text files
- A File System control for accessing files
- A Common Dialog control to provide the user with the ability to specify filenames as part of the process of opening and saving files

Now that you have an understanding of what the EasyEdit application is and what capabilities it has to offer we will turn our attention to the process of building the application.

You may want to remove this initial version of the EasyEdit program from your handheld computer at this time. The easiest way to accomplish this is through the Start menu, then Settings, Control Panel and finally Add/Remove Programs.

EasyEdit – The Construction

In the pages that follow you will be led through all nine steps of the creation process for the EasyEdit application. As with previous examples you may want to work along with the instructions to create your own copy of EasyEdit. You will note that for many of the steps I no longer provide step-by-step instructions. You can reference the Time Manager example in Chapter 2 for more detailed instructions.

*The file **Chapter 6\EasyEdit.vbp** contains a completed version of this project. Refer to Appendix A for instructions on downloading and installing the examples included in this book.*

Step 1 - Starting a New Project

Start Visual Basic and create a new Windows CE project.

Step 2 - Setting the Project Properties

Set the Project Name, Form Width, Remote Path and Run on Target properties to the values shown in the screenshot:

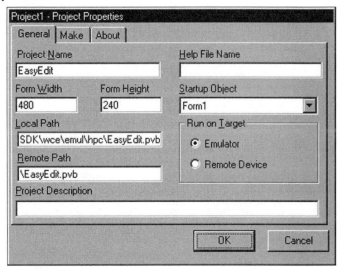

Step 3 - Constructing the User Interface

Add the following items to the EasyEdit form:

- Text Box control
- File control
- File System control.
- Common Dialog control
- Utility control

Construct a menu using the following information:

Menu Caption	Object Name	Enabled
&File	`mnuFile`	True
&New File	`mnuFileNew`	True
&Open File	`mnuFileOpen`	True
&Save File	`mnuFileSave`	True
Save &As...	`mnuFileSaveAs`	True
-	`mnuFileBar1`	n/a
&Error	`mnuFileError`	False
E&xit	`mnuFileExit`	True
&Edit	`mnuEdit`	True
Cu&t (add Ctrl+X shortcut)	`mnuEditCut`	True
&Copy (add Ctrl+C shortcut)	`mnuEditCopy`	True
&Paste (add Ctrl+V shortcut)	`mnuEditPaste`	True
-	`mnuEditBar1`	n/a
&Find	`mnuEditFind`	True
Find &Next	`mnuEditFindNext`	True
&Options	`mnuOptions`	True
&Font Size	`mnuOptionsFont`	True
&Help	`mnuHelp`	True
&Using EasyEdit	`mnuHelpUsing`	True
&About EasyEdit	`mnuHelpAbout`	True

The completed menu interface should look like the screenshot below. Also note the File, File System, Common Dialog and Utility controls:

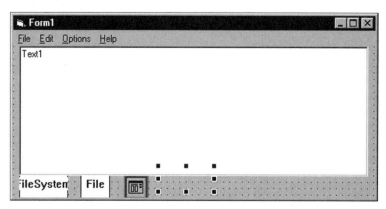

Step 4 - Setting the Form and Control Properties

Set the properties for the form and controls to match the following table:

Object	Property	Value
Form	Name	**frmEasyEdit**
	Caption	Larry Roof's EasyEdit
	WindowState	2 - Maximized
Text Box	Name	**txtFile**
	MultiLine	True
	ScrollBars	2 – Vertical
	Text	<blank>
File	Name	**ceFile**
FileSystem	Name	**ceFileSys**
Common Dialog	Name	**ceCommonDialog**
Utility	Name	**ceUtility**

Your form should now look like this:

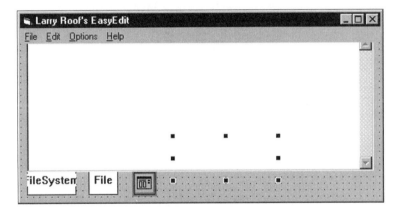

Finish this step by saving your project.

Step 5 - Adding your Coding

The next step in our development process is to add the code that will define how the EasyEdit application performs. I've broken this step down into logical components starting with the form-related events.

Starting and Stopping EasyEdit - The Form Events

There are two form events that are used by EasyEdit, the **Load** and **QueryUnload** events. The code for the **Load** event gets everything ready to start editing. The code in the **QueryUnload** makes sure that the active file has been saved before exiting the program.

The Form_Load Procedure

First let's take a look at the **Load** procedure which calls three routines:

```
Private Sub Form_Load()

' Fit the interface to the palmtop.
  AdjustControls

' Get initial configurations.
  GetConfigs

' Setup a new file.
  NewFile

' Put the user's focus back in the file contents.
  txtFile.SetFocus

End Sub
```

The **AdjustControls** routine handles fitting the application interface to the size of the user's handheld device screen. **GetConfigs** retrieves the user previous font setting. **NewFile** sets everything up to start editing a new, blank file. Finally the focus is set to the text box control where the user will be working.

The AdjustControls Procedure

The code for the **AdjustControls** routine is simple. Since the EasyEdit form has its WindowState property set to Maximized, the form will automatically adjust to the size of the display. This routine adjusts the size of the text box control as needed to fit the form size:

```
Sub AdjustControls()

' Extend the size of the interface to match the size of the
' display on the palmtop.
  txtFile.Width = frmEasyEdit.Width - txtFile.Left - 100

End Sub
```

The GetConfigs Procedure

The **GetConfigs** routine would be used to retrieve the last font size that was used. This feature allows the user to work in a selected font size from one time to the next. In this example this feature is not included.

```
Sub GetConfigs()

' This will be added later

End Sub
```

The NewFile Procedure

NewFile handles the preparation of the EasyEdit environment to begin editing a new, empty file.

It starts by making sure that the active file is saved. This protects the user against losing modifications that they failed to save. If the active file has already been saved a set of variables are initialized:

```
Sub NewFile()

' Make sure the current file is saved before starting a new file.
  If (FileIsSaved) Then
    txtFile.Text = ""
    strCurrentFile = ""
    frmEasyEdit.Caption = "Larry Roof's EasyEdit - Untitled"
    blnFileHasChanged = False

' The user must have changed their mind. Resume editing.
  Else

  End If

End Sub
```

This procedure also introduces the first two of our form level variables, **strCurrentFile** and **blnFileHasChanged**. We need to go back and declare these two variables in the General Declarations section:

```
Option Explicit

  Dim strCurrentFile
  Dim blnFileHasChanged
```

The FileIsSaved Function

The **FileIsSaved** function starts by checking to see if a file has been changed with the **blnFileHasChanged** flag. The only time that this flag will be true is when the user has made changes to the active file but has yet to save those changes.

In the event that there are unsaved changes the user is prompted to determine if they want to save the file. If they answer Yes, the file is saved. Answering No will cause the changes to be lost. Cancel simply causes the editing process to continue:

```
Function FileIsSaved()

  Dim intUsersAnswer
  Dim strFileNameCopy

' Are there unsaved changes? If so prompt the user to see what should
' be done.
  If (blnFileHasChanged) Then
    If (strCurrentFile = "") Then
      intUsersAnswer = MsgBox("The text in the untitled file has " _
                  & "changed." & vbCrLf & "Do you want to save the changes?", _
                vbExclamation + vbYesNoCancel + vbDefaultButton1, _
                "Larry Roof's EasyEdit")
```

```
        Else
            intUsersAnswer = MsgBox("The text in the " & strCurrentFile & _
                        " has changed." & vbCrLf & "Do you want to save the " _
                        & "changes?", vbExclamation + vbDefaultButton1 + _
                        vbYesNoCancel, "Larry Roof's EasyEdit")

        End If

' Does the user want to save the file before exiting?
    Select Case intUsersAnswer

' User wants to save the file.
        Case vbYes
            strFileNameCopy = strCurrentFile

            If (SaveFile(strFileNameCopy)) Then
                FileIsSaved = True
                strCurrentFile = strFileNameCopy

            Else
                FileIsSaved = False

            End If

' User doesn't want to save the file.
        Case vbNo
            FileIsSaved = True

' User wants to resume editing.
        Case vbCancel
            FileIsSaved = False

    End Select

' There are no unsaved changes. Simply return.
    Else
        FileIsSaved = True

    End If

End Function
```

The SaveFile Function

The **FileIsSaved** function calls upon still another function to physically save the active file. In saving the file, the **SaveFile** function handles getting the filename to use for the file and handling situations such as where the user has specified to overwrite an existing file:

```
Function SaveFile(strNameOfFile)

    Const lrFileOutput = 2

    Dim strDirectory
    Dim intUsersAnswer

' Setup the error handler.
    On Error Resume Next
```

The contents of the **strNameOfFile** argument control whether or not the user will be prompted for a filename. If it's either an empty string (**""**), or contains the words **SaveAs** the common dialog control will be displayed to allow the user to specify a name and directory for the file:

```
' Prompt the user for a filename if we don't already have one.
   If (strNameOfFile = "") Or (strNameOfFile = "SaveAs") Then
      ceCommonDialog.ShowSave
      strNameOfFile = ceCommonDialog.Filename

      If (strNameOfFile = "") Then
        SaveFile = False
        Exit Function

      End If

' Does this file already exist? If so, prompt the user to see if we
' should overwrite.
      If (strNameOfFile <> strCurrentFile) Then
         strDirectory = ceFileSystem.Dir(strNameOfFile)

         If strDirectory <> "" Then
           intUsersAnswer = MsgBox("The file " & strNameOfFile & _
                     "already exists." & vbCrLf & "Do you want to replace this " _
                     & "file?", vbExclamation + vbYesNo + vbDefaultButton1, _
                     "Larry Roof's EasyEdit")

            Select Case intUsersAnswer

' The user selected to overwrite the file. Nothing is needed to be
' done here. Simply continue.
            Case vbYes:

' The user doesn't want to overwrite the file so we will exit.
            Case vbNo:
                SaveFile = False
                Exit Function

            End Select

         End If

      End If

   End If
```

Finally at this point in the **SaveFile** function we are ready to save the file. Using the **Open** method of the File control, the file is opened for output. The **Err** object is checked to confirm that the file was successfully opened:

```
' Open the File.
   On Error Resume Next
   ceFile.Open strNameOfFile, lrFileOutput
```

```
      If Err <> 0 Then
        MsgBox "Error opening " & strNameOfFile & vbCrLf & _
               Err.Description, vbCritical, "Larry Roof's EasyEdit"
        Err.Clear
        SaveFile = False
        Exit Function

      End If
```

Write out the contents of the text box control, **txtFile**, to the file. The **LinePrint** method is used for this as it offers the best results. It writes the contents of the text box control out as is, adding a carriage return and line feed to the end of the file. A check is made after the write to the **Err** object to verify the success of the operation:

```
    ' Write out the file.
      ceFile.LinePrint txtFile.Text

      If Err <> 0 Then
        MsgBox "Error writing to " & strNameOfFile & vbCrLf & _
               Err.Description, vbCritical, "Larry Roof's EasyEdit"
        Err.Clear
        ceFile.Close
        SaveFile = False
        Exit Function

      End If
```

The **SaveFile** function completes by performing any cleanup that is required before returning:

```
    ' File has been saved so perform final cleanup.
      ceFile.Close
      strCurrentFile = strNameOfFile
      frmEasyEdit.Caption = "Larry Roof's EasyEdit - " & strCurrentFile
      blnFileHasChanged = False
      SaveFile = True

    End Function
```

The Form_QueryUnload Procedure

One of the worst things for an editor application to do is to allow the user to exit the program without saving changes that have been made to the active file. The **Form_QueryUnload** procedure contains code for handling just such a situation.

If you have not worked with the **Form_QueryUnload** event before, it's called whenever a form is about to be unloaded. This could be the result of the user tapping the close window button, your program has issued the **App.End** statement or any other event that would cause the form window to be unloaded. This is a particularly useful event to use when you want to make sure that an operation is performed before the form is unloaded. That is exactly the case we have with the EasyEdit program. We need to make sure that the file is saved before the form is unloaded.

So what happens if the user decides that they don't want a form to be unloaded? Let's say they accidentally tapped the Exit menu item. The **Cancel** argument to the **Form_QueryUnload** procedure is used to control just this type of situation. It's pretty simple. The value the **Cancel** argument has when the **QueryUnload** procedure completes determines whether or not the form will be unloaded. The user changes their mind and doesn't want to exit the application? Simply set the **Cancel** argument to **True**.

An example of this can be seen in the **Form_QueryUnload** procedure below. In the event that the form is being unloaded, a check is made to make sure that any changes made to the active file have been saved. If they have not, the **Cancel** property is set to **True**, which prohibits the program from exiting:

```
Private Sub Form_QueryUnload(Cancel, UnloadMode)

' Check if changes have been made before exiting.
  If (Not FileIsSaved) Then
    Cancel = True
  End If

End Sub
```

Working Around a Text Box Bug

As I documented earlier, the text box control has a bug in which the user is unable to move about the contents of the control using the arrow keys. EasyEdit makes use of the fix presented in that chapter to provide this functionality. Before we do this, however, let's code the **Change** event so that the form level variable **blnFileHasChanged** is set to **True** whenever the user changes the file in any way:

```
Private Sub txtFile_Change()

  blnFileHasChanged = True

End Sub
```

Here again is the code to get around the text box bugs:

```
Private Sub txtFile_KeyUp(KeyCode, Shift)

' If an arrow key was pressed process it.
  If (Shift = 0) Then

    Select Case KeyCode

      Case 37: ArrowLeft txtFile, ceUtility

      Case 38: ArrowUp txtFile, ceUtility

      Case 39: ArrowRight txtFile, ceUtility

      Case 40: ArrowDown txtFile, ceUtility

    End Select

  End If

End Sub
```

```vb
Private Sub ArrowUp(TextBox, Utility)
' Utility is the utility control.

  Dim intCharPos
  Dim intCRLFOffset
  Dim intCurLine
  Dim intCharsPriorToLine
  Dim intCursorPosOnLine
  Dim intPrevLineLen

  On Error Resume Next

' Find out where the cursor is presently at in the textbox.
  intCharPos = Utility.SendMessageLong(TextBox.hWnd, EM_LINEINDEX, -1, 0)
  intCurLine = Utility.SendMessageLong(TextBox.hWnd, _
              EM_LINEFROMCHAR, intCharPos, 0)

' The cursor is already at the first line. It can't move up.
  If (intCurLine = 0) Then Exit Sub

' Get more information on the cursor position.
  intCharsPriorToLine = Utility.SendMessageLong(TextBox.hWnd, _
                EM_LINEINDEX, intCurLine, 0)
  intCursorPosOnLine = TextBox.SelStart - intCharsPriorToLine
  intPrevLineLen = Utility.SendMessageLong(TextBox.hWnd, _
                EM_LINELENGTH, TextBox.SelStart - intCursorPosOnLine - 2, 0)

' Handle carriage return / line feed combinations that are
' encountered.
  If (Mid(TextBox.Text, intCharsPriorToLine - 1, 2) = vbCrLf) Then _
                intCRLFOffset = 2

' Set the new cursor position.
  If (intPrevLineLen < intCursorPosOnLine) Then
    TextBox.SelStart = intCharsPriorToLine - intCRLFOffset

  Else
    TextBox.SelStart = intCharsPriorToLine - (intPrevLineLen - _
                intCursorPosOnLine) - intCRLFOffset

  End If

' Make sure that the cursor is visible.
  ScrollTextBox TextBox, Utility

End Sub

Private Sub ArrowDown(TextBox, Utility)
' Utility is the utility control.

  Dim intCharPos
  Dim intCharsPriorToLine
  Dim intCurLine
  Dim intCursorPosOnLine
  Dim intNextLineLen
  Dim intTotalLines
```

```
      On Error Resume Next

' Find out where the cursor is presently at in the textbox.
      intTotalLines = Utility.SendMessageLong(TextBox.hWnd, _
                          EM_GETLINECOUNT, 0, 0)
      intCharPos = Utility.SendMessageLong(TextBox.hWnd, EM_LINEINDEX, -1, 0)
      intCurLine = Utility.SendMessageLong(TextBox.hWnd, _
                          EM_LINEFROMCHAR, intCharPos, 0)

' The cursor is already at the last line. It can't move down.
      If intCurLine = (intTotalLines - 1) Then Exit Sub

' Get more information on the cursor position.
      intCharsPriorToLine = Utility.SendMessageLong(TextBox.hWnd, _
                          EM_LINEINDEX, intCurLine, 0)
      intCursorPosOnLine = TextBox.SelStart - intCharsPriorToLine
      intCharsPriorToLine = Utility.SendMessageLong(TextBox.hWnd, _
                          EM_LINEINDEX, intCurLine + 1, 0)
      intNextLineLen = Utility.SendMessageLong(TextBox.hWnd, _
                          EM_LINELENGTH, intCharsPriorToLine, 0)

' Set the new cursor position.
      If (intCursorPosOnLine <= intNextLineLen) Then
        TextBox.SelStart = intCharsPriorToLine + intCursorPosOnLine

      Else
        TextBox.SelStart = intCharsPriorToLine + intNextLineLen

      End If

' Make sure that the cursor is visible.
      ScrollTextBox TextBox, Utility

End Sub

Private Sub ArrowLeft(TextBox, Utility)
' Utility is the utility control.

  Dim intCharPos
  Dim intCharsPriorToLine
  Dim intCurLine

  On Error Resume Next

' The cursor is already at the first character. It can't move left.
  If (TextBox.SelStart = 0) Then Exit Sub

' Get move information on the cursor position.
  intCharPos = Utility.SendMessageLong(TextBox.hWnd, EM_LINEINDEX, -1, 0)
  intCurLine = Utility.SendMessageLong(TextBox.hWnd, _
                      EM_LINEFROMCHAR, intCharPos, 0)
  intCharsPriorToLine = Utility.SendMessageLong(TextBox.hWnd, _
                      EM_LINEINDEX, intCurLine, 0)
```

```vb
' Set the new cursor position.
  If TextBox.SelStart - intCharsPriorToLine = 0 Then
    TextBox.SelStart = intCharsPriorToLine - 2

  Else
    TextBox.SelStart = TextBox.SelStart - 1

  End If

' Make sure that the cursor is visible.
  ScrollTextBox TextBox, Utility

End Sub
```

```vb
Private Sub ArrowRight(TextBox, Utility)
' Utility is the utility control.

  Dim intCharPos
  Dim intCharsPriorToLine
  Dim intCurLine
  Dim intCursorPosOnLine
  Dim intLineLen
  Dim intTotalLines

  On Error Resume Next

' Find out where the cursor is presently at in the textbox.
  intTotalLines = Utility.SendMessageLong(TextBox.hWnd, EM_GETLINECOUNT, 0, 0)
  intCharPos = Utility.SendMessageLong(TextBox.hWnd, EM_LINEINDEX, -1, 0)
  intCurLine = Utility.SendMessageLong(TextBox.hWnd, _
               EM_LINEFROMCHAR, intCharPos, 0)

' The cursor is already at the last line. It can't move down.
  If intCurLine = (intTotalLines - 1) Then

    If (TextBox.SelStart < Len(TextBox.Text)) Then TextBox.SelStart _
                                      = TextBox.SelStart + 1

    Exit Sub

  End If

' Get more information on the cursor position.
  intCharsPriorToLine = Utility.SendMessageLong(TextBox.hWnd, _
    EM_LINEINDEX, intCurLine, 0)
  intCursorPosOnLine = TextBox.SelStart - intCharsPriorToLine

  If (intCurLine = 0) Then
    intLineLen = Utility.SendMessageLong(TextBox.hWnd, EM_LINELENGTH, 0, 0)

  Else
    intLineLen = Utility.SendMessageLong(TextBox.hWnd, _
                 EM_LINELENGTH, intCharsPriorToLine + 2, 0)

  End If
```

```
' Set the new cursor position.
  If intCursorPosOnLine < intLineLen Then
    TextBox.SelStart = TextBox.SelStart + 1

  Else
    TextBox.SelStart = TextBox.SelStart + 2

  End If

' Make sure that the cursor is visible.
  ScrollTextBox TextBox, Utility

End Sub
```

```
Public Sub ScrollTextBox(TextBox, Utility)
' Utility is the utility control.

' This routine works around the textbox scrolloing bug by manually
' scrolling the text box so that the caret (cursor) is in view.
  Call Utility.SendMessageLong(TextBox.hWnd, EM_SCROLLCARET, 0, 0)

End Sub
```

Berfore this code will work remember to declare the constants:

```
Option Explicit
```

```
Const EM_LINEFORMCHAR = &HC9
Const EM_LINEINDEX = &HBB
Const EM_LINELENGTH = &HC1
Const EM_SCROLLCARET = &HB7
Const EM_GETLINECOUNT = &HBA

Dim strCurrentFile
Dim blnFileHasChanged
```

Implementing the EasyEdit Menu - The File Menu

The EasyEdit menu structure is comprised of four menus: File, Edit, Options and Help. In this section we will walk through each, examining the code used to provide functionality to the menus.

The File menu is used to implement all of the file management functions for the EasyEdit application. From this menu the user can create new files, save files and load existing files.

The New File Menu Item

The New File menu item allows the user to start a new file. I doubt that you will ever encounter an easier event procedure than this. It does two things. First, it calls the **NewFile** procedure that handles saving the existing file before creating a new file. This procedure was discussed earlier in this chapter. Secondly, it sets the focus back to the text box control so that the user can resume editing:

```
Private Sub mnuFileNew_Click()

  NewFile
```

```
' Put the user's focus back in the file contents.
  txtFile.SetFocus

End Sub
```

The Open File Menu Item

The procedure for the Open File menu item is as simplistic as that used for creating a new file. In this case though the **OpenFile** procedure is called to first check to see if the current file is saved before loading a new file:

```
Private Sub mnuFileOpen_Click()

  OpenFile

' Put the user's focus back in the file contents.
  txtFile.SetFocus

End Sub
```

The **OpenFile** routine handles the loading of existing files into EasyEdit. It begins by checking to make sure that the contents of the active file have been saved. This operation is performed by the **FileIsSaved** function that we reviewed earlier:

```
Sub OpenFile()

  Const lrFileInput = 1

  Dim strFileToOpen
  Dim strInputString

' Make sure the current file is saved before opening a file.
  If (FileIsSaved) Then
```

Opening the file is handled by first prompting the user for the file to open. Next the file is opened and the **Err** object checked to confirm the success of the **Open** operation:

```
' Get the name of the file to open.
' --- This needs to be replaced with File dialog.
    strFileToOpen = InputBox("File to open:", _
                   "Larry Roof's EasyEdit - Open File",  "")

' Open the selected file, if one was provided.
    If (strFileToOpen <> "") Then
      On Error Resume Next
      ceFile.Open strFileToOpen, lrFileInput

      If Err <> 0 Then
        MsgBox "Error opening " & strFileToOpen & vbCrLf & _
                  Err.Description, vbCritical, "Larry Roof's EasyEdit"
      Err.Clear
      Exit Sub

      End If
```

The complete contents of the selected file are then read into the variable **strInputString** using the **Input** method of the File object – one read for everything.

The **Err** object is then checked to confirm the success of the read operation. The next check may seem a bit odd. A check is made to see if the File control returned the right number of characters. Why? Because it has the habit of giving you a few more than are in the file. Bugs, you've got to love them!

Finally, the right two characters of the variable **strInputString** are examined to determine if they are a carriage return and line feed. If so, then they are removed. This trailing carriage return / line feed combo is a side effect of writing the file using the **LinePrint** method of the File Control. This method adds a carriage return / line feed combination to everything that it writes:

```
' Read in the file.
' Check and remove a trailing CRLF added during the saving of the
' file.
      strInputString = ceFile.Input(ceFile.LOF)

      If Err <> 0 Then
        MsgBox "Error reading from " & strFileToOpen & vbCrLf & _
                  Err.Description, vbCritical, "Larry Roof's EasyEdit"
        Err.Clear
        Exit Sub

      End If

' The file control has the habit of passing back trailing junk
' characters.
' Remove them if present.
      If(Len(strInputString) <> ceFile.LOF) Then
        strInputString = Mid(strInputString, 1, Len(strInputString) _
                  - (Len(strInputString) - ceFile.LOF))

      End If

' Check and remove a trailing CRLF added during the saving of the
' file.
      If (Right(strInputString, 2) = vbCrLf) Then
         strInputString = Mid(strInputString, 1, ceFile.LOF - 2)

      End If
```

At this point the file has been opened and read. The contents of the file are displayed in the text box control and final preparations are made to the editor, including:

- Loading the filename into the form-level variable **strCurrentFile**
- Setting the caption on the form so that it displays the name of the file being edited
- Resetting the form-level variable **blnFileHasChanged** to **False** (This variable is used to track when changes are made to the file)

```
' Display and setup the file.
    txtFile.Text = strInputString
    ceFile.Close
    strCurrentFile = strFileToOpen
    frmEasyEdit.Caption = " Larry Roof's EasyEdit - " & strCurrentFile
    blnFileHasChanged = False

' The user didn't provide a filename. Resume editing.
  Else

    End If

' The user must have changed their mind. Resume editing.
  Else

    End If

End Sub
```

The Save Menu Item

The event procedure for saving a file simply calls the **SaveFile** function passing the name of the current file that is being edited. A detailed analysis of this function was provided earlier in this chapter.

If this were a new file that was being saved for the first time the form-level variable **strCurrentFile** will be blank. The **SaveFile** function checks for this and will prompt the user to enter a filename:

```
Private Sub mnuFileSave_Click()

  SaveFile (strCurrentFile)

' Put the user's focus back in the file contents.
  txtFile.SetFocus

End Sub
```

The Save As... Menu Item

The **FileSaveAs** event procedure is identical to that used for the **FileSave** event with the exception that it passes the value **"SaveAs"** to the **SaveFile** function instead of the name of the current file being edited. The **SaveFile** function will then prompt the user for a new filename:

```
Private Sub mnuFileSaveAs_Click()

  SaveFile ("SaveAs")

' Put the user's focus back in the file contents.
  txtFile.SetFocus

End Sub
```

The Error Menu Item

The Error menu item is intended for development use only. It displays the number and description of the last runtime error that was encountered. Before releasing EasyEdit to users set the Visible property of the Error menu item to False. All it does is display a message box offering more detailed information about any error that arises:

```
Private Sub mnuFileError_Click()

  MsgBox "Error number " & Err.Number & vbCrLf & Err.Description

End Sub
```

The Exit Menu Item

The Exit menu item event procedure contains a single statement that invokes a procedure used to control exiting from EasyEdit:

```
Private Sub mnuFileExit_Click()

  ExitEditor

End Sub
```

In the **ExitEditor** procedure a check is made to see if the current file has been saved with the **FileIsSaved** function (see the discussion on this function earlier in this chapter). A positive response results in the application exiting via the **End** method of the **App** object.

```
Sub ExitEditor()

' Check to make sure that the contents of the current file have been
' saved before exiting.
  If (FileIsSaved) Then
    App.End

' The user must have changed their mind. Resume editing.
  Else

  End If

End Sub
```

The Edit Menu

The Edit menu provides the standard text manipulation and locator functions that you would expect to find in a text editor. This includes cutting, copying and pasting text plus a simplistic find feature.

The Cut Menu Item

The **EditCut** event procedure uses the **Clipboard** object for temporary storage of selected text. The procedure begins by clearing the current contents of the clipboard with the **Clear** method. Next the selected text is copied to the clipboard using the **SetText** method. Finally the text is removed from the file by setting the **SelText** property of the text box to an empty string `""`. The **SelText** property contains the text that the user has selected in the control:

```
Private Sub mnuEditCut_Click()

  Clipboard.Clear
  Clipboard.SetText txtFile.SelText
  txtFile.SelText = ""

' Put the user's focus back in the file contents.
  txtFile.SetFocus

End Sub
```

The Copy Menu Item

The **EditCopy** event procedure is identical to the **EditCut** procedure with the exception that it does not remove the selected text from the text box control. It only copies the selected text to the clipboard:

```
Private Sub mnuEditCopy_Click()

  Clipboard.Clear
  Clipboard.SetText txtFile.SelText

' Put the user's focus back in the file contents.
  txtFile.SetFocus

End Sub
```

The Paste Menu Item

The **EditPaste** event procedure handles retrieval of text from the clipboard. It inserts the text either in place of the text currently selected in the text box or at the current cursor position if no text is currently selected in the text box. The **Clipboard** object's **GetText** method provides this functionality:

```
Private Sub mnuEditPaste_Click()

  txtFile.SelText = Clipboard.GetText

' Put the user's focus back in the file contents.
  txtFile.SetFocus

End Sub
```

The Find Menu Item

The **EditFind** event procedure contains only the call to the **FindText** procedure, passing an empty string as the sole argument. The **FindText** procedure provides the functionality both to prompt the user for the string to locate or to find the string specified in its argument. This allows it to be used for both the Find and the Find Next menu items:

```
Private Sub mnuEditFind_Click()

  FindText ""

End Sub
```

The **FindText** procedure starts by checking the contents of the argument that was passed. If it's empty, the user is then prompted to enter the string that they are searching for. If it contains a value, that value is used for the search:

```
Sub FindText(strTextToUse)

  Dim strSelectedText
  Dim intTextPosition

' Either use the string passed to this routine or prompt the user for
' a string.
  If (strTextToUse = "") Then
    strSelectedText = InputBox("Find what:", _
                      " Larry Roof's EasyEdit - Find", strTextToFind)

  Else
    strSelectedText = strTextToUse

  End If
```

This routine introduces the third form level variable, **strTextToFind**, which we need to go back and declare:

```
Option Explicit

  Const EM_LINEFORMCHAR = &HC9
  Const EM_LINEINDEX = &HBB
  Const EM_LINELENGTH = &HC1
  Const EM_SCROLLCARET = &HB7
  Const EM_GETLINECOUNT = &HBA

  Dim strCurrentFile
  Dim blnFileHasChanged
  Dim strTextToFind
```

Before initiating the search for the specified text, the **FindText** procedure saves the string in the form-level variable **strTextToFind**. This enables the procedure to 'remember' the string if and when the user clicks on the Find Next menu item.

The VBCE **Instr** function is used to locate the position of the specified string within the file. This function returns a numeric value, which is in turn used to set the current file position with the **SelStart** property of the text box control. Selecting the requested text then highlights the specified string. This is accomplished by setting the **SelLength** property of the text box control equal to the length of the string being searched for:

```
' Find the string. This routine looks for the specifiec text from the
' current point of the text in txtFile, to the end of the text in
' txtFile.
' Anything before the current point is ignored.
  If (strSelectedText <> "") Then
    strTextToFind = strSelectedText
    intTextPosition = InStr(txtFile.SelStart + txtFile.SelLength _
                      + 1, txtFile.Text, strTextToFind)
```

```
        If (intTextPosition > 0) Then
          txtFile.SelStart = intTextPosition - 1
          txtFile.SelLength = Len(strTextToFind)

        Else
          MsgBox "Cannot find " & strTextToFind, vbInformation + _
                    vbOKOnly, "Larry Roof's EasyEdit"

        End If

      End If

    End Sub
```

The Find Next Menu Item

The **EditFindNext** event procedure is nearly identical to the **EditFind** procedure but instead of passing an empty string as the argument, it passes the contents of the form-level variable **strTextToFind**, which was set the last time the **FindText** procedure was called:

```
    Private Sub mnuEditFindNext_Click()

      FindText strTextToFind

    End Sub
```

The Options Menu

The Options menu provides a sole function, setting the size of the font that is used for the text window.

The Font Size Menu Item

The **OptionsFont** event procedure contains only a call to the **ChangeFont** procedure:

```
    Private Sub mnuOptionsFont_Click()

      ChangeFont

    End Sub
```

Within the **ChangeFont** procedure the common dialog control is used to display the current font configuration and allow the user to select a new configuration. The setting that the user specifies is then used to set the **FontSize** property of the text box control and is saved to the form-level variable **intCurrentFontSize**, which could be used to remember the font configuration between editing sessions:

```
    Sub ChangeFont()

    ' Font Constants
      Const cdlCFScreenFonts = &H1
      Const cdlCFEffects = &H100
      Const cdlCFLimitSize = &H2000
      Const cdlCFForceFontExist = &H10000
```

```
' Set the minimum and maximum font sizes.
  ceCommonDialog.Max = 30
  ceCommonDialog.Min = 8

' Set the dialog from the control.
  ceCommonDialog.FontBold = txtFile.FontBold
  ceCommonDialog.FontItalic = txtFile.FontItalic
  ceCommonDialog.FontName = txtFile.FontName
  ceCommonDialog.FontSize = txtFile.FontSize

  If ceCommonDialog.FontSize <> txtFile.FontSize Then
    ceCommonDialog.FontSize = ceCommonDialog.FontSize + 1
  End If

' Define what the font dialog should show. In this case we only want
' the Bold and Italic options displayed.
  ceCommonDialog.Flags = cdlCFForceFontExist Or cdlCFLimitSize Or _
                         cdlCFScreenFonts

' Display the dialog.
  ceCommonDialog.ShowFont

' Set the control from the dialog.
  txtFile.FontBold = ceCommonDialog.FontBold
  txtFile.FontItalic = ceCommonDialog.FontItalic
  txtFile.FontName = ceCommonDialog.FontName
  txtFile.FontSize = ceCommonDialog.FontSize
  intCurrentFontSize = txtFile.FontSize

End Sub
```

This routine also introduces the final form level variable, **intCurrentFontSize**, which we need to go back and declare:

```
Option Explicit

  Const EM_LINEFORMCHAR = &HC9
  Const EM_LINEINDEX = &HBB
  Const EM_LINELENGTH = &HC1
  Const EM_SCROLLCARET = &HB7
  Const EM_GETLINECOUNT = &HBA

  Dim strCurrentFile
  Dim blnFileHasChanged
  Dim strTextToFind
  Dim intCurrentFontSize
```

The Help Menu

The Help menu provides no functionality at this point. In Chapter 9 these items will be programmed to provide access to help topics.

Step 6 - Testing in the CE Emulator

Set the Run on Target project property to Emulator and run your project. Test out the various functionality of EasyEdit to create, modify, save and reload a file. Try adjusting the font size noting how the usability of the application improves or diminishes as the size is changed.

> You'll need to use the Control Manager to install the File, File System, Common Dialog and Utility controls onto both the emulator and your H/PC before running this test. See Chapter 4 for further details on using this utility.

Step 7 - Testing on a Handheld Computer

Set the Run on Target project property to Remote Device and run your project. As you did in the emulator, test out the functionality of the EasyEdit application. Find something that you don't like about the design? Change it. Is there a feature missing? Add it. That is the beauty of creating your own text editor.

Step 8 - Creating an Installation Program

Use the Application Install Wizard to generate an installation program for EasyEdit. If you need help with this wizard refer to Chapter 2 where a detailed explanation of the process is provided.

Step 9 - Test the Installation Program

As with previous examples, it is important that you test your installation program. It should install without error and allow you to completely remove the program.

Summarizing EasyEdit

There you have it, a complete text editor based upon VBCE's file input and output features. What I hope that you gather from this example is:

- ▲ That in the CE environment sequential files offer a viable alternative to databases
- ▲ There are useful applications that can constructed with minimal effort using VBCE

Feel free to use EasyEdit as a starting point for your own CE-based editors. Embellish upon its design to add features and functionality. It wouldn't take too much effort to create a text-based HTML editor or a note keeping application.

Summary

File input and output has been a part of the BASIC language since its conception. In this chapter, I demonstrated how it still has a use in today's applications. Sequential, random access and binary files can be used to provide both performance and functionality enhancements to your CE applications. Support for file I/O is provided through two controls, the File and File System controls. Together they allow you to create, manipulate and delete files.

As EasyEdit, this chapters' example program utilizes the two file controls along with the common dialog control to provide a comprehensive set of tools that can be used to incorporate files into your applications. You need to be comfortable with what these tools have to offer and when they would best used to improve your CE apps. For sequential, random access and binary files are not a thing of the past but a technique for improving your applications today.

Working with Databases

When the VBCE Toolkit was first released it was void of any form of database functionality. As such it was a pretty useless tool. I mean without a way to store and retrieve data what is an application to do? Thankfully this shortcoming has been corrected with the release of the **ActiveX Data Objects 1.0 SDK for Windows CE**. This control provides a subset of the Windows CE ADO allowing you to create and access databases on an H/PC.

Before you get too excited stop and remember that this is a CE tool. You're not going to find all of the functionality that you have come to expect from a desktop database. The ADO CE is a far cry from a relational database. What you will find is a tool that allows you to create tables, add, retrieve and delete records. Pretty basic stuff, but certainly enough to develop some effective CE applications.

In this chapter I will lead you through the process of working with the ADO CE. You will start by obtaining and installing the SDK. From there I will show you how to move databases to and from your H/PC and show you the key functionality that you can access from your CE applications including creating databases, adding, retrieving, modifying and deleting records. Finally I will show you how the ADO CE is used to store information that is gathered from the Time Manager application that was originally created back in Chapter 2.

What Does the ADO Provide?

Most simply stated, ADO provides access to databases on your H/PC. It allows you to create, manipulate and delete these structures from within your VBCE programs. The ADO CE implementation is a subset of the ADO standard and as such, it provides a limited amount of the functionality found in ADO in the form of a fairly complete implementation of the **Recordset** and **Field** objects.

The ADO CE SDK contains some additional tools that will aid you in the development and deployment of CE database applications:

- An ActiveSync module that synchronizes data between a desktop Access file and H/PC tables. This module determines when changes have been made to data on the desktop, H/PC, or both. Changes are synchronized between the two data sources. While this filter is in place, it will not be functional until the release of Windows CE 2.1.

- A utility that allows you to drag Access databases from your desktop to your H/PC. You can then choose which tables and fields that you wish to copy from the database.

- A utility that allows you to copy databases from your H/PC to an Access database on your desktop computer.

- A utility that allows you to copy databases from your desktop to the CE emulator.

▲ ADO CE and SQL documentation and sample code for both the Visual Basic and Visual C Toolkits for Windows CE.

▲ Support for moving data to and from SQL Server databases. This is provided through the Mobile Devices window.

What Does the ADO Not Provide?

The ADO CE does not provide access to the databases that come with your H/PC. That means you will not be able to add, modify, delete or even view data from the appointments, contacts or tasks databases that are used by Pocket Outlook. I know, I too would like to be able to get at those, but, for at least this version of the SDK, you can't do it.

Actually, it's a much broader omission than just those three databases. You cannot access any databases that were created using the API **CeCreateDatabase** function, the method that all CE applications written in C would use. This means most third-party applications' databases. Only if they use the ADO CE will you be able to access their data.

Acquiring the ADO CE SDK

The ActiveX Data Objects 1.0 SDK for Windows CE can be downloaded from Microsoft's web site.

It's a free download that's about 1 MB in size.

Installing the ADO CE SDK

The installation process used with the ActiveX Data Objects 1.0 SDK for Windows CE is fairly straightforward. It has a simple setup tool that performs the necessary configuration on both your desktop computer and your H/PC.

> The setup routine that is provided with the ActiveX Data Objects 1.0 SDK for Windows CE only handles installation on your development PC, not the client, or target PC. You must write your own setup application to install the ADO CE on the client's machine. I have included a brief discussion of such a program later in this chapter.

Requirements for Using the ADO CE

There are two sets of requirements that are needed for using the ActiveX Data Objects 1.0 SDK for Windows CE. One set of requirements is for your development machine. The other set is for the client machine that will be running your ADO enhanced applications.

For the Development Machine

The requirements for the development machine includes all of the tools used along with the ADO SDK in the process of creating CE applications. Most of the items in this list are requirements for running the VBCE Toolkit as well. The key difference is the need for Windows CE Services version 2.1:

- ▲ Windows NT Workstation version 4 with Service Pack 3

- ▲ Windows CE Services version 2.x; version 2.1 is recommended. The 2.1 version contains some enhancements that are utilized by the ActiveX Data Object

- ▲ An HPC running Windows CE version 2.0 or later

- ▲ Windows CE Platform SDK

- ▲ Visual Basic version 5 with Service Pack 2 or later

- ▲ Visual Basic for Windows CE Toolkit

For the Client Machine

The requirements for the client's machine are far less stringent than those needed for the development machine. Again, the key element is the Windows CE Services version 2.1:

- ▲ Windows CE Services version 2.x; version 2.1 is recommended. The 2.1 version contains some enhancements that are utilized by ActiveX Data Object v1.0.

- ▲ Windows NT Workstations version 4, Windows 95 or Windows 98

- ▲ An HPC running Windows CE version 2.0 or later

The Installation Procedure

The ADO CE SDK is packaged in a self-extracting zip file. When you run the executable it will create a new directory and copy the SDK installation files to that directory. You will then need to switch to this new directory and run the program **Setup.exe**. An opening dialog will be displayed followed by a licensing dialog. You will then come to the setup screen shown:

As you see there isn't anything for you to select or configure. Simply click the Install ADOCE button to continue.

Shortly after that you will be prompted for your only involvement in the installation process. With the following dialog you will be asked whether you want to install ADO for use with the CE emulator. I recommend that you do install this!

> There is a Visual Basic program included with the ActiveX Data Objects 1.0 SDK that handles the transferring of Access databases to the emulator. The default location for this application is:
>
> `C:\ProgramFiles\DevStudio\ADOCE\Samples\VB\EmulDB`

After you close the emulator dialog the installation will begin. A short process of copying files will occur. Upon completion the setup routine will attempt to connect to your H/PC to install the ActiveX Data Objects. If your H/PC is not currently connected you will be informed that it will be installed on the next mobile device connection.

The installation process is then completed.

> At this point you need to delete and recreate the partnership between your desktop computer and your H/PC. This allows ActiveSync to install the Table filters used with the ActiveX Data Objects. The easiest way to do this is:
>
> Disconnect your H/PC from your desktop if necessary.
>
> Open **Mobile Devices.**
>
> Select your H/PC in the **Mobile Devices** display and press the *Delete* key.
>
> Reconnect your H/PC.
>
> The new partnership process will automatically run.
>
> If you don't follow these instructions you will receive an error message saying **MicrosoftTable Service not instaled** every time that you connect your H/PC to your desktop.

Known Setup Bugs

There are few know bugs in the setup process. They are:

▲ You may have to stop the desktop sync manager for setup to work, although this should be done automatically for you.

▲ To uninstall the ActiveX Data Objects SDK you simply run the setup again. While this does remove all of the files from your desktop PC it doesn't remove files from your H/PC. You will need to use the Control Panel | Remove Programs utility on the H/PC for this. You will receive ActiveSync errors until this is done.

▲ The setup programs attempts to verify that you have either Visual Basic 5 or Visual C++ 5 installed on your development system before it will proceed with the installation. Sometimes the installation program fails to find these correctly:

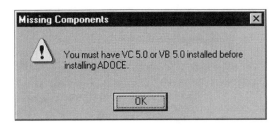

▲ The setup examines the values in the registry under the key of :

HKEY_LOCAL_MACHINE\Software\Microsoft\DevStudio\5.0\Directories

▲ If this key is not found then the Toolkit will not install correctly. A proper solution would be to uninstall your DevStudio products and reinstall them. However, just adding the missing key folder seems to allow install to complete.

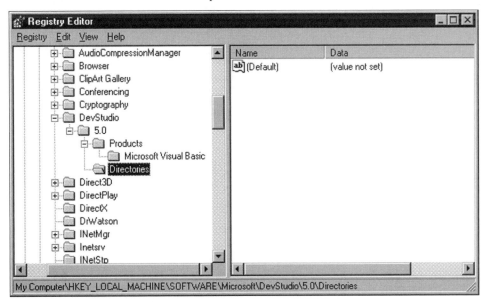

Working with the ADO CE Tools

As I stated earlier in this chapter the ADO CE SDK not only provides database functionality to your CE applications, but also includes a set of tools for management of databases between your desktop and H/PC computers. In this section I will show you what these tools have to offer and how they are used.

Copying Databases from the Desktop PC

The ADO CE SDK includes a tool that allows you to copy database tables from a Microsoft Access database on your desktop PC to your H/PC. The databases that it creates on the H/PC are in the standard Windows CE configuration (in other words, a single-hierarchical structured collection of data consisting of a number or records, each of which consists of one or more properties).

To copy a database from your desktop PC to your H/PC use the following steps:

Connect your H/PC device to your desktop PC.

Open the Mobile Devices window.

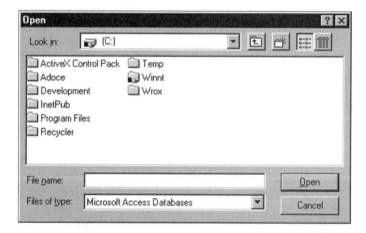

At this point you can either drag the Access database from an Explorer window to the Mobile Devices window or use the Tools | Import Database Tables menu item from the Mobile Device window to initiate the copy procedure. If you use the menu approach a dialog will be displayed from which you can select the Access database to copy.

A Synchronize File dialog may be displayed as shown in the figure below. If it is displayed select No. You just want to copy the tables to your H/PC.

The Import from Database to Mobile Device dialog will then be displayed:

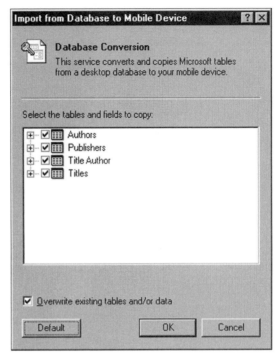

It is presenting you with a list of all of the tables contained in the database that you have selected to copy. At this point you can choose which tables that you want transferred to your H/PC. If you don't want a table transferred, simply deselect it from this dialog.

> **If by accident you copy tables to your H/PC that you do not want, DO NOT use one of the Windows CE delete database utilities to remove them. This would be really bad (see later). Instead you will need to delete them through the ADO CE as shown in the coding examples later in this chapter.**

The ADO CE SDK does not support relationships or joins between tables. Consider carefully how you intend to use various tables together before selecting them to be copied.

You can even select specific fields from tables that you want to copy, as shown in this screenshot:

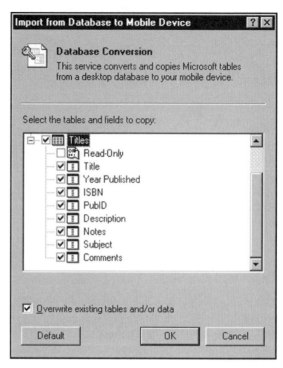

The <u>O</u>verwrite existing tables and/or data check box controls whether the copy will replace existing data on the H/PC.

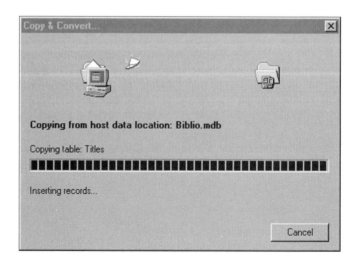

Once you have configured which tables and fields that you want to copy you initiate the copying procedure by clicking the OK button. The following dialog will be displayed to inform you on the progress of the transfer:

You should now see the selected tables appear as individual databases under the **\Databases** folder on your HPC.

Copying Databases from the H/PC

The ADO CE SDK includes a tool that allows you to copy database tables from your H/PC to a Microsoft Access database on your desktop PC.

You can copy a database from your desktop H/PC to your H/PC as follows:

Connect your H/PC device to your desktop PC.

Open the Mobile Devices window.

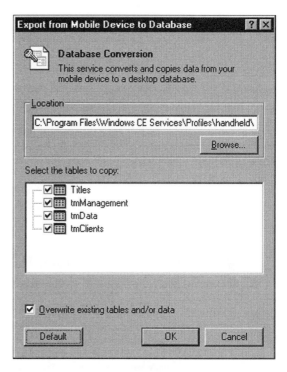

Use the Tools | Export Database Tables menu item from the Mobile Device window to initiate the copy procedure. The Export from Mobile Device to Database dialog will be displayed as shown:

This dialog has three distinct sections. The first is the location of the database on your desktop computer that will receive the data that is transferred from your H/PC.

The body of this dialog displays the tables that are present on the H/PC. You can select any tables that you wish to copy.

Finally the Overwrite existing tables and/or data check box allows you to control whether or not the data from the H/PC will overwrite existing data on your desktop computer.

Click the OK button to initiate the copying process. The dialog shown below will be displayed to show the progress of the copy procedure:

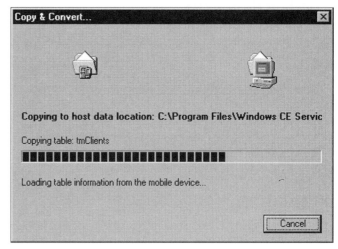

There is a log file created by this process named **ce2db.txt**. It will provide details on the transfer process. This file is located under the profile's directory of your H/PC device on your desktop computer. Typically this is:

`C:\Program Files\Windows CE Services\Profiles\Device Name`

> **This log file is overwritten with each copying process.**

Copying Data to an ODBC Data Source

You can optionally copy data to an ODBC data source instead of an Access database. This is accomplished by:

Selecting the Browse... button from the Export from Mobile Device to Database dialog. The Choose Your New Database Filename dialog will be displayed:

Select ODBC Database from the Save as type: combo box located at the bottom of the dialog.

The Select Data Source dialog will be display as shown in the screenshot below. Select the data source in which to copy your H/PC databases and click the OK button.

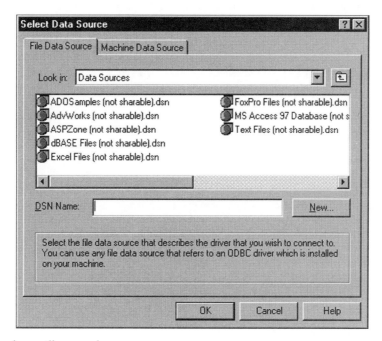

The copying procedure will proceed.

Copying Databases with Code

All of the examples of copying data between a desktop PC and an H/PC shown up to this point are for the most part a manual process. You have to drag or select files and configure a set of dialogs that specify how the copying procedure should be performed. That may be fine for you the developer but what if you want this to happen automatically from an end user's PC?

The answer is that there are two functions provided with the ADO CE SDK: **DeviceToDesktop** and **DesktopToDevice**. These functions are located in the **adofiltr.dll**. They can be used to copy databases to and from a H/PC and to and from a desktop PC.

There is a more detailed discussion on this in Chapter 8.

The Synchronization Process

The initial release of the ADO CE does not provide for any type of synchronization. So you might be wondering what the purpose of this section is. Well, it's here so that you can design your applications to make use of this functionality when it becomes available later this year with the release of Windows CE 2.1.

The key requirement for the synchronization process to occur is to have a unique, single column key with the name **PrimaryKey**. Obviously this index field needs to contain a unique value. Any table that does not have this configuration will not be synchronized and you will not receive any warning messages. I would recommend that you design all your ADO CE databases with this requirement in mind, so they are able to take advantage of future functionality.

Programming with the ADO CE SDK

In this next section we will delve into how to create and access databases from your CE applications using the ADO CE SDK. The materials in this section are presented in a sequential fashion, starting with creating a table, through adding and modifying records, retrieving records, and finishing with deleting records. In all you will find the key components that you will need to develop data-enabled applications using the VBCE Toolkit.

> *This section by no means presents everything that you can do with the ADO CE. For additional information reference the ADO CE Help that is included with the SDK.*
>
> *There is a sample program that is included with the ADO CE SDK that is a useful tool to aid in the development of your own ADO applications. It can be used to create, modify and delete tables, add data and examine records. This program is normally located in:*
>
> `C:\Program Files\DevStudio\Adoce\Samples\Vb\Adodemo`
>
> *I would recommend building a copy of this application and loading it onto your H/PC so that it is readily available. I found that expanding the number of fields that it displays from 3 to 6 significantly enhanced the usefulness of this program.*

Creating a Table

Now you may be wondering, "Why do I need to create a table? I thought that I could use the tools that were included with the ADO CE SDK to copy tables from my desktop PC". But how about the situation where you don't want to or can't create a table by copying from a desktop PC? Let's say, for instance, you have created an application using the VBCE Toolkit that uses the ADO SDK to work with a CE database. Now you want to market this application and distribute it from a web site. At this point it's no longer practical for you to copy the table from a desktop PC. You need to create the table from within your application.

> *An example of this is shown later in this chapter in the Time Manager example where three tables are created:* **tmClients**, **tmData** *and* **tmManagement**.

The following code fragment demonstrates the creation of a CE table:

```
Dim recEmployees

' Setup an error handler.
  On Error Resume Next

' Create the table.
  Set recEmployees = CreateObject("adoce.recordset")
  recEmployees.Open "CREATE TABLE xyEmployees (EmployeeID AS
      ↳ VARCHAR(9), Name VARCHAR(30), DateHired DATETIME, Evaluation
      ↳ TEXT)"

' Check to see if an error occurred while creating the table.
  If (Err.Number <> 0) Then
     MsgBox "An error occurred while creating the index." & vbCrLf _
          & Err.Number & " - " & Err.Description
     Err.Clear

  End If
```

This example begins by setting up an error handler. This is something that you should do in all of your procedures that include ADO code.

Next an instance of the ADO recordset object is created using the **recEmployees** variable:

```
Set recEmployees = CreateObject("adoce.recordset")
```

The **Open** method of the recordset object is then used to create the new table. The SQL **CREATE TABLE** statement is used for this purpose. In the case of this example the table name is **xyEmployees**. It will have four fields: **EmployeeID**, **Name**, **DateHired** and **Evaluation**. **EmployeeID** is the employee's Social Security number minus the hyphens that will be used as the primary key for this table; **Name** is a string of 30 characters, **DateHired** will store a date and **Evaluation** is a text field that is similar to the Access memo field.

This table will be created in the **\Database** directory on the H/PC. You do not have the option to specify its creation in another directory.

> *I like to use a prefix with all of my table names. Since they will all be created in the* **\Database** *directory on the H/PC there is the possibility that there will be a conflict with existing or future databases. Using a two-letter prefix reduces the chance that this will occur.*
>
> *For instance the tables that are used by the Note Manager application in Chapter 10 are* **nmFolders**, **nmNotes** *and* **nmManagement**, *where* **nm** *stands for Note Manager.*

Creating an Index

The tables that you create should all include at least a Primary Key index. They can improve the efficiency of your ADO code. They also will allow your table to be synchronized with desktop tables in future versions of the ADO CE SDK.

The following code fragment demonstrates creating an index:

```
Dim recEmployees

' Setup an error handler.
  On Error Resume Next

' Create the table.
  Set recEmployees = CreateObject("adoce.recordset")
  recEmployees.Open "CREATE TABLE xyEmployees (EmployeeID AS
            ↳ VARCHAR(9), Name VARCHAR(30), DateHired DATETIME, Evaluation
            ↳ TEXT)"

' Check to see if an error occurred while creating the table.
  If (Err.Number <> 0) Then
      MsgBox "An error occurred while creating the index." & vbCrLf
            ↳ & Err.Number & " - " & Err.Description
      Err.Clear

  End If

  recEmployees.Open "CREATE INDEX PRIMARYKEY ON xyEmployees
            ↳ (EmployeeID) "

' Check to see if an error occurred while creating the index.
  If (Err.Number <> 0) Then
      MsgBox "An error occurred while creating the index." & vbCrLf
            ↳ & Err.Number & " - " & Err.Description
      Err.Clear

End If
```

This example continues on from the previous example where we created a table. This is a common practice, as you will typically want to follow up the creation of a table with the creation of at least a Primary Key index.

Again the recordset **Open** method is used but in this case to create the index. The SQL **CREATE INDEX** statement is used for this purpose. The name of this index is **PRIMARYKEY**. It's creating the index for the **xyEmployees** table. The field on which it will be indexed is **EmployeeID**.

Also note that another check is made to see if an error occurred during the creation of this index.

> *Remember, even though synchronization is not supported in the first release of the ADO CE SDK, there are plans to include it in the next release scheduled to be bundled with Windows CE 2.1. For synchronization to occur, your tables must have an index named* **PrimaryKey** *based upon a single, unique-value field.*

Determining If a Table Exists

If your application is going to create the table(s) that it uses, it will need to first check to see if a table exists. There are three ways that this can be accomplished:

- With the File System control's **Dir** method
- By looking in the **MSysTables** table. This is the table used by ADO to store table names.
- By setting an error handler, attempting to open the table and then check for an error signifying that the table does not exist

In this example we will be using the second method where we will search **MSysTables** for the table in question. The following code will perform this function:

```
Private Function DoesTableExist(strTableName)

  Dim recSystemTable
  Dim strSQL

' Setup an error handler.
  On Error Resume Next

' Open the table.
  Set recSystemTable = CreateObject("adoce.recordset")
  strSQL = "SELECT TableName FROM MSysTables WHERE TableName = '" _
          & strTableName & "'"
  recSystemTable.Open strSQL, "", adOpenKeyset, adLockOptimistic

' Check to see if an error occurred while opening the table.
  If (Err.Number <> 0) Then
    MsgBox "An error occurred while opening the table." & vbCrLf & _
          Err.Number & " - " & Err.Description
    Err.Clear
    DoesTableExist = False
    Exit Function

  End If

' Determine if we have found any matches
  If recSystemTable.EOF = True Then
    'There is no matching table name
    DoesTableExist = False

  Else
    'Table name found
    DoesTableExist = True

  End If

  'Close Down system table
  recSystemTable.Close
  Set recSystemTable = Nothing

End Function
```

This code begins by setting up an error handler. It then opens the table, **MSysTables**, which is used by ADO to track the tables that it has created.

A SQL select statement is then assembled to return a single column recordset consisting of the **TableName** of all the ADO CE tables that match the name passed to the function. Because SQL is case insensitive we don't have to worry about the name of the table being correctly cased. The recordset that is created will contain at most one row from the **MSysTables** table. All that is left to do is to find out if the recordset is empty by checking to see if the **EOF** property is **True**. If it is **True** then the table does not exist, otherwise we have a match and the **DoesTableExist** function can return **True**.

Dropping a Table

Tables that are created with the ADO CE SDK need to be deleted with the ADO CE SDK. Failure to do this will have very bad results as it corrupts the table management function of ADO. The fix to this condition is to completely remove ADO and reinstall it from scratch.

> **Dropping tables is irreversible. Make absolutely sure that this is the action you want to take before doing it.**

The following code can be used to drop a table:

```
Dim recTables

' Setup an error handler.
On Error Resume Next

' Drop the table.
Set recTables = CreateObject("adoce.recordset")
recTables.Open "DROP TABLE xyEmployees"

' Check to see if an error occurred while deleting the table.
If (Err.Number <> 0) Then
    MsgBox "An error occurred while deleting the table." & vbCrLf _
            & Err.Number & " - " & Err.Description
    Err.Clear

End If

' Destroy the recordset variable.
Set recTables = Nothing
```

This example begins by setting an error handler. The **Open** method of the recordset object is then used to drop the table. The SQL **DROP TABLE** statement is used for this purpose. A check is then made to see if an error occurred during the dropping of the table.

Finally the object variable used for the recordset is destroyed, freeing up its resources.

Dropping tables is a task that you will need to incorporate into the uninstall procedures for your ADO-enabled applications.

Opening a Table

Now that you have a table to work with next up is opening the table. You have already seen the **Open** method used in examples earlier in this chapter. Now we will look at it in a bit more detail. The syntax for the **Open** method is:

```
recordset.Open Source, Active Connection, Cursor Type, Lock Type, Options
```

The descriptions of these arguments are:

Source is a required argument that is either the name of the table that is to be opened, or a SQL statement. When using the name of a table all records in that table are part of the recordset. Using a SQL statement allows you to exclude particular records.

Active Connection has only one valid value: **""** (an empty string). This argument is optional.

Cursor Type specifies how you will be able to move about the recordset. This argument is optional. It has two acceptable values:

- **adOpenForwardOnly** that has the value of 0 only allows you to move forward through the recordset. This is the default value.

- **adOpenKeyset** that has the value of 1 allows you to move any direction through the recordset.

Typically, if you are just reporting on records and as such need to make only a single pass through the records, you would use **adOpenForwardOnly**. If you are creating an application that allows the user to scroll forward and backwards through records, you will want to use **adOpenKeyset**.

> *The constants used with the examples shown in this book are defined in the file* **ADOdeclarations.bas** *included with the examples for this book. You may include all or part of this module in any CE applications that are using ADO.*

Lock Type specifies which type of locking is used when opening the recordset. This argument is optional. It has two acceptable values:

- **adLockReadOnly** that has the value of 1 allows you to only read records. This is the default value.
- **adLockOptimistic** that has the value of 3 allows you to add, modify and delete records.

Typically, if the user isn't going to be modifying any records in your application use **adLockReadOnly**. Otherwise use **adLockOptimistic**.

Options tells ADO what is in the **Source**, or first argument. This argument is optional. It has the following acceptable values:

- ▲ **adCmdText** that has the value of 1 tells ADO that the **Source** argument is an SQL statement.

- ▲ **adCmdTable** that has the value of 2 tells ADO that the **Source** argument is a table name.

- ▲ **adCmdStoredProc** that has the value of 4 tells ADO that the **Source** argument is a stored procedure. *Stored procedures are not presently supported in the ADO CE.*

- ▲ **adCmdUnknown** that has the value of 8 tells ADO that the contents of the **Source** argument are unknown. This is the default value.

The following example demonstrates the use of the **Open** method:

```
Dim recEmployees

' Setup an error handler.
On Error Resume Next

' Open the table.
Set recEmployees = CreateObject("adoce.recordset")
recEmployees.Open "xyEmployees", "", adOpenKeyset, adLockOptimistic

' Check to see if an error occurred while opening the table.
If (Err.Number <> 0) Then
    MsgBox "An error occurred while opening the table." & vbCrLf _
        & Err.Number & " - " & Err.Description
    Err.Clear

End If
```

In this example the **xyEmployees** table is opened with the **Cursor Type** that will allow movement in any directory through the recordset and the **Lock Type** that will allow adding, modifying and deleting records. This would be the argument combination that you would typically use if you were creating an application where the user would be able to browse through and modify records.

Managing Your Recordsets

As I stated in the discussion of the **Open** method you could use a SQL statement as the **Source** for the recordset you are creating. Now I'm not going to attempt to teach you SQL in the course of this chapter, but only show you examples of a couple of simple statements that you can use to restrict and order your recordsets.

For a detailed tutorial on SQL see the Wrox title "Instant SQL Programming" by Joe Celko.

The ADO Help includes a detailed list of the SQL statements that are supported by the ADO CE.

> **You should note that ADO CE does not allow you to join tables.**

Selecting the Records to Return

The most common reason for using a SQL statement to create a recordset is where you want to restrict, or limit, the number of records that are returned. By adding the **WHERE** clause of the **SELECT** statement you can specify that the records must match.

Take the following example for instance:

```
    Dim recEmployees

 ' Setup an error handler.
   On Error Resume Next

 ' Create a recordset.
   Set recEmployees = CreateObject("adoce.recordset")
   recEmployees.Open "SELECT * FROM xyEmployees WHERE Name = '"
       ↳ & txtName.Text & "'"
```

In this example a SQL statement is used to return the record for the employee, using the name that the user has entered in the text box called **txtName**.

> *Note the use of apostrophes around the value of the text box control.*

For example, if name that the user enters is "Larry Roof", the SQL statement that is passed to ADO is:

```
   SELECT * FROM xyEmployees WHERE Name = 'Larry Roof'
```

Optionally you could use the **LIKE** clause, which allows you to do a wildcard search or one where you are only looking for a match of part of a value. Take for instance the following example:

```
    Dim recEmployees

 ' Setup an error handler.
   On Error Resume Next

 ' Create a recordset.
   Set recEmployees = CreateObject("adoce.recordset")
   recEmployees.Open "SELECT * FROM xyEmployees WHERE Name LIKE
       ↳ 'Larry%'"
```

Notice how the **%** character is used as a wildcard character. The recordset generated by this example will include all of the employees with a first name of **Larry**.

Restrictions of the WHERE Clause

The **WHERE** clause supported by ADO CE has a few more restriction than you may be used to. If you are familiar with SQL from the desktop environment you may have used the **BETWEEN** predicate to restrict a recordset to those records with values between a pair of arguments. For example:

```
   SELECT * FROM Orders WHERE OrderValue BETWEEN 1000 AND 2000
```

This is not supported by ADO CE. However, you can build up a complex expression with **AND** and **OR** boolean logic. So the above statement could be achieved by:

```
SELECT * FROM Orders WHERE (OrderValue >= 1000 AND OrderValue <= 2000)
```

In this simple case this is no great problem, but if you start to build up more complex expressions you will have to be careful. Use parentheses liberally to make sure you get the result you intend!

> *Another type of comparison not supported in this release of the Toolkit is the* **IN** *operator. If want to select records from known lists then you will have to either make up a really complex expression, or expect to get a bigger recordset and always check that the records in it are useful to you in code.*

Sorting the Recordset

Sorting is another common use for SQL statements. For instance, let's say you wanted to fill a grid control with all of your employees ordered by the date that they were hired. This can be accomplished with a SQL statement containing an **ORDER BY** clause.

Take the following example for instance:

```
Dim recEmployees

' Setup an error handler.
On Error Resume Next

' Create a recordset.
Set recEmployees = CreateObject("adoce.recordset")
recEmployees.Open "SELECT * FROM xyEmployees ORDER BY DateHired
    DESC"
```

In this example a SQL statement is used to construct a recordset of all of your employees, ordered by the date that they were hired, sorted in a descending order. You could optionally sort them in an ascending order by using the descriptor **ASC**. ADO CE will accept a sort on up to three columns.

Navigating Through a Recordset

Building a recordset is only part of the process. You typically will want to be able to move about in, or navigate through, the recordset. The ADO CE provides a set of methods and properties for doing just this.

MoveFirst, MoveLast, MoveNext and MovePrevious

These four methods can be used to move about a recordset. As their names suggest, they move to the first, last, previous or next record in the current recordset.

> To make use of the `MovePrevious` and `MoveFirst` methods you must open the recordset with the Cursor Type of `adOpenKeyset` that enables you to move in any direction within the recordset.

For example, assume that you have an application that displays employee records. Part of the interface is four command buttons with the captions First, Last, Previous and Next. The event procedures for each of these buttons might contain code similar to the following:

```
Private Sub cmdFirst_Click()

  mrecEmployees.MoveFirst
  UpdateDisplay

End Sub

Private Sub cmdLast_Click()

  mrecEmployees.MoveLast
  UpdateDisplay

End Sub

Private Sub cmdPrevious_Click()

  mrecEmployees.MovePrevious
  UpdateDisplay

End Sub

Private Sub cmdNext_Click()

  mrecEmployees.MoveNext
  UpdateDisplay

End Sub
```

The procedure **UpdateDisplay** is responsible for displaying the fields of the current record in the controls that are part of this interface. Unlike Visual Basic that offers data-bound controls with the VBCE Toolkit, it is you that is responsible for updating the display. For example the **UpdateDisplay** procedure might look something like the following:

```
Private Sub UpdateDisplay()

  txtName.Text = mrecEmployees.Fields("Name")
  txtDateHired.Text = mrecEmployees.Fields("DateHired")
  txtEvaluation.Text = mrecEmployees.Fields("Evaluation")

End Sub
```

BOF and EOF Properties

There is a small problem in the **Move** code examples above. The procedures used to move to the previous and next records have the possibility of generating an error. For example let's say that you have a recordset of employees. Presently the first record in this record is the active record. If the user then clicks the Previous button the event procedure for that button will attempt to move back one record, or past the start of the recordset. When the **UpdateDisplay** procedure is then called it will generate an error by attempting to access the fields of the current record.

One way that you can prohibit this from occurring is through the use of the **BOF** (beginning of file) and **EOF** (end of file) properties of a recordset. Take for example the modified procedures used by the Previous and Next command buttons:

```
Sub cmdPrevious_Click()

  mrecEmployees.MovePrevious

' Check to make sure that you are not parked on the BOF.
  If (mrecEmployees.BOF = True) Then
    mrecEmployees.MoveNext
    Exit Sub

  End If

' The record has changed so update the display.
  UpdateDisplay

End Sub
```

```
Sub cmdNext_Click()

  mrecEmployees.MoveNext

' Check to make sure that you are not parked on the EOF.
  If (mrecEmployees.EOF = True) Then
    mrecEmployees.MovePrevious
    Exit Sub

  End If

' The record has changed so update the display.
  UpdateDisplay

End Sub
```

As you can see in these revised versions now after repositioning the record pointer, a check is made to make sure that we haven't moved onto the **BOF** or **EOF**. If we have then the record pointer is set back to where we started and the routine is exited. We didn't need to make a call to **UpdateDisplay** because that record is already being displayed.

Adding a Record

There are two ways that you can use to add new records to a database – with the **AddNew** method of a recordset and with the SQL **INSERT** statement. In this section we will look at each of these ways.

Using The SQL INSERT Statement

The SQL **INSERT** statement provides a simple way to add a record to a database. It's used in conjunction with the recordset **Open** method. For example:

```
    Dim recEmployees

  ' Setup an error handler.
    On Error Resume Next

  ' Add the record.
    Set recEmployees = CreateObject("adoce.recordset")
    recEmployees.Open "INSERT INTO xyEmployees (EmployeeID, Name,
      ⮑ DateHired, Evaluation) VALUES ('" & txtEmployeeID.Text &
      ⮑ "', '" & txtName.Text & "', '" & txtDateHired.Text &
      ⮑ "', '" & txtEvaluation.Text & "')"
```

This code fragment demonstrates adding a new record to the **xyEmployees** table using the contents of four text box controls (**txtEmployeeID**, **txtName**, **txtDateHired** and **txtEvaluation**) as the field values for the fields of **Name**, **DateHired** and **Evaluation**.

Using AddNew Method

Adding records to a recordset is simple using the recordset **AddNew** method. Actually it involves the use of two methods, **AddNew** and **Update**, sandwiched around a series of statements that load field values into the new record. Take for instance the following code fragment:

```
    Dim recEmployees

  ' Setup an error handler.
    On Error Resume Next

  ' Open the table.
    Set recEmployees = CreateObject("adoce.recordset")
    recEmployees.Open "xyEmployees", "", adOpenKeyset, adLockOptimistic

  ' Add the record.
    recEmployees.AddNew
    recEmployees.Fields("EmployeeID") = txtEmployeeID.Text
    recEmployees.Fields("Name") = txtName.Text
    recEmployees.Fields("DateHired") = txtDateHired.Text
    recEmployees.Fields("Evaluation") = txtEvaluation.Text
    recEmployees.Update
```

This example begins by creating a recordset. Note that the recordset is opened for read and write by using the **adLockOptimistic** argument. The use of the **AddNew** method creates the new record. The three statements that follow load the fields of the new record with values taken from the interface. Finally the **Update** method saves these values for this new record.

Handling the Absence of AutoNumbering

Earlier during the discussion of creating tables I mentioned that every table should have an index named **PrimaryKey** that is based upon a field containing unique values. Now in your tables you may have an obvious field for this purpose, such as an Employee's Social Security number as shown in the examples from this chapter. But what if you don't?

The ADO CE does not provide an **AutoNumber** field type as found in Microsoft Access. If you haven't worked with AutoNumber before the beauty of this type of field is that a unique number is generated for you as each new record is added. With ADO CE, it's up to you to create the field ID's.

To work around this shortcoming I 'create' my own unique IDs through a bit of ADO manipulation as shown in the function below:

```
Private Function NextID()

  Dim recTemp

' Retrieve the Management record.
  Set recTemp = CreateObject("adoce.recordset")
  recTemp.Open "SELECT * FROM xyManagement", "", adOpenKeyset,
    ↳ adLockOptimistic

' Increment the record counter by 1 and write it back out to the
' database.
  recTemp.Fields("LastIDUsed").Value = recTemp.Fields("LastIDUsed")  + 1
  rectemp.Update
  NextID = recTemp.Fields("LastIDUsed")

' Close the temporary recordset.
  recTemp.Close
  Set recTemp = Nothing

End Function
```

The **xyManagement** table has a single record table that I use to track the ID numbers for my tables. It will have a field for each table in my application for which I am generating IDs. To get the next number I start by opening the table. Next, I increment the ID and write it back to the **xyManagement** table. At this point the contents of this field is my new ID. Finally, I pass this new incremented value back to the calling routine so that it can be used in the new record.

While this is not a painless approach to the auto numbering problem, it's fairly easy to use once you have created the **NextID** function.

Modifying Records

Changing, or modifying a record with the ADO CE is similar to the process used to add a new record. You simply update the field values for the current record and issue the recordset's **Update** method as shown in the following code fragment:

```
' Update the record.
  recEmployees.Fields("Name") = txtName.Text
  recEmployees.Fields("DateHired") = txtDateHired.Text
  recEmployees.Fields("Evaluation") = txtEvaluation.Text
  recEmployees.Update
```

*Remember to open the recordset for reading and writing when using the **Update** method. If you fail to do this you will generate a runtime error.*

Deleting Records

Deleting records, like adding records offers two approaches: a SQL statement and using the recordset's **DELETE** method.

Using SQL DELETE Statement

The SQL **DELETE** statement provides a simple way to delete records from a database based on some selection criteria. Like the **INSERT** statement, it's used in conjunction with the recordset **Open** method. For example:

```
  Dim recEmployees

' Setup an error handler.
  On Error Resume Next

' Add the record.
  Set recEmployees = CreateObject("adoce.recordset")
  recEmployees.Open "DELETE xyEmployees WHERE EmployeeID = '" &
     txtEmployeeID.Text & "'"
```

In this example the record that has an Employee ID that matches the value of the text box **txtEmployeeID** will be deleted. A less restrictive **WHERE** clause could be used to remove several records from the database. If you were to leave out the **WHERE** clause all together then every record would be removed from the table.

> Using the DELETE SQL statement in this way does not remove the table itself, it just removes all the records stored within it.

Using The Delete Method

Deleting records from an open recordset with the **Delete** method involves two steps: first the record must be deleted; second you must move to a new record. The reason behind the second step is that even though you have deleted a record that record remains as the current record. It's not until you move off that record that it becomes no longer accessible, i.e. deleted.

The following example demonstrates this two step process:

```
' Delete the current record.
  recEmployees.Delete

' Move to a new record and display its contents on the interface.
  recEmployees.MoveNext
  If (recEmployees.EOF = True) Then recEmployees.MoveLast
  UpdateDisplay
```

This example starts by using the **Delete** method to remove the current record. Next we move off the deleted record by issuing the **MoveNext** method. We also need to make a check to see if we have moved onto the end of the file. If we have, we simply issue the **MoveLast** method. Finally the **UpdateDisplay** procedure is called to load the interface with the values from the new record.

TableView – A Step-By-Step Example

A frequent use of databases is to show data in a tabular format. This can easily be achieved with the ActiveX Control Pack Grid control that you saw in Chapter 4. I have built a small demonstration of doing just this.

TableView – The Completed Project

Before we start constructing the TableView application, let's take a look at the completed project. I use this approach because I believe that seeing the finished product aids in understanding discussions on its development.

To install TableView on your handheld computer follow these steps:

▲ Establish a connection between you desktop and handheld computers

▲ Using the instructions laid out in Appendix A, find the version of TableView for Chapter 7

▲ Follow the installation directions.

Using TableView

Once you have completed the installation of this example, run it on your handheld computer. The TableView interface should be displayed as shown in the screenshot below:

TableView offers a read only look at the data in your ADO CE tables. The above screenshot shows a display of the **MSysTables** table, which contains relevant information about every other table known to ADO CE.

TableView – The Requirements

The purpose for TableView is to provide a read only view of data in a tabular format:

▲   The application should allow you to query the data in any database managed by ADO CE.

TableView – The Design

The TableView application has a fairly simple design. All that is really needed is a grid for data display and a method of selecting the database table to view. The user interface consists of:

▲   A single form

▲   A Grid control to display the data

▲   A text box to enter the name of the data table to view

▲   A couple of command buttons to control the application.

> *You may want to remove this initial version of the TableView program from your handheld computer at this time. The easiest way to accomplish this is through the* Start *menu, then* Settings | Control Panel *and finally* Remove Programs.

TableView – The Construction

In the pages that follow you will be led through all nine steps of the creation process for the TableView application. As with previous examples you may want to work along with the instructions to create your own copy of TableView. You will note that for many of the steps I no longer provide step-by-step instructions.

> *The Chapter 7 version of* **TableView.vbp** *contains a completed version of this project. Refer to Appendix A for instructions on downloading and installing the examples included in this book.*

Step 1 - Starting a New Project
Start Visual Basic and create a new Windows CE project.

Step 2 - Setting the Project Properties
Set the Project Name, Form Width, Remote Path and Run on Target properties to the values shown in the screenshot below:

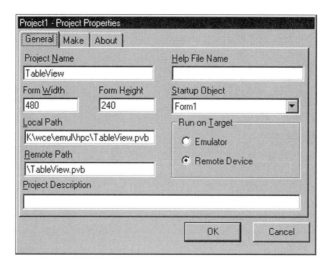

Step 3 - Constructing the User Interface

Add the following items to the TableView form:

- Text Box control
- Grid control
- Two Command buttons

The exact placement of the controls is irrelevant since they will be positioned during run-time startup. The user interface should look a little like the following screenshot:

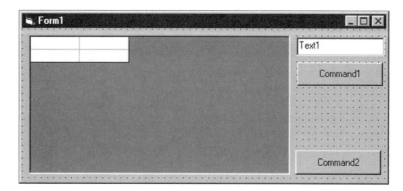

Step 4 - Setting the Form and Control Properties

Set the properties for the form and controls to match the following table:

Object	Property	Value
Form	Name	**frmTableView**
	Caption	ADO CE Tables
	WindowState	2 – Maximized
Text Box	Name	**txtTable**
	Font	MS Sans Serif, 10 Pt Bold
Command2	Name	**cmdExit**
	Caption	E&xit
	Cancel	True
	Font	MS Sans Serif, 10 Pt Bold
Command1	Name	**cmdRead**
	Caption	&Read
	Default	True
	Font	MS Sans Serif, 10 Pt Bold
Grid	Name	**grdData**

The completed user interface should look somewhat like this:

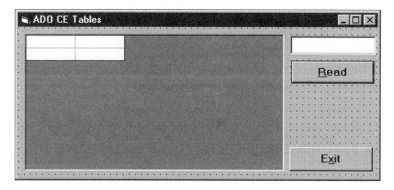

Finish this step by saving your project.

Step 5 - Adding your Coding

The next step in our development process is to add the code that will define how the TableView application queries and displays the data held in the ADO CE databases. To make coding a little more readable I have used a bunch of constant declarations found in the **BAS** module, **ADODeclarations.bas**. This file can found in the source code for this book. You will need to add it to your project.

Starting and Stopping TableView – The Form Events

The obvious event handlers that need to be coded are the Exit button and the form **Load**. In some database applications you may find that you need to maintain open recordset objects in form level variables. If that were the case here I would put any clean up code in the event handler for the Exit button. All I need do here is use the **End** method of the **App** object:

```
Private Sub cmdExit_Click()

  App.End

End Sub
```

The **Form_Load** event is similar to many others I have used so far:

```
Private Sub Form_Load()

' Purpose: Size and fill the grid with data of known tables
  AdjustControls
  txtTable.Text = "MSysTables"

' Invoke a click of the read button
  cmdRead.Value  = True

End Sub
```

The **AdjustControls** routine resizes the Grid control to take up most of the form space, and positions the text box and command buttons to the right-hand edge:

```
Private Sub AdjustControls()

  Const BORDER = 30 'Gives a nice edge from the form border

  On Error Resume Next

' Grid
  grdData.Left = BORDER
  grdData.Top = BORDER
  grdData.Height = Me.ScaleHieght - 2 * BORDER
  grdData.Width = Me.Width - 3 * BORDER - txtTable.Width

' Text Box
  txtTable.Left = grdData.Width + 2 * BORDER
  txtTable.Top = BORDER

' Read Button
  cmdRead.Top = txtTable.Top + txtTable.Height + BORDER
  cmdRead.Left = txtTable.Left

' Exit Button
  cmdExit.Top = Me.ScaleHeight - cmdExit.Height - BORDER
  cmdExit.Left = txtTable.Left

End Sub
```

Displaying Table Data

The rest of the code for this sample is executed from the **Click** event of the **cmdRead** button.

```
Private Sub cmdRead_Click()

'Fill the grid with the contents of the Table
  Dim recTable
  Dim strRow
  Dim intCol
  Dim fldHeader

  On Error Resume Next

  If DoesTableExist(txtTable.Text) Then
```

As normal when doing any database work I always use an error handler. The main bulk of the code is controlled by the result of the **DoesTableExist** function called. This was described earlier in the chapter. The form **Load** event sets the value of the text box to **MSysTables**, this is one of the few tables that you can be certain of finding when ADO CE is installed:

```
' Prepare recordset
  Set recTable = CreateObject("ADOCE.Recordset")

' Open the table
  recTable.Open txtTable.Text, "", adOpenForwardOnly,
        ↳ adLockReadOnly, 2
```

The first thing to do is prepare a recordset. In this case all that is needed is a forward only recordset as all the display will be done in a single pass of the data:

```
' Reset grid first
  grdData.Clear
  grdData.Rows = 0
  grdData.Cols = 0

' How Many Columns
  grdData.Cols = recTable.Fields.Count

' Add a row for column headers
  For intCol = 0 To recTable.Fields.Count - 1
      strRow = strRow & recTable.Fields(intCol).Name & Chr(9)
  Next

' Chop off the trailing Tab character
' Use Mid because Left causes a Bug in a form!
  strRow = Mid(strRow, 1, Len(strRow) - 1)

  grdData.AddItem strRow
```

Before adding rows to the grid I have to reset the number of columns and rows back to zero. This is because of the way that the **AddItem** method of the Grid control appends data. If the grid was left with more columns than necessary to display a whole row, the excess columns would be filled with data from a subsequent row leaving an unreadable mishmash of data.

The **Fields** collection of the recordset is then used to configure the number of columns. Unlike collections you may be used to from the desktop VB environment, this collection is zero based. We use a **For** loop to build up a string of column names separated by tab characters. This string has the last tab trimmed off and is used in the **AddItem** method of the grid:

```
' Now Add all the data
Do Until recTable.EOF

' Add Row
    strRow = ""

    For intCol = 0 To recTable.Fields.Count - 1
        strRow = strRow & recTable.Fields(intCol).Value & Chr(9)
    Next

    strRow = Mid(strRow, 1, Len(strRow) - 1)
    recTable.MoveNext
    grdData.AddItem strRow

Loop
```

The data from the table is extracted by using a **Do** loop that finishes when the **EOF** property of the recordset is **True**. A tab separated string is built up exactly as the header row and appended to the grid:

```
' Close the table
    recTable.Close

' Destroy the object
    Set recTable = Nothing
```

The last thing to do is to close the recordset:

```
Else
    MsgBox "The table " & txtTable.Text & " does not exist!", _
        vbCritical, App.Title

End If

End Sub
```

In the case that a bad table name is typed into the text box, the **DoesTableExist** function would have returned **False**, leaving us to give the user a simple message.

Step 6 - Testing in the CE Emulator

For this example I would only test on the emulator if you elected to install the ADO CE Toolkit. This is an optional part of the setup. If you do want to test on the emulator then ensure that the Run on Target project property is set to Emulator.

Step 7 - Testing on a Handheld Computer

Set the Run on Target project property to Remote Device and run your project. Remember, this example is using a control from the ActiveX Control Pack so you may need to install the Grid control onto the handheld before testing. Try viewing the other system tables that are part of the initial installation of the Toolkit (e.g. **MSysFields** or **MSysIndexes**) It never hurts to give yourself an understanding of the way the database works under the hood.

Step 8 - Creating an Installation Program

You can generate an installation for the program **.pvb** file itself, but you would find it failed to install correctly with a clean H/PC. There are some other issues with installing ADO distributable files. These will be discussed next. You would also have to remember to distribute the Grid control.

Step 9 - Test the Installation Program

As with previous examples, it's important that you test your installation program. It should install without error and allow you to completely remove the program.

Summarizing TableView

This small example demonstrates just how easy it is to read through a set of data. It could very easily be enhanced to allow you to enter your own SQL in the text box and become a very useful tool. I will leave this up to you as an exercise.

Distributing Programs That Use ADO

When you are ready to distribute an application that makes use of the ADO CE you will need to create a setup program that will update both the user's desktop computer and their H/PC. The Help that is included with the ADO CE SDK has information on this process under Distributing ADOCE Applications, which is located under the Programmer's Guide section. There you will find examples of a custom setup program that will install files and modify the registry of the desktop computer.

The tasks that such a program needs to do are:

- Determine whether the *target desktop* machine has a recent enough version of Windows CE Services installed.

- Copy the desktop component files to the Windows CE Services folder. This location can be determined by examining the registry of the desktop.

- Register the ActiveX component **adofiltr.dll**

- Add custom menu entries to the Mobile Devices Tools menu. In this case it is the Import and Export database menu options. These are configured in the registry under the key of:

    HKEY_LOCAL_MACHINE\Software\Microsoft\Windows CE Services\CustomMenus.

▲ Each menu item is configured as a subkey of the above having keys of: Command, DisplayName, StatusHelp and Version.

▲ Finally, shell the CE application manager with a parameter specifying a configuration file for the handheld components. In the case of ADO CE this **INI** file specifies which cabinet files to use and which **DLL** components to install on the device.

We shan't go into more depth than this here. The documentation that the SDK installs to the Books Online is good, but if you're in a hurry to create a setup program to run a user installation, we have made a small executable to install the necessary components to both the desktop and the handheld device. Appendix A has instructions on how to get it.

> This shows an important technique for writing a desktop companion program. If you want your user to be able to start your complimentary desktop application from the Mobiles Devices Tools menu all you have to do is add a few registry entries to the desktop machine in your setup program under the Custom menus section of the Windows Services registry entries. See Books Online for more details.

Updating Time Manager

In the pages that follow I will show you how ADO is used to add database functionality to the Time Manager application that was first introduced in Chapter 2. It's a simple application that provides the capability to track the amount of time that is spent with clients. In this following section we will modify the Time Manager application, augmenting its features to:

▲ Add a list of clients from which to select

▲ Store billing information for future processing

Using Time Manager

Before we look into the details of how database functionality was added to the Time Manager application, let's take a look at the program with this additional feature. This approach is used so that you can better understand the discussions on its development.

To install the revised version of Time Manager on your handheld computer follow these steps:

▲ Establish a connection between your desktop and handheld computers

▲ Using the instructions laid out in Appendix A, find the version of Time Manager for Chapter 7

▲ Follow the installation directions

> This setup program does not install the ADO CE files themselves. You must already have them installed on your machine for this example to work.

Using The Revised Time Manager

Once you have completed the installation of this example, run it on your handheld computer. The Time Manager interface should be displayed.

Test out the new features that have been added to this application. Use the drop down box to select a client for which this session will be billed to as shown in the screenshot below. Start the timer by clicking the S̲tart button, let it run for a while and then stop the timer by clicking the Sto̲p button. Select the time interval that you want to bill to using the O̲ptions | R̲ound Billing To Nearest menu item. Type a note into the large text box on the right of the screen. Click the Lo̲g button to save the details for this session to the database.

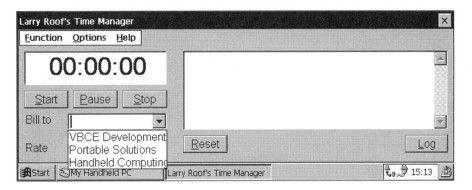

Time Manager – The Requirements

This revised version of the Time Manager application is a rework of the version presented in Chapter 3. Its primary purpose is to demonstrate how to incorporate database functionality into your applications. The only requirements for this version are to provide:

- A list of clients from which to bill
- The ability to save session data to a database

Time Manager – The Design

This third version of the Time Manager application, like the first two, has a fairly simple design. The modifications that are needed for this version are:

- Create the ADO tables that will be used by this application
- Loading clients into the Bill to combo box control
- Calculating the bill according to the time interval set in the R̲ound Billing To Nearest menu item
- Saving session data

With these design criteria specified we can begin the process of modifying the Time Manager application.

> *You may want to remove the revised version of the Time Manager program from your handheld computer at this time. The easiest way to accomplish this is through the* Start *menu, then* Settings | Control Panel *and finally* Remove Programs.

Time Manager – The Construction

In the pages that follow you will be led through the nine steps creation process to modify the previous version of the Time Manager application as we left it in Chapter 3. You can gain the most benefit from this section by working along with the instructions to create your own copy of the Time Manager application.

> *The Chapter 7 version of* **Time Manager.vbp** *contains a completed version of this project. Refer to Appendix A for instructions on downloading and installing the examples included in this book.*

Step 1 - Starting a New Project

Since we will be using the previous version of Time Manager as a starting point this step is unneeded. Instead simply load the project you created in Chapter 3 or the finished solution from the source code for the Chapter 3 version of **Time Manager.vbp**. See the note above for instructions on accessing example applications.

Step 2 - Setting the Project Properties

As was the case with Step 1, this step is unneeded since we are making use of an existing project.

Step 3 - Constructing the User Interface

There is nothing that needs to be done to the interface for the Time Manager application.

Step 4 - Setting the Form and Control Properties

There is nothing that needs to be done to the properties for the Time Manager application.

Step 5 - Adding your Coding

The next step in our development process is to add the code that will provide the new functionality for the Time Manager application. This section is broken down into several parts, one for each new function that is being added.

> *You will also need to add the* **ADODeclarations.bas** *module.*

Coding the Creation of the Time Manager Tables

The most complicated piece of code that we are adding to Time Manager involves the creation of the three tables that are used in this revised version of the application. This procedure is called from the **Form_Load** event procedure:

```
Private Sub Form_Load()

' Fit the interface to the palmtop.
  AdjustControls

' Initialize the controls on the form.
  msngDefaultRate = 100
  txtRate.Text = FormatCurrency(msngDefaultRate)

' Initialize the database
  InitializeDatabase

End Sub
```

The first table is the **tmClients** table. It's used to store a list of the clients that subsequently are used to propagate the Bill to combo box control.

The second table is the **tmData** table, which is used to store session information.

The third table is the **tmManagement** table. This is a support table that is used to generate unique record numbers to use with records being stored in the **tmData** table.

The purpose of the **InitializeDatabase** procedure is to check if the three tables exist and to create them if they are not present. The procedure begins by setting an error handler. This is an important step, as the first time this application runs we will be attempting to open tables that don't exist:

```
Private Sub InitializeDatabase()

  Dim recClients
  Dim recData
  Dim recManagement

' Set up error handler.
  On Error Resume Next
```

A recordset object is then created for each of the three tables – **tmClients**, **tmData** and **tmManagement**:

```
' Create recordset objects for the three tables used by this
' application.

  Set recClients = CreateObject("adoce.recordset")
  Set recData = CreateObject("adoce.recordset")
  Set recManagement = CreateObject("adoce.recordset")
```

Now we are ready to check for the first table – the **tmClients** table. You should note that we are using a fairly crude method here involving opening a file to determine if it exists. You could also look in the ADO **MSysTables** table to see if the **tmClients** table is present:

```
' Check to make sure the clients table is present.
' If it is not, create it.
  Err.Clear
  recClients.Open "tmClients"
```

If an error was generated we assume that it was because the table does not exist because we have used **Err.Clear** to explicitly ignore any prior errors. Having discovered an error we create the table. The command to create the two-field **tmClients** table is issued:

```
If (Err <> 0) Then
  Err.Clear
  recClients.Open "CREATE TABLE tmClients (ClientID INTEGER,
        ⇨ Name VARCHAR(30))"

  If Err.Number <> 0 Then
    MsgBox "Error creating Clients table." & vbCrLf & Err.Number &
          ⇨ " - " & Err.Description
    App.End

  End If
```

Add an index to the table to enable it to use the synchronization feature planned for the next release of the ADO CE:

```
recClients.Open "CREATE INDEX PrimaryKey ON tmClients (ClientID)"
```

Finally add some default records to the table. If you wanted to you could expand the functionality of Time Manager to enable the user to add new clients. Note that I'm using the **AddNew** method of the recordset object. You could just as easily use the SQL **INSERT** statement:

```
' Add a set of default clients into the table.
    recClients.Open "tmClients", , adOpenKeyset, adLockOptimistic

    recClients.AddNew
    recClients.fields("ClientID").Value = 1
    recClients.fields("Name").Value = "Handheld Computing"
    recClients.Update

    recClients.AddNew
    recClients.fields("ClientID").Value = 2
    recClients.fields("Name").Value = "Portable Solutions"
    recClients.Update

    recClients.AddNew
    recClients.fields("ClientID").Value = 3
    recClients.fields("Name").Value = "VBCE Development"
    recClients.Update

    If Err.Number <> 0 Then
      MsgBox "Error adding to Clients table." & vbCrLf & Err.Number _
            & " - " & Err.Description
      App.End

    End If

  End If

  recClients.Close
```

Next a check is made to see if the **tmData** table is present:

```
' Check to make sure the data table is present.
' If it is not, create it.
  Err.Clear
  recData.Open "tmData"
```

If the **tmData** table is not found it is created as with the **tmClients** table. Pay particular attention to the field types for the **Rate** field (a currency value that is stored as a double) and the **Billed** field (a Boolean value stored as a bit). This demonstrates how you must adjust your data types to fit those provided by the ADO CE.

The **Billed** field not used by the Time Manager application but is instead would be set by a desktop application as each record is processed:

```
If (Err <> 0) Then
  Err.Clear
  recData.Open "CREATE TABLE tmData (RecordID INTEGER, BillTo
          ↳ VARCHAR(30), Rate FLOAT, TimeUsed DATETIME, Bill FLOAT,
          ↳ Notes TEXT, Billed BIT)"

  If Err.Number <> 0 Then
    MsgBox "Error creating Data table." & vbCrLf & Err.Number & _
          " - " & Err.Description
    App.End

  End If
```

An index is created for the **tmData** table as well:

```
  recData.Open "CREATE INDEX PrimaryKey ON tmData (RecordID)"

End If

recData.Close
```

Finally a check is made for the **tmManagement** table. As with the previous two tables this check is performed by attempting to open the table:

```
' Check to make sure the Management table is present.
' If it is not, create it.
  Err.Clear
  recManagement.Open "tmManagement"
```

If the table does not exist it is created:

```
If (Err <> 0) Then
  Err.Clear
  recManagement.Open "CREATE TABLE tmManagement (RecordID INTEGER,
          ↳ LastIDUsed INTEGER)"
```

```
      If Err.Number <> 0 Then
        MsgBox "Error creating Management table." & vbCrLf & _
              Err.Number & " - " & Err.Description
        App.End

      End If
```

An index is added:

```
      recManagement.Open "CREATE INDEX PrimaryKey ON tmManagement
            ↳ (NoteID)"
```

A single record is added to this table and the field used to generate record numbers is initialized to **0**. For more information on this technique refer to the section on "Handling the Absence of AutoNumbering" earlier in this chapter:

```
   ' Create the only record used in this table and initialize the
   ' counter.
      recManagement.Open "tmManagement", , adOpenKeyset,
              ↳ adLockOptimistic

      recManagement.AddNew
      recManagement.fields("RecordID").Value = 1
      recManagement.fields("LastIDUsed").Value = 0
      recManagement.Update

   End If

   recManagement.Close
```

The procedure ends with the deletion of the three recordset objects:

```
   ' Destroy the recordset objects used for the three tables.
   Set recClients = Nothing
   Set recData = Nothing
   Set recManagement = Nothing

End Sub
```

Coding the Loading of the Client List

The second procedure that needs to be added to Time Manager handles the loading of clients into the Bill to combo box control. It starts by setting an error handler. This procedure is also called from the **Form_Load** event procedure:

```
Private Sub Form_Load()

' Fit the interface to the palmtop.
  AdjustControls

' Initialize the controls on the form.
  msngDefaultRate = 100
  txtRate.Text = FormatCurrency(msngDefaultRate)
```

```
' Initialize the database
  InitializeDatabase
```

```
' Load clients into combo box
  LoadClients
```

```
End Sub
```

```
Private Sub LoadClients()

  Dim recClients

' Setup error handler.
  On Error Resume Next
```

Next a recordset is created containing all of the records from the **tmClients** table:

```
' Create a recordset of the folders.
  Set recClients = CreateObject("adoce.recordset")
  recClients.Open "SELECT * FROM tmClients", , adOpenForwardOnly,
         ↳ adLockReadOnly

  If Err Then
    MsgBox "Error retrieving client information."
    Exit Sub

  End If
```

We then run through this recordset adding each client into the Bill to combo box control. Note how the **EOF** property is used to determine when we have reached the end of the recordset and how the **MoveNext** method is used to work through the recordset:

```
' Load the display with the folders.
  Do While Not (recClients.EOF)
    cboBillTo.AddItem recClients.Fields("Name")
    recClients.MoveNext
  Loop
```

This procedure ends with the deletion of the recordset object:

```
' Destroy the recordset objects used for the clients table.
  Set recClients = Nothing

End Sub
```

Coding the Saving of Session Data

The final procedure that is being added to the Time Manager application performs the saving of session data. This routine is called from the Log command button **Click** event:

```
Private Sub cmdLog_Click()

' Set the availability of buttons
  cmdStart.Enabled = False
  cmdPause.Enabled = False
```

```
    cmdStop.Enabled = False
    cmdReset.Enabled = True
    cmdLog.Enabled = False

' Set the availability of menu items
    SetMenuItems

' Save the information
    SaveSession

End Sub
```

It begins just as the other two did, by setting up an error handler:

```
Private Sub SaveSession()

    Dim recData

' Set up error handler.
    On Error Resume Next
```

Next a recordset object is created:

```
' Create recordset object for the data table.
    Set recData = CreateObject("adoce.recordset")
```

Finally the data from this session is saved. Note how the record number is determined by calling the **NextID** function. An example of this procedure was presented earlier in this chapter in the section on "Handling the Absence of AutoNumbering". You'll need to remember to rename **xyManagement** to **tmManagement**.

You could just as well use the SQL **INSERT** statement here to store this session data:

```
' Save the session data.
    recData.Open "tmData", , adOpenKeyset, adLockOptimistic

    recData.AddNew
    recData.Fields("RecordID").Value = NextID
    recData.Fields("BillTo").Value = cboBillTo.Text
    recData.Fields("Rate").Value = CDbl(Right(txtRate.Text,
        ⮡ Len(txtRate.Text) - 1))
    recData.Fields("TimeUsed").Value = mdtmElapsedTime
    recData.Fields("Bill").Value = CalculateBill
    recData.Fields("Notes").Value = txtNotes.Text
    recData.Fields("Billed").Value = False
    recData.Update
```

This routine completes by destroying the recordset object:

```
' Destroy the recordset objects used for the tables.
    Set recData = Nothing

End Sub
```

In order to have a time to save we need to add an extra line to the **cmdStop_Click** event:

```
Private Sub cmdStop_Click()

' Set the availability of buttons
  cmdStart.Enabled = False
  cmdPause.Enabled = False
  cmdStop.Enabled = False
  cmdReset.Enabled = True
  cmdLog.Enabled = True

' Set the availability of menu items
  SetMenuItems

' Turn off the clock
  tmrClock.Enabled = False
```

```
  mdtmElapsedTime = Now - mdtmStartTime + mdtmElapsedTime
```

```
End Sub
```

Coding the CalculateBill Function

We still need to actually calculate the total of the bill by working out the billing time and multiplying it by the rate. We first need get the rate from the **txtRate** text box, but minus the currency symbol. We also calculate the number of seconds used from the **mdtmElapsedTime** variable:

```
Private Function CalculateBill()

Dim intBillingPeriod
Dim intSeconds
Dim dblRate

dblRate = Right(txtRate.Text, Len(txtRate.Text) - 1)
intSeconds = DateDiff("s", 0, mdtmElapsedTime)
```

Now that we have the time to be billed we need to work out what the user has set the billing period to in the Round Billing To Nearest menu item. The **mstrBillToNearest** variable will be set shortly in the appropriate menu item's **Click** event:

```
Select Case mstrBillToNearest
```

Finally, we then use the number of seconds to calculate the bill:

```
Case "Hour"

    intBillingPeriod = intSeconds \ 3600
    If intSeconds Mod 3600 >= 1800 Then
        intBillingPeriod = intBillingPeriod + 1
    End If

    CalculateBill = (intBillingPeriod * dblRate)
```

```
Case "Half"

    intBillingPeriod = intSeconds \ 1800
    If intSeconds Mod 1800 >= 900 Then
        intBillingPeriod = intBillingPeriod + 1
    End If

    CalculateBill = (intBillingPeriod * dblRate)

Case "Quarter"

    intBillingPeriod = intSeconds \ 900
    If intSeconds Mod 900 >= 450 Then
        intBillingPeriod = intBillingPeriod + 1
    End If

    CalculateBill = (intBillingPeriod * dblRate)

Case "Minute"

    intBillingPeriod = intSeconds \ 60
    If intSeconds Mod 60 >= 30 Then
        intBillingPeriod = intBillingPeriod + 1
    End If

    CalculateBill = (intBillingPeriod * dblRate)

End Select

End Function
```

Before we can finish this update to Time Manager we need to declare the **mstrBillToNearest** variable and set it in the appropriate menu **Click** events:

```
Option Explicit

Dim msngDefault           ' The Standard rate to charge clients
Dim mdtmElapsedTime       ' Used to track the time that has elapsed
Dim mdtmStartTime         ' Holds the time that the timer was started
Dim mstrBillToNearest     ' Holds the billing interval

Private Sub mnuOptionsHour_Click()

  If Not mnuOptionsHour.Checked Then
    mnuOptionsHour.Checked = True
    mnuOptionsHalf.Checked = False
    mnuOptionsQuarter.Checked = False
    mnuOptionsMinute.Checked = False

  End If

  mstrBillToNearest = "Hour"

End Sub
```

```
Private Sub mnuOptionsHalf_Click()

  If Not mnuOptionsHalf.Checked Then
    mnuOptionsHour.Checked = False
    mnuOptionsHalf.Checked = True
    mnuOptionsQuarter.Checked = False
    mnuOptionsMinute.Checked = False

  End If

    mstrBillToNearest = "Half"

End Sub

Private Sub mnuOptionsQuarter_Click()

  If Not mnuOptionsQuarter.Checked Then
    mnuOptionsHour.Checked = False
    mnuOptionsHalf.Checked = False
    mnuOptionsQuarter.Checked = True
    mnuOptionsMinute.Checked = False

  End If

    mstrBillToNearest = "Quarter"

End Sub

Private Sub mnuOptionsMinute_Click()

  If Not mnuOptionsMinute.Checked Then
    mnuOptionsHour.Checked = False
    mnuOptionsHalf.Checked = False
    mnuOptionsQuarter.Checked = False
    mnuOptionsMinute.Checked = True

  End If

    mstrBillToNearest = "Minute"

End Sub
```

Step 6 - Testing in the CE Emulator

I would recommend skipping the testing on the emulator as that would require additional configuration to be able to make use of the ADO.

Step 7 - Testing on a Handheld Computer

Set the Run on Target project property to Remote Device and run your project. Test out the new functionality that was added to Time Manager by selecting a client from the Bill to combo box control and logging the data from a session. You can check that it has worked successfully by using the TableView application to view the **tmData** database.

Step 8 - Creating an Installation Program

Use the Application Install Wizard to generate an installation program for Time Manager. If you need help with this wizard refer to Chapter 2, where a detailed explanation of the process is provided.

Don't forget, if you are distributing copies of this application to client's you must also provide an installation routine that will handle installing ADO on their H/PC.

Step 9 - Test the Installation Program

As with previous examples, it's important that you test your installation program. It should install without error and allow you to completely remove the program. Your testing should also encompass the ADO setup routine.

Summarizing the Revised Time Manager

This revised version of Time Manager presents a simple example of how the ADO CE can be used to enhance the functionality of an application. In particular it demonstrates one technique that you should consider adding into your own database applications – it creates its own tables.

You may want to further explore the use of the ADO CE with the Time Manager application. One feature that you could add is the ability to add new customers to the Clients table. Another would be to provide a way to retrieve and display data from previous sessions.

As this chapter demonstrates, adding database functionality to a CE application is not difficult nor does it require a substantial amount of code.

Summary

The ADO CE SDK allows you to develop applications that incorporate database functionality with minimal programming effort. It allows you to create tables, add, modify and delete records and retrieve data for displaying. While the Windows CE version of ADO does not offer everything that you would find in the desktop version it still provides a solid set of features.

The next release of the ADO CE SDK is scheduled to include the ability to synchronize data between a desktop computer and an H/PC. CE databases that you design today should be constructed in such a way that they will be able to make use of this feature when it becomes available. In order to prepare for this, remember to create an index named PrimaryKey for each of your tables.

Further Information on the ADO CE

As you work with the ADO CE you may find that you need more information than is provided with the SDK. You can find additional information through Microsoft's ADO CE newsgroup or Microsoft's Universal Data Access web site at **www.microsoft.com/ado**. While this site doesn't specifically target the ADO CE SDK it does provide useful information on ADO in general.

Moving Data Between Devices

One of the most challenging problems that CE application developers face is how to manage the transfer of data between a desktop computer and an H/PC. It's often the key issue in the effective use of H/PCs as data gathering devices. In addressing this problem, you must consider how the application will be used, where it will be used, what type of data you need to store, how the H/PC and desktop computer will communicate, as well as other issues specific to each application.

In this chapter, we'll be looking at a number of alternatives for moving data between a desktop computer and an H/PC. Each alternative begins with a table that outlines the specifications of that method. These tables are provided simply as a reference so that you can quickly find the alternative that's best suited for your particular need. The information provided by the tables include the ease of implementing the method, what it's best suited for, what kinds of data structures it will work with and an example program that makes use of the method. Here's an example table:

Ease of implementation:	Simple
Best suited for:	Data that does not need to be synchronized, only transferred.
Data structure:	Sequential or random access files.
Example program:	The Inventory Manager case study.

Options for Moving Data

This chapter is all about the options of how to move data between a desktop computer and an H/PC. You should note that there is no single 'right way'. There are only methods that are more or less appropriate for a given set of conditions. You may even find that for your application you need to combine two or more of the approaches listed here to achieve the desired effect.

When you are designing an application that will involve the transfer of data between a desktop computer and an H/PC it's imperative that you consider the following items during the early stages of designing your application:

- Where will the H/PC be used? The "where" will often dictate which methods of data transferal are applicable.

- What type of data is being transferred? The type of data may determine what methods of data storage are required which in turn can determine which types of data transferal are applicable.

- Is data synchronization required? By synchronized we mean that there needs to be identical copies of the data on both the desktop computer and the H/PC. Don't be fooled by this one. It is a mistake to think that all data needs to be synchronized.

- How will the desktop computer and H/PC communicate? Will it be by direct connection? Via a modem? Over the Internet? The method that the two machines use to communicate can dictate what approaches of data transfer will work.

The remainder of this chapter presents the various options for data transferal. Each option will include information on what a particular method is best suited for. I would recommend that you work through each option so that you are comfortable with what they have to offer and how they are implemented. You'll find this information invaluable in the design of successful CE applications.

Using the Synchronized Files Folder

We'll start with what I consider to be the simplest approach. It's best suited for situations where data needs to be transferred from one system to the other for processing but does not need to be synchronized. It uses the built-in **Synchronized Files** folder feature of the Windows CE Services to copy files to and from the H/PC.

For instance, let's say you were developing a CE application that gathers data. The H/PC on which the data is gathered never makes use of the data. It simply stores the data in a sequential file that is subsequently sent to a desktop computer for processing at a later time.

This is a perfect situation to use this simple approach of moving data via the **Synchronized Files** folder. All your application needs to do is create the file in the appropriate directory and to perform some basic file existence checks.

The specifications for this method of data transferal are as follows:

Ease of implementation:	Simple
Best suited for:	Data that does not need to be synchronized, only transferred.
Data structure:	Sequential or random access files.
Example program:	The Check Files example application.

The key criteria for the use of this method are:

- That the data does not need to be synchronized. No synchronization occurs using this approach. Whole files are copied, processed and deleted.
- That sequential or random access files can be used to store the data. This approach is best suited for when you have a CE application that is only responsible for gathering data and not involved in the data processing. This write-and-never read approach is an ideal situation for the use of sequential files.

Working with the Synchronized Files Folder

The trickiest part (if you can even call it that) of working with the **Synchronized Files** folder is how you want to manage the files in that folder. For example, let's say you want to gather data via a form and store the data in a series of records in a sequential file. The data file will be created in **\My Documents\Synchronized Files**. The process that will be used to gather and transfer the data to a desktop computer will be:

- The file is created on the H/PC
- Once the data gathering process has completed the H/PC is connected up to the desktop computer via a docking cradle

▲ For this example the Windows CE Services are configured such that synchronization will occur automatically

▲ The data file is copied to the desktop computer and stored in its synchronized files folder

▲ The H/PC is disconnected from the desktop computer

▲ A desktop application is run which opens the data file and processes the data

▲ The file is deleted from the desktop's synchronization folder upon completion of the processing

At this point there is only a copy of the file on the H/PC. But what happens if the H/PC is connected back up to the desktop computer? Does it send the data file again? The answer is that it doesn't resend the file. The synchronization process built into the Windows CE Services is smart enough to not repetitively copy the same file. This is the key point to making this process work.

Checking the Synchronized Files Folder

The key to this whole process is the handling of files in the **Synchronized Files** folder. To better understand this function lets take a look at a simple example called **Check Files** that checks the **Synchronized Files** folder for a specific file.

Using the Check Files Program

To install the Check Files program on your handheld computer follow these steps:

▲ Establish a connection between your desktop and handheld computers

▲ Using the instructions laid out in Appendix A run the setup program for Check Files

▲ Follow the installation directions.

Once you have completed the installation of this example, run it on your handheld computer. The Check Files interface will be displayed as shown in the screenshot below:

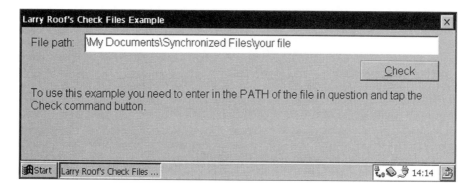

Replace the your file part of the path in the text box with a file that exists in the **Synchronized File** folder of your H/PC and click the Check button. The following message box dialog should be displayed:

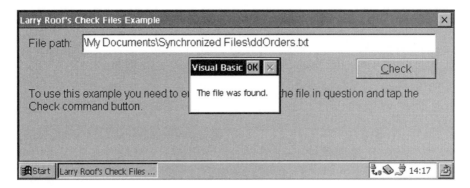

Try checking for a file that does not exist in the **Synchronized Files** folder on your H/PC. A dialog will be displayed with the message The file was not found:

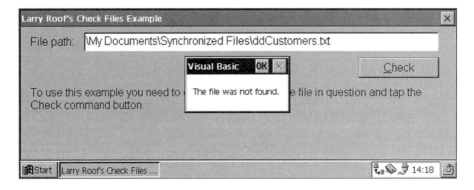

You may want to remove the Check Files example program from your handheld computer at this time. The easiest way to accomplish this is through the Start *menu, then* Settings, Control Panel *and finally* Remove Programs.

Examining the Check Files Program

This is a painfully simple example comprised of two pieces of code, one in the **Click** event procedure for the Check button and the other being the **CheckForFile** function.

The file **CheckFiles.vbp** *contains a completed version of this example. Refer to Appendix A for instructions on downloading and installing the examples included in this book.*

The Check Button Click Event Procedure

The **Click** event procedure of the Check button (**cmdCheck**) starts by calling the **CheckForFile** function, passing the path of the file in question. The value returned from this function is then used to determine which of two messages to display:

```
Private Sub cmdCheck_Click()

  Dim blnFileFound

' See if the specified file exists.
  blnFileFound = CheckForFile(txtFilePath.Text)

' Display the results.
  If (blnFileFound) Then
    MsgBox "The file was found."

  Else
    MsgBox "The file was not found."

  End If

End Sub
```

The CheckForFile Function

This function is the heart of the Check Files program. It uses the File System control's **Dir** method to determine whether or not a file exists. The file is passed as the lone argument to the function:

```
Function CheckForFile(strFileToFind)

' NOTE - This routine requires that you have a File System control
' named "ceFileSystem" on the form from which this function is called.

  Dim strFileFound

' Set up an error handler.
  On Error Resume Next

' Use the File System control to check for the file in question.
  strFileFound = ceFileSystem.Dir(strFileToFind)

' If an error was generated then return false AND display a message
' so that the developer knows that there is a problem.
  If (Err.Number <> 0) Then
    CheckForFile = False
    Err.Clear
    MsgBox "An error was encountered while attempting to locate the file."
    Exit Function

  End If
```

The **Dir** method will return an empty string if the file doesn't exist. The appropriate value is returned to the calling procedure based upon this:

```
' The DIR method of the File System object returns a string if the
' file in question was found. If the string is empty the file does not ' exist.
  If (strFileFound = "") Then
    CheckForFile = False

  Else
    CheckForFile = True

  End If

End Function
```

Using this Method in Your Applications

Now that you have an understanding of how to check the **Synchronized Files** folders for a file, let's examine exactly what you would have to do to make use of this form of data transfer with your CE applications.

Step 1 - Checking for a Previous File

When your application starts you will need to check for a previous version of the data file in the **Synchronized Files** folder. You could use the **CheckForFile** function for this. If the file is found you may need to prompt the user to see if they want to continue adding to this file or start a new file.

Step 2 – Deleting a Previous Version of the File

If you find a previous version of your data file you could use the **Kill** method of the File System control to delete it. I prefer this method to simply opening the file using the mode of output, which will overwrite the existing file, but is a less clear approach.

Step 3 – Opening the File

Now you are ready to open the data file in the **Synchronized Files** folder using the File control's **Open** method.

Step 4 – Writing to the File

As the user gathers data it is written to the file in the **Synchronized Files** folder.

Step 5 – Closing the File

Before your CE application exits you should close the file. At this point everything that you need to do in your application is done. The rest of the process is handled by the Windows CE Services.

Summarizing the Synchronized Files Method

As this section demonstrates using the **Synchronized Files** folder along with the Windows CE Services is simple to do. The only code that you may have to add to your application to make use of this feature is to check for a previous version of your data file. I can't think of a method that would be any easier.

Letting ADO Handle it

The next method of data transfer that I'll be examining is the automatic synchronization feature provided with the ADO CE. Actually, this feature is not presently available, but will be included in the next release of Windows CE scheduled for late 1998. I decided to include it in this chapter because ADO CE can presently be used to create database-enabled CE applications, and for the functionality it will offer the CE developer.

For additional information on the use of the ADO CE see Chapter 7 – Working with Databases.

This approach is best suited for situations where data needs to be synchronized with desktop databases. The specifications for this method of data transfer are as follows:

Ease of implementation:	Simple
Best suited for:	Data that needs to be synchronized, though it can also be used to transfer data that does not require synchronization.
Data structure:	ADO CE database on the H/PC and an Access database on the desktop PC.
Example program:	None as this feature is not yet supported

Using this Method in Your Applications

As I said at the start of this section this feature is not presently available in the ADO CE SDK. There are some steps though that you can take now to prepare your CE applications for when it becomes available.

What you need to do to Your CE Databases

The key item that you need to incorporate into your CE database applications today is the use of a database index made up of a single field of numeric integer data. This key needs to be named **PrimaryKey** and must also be unique.

Primary Keys and AutoNumbering

The ADO CE SDK does not support the autonumbering feature found in Microsoft Access. For those of you that are not familiar with this feature, Access provides a field data type called **AutoNumber**. This is a special data type, which causes Access to generate a unique, sequential identification number for each record it adds. This is particularly useful in situations where your data does not contain a unique ID or at least not a single field unique identifier.

Since the ADO CE does not provide for autonumbering you are forced to create this functionality on your own (see Chapter 7 for more details on this technique). The downside of using this approach with synchronization is that there is no good way then to handle situations where records are added on both the desktop and H/PC versions of the database. You simply can't control the autonumbers.

The best workaround that I have found for this problem is to restrict the creation of new records to either the H/PC or the desktop database. This means that only one side needs to keep track of the automatically assigned IDs while both sides can use and modify the data.

Summarizing the ADO Synchronization Method

When this functionality becomes available I believe that it will be the method of choice for CE developers that wish to move data between a desktop computer and an H/PC. It requires no additional coding on your part and provides the additional feature of synchronizing data between the two devices.

Copying Tables via the ADO CE

The third method of data transfer that we will be examining demonstrates the copy table functionality provided with the ADO CE SDK. It's accessible in two forms, **manual** and **programmatic**. The manual form is through the Mobile Devices application. The programmatic form uses the ADO CE API.

The specifications on this method of data transfer are as follows:

Ease of implementation:	Average
Best suited for:	Data stored in ADO CE databases tables but does not need to be synchronized only transferred.
Data structure:	ADO CE database tables on the H/PC and an Access database on the desktop PC.
Example program:	Although none are provided the code examples in this section provide all the information that you need.

Adding ADO CE Functionality to Mobile Devices

When you install the ADO CE SDK on your desktop system (see Chapter 7 for more details on this subject) it augments the functionality of the Mobile Devices application that is delivered as part of the Windows CE Services. It adds two menu items under the Tools menu of this application for importing and exporting database tables between a desktop computer and an H/PC:

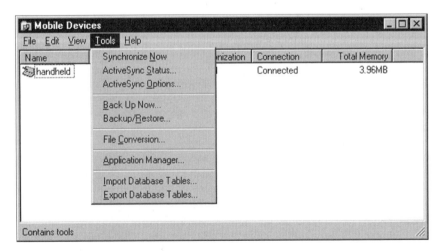

The Import Database Tables... function allows you to transfer a database table from the desktop computer to the H/PC. The Export Database Tables... function can be used to transfer a database table from an H/PC to a desktop computer. The use of both of these functions is covered in Chapter 7.

In addition to this manual approach both the Import and Export functionality of the ADO CE can be accessed from a desktop application allowing you to create applications that will programmatically transfer data between a desktop computer and an H/PC.

Using the Manual Method

I'm not going to present the use of the manual method here as it's detailed in Chapter 7. Instead what I will do is to briefly discuss what you need to consider before implementing this approach to data transfer in your CE applications.

Anytime that you involve a manual process in your application you need to consider what is required of the user and how to record whether or not the process has been performed correctly. The use of the Mobile Devices manual method is questionable on both of these counts.

Ease of use – While it is easy enough for a user to bring up the Mobile Devices application and establish communications to an H/PC, using the Import and Export database features requires them to have a solid understanding of the relationship between desktop databases and H/PC tables. In addition, the use of these utilities may require the user to select specific tables and fields presenting an opportunity for error.

Determining if the process was performed – Even if the users of your application are capable of performing this manual task there is no good way from your CE program to determine whether or not this process was performed.

>   *Given the potential problems that are involved with the use of this manual method I wouldn't recommend that it be used other than for applications that will be used by you alone.*

Using the Programmatic Method

While the manual method of using the Mobile Devices application doesn't offer much, the programmatic method does. It presents a fairly easy to implement and controllable method for transferring data between a desktop PC and an H/PC. To better understand this functionality lets take a look at a simple example called **Copy Tables** that demonstrates copying files to and from an H/PC.

Using the Copy Tables Program

To install the Copy Tables program on your desktop computer follow these steps:

- ▲ Using the instructions laid out in Appendix A run the setup program for Copy Tables
- ▲ Follow the installation directions

Once you have completed the installation, use the Start menu on your *desktop* computer to run this example. The Copy Tables interface will be displayed as shown in the screenshot below:

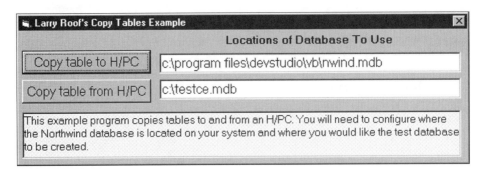

The Copy table to H/PC button will trigger the copying of the **Employees** table from the Northwind database to your H/PC. The Copy table from H/PC button initiates the copying of the **Employees** table from your H/PC to a new database on your desktop PC. You may need to adjust the two default paths to match the location of the databases on your system.

Now that we have seen what this application does, lets look at how it was constructed.

> *You may want to remove the Copy Tables example program from your desktop computer at this time. The easiest way to accomplish this is through the Start menu, then Settings, Control Panel and finally Remove Programs.*

> *You may also want to delete the copy of the Employees database from your H/PC. **DO NOT** use one of the Windows CE delete database utilities to remove it. As we saw in the previous chapter, this would be really bad. Instead you will need to delete them through the ADO CE as shown in the coding examples in Chapter 7.*

Using the ADO CE API

Included in the installation of the ADO CE SDK is the file **adofiltr.dll**. This dynamic link library contains two functions, **DesktopToDevice** and **DeviceToDesktop** that can be used to copy tables to and from an H/PC. These are the same functions that are used with the Mobile Devices application.

> *The file **CopyTables.vbp** contains a completed version of this example. Refer to Appendix A for instructions on downloading and installing the examples included in this book.*

Copying Tables to the H/PC

The function **DESKTOPTODEVICE** is used to copy tables from the desktop computer to the H/PC. The syntax for this function is:

```
DESKTOPTODEVICE (DesktopLocn, TableList, Sync, Overwrite, DeviceLocn)
```

Where:

DesktopLocn   The path and file name of the Access database that contains the tables to be transferred. Optionally this can be a DSN in the case where ODBC is being used.

TableList   The list of tables and fields that will be copied to the H/PC. This argument is in the
                  form of:

                  `[!]table name.field name..`

                  The leading `!` states that the table is to be read only. Following that, you will provide a
                  table name. After the table name you may list individual fields from the table that you
                  want to copy. Each field is separated by a period. If you do not list any fields all of the
                  fields in the table will be copied. Each table definition is ended with two periods. You
                  may include multiple table definitions in this single argument by simply appending them
                  together.

                  For example:

                  `!Customers..Orders.OrderID.CustomerID..`

                  Would copy the complete `Customers` table and the `OrderID` and `CustomerID` fields
                  from the `Orders` table. The `Customers` table would be read only on the H/PC.

Sync   The argument is always `False`. It is provided for future compatibility.

Overwrite   This argument specifies whether or not to overwrite existing tables of the same name. It
                  is `True` by default.

DeviceLocn   This argument is always an empty string (`""`). It is provided for future compatibility.

The syntax of the declaration that you would use with this function is as follows:

```
Declare Function DESKTOPTODEVICE Lib _
        "c:\program files\windows ce services\adofiltr.dll" _
        (ByVal DesktopLocn As String, _
        ByVal TableList As String, _
        ByVal Sync As Boolean, _
        ByVal Overwrite As Integer, _
        ByVal DeviceLocn As String) As Long
```

The **Click** event procedure for the Copy table to H/PC command button (**cmdToHPC**) demonstrates the
use of the **DEVICETODESKTOP** function:

```
Private Sub cmdToHPC_Click()

  Dim lngStatus As Long

' Setup an error handler.
  On Error GoTo ehToHPC

' Copy the Employees table from the Northwind database.
  lngStatus = DESKTOPTODEVICE(txtToHPC.Text, "!Employees..", False, True, "")

' Check whether the table was copied successfully.
  If (lngStatus <> 0) Then
    MsgBox "An error occurred transferring the table."
```

```
    Else
      MsgBox "The Employees table was successfully copied to the H/PC."

    End If

    Exit Sub

  ' Process errors here.
  ehToHPC:
    MsgBox "The following error occurred: " & vbCrLf & "Error number " _
      & Err.Number & vbCrLf & Err.Description

  End Sub
```

The key to this procedure is the line:

```
  lngStatus = DESKTOPTODEVICE(txtToHPC.Text, "!Employees..", False, True, "")
```

Which says copy the **Employees** table to the H/PC and make it read only. Since no fields are specified all of the fields from the table are included. Also note the required two trailing periods. The status returned by this function is then checked to determine whether the table was successfully copied.

Copying Tables from the H/PC

The function **DEVICETODESKTOP** is used to copy tables from the H/PC to a desktop computer. The syntax for this function is:

DEVICETODESKTOP (DesktopLocn, TableList, Sync, Overwrite, DeviceLocn)

Where:

DesktopLocn   The path and file name of the Access database that will receive the tables that are transferred. Optionally this can be a DSN in the case where ODBC is being used. A new database will be created if it does not already exist.

TableList   The list of tables that will be copied to the H/PC. You cannot specify specific fields. This argument is in the form of:

Table name..

Each table name is terminated with two periods. You can include multiple tables in this single argument by appending them together.

For example:

Customers..Orders..

Would copy both the **Customers** and **Orders** table.

Sync   The argument is always **False**. It is provided for future compatibility.

Overwrite   This argument specifies whether or not to overwrite existing tables of the same name. It is **True** by default.

DeviceLocn   This argument is always an empty string (**""**). It is provided for future compatibility.

The syntax of the declaration that you would use with this function is as follows:

```
Declare Function DEVICETODESKTOP Lib _
        "c:\program files\windows ce services\adofiltr.dll" _
        (ByVal DesktopLocn As String, _
        ByVal TableList As String, _
        ByVal Sync As Boolean, _
        ByVal Overwrite As Integer, _
        ByVal DeviceLocn As String) As Long
```

The **Click** event procedure for the Copy table from H/PC command button (**cmdFromHPC**) demonstrates the use of the **DEVICETODESKTOP** function:

```
Private Sub cmdFromHPC_Click()

  Dim lngStatus As long

' Setup an error handler.
  On Error GoTo ehFromHPC

' Copy the Employees table from the H/PC.
  lngStatus = DEVICETODESKTOP(txtFromHPC.Text, "Employees..", False, True, "")

' Check whether the table was copied successfully.
  If (lngStatus <> 0) Then
    MsgBox "An error occurred transferring the table."

  Else
    MsgBox "The Employees table was successfully copied from the H/PC."

  End If

  Exit Sub

' Process errors here.
ehFromHPC:
  MsgBox "The following error occurred: " & vbCrLf & "Error number " _
    & Err.Number & vbCrLf & Err.Description

End Sub
```

The key to this procedure is the line:

```
lngStatus = DEVICETODESKTOP(txtFromHPC.Text, "Employees..", False, True, "")
```

Which says copy the **Employees** table to the desktop. Note the required two trailing periods. The status returned by this function is then checked to determine whether the table was successfully copied.

Summarizing the ADO CE Table Copy Method

The ADO CE table copy features presents the developer with a solid set of tools for transferring data between a desktop computer and an H/PC. While the manual method for copying tables doesn't offer the controllability that would be needed by most applications the programmatic method does. These tools are best suited for situations where you need to transfer complete tables between devices rather than synchronizing individual records.

Over the Internet

Up to this point all of the methods that we've looked at have been based upon functionality provided by either the Windows CE Services or the ADO CE. In this example I'll look at the first total programming alternative. It demonstrates how the Winsock control can be used to transfer data to and from an Internet web server.

The specifications for this method of data transfer are as follows:

Ease of implementation:	Complex
Best suited for:	Where the H/PC and server PC are physically separated and there is an established web site used to manage data.
Data structure:	Database, sequential or random access file
Example program:	The ASP Client example application.

Writing Web-Enabled CE Applications

One of the coolest features that you have at your disposal as a CE developer is the Winsock control. It enables you to access web servers from your applications for the purpose of transferring and retrieving data. All that's required to incorporate this functionality into your applications is a good understanding of HTML, simple Visual Basic parsing techniques, and optionally, the use of Active Server Pages.

Although I mentioned that the use of Active Server Pages (ASP) is an optional component of this method I prefer to use ASP as it allows me to easily request data from, and send data to, a web server. You may, however, choose to use CGI, IDC or other techniques that allow you to generate dynamic HTML pages that can be interpreted by your CE applications.

The ASP Client Example

To better understand this functionality lets take a look at a simple example program called **ASP Client** that demonstrates sending data to, and receiving data from, a web server.

> There are numerous bugs with the Winsock control, which means that you may experience some problems running this app. For example, it tends to only work with a dial-up connection not a network connection. See Appendix B for more details on bugs.

Using the ASP Client Program

To install the ASP Client program on your desktop computer follow these steps:

- Establish a connection between your desktop and handheld computers
- Using the instructions laid out in Appendix A run the setup program for ASP Client
- Follow the installation directions.

> *To run this example you will need access to a web server that's running Active Server Pages. This example makes use of two server-based ASP files -***ReceiveData.asp*** *and* **SendData.asp**. *You will need to copy these files from the folder on your H/PC where the ASP Client is installed to an appropriate directory on your web server.*

> Developing a Winsock application can be a pain; you need a connection to your desktop computer to transfer the program and another connection to the Internet for testing. Something that I have found that works well is the Ethernet / Serial Combo PC card from Socket Communications. This card is a combination of an Ethernet card and a serial communications port. With this card you can use an Ethernet connection for transferring your program and the serial port to access a modem so that you can load and test without having to change connections. The card is designed to use minimal power. For more information on this product visit Socket's site at www.socketcom.com.

Once you have completed the installation of this example, establish a modem connection to your web server and then run the application on your handheld computer. The ASP Client interface will be displayed as shown in the screenshot below.

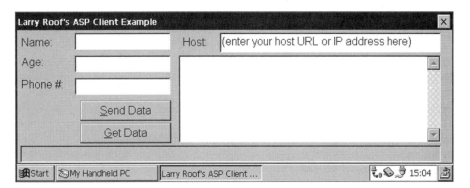

Enter the URL for your web server host (for example **www.myserver.com**), the name "Joe+Smith" in the Name text box and tap the <u>G</u>et Data command button. If you have everything configured correctly you will receive a web page containing data on Joe Smith. The HTML source for the page will be displayed in the large text box at the right of the application interface. The Age and Phone # fields will be filled with data that is parsed from the HTML.

Next, try sending some data to the web server. First enter a name, age and phone number. Then tap the Send Data command button. After a brief pause the contents of the response from the web server will be displayed in the large text box.

Now that we have seen what this application does, let's look at how it was constructed.

> *You may want to remove the ASP Client example program from your handheld computer at this time. The easiest way to accomplish this is through the* Start *menu, then* Settings, Control Panel *and finally* Remove Programs.

Using the Winsock Control

The key to the ASP Client application is the use of the Winsock control. In the following sections we will examine the code used to connect to a web server, send data to a server and parse HTML text that is returned from the server.

> *The file* **ASPClient.vbp** *contains a completed version of this example. Refer to Appendix A for instructions on downloading and installing the examples included in this book.*

You can find detailed information on obtaining and using the Winsock control in Chapter 5.

Sending Data to an ASP Page

The Send Data command button's **Click** event procedure contains the code that sends data to a web server. It begins by setting a flag called **mstrMode** to **"sending"**. This flag is used by the parsing routine **ProcessPage** to determine how to process HTML documents received from the web server:

```
Private Sub cmdSend_Click()

' Set the operating mode.
  mstrMode = "sending"
```

Next, it configures a connection with the web server via port **80**, the default port for web communication:

```
' Configure the winsock control.
  ceWinsock.RemoteHost = txtHost.Text
  ceWinsock.RemotePort = 80
```

The connection is opened to the server using the Winsock control's **Connect** method:

```
' Establish a connection to the host.
  ceWinsock.Connect
```

Finally, the data from the ASP Client's form is sent to the web server. The data is passed as part of a request for the **ReceiveData** page. Each field from the form is concatenated together with **&** characters to form a query string:

```
    ' Send a request for the selected page.
    ceWinsock.SendData "GET ReceiveData.asp?txtName=" & txtName.Text &
        ↳ "&txtAge=" & txtAge.Text & "&txtPhone=" & txtPhone.Text &
        ↳ vbCrLf & vbCrLf

End Sub
```

The ASP page `ReceiveData.asp` parses the request from the client to extract the data. In this example the data is simply echoed to the ASP client. In a real-life application there would be additional code that would handle the storage of the data, typically in a database.

The ASP `Request` object's `QueryString` collection is used to extract the data that was passed. Note how the names `txtName`, `txtAge` and `txtPhone` match the values passed in the query string from the ASP Client:

```
<% @ Language="VBSCRIPT" %>
<!-- Server Code will be VBScipt -->
<HTML>

<BODY>
<H2> Status - Success***</H2>
  The name provided was <% = Request.Querystring("txtName") %><BR>
  The age provided was <% = Request.Querystring("txtAge") %><BR>
  The phone number provided was <% = Request.Querystring("txtPhone") %><BR>
</BODY>

</HTML>
```

> When using the `Querystring` method to send data it's important that the items of data are in a particular format. The format is described in the HTTP 1.1 specification that can be obtained from www.w3.org. The example above will work as long as the data in the text box contains only simple alphanumeric characters with no spaces or punctuation such as ampersands, which have a special meaning to the web server that handles the request. To use more general data you would need to ensure that all the characters after the '?' are first URL encoded.

Requesting Data from an ASP Page

The Get Data command button's `Click` event procedure contains the code that retrieves data from a web server. It begins by setting a form level variable called `mstrMode` to `"retrieving"`. This flag is used by the parsing routine `ProcessPage` to determine how to process HTML documents received from the web server:

```
Private Sub cmdGet_Click()

' Set the operating mode.
  mstrMode = "retrieving"
```

Next it configures a connection with the web server via port **80**, the default port for web communication:

```
' Configure the winsock control.
  ceWinsock.RemoteHost = txtHost.Text
  ceWinsock.RemotePort = 80
```

The connection is opened to the server using the Winsock control's **Connect** method:

```
' Establish a connection to the host.
  ceWinsock.Connect
```

Finally, the name to find is taken from the ASP Client's form and is sent to the web server. The data is passed as part of a request for the **SendData.asp** page:

```
' Send a request for the selected page.
  ceWinsock.SendData "GET SendData.asp?txtName=" & txtName.Text & vbCrLf & vbCrLf

End Sub
```

The ASP page **SendData.asp** parses the request from the client to extract the name. In this example I've hard coded several names into the ASP procedure. In a real-life application you would typically retrieve this information from a database.

The ASP **Request** object's **QueryString** collection is used to extract the name that was passed. Note how the name **txtName** matches the values passed in the query string from the ASP Client:

```
<% @ Language="VBSCRIPT" %>
<!-- Server Code will be VBScipt -->
  <HTML>

  <BODY>

  <% Select Case Request.Querystring("txtName") %>
  <%    Case "Joe Smith" %>
        - data returned - <BR>
        Age = 35 <BR>
        Phone = 555-1212
  <%    Case "John Doe" %>
        - data returned - <BR>
        Age = 40 <BR>
        Phone = 555-1234
  <%     Case Else %>
        - no data available - <BR>
  <% End Select %>

  </BODY>

  </HTML>
```

To actually get data on 'John Doe' the value entered into the `txtName` text box would have to be "**John+Doe**" since a plus symbol in the query string indicates a value of a single space. Sending data with a space in would cause the web server to return a page describing an error.

Parsing HTML for Data

When data is received from the web server the **DataArrival** event of the Winsock control is fired. Normally when this occurs all that you would need to do is use the Winsock's **GetData** method to get the document. Unfortunately the current version of the CE Winsock control has a bug that requires that you first close the connection, and then reopen the connection before you can get the data.

You can simplify the parsing process by structuring the HTML pages generated by your ASP code. Include headers that are easy to locate and statements that identify whether or not an operation completed successfully.

```
Private Sub ceWinsock_DataArrival(ByVal bytesTotal)

' There is a bug in the winsock control. It doesn't tell you that data
' has arrived until after the connection has begun to be closed.
' In this state the data can not be read from the winsock control.
' The work around to this bug is to close the control and reconnect
' the control so that you can get access to the data that was
' returned.

  On Error Resume Next

  ceWinsock.Close

  If (Err.Number <> 0) Then
    MsgBox "Error closing the first time, Err #" & Err.Number & _
                   " - " & Err.Description
    Err.Clear

  End If

  ceWinsock.Connect

  If (Err.Number <> 0) Then
    MsgBox "Error reconnecting, Err #" & Err.Number & " - " & Err.Description
    Err.Clear

  End If
```

The HTML data returned from the web server is read into the form variable **mstrHTML**:

```
ceWinsock.GetData mstrHTML
txtPage.Text = mstrHTML
```

```
If (Err.Number <> 0) Then
  MsgBox "Error retrieving data, Err #" & Err.Number & " - " & Err.Description
  Err.Clear

End If

ceWinsock.Close

If (Err.number <> 0) Then
  MsgBox "Error closing the second time, Err #" & Err.number & _
             " - " & Err.Description
  Err.Clear

End If
```

It's then sent off to the **ProcessPage** procedure where it will be parsed for information:

```
' Process the page that was received.
ProcessPage

End Sub
```

The **ProcessPage** procedure is a universal routine that processes pages returned from the web server. It determines how to process the HTML document by checking the **mstrMode** flag that was set in the **Click** event procedures for the <u>G</u>et Data and <u>S</u>end Data command buttons:

```
Sub ProcessPage()

  Dim intStartLocation
  Dim intEndLocation

' Process the page that was returned.
  Select Case mstrMode
```

If this is a send operation, where the client has sent data to the server for processing we simply parse the returned HTML to determine the status of the request. The Visual Basic **InStr** function is used to locate the keyword **Status - :**

```
' This page was received back after we sent some data to the web
' server.
  Case "sending"
    intStartLocation = InStr(1, mstrHTML, "Status - ", vbTextCompare)

    If (intStartLocation = 0) Then
      lblStatus.Caption = "An error occurred processing data."

    Else
      intEndLocation = InStr(intStartLocation, mstrHTML, "***", vbTextCompare)
      lblStatus.Caption = Mid(mstrHTML, intStartLocation + 9, _
          intEndLocation - intStartLocation - 9)

    End If
```

If this is a get operation, where the client has requested data from the server, the returned HTML needs to be parsed to extract the data. Again the **InStr** function is used to locate the data:

```
' This page was received back after we requested
' some data from the web server.
   Case "retrieving"

' Was there data returned?
    intStartLocation = InStr(1, mstrHTML, "- data returned -", vbTextCompare)
```

If the **InStr** function returns an empty string that means that there is no data available for the name you requested:

```
' No there was no data returned.
    If (intStartLocation = 0) Then
       lblStatus.Caption = "No data is available on this individual."
       txtAge.Text = ""
       txtPhone.Text = ""
```

If data was returned both the age and phone number are parsed out of the HTML string and loaded into the ASP Client's interface:

```
' Yes there was data returned so display it.
    Else
       lblStatus.Caption = ""
       StartLocation = InStr(intStartLocation, mstrHTML, "Age = ", vbTextCompare)
       txtAge.Text = Mid(mstrHTML, intStartLocation + 6, 2)
       intStartLocation = InStr(intStartLocation, mstrHTML, _
                          "Phone = ", vbTextCompare)
       txtPhone.Text = Mid(mstrHTML, intStartLocation + 8, 8)

    End If

  End Select

End Sub
```

Summarizing the Internet Method

The ability to add web access to your CE applications gives you the flexibility to create programs that can be used anywhere that there's an Internet connection. This can be a powerful feature. The combination of the VBCE Toolkit, the Winsock control and Active Server Pages offers a wealth of options for you to use in your applications.

The drawbacks of this method are that it requires a bit of coding and a good understanding of HTML. But *man* you can do some seriously cool things with this. The sample ASP pages that I have used here return data as an HTML stream, however, there is nothing to prevent you using ASP to send back other forms of structured text data or even binary data.

Via the Serial Communications Port

The final method that I'll be examining demonstrates how a modem connection can be used to transfer data to and from an H/PC. This method makes use of simple, serial port communication techniques that can be easily implemented into your CE applications.

The specifications on this method of data transfer are as follows:

Ease of implementation: Average
Best suited for: Where the H/PC and server PC are physically separated and there is not
                           an established web site used for managing data.
Data structure: Database, sequential or random file.
Example program: Although none are provided the code examples in Chapter 5 demonstrate
                           how to read and write data using the Comm control.

Creating Communication-Enabled CE Applications

Computer serial ports have been used to communicate data for years. This method is nothing more than a CE version of those time-tested techniques. At first glance you may think that this approach isn't very useful. After all it doesn't offer the functionality of the ActiveSync component of the Windows CE Services. Nor can it match the synchronization capabilities of the ADO CE. And it's nowhere near as cool or flexible as what you can do with the Winsock control. What it does offer, however, is a solid, configurable method for communicating data from anywhere there is a phone connection. That alone makes this an option to consider.

Using the Comm Control

The tool that the VBCE Toolkit provides to access the serial port on an H/PC is the Comm control. While it's a fairly simple control to utilize, the development of effective communication applications often requires a good deal of coding. Code is typically required for:

▲ Establishing a connection to a desktop system

▲ Communicating non-data instructions between the two devices

▲ Transferring data

▲ Confirming data transferal

▲ Error handling

The good side of all of this is that with some planning and careful coding you can reuse much of your work in subsequent applications.

In the following sections I will briefly discuss what is involved in, and how you can handle, each of these communication tasks. These are not coding examples but rather approaches that you can use to create effective communication-enabled applications.

> Detailed examples on using the Comm control are available in Chapter 5. The Chat program in its CE version and desktop equivalent demonstrate the use of this control. Additionally, there is sample available on the Wrox Web site for this book that shows how to use the control with a GPS unit.

Establishing Connection

The process of establishing a connection between a desktop PC and an H/PC is not very difficult. The desktop application needs to be monitoring the modem waiting for connections. The H/PC application must open the serial port and send a modem control string to dial the desired number. Thankfully most modem manufacturers still support the Hayes command set. This allows you to dial a number with something as simple as the statement below:

```
ceComm.Output = "ATDT 1,800,5551212"
```

Obviously you need to put enough error handling in your applications to handle busy telephone lines, failures to answer and other typical problems. If you wrap your dialing process up in a function you will be able to use it over and over again. All that you need to pass to the function is the number to dial.

Communicating Instructions

You may find that you need to pass commands or instructions between the desktop computer and your H/PC in addition to the data that is being transferred. What I have found to be the most effective approach to this requirement is to create a simple command set that encompasses all of the features that you desire. This does not need to be complicated. For example you could make use of something as simple as the following:

B	Beginning of data packet
E	End of data packet
C	Checksum value
I	Invalid data was received.
R	Resend last message
S	Data was successfully received
T	Terminating communications

Each data packet sent would start with a command. The receiving program then looks for the command by parsing the data and responds accordingly. As I recommended in the discussion on establishing communications, I would suggest that you create a universal message processing function, to handle the various types of commands that your applications require. That way you can quickly create communication-enabled applications by including this module.

Passing Data

You will probably find that the most straightforward part of your communication applications involves sending the data. It normally comes down to a single statement similar to the one below:

```
ceComm.Output = strDataBlock
```

This step can become more complicated as you add commands and checksum values to your messages.

Confirming Successful Data Transmission

The approach that I like best for verifying successful data transmission involves the use of **checksum** values. Checksums are nothing more than a tool to confirm that what was sent from one device was indeed what was received on the other device. Typically checksums are calculated by summing up the ASCII codes of every character that is sent. You can incorporate checksums into your communication applications with something as simple as the following function:

```
Function CalculateChecksum (StringToSend)

  Dim intCounter
  Dim intTotalValue

' Calculate the checksum.
  For intCounter = 1 To Len(StringToSend)
    intTotalValue = intTotalValue + Asc(Mid(StringToSend,intCounter,1))
  Next

' Return the calculated checksum.
  CalculateChecksum = intTotalValue

End Function
```

All that you have to do then is append the checksum value onto the data that you are transferring. For example:

```
intChecksumValue = CalculateChecksum(strMyData)
ceComm.Output = strMyData & "|" & intChecksumValue
```

Using something as simple as the "|" character makes for easy location of the checksum by the receiving application. All that they have to do then is to perform their own checksum calculation on the data string to verify the data integrity.

Handling Errors in your Communication Routines

No set of communication routines can be complete without a comprehensive set of error handling functions. This is a particularly difficult task to implement with the limited error handling tools provided with the VBCE Toolkit. What I recommend is that you write a set of functions for establishing, sending and receiving data. Within those routines you check everything. That way you can afford to invest the time to develop detailed error-handling routines that can be reused in your future applications.

Summarizing the Serial Port Method

The serial communications port allows you to create applications that can be used anywhere that there is a phone line. With the availability of cellular modems this means just about everywhere. That's a powerful capability. That's not to say that you should implement serial communications as the primary form of data transfer in your CE applications. It requires more coding than the other methods and typically is more prone to error. But with some careful modular coding you will find that you will be able to create solid, stable CE applications.

Summary

As this chapter demonstrated there are several options available to you for transferring data between a desktop computer and an H/PC. Each option has particular situations for which it's best suited.

The **Synchronized Files** folder approach is by far the simplest method allowing you to effortlessly transfer sequential and random access files between devices.

The two ADO methods are ideal for use with CE databases.

The Winsock approach brings the power and flexibility of the Internet into your CE applications.

The serial communications port method provides the greatest area of use.

You would be best to familiarize yourself with each of these methods so that you can apply the appropriate method to meet each of your application's needs.

Using Help Files with Your CE Applications

No Windows CE application is complete without a supporting help file. It's the first and often the only instructional information that most users will reference. While manuals may be able to offer a far greater level of detail than a help file, they are often left behind when the user takes their handheld computer away from their desk.

The first thing that you'll notice about Windows CE help is that it's fairly simplistic in comparison to the help system offered under Windows 95 or Windows NT. The CE help system, called Pocket Help, has been scaled down, just as Pocket Word and Pocket Excel have been scaled down from their desktop counterparts. The limited resources of a CE machine simply cannot support the overhead required by a desktop help system. What remains is a fairly simplistic HTML-based architecture that provides just a minimal platform for development. Still, even with these limitations you will find that with careful planning and design that you'll be able to create effective help files.

In this chapter I will teach you about the Windows CE help system. This overview will include everything from how to access and use a help file, to reviewing the structure of CE help files and finally how to incorporate CE help files into your applications. At the end of the chapter I will lead you, step-by-step, through the construction of two help systems, one for the EasyEdit application and the second for the Time Manager application.

Windows CE Help Files

While the purpose behind Windows CE and Windows 95 help files may be the same, the method in which they are implemented differs dramatically. Windows CE help files offer none of the robustness found in Windows 95 help files. Gone is support for multimedia objects, built in search-capabilities, pop-up definitions and graphical hot spots. Instead Windows CE offers a simplistic help system that is built upon HTML, the language more commonly used to construct web pages. In fact, if you're familiar with HTML you should have no problem constructing CE help files. For that is all they are – a set of HTML files that are linked together with HTML anchor tags.

In the following section I will teach you how to access, work with and construct CE help files. Plus how to create a help system comprised of a set of contents and topic files. I will also provide you with a list of supported HTML tags that you can incorporate into your HTML help files.

> **Help System** is the term I use to refer to a set of related help files. As you will learn shortly, a help system is comprised of a single Contents file and one or more Topic files.

Ways to Access CE Help

Let's start our examination of the Windows CE help system from the users point of view. There are three methods provided to the user for accessing a CE help system:

▲ Through the Help command on the Start menu. When you use this method the system help file will be displayed. It will provide links to the various help systems that are present on the H/PC.

▲ By tapping the question mark button on a window. This will cause the help file for the active application to be displayed. This functionality is not provided for CE applications built using the VBCE Toolkit.

▲ By pressing the *Alt+H* shortcut key combination. As with the question mark, the help file for the active application is displayed. This feature is also not supported for CE applications built with the VBCE Toolkit.

These methods provide access to Windows CE help by both keyboard and stylus, one of the key input features we discussed in Chapter 3.

Using CE Help

Upon activation, a Help dialog similar to the one below will be displayed:

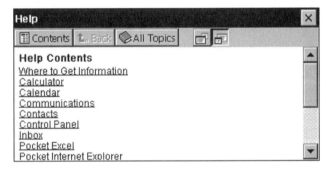

At the top of the Help dialog is a set of navigational buttons. The function of each button is detailed below:

    Displays the Contents page for the current help topic. The feature is provided since the CE help system allows you to move between the help files for various topics.

    Returns to the previous viewed page. Subsequent use of this button will continue to work back through past pages in the order they were viewed.

    Brings up a Contents page that lists all of the standard CE help topics. This page includes a link to other help systems that have been installed on this H/PC along with third-party software applications.

    Switches the help system display to full screen mode.

    Switches the help system display to a dialog, or small window mode.

You navigate about Windows CE help just as you would within a browser. Tapping on the hyperlinks displayed in the dialog loads subsequent help pages. A help page may also include simple graphics that can be used to provide access to other pages.

The Components of the CE Help System

A Windows CE help system is comprised of two types of files – **Contents** and **Topics**. The relationship between these two types of files is that there will be a single Contents file along with one or more Topic files. The purpose of the Contents file is to provide links to the Topic files. The diagram below shows this relationship:

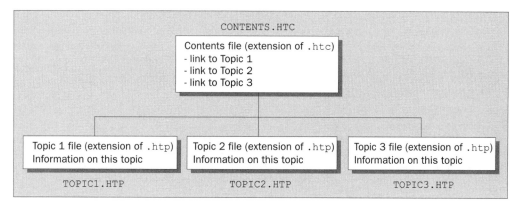

In this example, the Contents file, **CONTENTS.HTC**, has links to three Topic files, **TOPIC1.HTP**, **TOPIC2.HTP** and **TOPIC3.HTP**.

Next we'll take a more detailed look at each of these file types.

The Contents File

The Contents file serves as a menu to the topics that comprise a particular help system. It will have a series of links, one for each topic. Two rules apply to Contents files:

- They should have a **.htc** file extension
- They should be located in the **Windows** folder

You can create a help system that is comprised of only the Contents file. In this case instead of providing links the Contents file would contain content.

The Layout of the Contents File

The easiest way to gain an understanding of
the layout of a Contents file is by working
through an example file. The file that we'll be
examining produces the help display shown in
the screenshot:

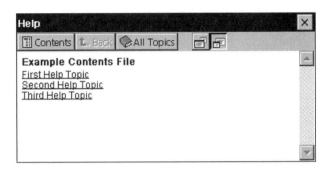

The following source was used to produce this file. As you can see, it's nothing more than straight HTML
code. In fact, you could view this file in a web browser with the result being similar to that shown above:

```
<HTML>
<HEAD>
</HEAD>
<BODY>
<H5>Example Contents File</H5>
<A HREF="FILE:Topic1.htp">First Help Topic</A><BR>
<A HREF="FILE:Topic2.htp">Second Help Topic</A><BR>
<A HREF="FILE:Topic3.htp">Third Help Topic</A><BR>
</BODY>
</HTML>
```

A contents file, like any other HTML document, begins with a `<HTML>` tag and ends with a `</HTML>` tag.
Within these tags will be two sections, a **header** section and a **body** section.

The header section begins with a `<HEAD>` tag and ends with a `</HEAD>` tag. It serves little use for the
purpose of CE help files. In fact it doesn't even need to be included. I personally include the header
section just to provide a valid HTML structure to my help files.

The body section is where we'll focus our attention. The body section begins with a `<BODY>` tag and ends
with a `</BODY>` tag. Between these two tags is where you place the HTML code that will be used to
construct the display of the Contents file. In the example above this consisted of four lines:

```
<H5>Example Contents File</H5>
<A HREF="FILE:Topic1.htp">First Help Topic</A><BR>
<A HREF="FILE:Topic2.htp">Second Help Topic</A><BR>
<A HREF="FILE:Topic3.htp">Third Help Topic</A><BR>
```

The first line is a header style as designated by the `<H5>` tag. The number after the `<H` specifies how large
of font should be used for the header (the number does not designate the font size though). The smaller
the number, the larger the text. The text between the `<H5>` tag and the `</H5>` tag is displayed to the
user. If you look back to the figure of this file you will see Example Contents File displayed at the top.

The second, third and fourth lines define links to topic files. Links are created with the **<A>**, or **anchor** tag. This tag is used to create hyperlinks between text strings and Topic files. The first part of the tag specifies the Topic file. In the example HTML fragment above you'll see that there is a link defined using the **HREF** argument. This argument defines a link for the file **Topic1.htp**. The second and third lines create links to **Topic2.htp** and **Topic3.htp** respectively. The **</A>** tag marks the end of an anchor. Between the **<A HREF="FILE:Topic1.htp">** and the **</A>** tag is the text that will be displayed to the user.

Finally, at the end of the second through fourth lines are **
** tags that specify to start a new line of text. Without these tags all three of our links would be on the same line.

Not familiar with HTML? Don't sweat it. Just follow these simple steps to create your own Contents file:

Make a copy of the **Contents.htc** *file that can be found in source code for this book under* **Chapter 9**.

To create your own header simply place the heading that you want displayed between the **<H5>** *and* **</H5>** *tag.*

To create your own topic links place the name of you topic file after **<A HREF="FILE**: *and place the text you want displayed between the* **<A>** *and* **</A>** *tags.*

The Topic File

The Topic file is used to provide detailed information on a particular part of your application. Typically, you will have a separate Topic file for each distinct component of your app. Two rules apply to Topic files:

- ▲ They should have a **.htp** file extension
- ▲ They should be located in the **Windows** folder

The Layout of the Topic File

As with the Contents file the easiest way to gain an understanding of the layout of a Topic file is by working through an example file. The file that we'll be examining produces the Help display shown in the screenshot below:

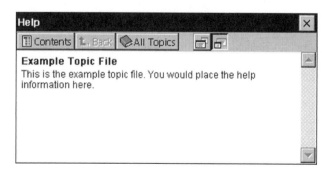

The following source was used to produce this file. As with the Contents example file, you can see that it is nothing more than straight HTML code:

```
<HTML>
<HEAD>
</HEAD>
<BODY>
<H5>Example Topic File</H5>
<P>
This is the example topic file. You would place the help  information here.
</P>
</BODY>
</HTML>
```

A Topic file, like any other HTML document, begins with a **<HTML>** tag and ends with a **</HTML>** tag. Within these tags will be two sections, a head section and a body section.

The header section begins with a **<HEAD>** tag and ends with a **</HEAD>** tag. As I explained earlier, it serves little use for the purpose of CE help files. If you don't want it, simply leave it out.

The body section is where the content of the Topic file is. The body section begins with a **<BODY>** tag and ends with a **</BODY>** tag. Between these two tags is where you place the HTML code that will be used to construct the display of the topic file. In the example above this consisted of four lines:

```
<H5>Example Topic File</H5>
<P>
This is the example topic file. You would place the help  information here.
</P>
```

The first line is a header style as designated by the **<H5>** tag. The third and fourth lines provide the text for this help topic. A new paragraph is defined with the **<P>**, or **paragraph** tag. The text after this tag is the content for the paragraph. The paragraph ends with the **</P>** tag.

Now this is an incredibly simple example of a Topic file. Typically you would have multiple paragraphs, include bolded text, lists and possibly even pictures. You will see more complex examples in the help files that are created later in this chapter for the EasyEdit and Time Manager applications.

Haven't worked with HTML? Don't worry. Simply follow these steps to create your own Topic file:

Make a copy of the **Topic.htp** *file that can be found in source code for this book under* **Chapter 9**.

To create your own header simply place the heading that you want displayed between the **<H5>** *and* **</H5>** *tag.*

Add the information for this topic between the **<P>** *and* **</P>** *tags.*

HTML Tags Supported by CE Help

The Windows CE help system supports a subset of the HTML language. In the following table I list the tags that I have found useful in developing CE help systems. For a complete list of the supported tags see the Pocket Internet Explorer HTML Reference on the Microsoft web site.

Tag	Description
<!-- -->	Comment line
<A>	Anchor, used to create hyperlinks
<B>	Bold the text
<BASEFONT>	Set the default font to use for the file
<BIG>	Displays the text in a larger font
<BLINK>	Displays blinking text
<BODY>	Specifies the beginning of the body section of the file
 	Inserts a line break, the equivalent of a carriage return and line feed
<CAPTION>	Adds a caption to a table
<CENTER>	Centers the specified text on the display window
<DD>	Defines the data for an item in a data definition list
<DL>	Defines a title for an item in a data definition list
<DT>	Defines a heading for a data definition list
<FONT>	Allows you to manipulate the font used with your display
<H#>	Specifies the size of heading to use
<HEAD>	Defines the area containing information about the HTML document
<HR>	Creates a horizontal line across the display
<HTML>	Specifies the beginning of the HTML document
<I>	Displays text in italics
<IMG>	Used to include a graphic into your help page
<LI>	Adds an item to a list
<OL>	Provides a numerically ordered list
<P>	Starts a new paragraph
<TABLE>	Defines the start of a table
<TD>	Defines a cell in a table
<TH>	Defines a heading for a table
<TR>	Defines a row in a table
<UL>	Provides an unordered list

Building Successful CE Help Systems

There are no two ways around it. If you want to build successful help systems you are going to have to have a sound understanding of HTML. Other than that here are some general rules of thumb that I recommend you keep in mind while developing your help systems:

▲ **Keep each Topic file as simple as possible.** You don't want to create Topic files that resemble detailed white papers. Instead, construct pages that provide specific information using as few words as possible.

▲ **Keep graphics at a minimum.** Remember, this isn't a desktop help system that you are creating here. Always keep in mind the limitations of the CE platform. Don't consume all of the system RAM with your screenshots and clipart.

▲ **Be consistent.** Each individual topic file that is part of a help system should look and feel the same as the other pages.

▲ **Have a minimum hierarchy of files.** Be careful not to create a multiple-level hierarchy that becomes a headache for the user to navigate. I've found that the most effective structure is a single Contents file with all Topic files one level below.

▲ **Bigger is better.** This is a carryover from Chapter 3. Just as you can improve the usability of your application's interface by increasing the size of font that you use, you can improve your help system by making use of larger fonts. For example the following HTML fragment will change the size of the text used to display the words Important News, increasing it by **2**.

```
<FONT SIZE=+2>Important News</FONT>
```

Accessing Help From Your CE Applications

Now that you have a fundamental understanding of how to construct a Windows CE help system, the next problem is making it accessible from your VBCE application. There are two methods to accomplish:

▲ By using the Utility control included with this book

▲ By using the Common Dialog control from Microsoft

Which control should you use? My rule of thumb says use whichever control that you are using for other purposes in your application. It all has to do with how much space is being used on the handheld computer.

In this section you will learn how to use both methods.

With the Utility Control

Using the Utility control to access help offers two advantages over the common dialog control. It's easier to use and requires less space on the handheld computer. In situations where you don't need the additional functionality provided by the common dialog control (to open files, save files, change fonts, etc.) I would recommend using the Utility control to access your help system.

> *For details on adding the Utility control to your project and for additional information on its properties, methods and events see Chapter 5.*

The Utility Control Example

As I stated above, the Utility control undoubtedly offers the easiest way to access help. With a single line of code you can start Pocket Help and load a help file of your choice. An example of this is shown in the code fragment below:

```
Private Sub mnuHelpUsing_Click()

  Dim intReturnValue

  intReturnValue = utlLaunchHelp.Shell("\Windows\Peghelp.exe", "\Windows\MyHelp.htc")

  If (intReturnValue = False) Then
    MsgBox "Help is not available."
  End If

End Sub
```

In the case of this example an instance of the Utility control has been named **utlLaunchHelp**. The **Shell** method of this control is used to launch **Peghelp.exe**, which is the Pocket Help executable. One argument is provided which is our help file. Finally the return status is checked to confirm that the help system was launched successfully.

With the Common Dialog Control

The common dialog control offers similar functionality to the Utility control in accessing help systems. It also provides access to the CE File Open, Save, Font, and Color dialogs. In situations where I need any of the other features that the common dialog control has to offer in addition to the need for accessing help systems I use the common dialog control.

The Common Dialog Control Example

Using the common dialog control to access help is no more complicated than the Utility control. All that you need to do is to set a single property and issue a single method:

```
Private Sub mnuHelpUsing_Click()

  ceCommonDialog.HelpFile = "MyHelp.htc"
  ceCommonDialog.ShowHelp

End Sub
```

Adding Help to EasyEdit

Before we look into the details of how help was added to the EasyEdit application, let's take a look at the program with this additional feature. This approach is used so that you can better understand the discussions on its development.

To install the revised version of EasyEdit on your handheld computer follow these steps:

▲ Establish a connection between your desktop and handheld computers

▲ Using the instructions laid out in Appendix A find the version of EasyEdit for Chapter 9

▲ Follow the installation directions

Using the Revised EasyEdit

Once you have completed the installation of this example, run it on your handheld computer. The EasyEdit interface should be displayed as shown in the screenshot below.

> There have not been any changes made to the appearance of this interface since the previous version.

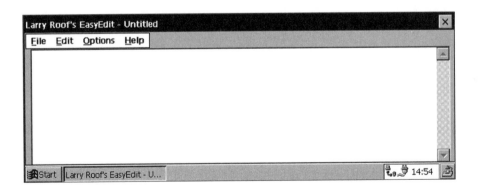

Test out the help feature that has been added to this application. Under the <u>H</u>elp menu select the <u>U</u>sing EasyEdit and <u>A</u>bout EasyEdit menu items. An example of the <u>U</u>sing EasyEdit help is shown in the screenshot:

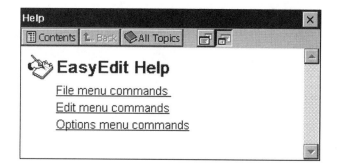

EasyEdit – The Requirements

This revised version of the EasyEdit application is a rework of the version presented in Chapter 6. Its primary purpose is to demonstrate how to integrate a Windows CE help system into your applications. The only requirements for this version are to provide:

- A help system for using EasyEdit
- A simple <u>A</u>bout EasyEdit box

EasyEdit – The Design

This second version of the EasyEdit application, like the first, has a fairly simple design. In fact the actual modifications that are needed to the application itself are minimal, just a few lines of code to add to the click events of two menu items. Therefore, the design issues presented in this section will for the most part focus on the EasyEdit help system.

The help system for the EasyEdit application is going to be extremely simple, just the bare necessities. It will provide:

- A Contents page with links to pages on using the <u>F</u>ile menu, <u>E</u>dit menu and <u>O</u>ptions menu
- An About page that will provide the information normally found in an about box including the version number and copyright

With these design criteria specified we can begin the process of adding help to the EasyEdit application.

You may want to remove the revised version of the EasyEdit program from your handheld computer at this time. The easiest way to accomplish this is through the Start *menu, then* <u>S</u>ettings, <u>C</u>ontrol Panel *and finally* Remove Programs.

EasyEdit – The Construction

In the pages that follow I will lead you through the nine step creation process to modify the previous version of the EasyEdit application as we left it in Chapter 6. You can gain the most benefit from this section by working along with the instructions to create your own copy of the EasyEdit application.

> *The Chapter 9 version of* **EasyEdit.vbp** *contains a completed version of this project. Refer to Appendix A for instructions on downloading and installing the examples included in this book.*

Step 1 - Starting a New Project

Since we will be using the previous version of EasyEdit as a starting point this step is unneeded. Instead simply load the project you created in Chapter 6 or the finished solution from the source code for Chapter 6. See the note above for instructions on accessing example applications.

Step 2 - Setting the Project Properties

As was the case with Step 1, this step is unneeded since we are making use of an existing project.

Step 3 - Constructing the User Interface

While there is nothing that we need to do to the EasyEdit Application interface, we do need to construct the interfaces to the EasyEdit help system. But since the help interface is constructed from HTML code we will leave this task to Step 5.

> Note that the common dialog control that will provide the link to the help files was added in Chapter 6 to make use of the **FileOpen** and **FileSave** methods of that control.

Step 4 - Setting the Form and Control Properties

The are no form or control properties to be set here. They were set in Chapter 6 during the construction of the first version of the EasyEdit application.

Step 5 - Adding Your Coding

This coding step is divided into two parts. The first part examines the code needed to link the EasyEdit application to its help system. This part is fairly simple. In the second part I walk you through the construction of the EasyEdit help system which is a bit more complex, though by no means difficult.

Coding the EasyEdit Help Link

There are two pieces of code to add to the EasyEdit application. One, which will provide access to the help system and the other that, will bring up the About information.

Add the code that uses the common dialog control to access the Using EasyEdit help. It starts by setting the name of the help file that is to be displayed. Then it issues the **ShowHelp** method to display the file:

```
Private Sub mnuHelpUsing_Click()

' Display the contents, or using help.
  ceCommonDialog.HelpFile = "EasyEdit.htc"
  ceCommonDialog.ShowHelp

End Sub
```

Add the code that uses the common dialog control to access the EasyEdit About information. As with the previous example you simply load the help file name into the **HelpFile** property and then use the **ShowHelp** method:

```
Private Sub mnuHelpAbout_Click()

' Display the About help.
  ceCommonDialog.HelpFile = "EasyEdit About.htp"
  ceCommonDialog.ShowHelp

End Sub
```

> Note that I made use of a help file rather than the more traditional dialog form to display the EasyEdit About information. I simply prefer to not have the overhead associated with adding another form to the application just to display this information.

Coding the EasyEdit Help Files

There are five individual help files that comprise the EasyEdit help system. This section will focus on the coding of each.

The EasyEdit help **Contents File** is the first file that will be constructed. The purpose of this file is to provide links to the other files that are part of the help system. Follow these instructions to create this file:

On your handheld computer create a new file using the completed version of EasyEdit or your favorite text editor.

> I have found that creating help files on a handheld computer is the easiest approach. Use a simple text editor to construct the files - EasyEdit will work just fine for this. Create the help file and save it, but stay in the editor. Then use the CE Explorer to launch the help file. Review how your work looks. You can then switch between the editor and Explorer to refine the appearance of your help file. This method also saves you the effort of having to download the help files to your handheld.

Add the HTML code for the help Contents file:

```
<HTML>
<BODY>
<TABLE>
<TR>
<TD><IMG SRC="EasyEdit.2bp" ></TD>
<TD><H2>EasyEdit Help</H2></TD>
</TR>
<TR>
<TD></TD>
<TD><FONT SIZE=+2>
<A HREF="FILE:EasyEdit File Menu.htp">File menu commands</A>
</FONT></TD>
</TR>
<TR>
<TD></TD>
<TD><FONT SIZE=+2>
<A HREF="FILE:EasyEdit Edit Menu.htp">Edit menu commands</A><BR>
</FONT></TD>
</TR>
<TR>
<TD></TD>
<TD><FONT SIZE=+2>
<A HREF="FILE:EasyEdit Options Menu.htp">Options menu  commands</A><BR>
</FONT></TD>
</TR>
</TABLE>
</BODY>
</HTML>
```

This code begins by creating a two-column table. This is accomplished with the **<TABLE>**, **<TR>** and **<TD>** tags. The two columns are specified by the use of two sets of **table definition <TD>** tags between the **<TR>** and **</TR> table row** tags. In the first table cell (the left cell of the first row of the table) the graphic **EasyEdit.2bp** is placed. I decided to add a graphic here to enhance the appearance of the help system but at the same time I kept the size of the graphic small to minimize the impact on the CE resources. The header **EasyEdit Help** is placed in the right cell of the first row using the **<H2>** tag. This is a fairly large header that I think is perfect for viewing on a small CE screen:

> The graphical file, **EasyEdit.2bp**, is a graphical image stored using the CE bitmap format. You can just as well use standard Windows bitmap files that you have copied to your H/PC.

```
<HTML>
<BODY>
<TABLE>
<TR>
<TD><IMG SRC="EasyEdit.2bp" ></TD>
<TD><H2>EasyEdit Help</H2></TD>
</TR>
```

Next three links are defined using **<A>**, or anchor, tags. I'm only going to discuss the first of the links here as the others are implemented in exactly the same fashion. They are placed in the right column of our two-column table. The left column is empty as defined by the **<TD>   </TD>** set of tags. Note that there is also a larger font in use here as specified by the **<FONT>** tag that increases the size of the font for this section by **2**.

```
<TR>
<TD></TD>
<TD><FONT SIZE=+2>
<A HREF="FILE:EasyEdit File Menu.htp">File menu commands</A>
</FONT></TD>
</TR>
```

Save the completed file as **EasyEdit.htc** in the **\Windows** directory of your handheld computer.

The EasyEdit **File Menu Topic File** is the next file that will be constructed. This file explains the purpose of each of the menu items that comprise the File menu. Follow these instructions to create this file:

On your handheld computer create a new file.

Add the HTML code for the File menu help file:

```
<HTML>
<BODY>
<TABLE>
<TR>
<TD WIDTH=70>
<IMG SRC="EasyEdit.2bp">
</TD>
<TD><H2>File Menu</H2></TD>
</TR>
<TR><FONT SIZE=+1>
<TD><B>New File</B></TD>
</FONT></TD>
<TD><FONT SIZE=+1>
Starts a new file.
</FONT></TD>
</TR>
<TR><FONT SIZE=+1>
<TD><B>Open File</B></TD>
</FONT></TD>
<TD><FONT SIZE=+1>
Opens and loads an existing file.
</FONT></TD>
</TR>
<TR><FONT SIZE=+1>
<TD><B>Save File</B></TD>
</FONT></TD>
<TD><FONT SIZE=+1>
Saves the current file.
</FONT></TD>
</TR>
<TR><FONT SIZE=+1>
<TD><B>Save As...</B></TD>
```

```
</FONT></TD>
<TD><FONT SIZE=+1>
Saves the current file under a different filename.
</FONT></TD>
</TR>
<TR><FONT SIZE=+1>
<TD><B>Exit</B></TD>
</FONT></TD>
<TD><FONT SIZE=+1>
Exits EasyEdit after saving changes to the current file.
</FONT></TD>
</TR>
</TABLE>
</BODY>
</HTML>
```

Like the previous example, this file starts by defining a two-column table. Here though we are also controlling how wide we want the first, or left, column of the table to be. The **WIDTH** argument is used with the **<TD>** tag to accomplish this. I'm specifying the width so that I can better control the appearance of the help file. This width will be used throughout the table. In the left column I include the **EasyEdit.2bp** image. In the right column is the header **File Menu**:

```
<HTML>
<BODY>
<TABLE>
<TR>
<TD WIDTH=70>
<IMG SRC="EasyEdit.2bp">
</TD>
<TD><H2>File Menu</H2></TD>
</TR>
```

The remainder of the page builds the definitions for each menu item of the File menu. I'm only going to discuss the first item as the rest are implemented in exactly the same way:

```
<TR><FONT SIZE=+1>
<TD><B>New File</B></TD>
</FONT></TD>
<TD><FONT SIZE=+1>
Starts a new file.
</FONT></TD>
</TR>
```

A new row is defined for each menu item. In the left cell of that row is the title from the menu item itself. This matches the caption property from the EasyEdit application. Note the use of **<B>** and **</B>** here to highlight this text. The right cell holds the description for each menu item.

The result of this technique can be seen in the screenshot here:

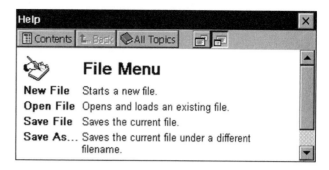

Save the completed file as **EasyEdit File Menu.htp** in the **\Windows** directory of your handheld computer.

The help Topic files for both the Edit and Options menus are nearly the identical to the File menu help. As such I will not spend time discussing them here. The code should be fairly self evident:

The EasyEdit **Edit Menu Topic File**:

```
<HTML>
<BODY>
<TABLE>
<TR>
<TD WIDTH=70>
<IMG SRC="EasyEdit.2bp">
</TD>
<TD><H2>Edit Menu</H2></TD>
</TR>
<TR><FONT SIZE=+1>
<TD><B>Cut</B></TD>
</FONT></TD>
<TD><FONT SIZE=+1>
Removes the selected text and places it on the clipboard.
</FONT></Td>
</TR>
<TR><FONT SIZE=+1>
<TD><B>Copy</B></TD>
</FONT></TD>
<TD><FONT SIZE=+1>
Copies the selected text to the clipboard.
</FONT></TD>
</TR>
<TR><FONT SIZE=+1>
<TD><B>Paste</B></TD>
</FONT></TD>
<TD><FONT SIZE=+1>
Pastes the contents of the clipboard into the current file.
</FONT></TD>
</TR>
<TR><FONT SIZE=+1>
<TD><B>Find</B></TD>
</FONT></TD>
<TD><FONT SIZE=+1>
```

```
Find a specified string within the file.
</FONT></TD>
</TR>
<TR><FONT SIZE=+1>
<TD><B>Find Next</B></TD>
</FONT></TD>
<TD><FONT SIZE=+1>
Find the next occurrence of a string within this file..
</FONT></TD>
</TR>
</TABLE>
</BODY>
</HTML>
```

Save as **EasyEdit Edit Menu.htp**.

This should create this help file:

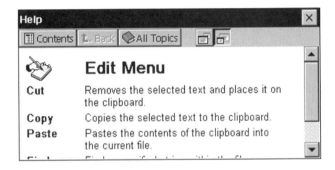

The EasyEdit **Options Menu Topic File**:

```
<HTML>
<BODY>
<TABLE>
<TR>
<TD WIDTH=70>
<IMG SRC="EasyEdit.2bp">
</TD>
<TD><H2>Options Menu</H2></TD>
</TR>
<TR><FONT SIZE=+1>
<TD><B>Font Size</B></TD>
</FONT></TD>
<TD><FONT SIZE=+1>
Adjusts the size of the font being used.
</FONT></TD>
</TR>
</TABLE>
</BODY>
</HTML>
```

Save as **EasyEdit Options Menu.htp**.

This should create this help file:

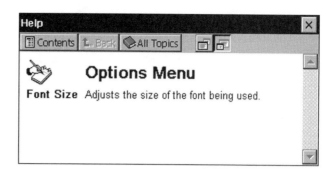

The EasyEdit **About File** is my help file implementation of the About dialog form.

Follow these instructions to create this file:

On your handheld computer create a new file.

Add the HTML code for the **About** help file:

```
<HTML>
<BODY>
<TABLE>
<TR>
<TD><IMG SRC="EasyEdit.2bp" ></TD>
<TD><H2>About EasyEdit</H2></TD>
</TR>
<TR>
<TD></TD>
<TD><FONT SIZE=+2>
Larry Roof's EasyEdit version 1.0
</FONT></TD>
</TR>
<TR>
<TD></TD>
<TD><FONT SIZE=+2>
Copyright &copy;1998 Larry Roof<BR>
</FONT></TD>
</TR>
<TR>
<TD></TD>
<TD><FONT SIZE=+2>
All rights reserved.
</FONT></TD>
</TR>
</TABLE>
</BODY>
</HTML>
```

As with the previous examples here a two-column table is used. The same image file is presented along with some minimal text.

> Note that I have used the special HTML escape sequence © for the copyright
> character. There are many such substitution sequences for difficult to type
> characters and those that may have special meaning to the HTML browser. If you
> want to display a character from the ASCII set use &#???; where ??? is the
> decimal number of the character you want. Other common short cuts you may need
> are < for the less than symbol (<) and > for the greater than (>) symbol.

Save the completed file as **EasyEdit About.htp** in the **\Windows** directory of your handheld
computer.

This file when presented will appear as
shown here:

Step 6 - Testing in the CE Emulator

I would recommend skipping the testing on the emulator here as the help files are already resident on the
handheld computer.

If you do want to try to your help files out in the emulator then you'll need to use a utility called
EMPFILE.EXE which can be located in the **Windows** directory for the emulator. You can use this to
synchronize the object stores.

Step 7 - Testing on a Handheld Computer

This is the only item that we are concerned with here: when you select the Help menu items is the
appropriate help displayed? Make sure to test out not only both the Using EasyEdit and About EasyEdit
help but also each individual help file.

Step 8 - Creating an Installation Program

While I'm not going to go through the complete process of generating an installation file here, remember
that when you add help files to your application that you need to explicitly include those files during the
generation of the installation program. The CE Application Install Wizard will not automatically include
them for you.

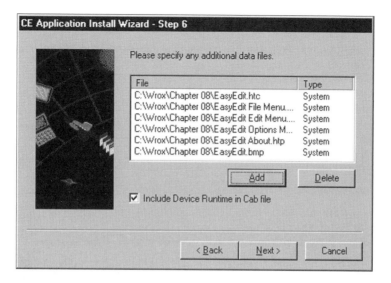

Step 9 - Test the Installation Program

As with previous examples, it's particularly important that you test your installation program to verify that the help files are functional.

Summarizing the Revised EasyEdit

That's everything, both on the VBCE side and on the HTML help file side that is required to add help capabilities to the EasyEdit application. As you saw, adding help is painfully simple from the VBCE side but requires a bit of HTML knowledge on the side of the help files.

Adding Help to Time Manager

I'm not going to go into a detailed discussion of how help was added to the Time Manager application. The reason for this is that it was implemented in exactly the same manner as was used with the EasyEdit application. You should not have any problem understanding either the VBCE and HTML code if you have worked through the EasyEdit example above.

The Contents File (**Time Manager.htc**):

```
<HTML>
<BODY>
<TABLE>
<TR>
<TD><IMG SRC="Time Manager.2bp" ></TD>
<TD><H2>Time Manager Help</H2></TD>
</TR>
<TR>
<TD></TD>
<TD><FONT SIZE=+2>
<A HREF="FILE:Time Manager Overview.htp">An overview of Time Manager</A>
</FONT></TD>
```

```
</TR>
<TR>
<TD></TD>
<TD><FONT SIZE=+2>
<A HREF="FILE:Time Manager Quick Start.htp">Get a quick start with
    Time Manager</A><BR>
</FONT></TD>
</TR>
<TR>
<TD></TD>
<TD><FONT SIZE=+2>
<A HREF="FILE:Time Manager Function Menu.htp">Function menu commands</A>
</FONT></TD>
</TR>
<TR>
<TD></TD>
<TD><FONT SIZE=+2>
<A HREF="FILE:Time Manager Options Menu.htp">Options menu commands</A><BR>
</FONT></TD>
</TR>
<TABLE>
</BODY>
</HTML>
```

This should look like this:

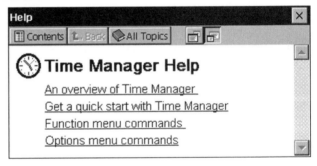

The Function Menu Topic File (**Time Manager Function Menu.htp**):

```
<HTML>
<BODY>
<TABLE>
<TR>
<TD WIDTH=70>
<IMG SRC="Time Manager.2bp">
</TD>
<TD><H2>Function menu</H2></TD>
</TR>
<TR><FONT SIZE=+1>
<TD><B>Start timer</B></TD>
</FONT></TD>
```

```
<TD><FONT SIZE=+1>
Starts timing a new session.
</FONT></TD>
</TR>
<TR><FONT SIZE=+1>
<TD><B>Pause timer</B></TD>
</FONT></TD>
<TD><FONT SIZE=+1>
Temporarily halts the timing of the current session. Tap the
    <I>Start</I> button or <I>Start timer</I> menu item to
    resume timing the session.
</FONT></TD>
</TR>
<TR><FONT SIZE=+1>
<TD><B>Stop timer</B></TD>
</FONT></TD>
<TD><FONT SIZE=+1>
Stops the timer. Once stopped the timer cannot be restarted, only reset.
</FONT></TD>
</TR>
<TR><FONT SIZE=+1>
<TD><B>Reset timer</B></TD>
</FONT></TD>
<TD><FONT SIZE=+1>
Resets the timer to start a new session.
</FONT></TD>
</TR>
<TR><FONT SIZE=+1>
<TD><B>Log record</B></TD>
</FONT></TD>
<TD><FONT SIZE=+1>
Stores the data from the current session.
</FONT></TD>
</TR>
<TR><FONT SIZE=+1>
<TD><B>Upload data</B></TD>
</FONT></TD>
<TD><FONT SIZE=+1>
Transfers session data from your handheld computer to a desktop
    computer for processing.
</FONT></TD>
</TR>
<TR><FONT SIZE=+1>
<TD><B>Exit</B></TD>
</FONT></TD>
<TD><FONT SIZE=+1>
Exits time manager after saving the active session.
</FONT></TD>
</TR>
</TABLE>
</BODY>
</HTML>
```

This should look like this:

The Options Menu Topic File (**Time Manager Options Menu.htp**):

```
<HTML>
<BODY>
<TABLE>
<TR>
<TD WIDTH=70>
<IMG SRC="Time Manager.2bp">
</TD>
<TD><H2>Options menu</H2></TD>
</TR>
<TR><FONT SIZE=+1>
<TD><B>Database To Use</B></TD>
</FONT></TD>
<TD><FONT SIZE=+1>
Specifies what database to use as a source of client information.
</FONT></TD>
</TR>
<TR><FONT SIZE=+1>
<TD><B>Round Billing To Next</B></TD>
</FONT></TD>
<TD><FONT SIZE=+1>
Sets how to round the time from a session.
</FONT></TD>
</TR>
<TR><FONT SIZE=+1>
<TD><B>Set Default Rate...</B></TD>
</FONT></TD>
<TD><FONT SIZE=+1>
Sets the default hourly rate to bill clients.
</FONT></TD>
</TR>
</TABLE>
</BODY>
</HTML>
```

This should result in the following help file:

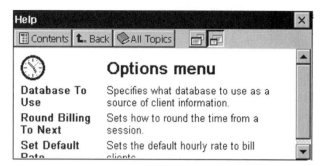

The Overview help file that provides the user with a brief overview of Time Manager (**Time Manager Overview.htp**):

```
<HTML>
<BODY>
<TABLE>
<TR>
<TD WIDTH=70>
<IMG SRC="Time Manager.2bp">
</TD>
<TD><H2>Overview</H2></TD>
</TR>
<TR><FONT SIZE=+1>
<TD></TD>
</FONT></TD>
<TD><FONT SIZE=+1>
The time manager application is a utility for tracking and
    billing of hours. It allows you to keep a log of your
    activities including the time spent, client's name, rate
    to bill at and notes that were made during conversations.
    Subsequently you can transfer billing information to a
    desktop system for processing.
</FONT></TD>
</TR>
</TABLE>
</BODY>
</HTML>
```

The overview should look like this:

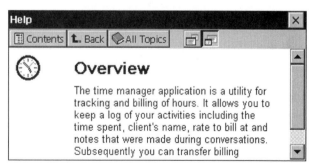

Finally the Quick Start help file (**Time Manager Quick Start.htp**) which demonstrates a feature that I like to include in my handheld applications, that of a Quick Start Tutorial. Just something to help get the user up, running and familiar with an application:

```
<HTML>
<BODY>
<TABLE>
<TR>
<TD WIDTH=70>
<IMG SRC="Time Manager.2bp">
</TD>
<TD><H2>Quick Start</H2></TD>
</TR>
<TR><FONT SIZE=+1>
<TD></TD>
</FONT></TD>
<TD><FONT SIZE=+1>
The following set of instructions provide a brief introduction
    in the use of Time Manager.
</FONT></TD>
</TR>
<TR><FONT SIZE=+1>
<TD><B>Select database</B></TD>
</FONT></TD>
<TD><FONT SIZE=+1>
You need to select the database that will provide your client
    list. This information is used to fill the "bill to:"
    field. Under the <I>Options</I> menu select <I>Database
    To Use</I> then either <I>Contacts</I> to use the outlook
    contacts database or <I>Time Manager</I> to use the
    database provided with Time Manager.
</FONT></TD>
</TR>
<TR><FONT SIZE=+1>
<TD><B>Set Billing Method</B></TD>
</FONT></TD>
<TD><FONT SIZE=+1>
Customer billing can be configured to round time to the next
    minute, 15 minutes, half hour or hour. under <I>Options
    </I> select <I>Round Billing To Next</I> and then select
    the desired interval.
</FONT></TD>
</TR>
<TR><FONT SIZE=+1>
<TD><B>Set Default Rate..</B></TD>
</FONT></TD>
<TD><FONT SIZE=+1>
Time Manager allows you to specify a default rate which to
    bill clients. This is the rate that will be used when
    starting a new session. To set this rate select
    <I>Options</I> then <I>Set Default Rate...</I>. Enter
    your default rate in the dialog.
</FONT></TD>
</TR>
<TR><FONT SIZE=+1>
```

```
<TD><B>Set Bill To</B></TD>
</FONT></TD>
<TD><FONT SIZE=+1>
From the <I>Bill To</I> combo box select the client to bill for this session.
</FONT></TD>
</TR>
<TR><FONT SIZE=+1>
<TD><B>Adjust RatE</B></TD>
</FONT></TD>
<TD><FONT SIZE=+1>
In the <I>Rate</I> input field the default rate should
    already be set. Adjust this value if needed.
</FONT></TD>
</TR>
<TR><FONT SIZE=+1>
<TD><B>Start the timer</B></TD>
</FONT></TD>
<TD><FONT SIZE=+1>
Tap the <I>Start</I> button to start the timer.
</FONT></TD>
</TR>
<TR><FONT SIZE=+1>
<TD><B>Pause the timer</B></TD>
</FONT></TD>
<TD><FONT SIZE=+1>
If needed you can pause the timer during a session by tapping
    the <I>Pause</I> button.
</FONT></TD>
</TR>
<TR><FONT SIZE=+1>
<TD><B>Enter notes</B></TD>
</FONT></TD>
<TD><FONT SIZE=+1>
During the session you can keep notes in the text window on
    the right of Time Manager's interface. These notes will
    be saved when you log the session.
</FONT></TD>
</TR>
<TR><FONT SIZE=+1>
<TD><B>Stop the timer</B></TD>
</FONT></TD>
<TD><FONT SIZE=+1>
To complete a session tap the <I>Stop</I> button.
</FONT></TD>
</TR>
<TR><FONT SIZE=+1>
<TD><B>Log the session</B></TD>
</FONT></TD>
<TD><FONT SIZE=+1>
After completing a session it can be logged for later billing
    and reference. To log a session tap the <I>Log</I> button.
</FONT></TD>
</TR>
```

```
<TR><FONT SIZE=+1>
<TD><B>Upload Data</B></TD>
</FONT></TD>
<TD><FONT SIZE=+1>
Session information can be uploaded to a desktop computer for
    storage and billing. simply select <I>Upload Data</I>
    from the <I>Function</I> menu. Your handheld computer
    must be connected to a desktop computer for this to be
    performed.
</FONT></TD>
</TR>
<TR><FONT SIZE=+1>
<TD><B>Reset the timer</B></TD>
</FONT></TD>
<TD><FONT SIZE=+1>
To start a new session tap the <I>Reset</> Button which will
    prepare the Time Manager interface to begin a new session.
</FONT></TD>
</TR>
</TABLE>
</BODY>
</HTML>
```

The Time Manager Quick Start help is shown in the screenshot below:

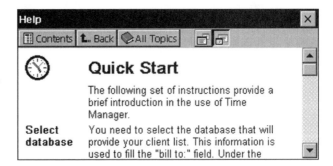

Then there is the About information (**Time Manager About.htp**):

```
<HTML>
<BODY>
<TABLE>
<TR>
<TD><IMG SRC="Time Manager.2bp" ></TD>
<TD><H2>About Time Manager</H2></TD>
</TR>
<TR>
<TD></TD>
<TD><FONT SIZE=+2>
Larry Roof's Time Manager version 1.0
</FONT></TD>
</TR>
<TR>
<TD></TD>
<TD><FONT SIZE=+2>
Copyright &COPY; 1998 Larry Roof<BR>
```

```
</FONT></TD>
</TR>
<TR>
<TD></TD>
<TD><FONT SIZE=+2>
All rights reserved.
</FONT></TD>
</TR>
</TABLE>
</BODY>
</HTML>
```

The About dialog should now look like this:

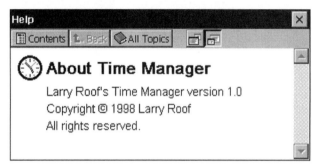

Finally we need to add the code to the menu **Click** events so that these help files are launched when the user selects the appropriate menu item. I have elected to use the common dialog, named **dlgHelp**, to access the help files:

```
Private Sub mnuHelpUsing_Click()

  ceHelp.HelpFile = "Time Manager.htc"
  ceHelp.ShowHelp

End Sub
```

```
Private Sub mnuHelpAbout_Click()

  ceHelp.HelpFile = "Time Manger About.htp"
  ceHelp.ShowHelp

End Sub
```

Testing Out The Revised Time Manager

To install the revised version of Time Manager on your handheld computer follow these steps:

- Establish a connection between you desktop and handheld computers
- Using the instructions laid out in Appendix A find the version of Time Manager for Chapter 9
- Follow the installation directions

You may want to remove the revised version of the Time Manager program from your handheld computer at this time. The easiest way to accomplish this is through the Start *menu, then* Settings, Control Panel *and finally* Remove Programs.

Summary

Well that's it. Everything that you need to know to add help files to your applications. As you learned, it was more a lesson in HTML than in VBCE. I personally like the CE help file structure. It's far easier to create help systems for CE than it is for Windows 95. Well, that is unless you want to invest several hundred dollars for Windows 95 help editing tools.

The key points that you should remember from this chapter are:

- There are two methods to add help functionality to your applications: with either the Utility or common dialog control. While the Utility control requires less resources, if you are already using the common dialog control with your application you might as well stick with it for help.

- Help systems are made up of a set of files that have the file extensions of **.htc**, for Contents files, and **.htp**, for Topic files. These files are usually stored in the **\Windows** directory of your handheld computer.

- Windows CE makes use of a special type of bitmap file that has the file extension of **.2bp**. All of your images should be converted to this format for use with your applications.

.

Case Studies

While the first part of this book focused on the VBCE language, its usage and practical techniques, this second part presents complete CE applications. These applications are built using many of the skills detailed in the first half along with a healthy dose of new tricks, techniques and tips.

We kick off the second part with the **Inventory Manager** application. Inventory Manager is a tool for gathering and storing inventory information using a handheld computer and a barcode scanner. This application is built using the simplest of tools. Its data is stored in comma-delimited sequential files. The Windows CE Services are used to transfer the data files to a desktop computer. There is a minimal amount of coding required to construct this app. My intention here is to demonstrate how to create useful applications that are quick and easy to build.

Next is the **Note Manager** application. This application is slightly more complex than the Inventory Manager. Note Manager is a utility program that allows you to store and organize notes. It uses an ADO CE database to store its notes and index, which provides for some interesting examples in retrieving records. The interface for Note Manager demonstrates the use of the TreeView and ImageList controls.

At the beginning of each case study, you will find a table that outlines the specifications of that application. These tables are provided as a reference so that you can quickly find examples to help you with your programs. They detail the difficulty of the application, how it stores and transfers data, which controls it uses, and other unique features. An example of one of these tables is shown below:

Level of application:	NOVICE - basic understanding of CE, VB and Access
Data storage – Local:	Sequential, comma-delimited file
Data storage – Desktop:	Access database
Transferal method:	auto-transferal using **Synchronized Files** folder
Desktop update method:	Access query
Controls used:	File, File System and Common Dialog
Unique features:	uses a barcode scanner

VBCE can be used to address a wide variety of needs as is demonstrated with these case studies. I would recommend that you work through all of these applications. Each demonstrates different techniques and resources that you can use in your own applications.

By the time your are finished, you'll have a solid understanding of how VBCE can be used to construct your own applications. I wish you good fortune in all your future VBCE projects!

The Inventory Manager: Scanning and Recording Data

One of the key features of the handheld computer is that it's portable. Combine that with the ease in which adding a barcode scanner can extend its functionality, and you have the perfect inventory tool. That is the focus of this case study. The Inventory Manager application is intended to provide a simple tool for scanning and recording data. In this example, the data we'll be gathering is book orders that are being processed in a warehouse. Before the chapter is over, you'll see how the combination of a handheld computer, a barcode scanner and the Visual Basic for Windows CE Toolkit can be applied to provide solutions to your inventory needs.

The Application Specifications

The Inventory Manager is a simple case study. It's built upon a single form with only a handful of controls. It uses the automatic synchronization feature of the Windows CE Services to transfer order lists and completed orders between a desktop PC and a H/PC. The specifics on this application are:

Level of application:	NOVICE - basic understanding of CE, VB and Access
Data storage – Local:	Sequential, comma-delimited file
Data storage – Desktop:	Access database
Transferal method:	Auto-transferal using the **Synchronized Files** folder
Desktop update method:	Access query
Controls used:	File, File System and Common Dialog
Unique features:	Uses a barcode scanner

The Inventory Manager – Step-By-Step

In the following sections, you'll be led through the process used to create the Inventory Manager application. This application demonstrates how simple it can be to create a fully functional program that uses both the processing and portability features found in H/PCs. It also displays techniques that you can use to streamline user input for handheld applications.

> The corresponding desktop applications used to create `Orders.inv` and process `Completed.inv` are not provided as part of this discussion. Simple Visual Basic or Access programs could be developed to provide this functionality.

Using the Inventory Manager

We will begin our examination of Inventory Manger by looking at the finished product.

Installing the Inventory Manager

To install Inventory Manager on your handheld computer follow these steps:

- Establish a connection between your desktop and handheld computers
- As laid out in the instructions of Appendix A, find the Inventory Manager app setup file
- Follow the installation directions

Installing Optional Hardware

If you have a barcode scanner to use with your H/PC you should install the hardware and software before running the Inventory Manager application. See the reference later in this chapter for additional information regarding barcode scanners for Windows CE.

> *You don't actually need a barcode scanner to try out this application as the scanner mimics typing the barcode number into a text box.*

> **Before you can run the Inventory Manager application you'll need to manually copy the file Orders.inv to the Synchronized Files folder. This file contains a set of test orders that can be processed by Inventory Manager.**

Running the Inventory Manager

Once you have completed the installation of this example run it on your handheld computer by selecting the Inventory Manager item from the Start menu. The Inventory Manager interface should be displayed as shown in the screenshot below:

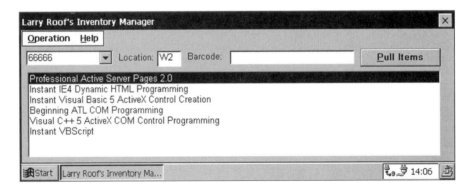

To test out the features of this application, try the following:

▲ Selecting orders from the combo box located in the upper left corner of the user interface. As you select different orders the list of order items will be updated.

▲ Either scan or type in the barcode for the books specified in an order. As you complete each barcode the item will be removed from the list. Barcodes for the books included in the example order file are included below.

▲ Access the help system. You will find additional information on using Inventory Manager under the Quick Start For Inventory Manager help item.

▲ After exiting the Inventory Manager application examine the contents of the **Synchronized Files** folder on your H/PC. Notice the addition of the **Completed.inv** file. This file contains a list of the items that you processed.

Title	Barcode
Beginning Visual Basic 5	9 781861 000392
Professional Active Server Pages 2.0	9 781861 001269
Instant VBScript	9 781861 000446
Instant Visual Basic 5 ActiveX Control Creation	9 781861 000231
Beginning ATL COM Programming	9 781861 000118

Table Continued on Following Page

Title	Barcode
Visual C++ 5 ActiveX COM Control Programming	9 781861 000378
Instant IE4 Dynamic HTML Programming	9 781861 000682

Removing the Inventory Manager

You may want to remove the Inventory Manager application from your H/PC after you have finished evaluating the finished product. This can be accomplished via the Start menu by selecting Settings, then Control Panel and finally Remove Programs. Select Inventory Manager from the Remove Programs interface.

The Inventory Manager – The Requirements

The purpose for Inventory Manager is to provide a portable order processing application that is easy to use. The requirements for this application are to:

▲ Incorporate a barcode scanner to simplify input

▲ Make use of existing functionality found in the Windows CE Services to transfer data between the H/PC and the desktop

▲ Use simple file input and output techniques

▲ Require only minimal user interaction to process an order

▲ Offer several ways to input barcode information

The Inventory Manager – The Design

The Inventory Manager application has a fairly simple design. That is because the File, File System and Common Dialog controls provide most of its functionality. The design of Inventory Manager includes the following:

▲ The adoption of Windows CE Service's ActiveSync feature to transfer order data between the desktop computer and the H/PC

▲ Three methods to process an order item: by barcode scanner, using keyboard entry, using command button

▲ A single form that is composed primarily of a large list box control used to display order items

▲ A simple menu structure including only Operation and Help menus

▲ A File control for reading and writing sequential text files

▲ A File System control for querying file information

▲ A Common Dialog control used to display help files

▲ A combo box used to display orders

▲ A label used to display the location of order items

▲ A text box used for entry of the barcode for each order item

The Inventory Manager application will make use of two data files. The first file, **Orders.inv**, will be created on a desktop PC and then transferred to the H/PC via the ActiveSync feature of the Windows CE Services. It is a sequential file comprised of a series of records, with each new line in the file being a new record. Each record has five fields. The fields are, in order:

▲ Order number

▲ Item number

▲ Book title

▲ Barcode

▲ Location

The second file, **Completed.inv**, will be created by the Inventory Manager application itself. It will in turn be transferred to the desktop PC via the ActiveSync feature of the Windows CE Services. It is also a sequential file comprised of a series of records with each new line in the file being a new record. Each record has a single field. This field is:

▲ Item number

Now that you have an understanding of what the Inventory Manager application is and what capabilities it has to offer we will turn our attention to the process of constructing the application.

The Inventory Manager – The Construction

In the pages that follow you will be led through all nine steps of the creation process for the Inventory Manager application. As with the previous examples in the first part of this book you may want to work along with the instructions to create your own copy of Inventory Manager.

> *The file **Inventory Manager.vbp** in the source code for this book contains a completed version of this project. Refer to Appendix A for instructions on downloading and installing the source code.*

Step 1 - Starting a New Project

Start Visual Basic and create a new Windows CE project.

Step 2 - Setting the Project Properties

Set the Project Name, Form Width, Remote Path and Run on Target properties to the values shown in this screenshot:

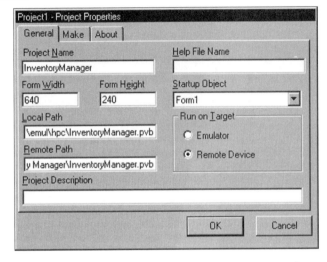

The setting for Remote Path is **\Program Files\Inventory Manager\Inventory Manager.pvb**. This is the location on your H/PC where the application program will be created. If you ran the installation program for the previous step then this directory will have been created, otherwise you'll need to do it yourself.

> *This application does not support the 'narrow screen' H/PCs. It could be easily modified though to incorporate the auto resizing techniques demonstrated with other applications.*

Step 3 - Constructing the User Interface

Add the following items to the Inventory Manager form:

- Combo box control for displaying orders
- Label control to display Location:
- Label control that will display location information on each order item
- Label control to display Barcode:
- Text box control that will allow the user to enter barcodes
- Command button that provides an alternative method for processing an order item
- File control for reading the **Orders.inv** file
- File control for writing completed items file
- File System control used to check for the existence of the **Orders.inv** file
- Common dialog control used to display help

The user interface should look something like this:

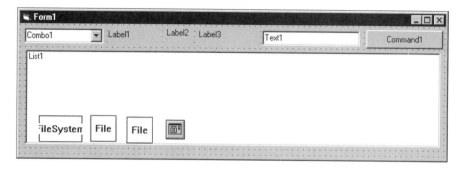

Construct a menu using the following information:

Menu Caption	Object Name	Enabled
&Operation	mnuOperation	True
&Error	mnuOperationError	False
E&xit	mnuOperationExit	True
&Help	mnuHelp	True
&Using Inventory Manager	mnuHelpUsing	True
&Quick Start For Inventory Manager	mnuHelpQuickStart	True
-	mnuHelpBar1	N/A
&About Inventory Manager	mnuHelpAbout	True

Step 4 - Setting the Form and Control Properties

Set the properties for the form and controls to match the following table:

Object	Property	Value
Form	Name	frmInventoryManager
	Caption	Larry Roof's Inventory Manager
	WindowState	2 – Maximized
Combo box	Name	cboOrders
	Style	2 – Dropdown List
Label 1	Caption	Location:
Label 2	Name	lblLocation
	BackColor	<White>
	BorderStyle	1 – Fixed Single
	Caption	<blank>)
Label 3	Caption	Barcode:

Object	Property	Value
Text box	Name	**txtBarcode**
	Text	<blank>
Command button	Name	**cmdPullItem**
	Caption	**&Pull Item**
List box	Name	**lstOrderItems**
File System control	Name	**ceFileSystem**
File	Name	**ceFileInput**
File	Name	**ceFileOutput**
Common dialog	Name	**ceCommonDialog**

I could easily have used a single File control to read from the **Orders.inv** *file and write to the* **Completed.inv** *file. I chose to use two controls so that it would be easier to understand what is happening. If this were a real-world application I would use a single control.*

The completed user interface should now look like this:

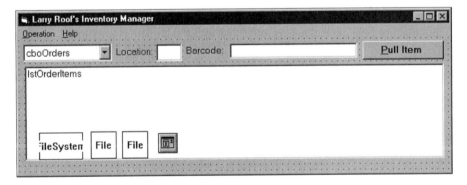

Finish this step by saving your project.

Step 5 - Adding your Coding

The next step in our development process is to add the code that will define how the Inventory Manager application performs. I've broken this step down into logical components. The application makes use of two module level variables and two constants:

```
Option Explicit

Const lrFileModeAppend = 8
Const lrFileModeInput = 1

Dim mintNumberOfItems
Dim mavntOrderInformation()
```

Starting the Inventory Manager – The Form_Load Event Procedure

The primary function of this procedure is to load the contents of the **Orders.inv** file into Inventory Manager. Calling the **LoadOrders** procedure performs this operation:

```
Private Sub Form_Load()

' Load the list of orders to process.
  LoadOrders

End Sub
```

The LoadOrders Procedure

This procedure makes use of the most involved and complicated code found in the Inventory Manager application. Even then it is nothing to break a sweat over. It begins by initializing a couple of variables used to track information:

```
Private Sub LoadOrders()

   Dim strLastOrder
   Dim avntOrderRecord

' This routine loads the list of orders to process.
' Initialize the variable used to track when the order # changes.
   strLastOrder = ""
   mintNumberOfItems = 0
```

Then it calls the **OpenDataFiles** procedure to open the **Orders.inv** file. This procedure is used here to encapsulate the code that is used to open the file and to simplify this procedure's code. A detailed examination of the **OpenDataFiles** procedure immediately follows the coverage of the **LoadOrders** procedure:

```
' Start by opening the data files.
  OpenDataFiles
```

Once the file is opened a loop is begun that will be used to process each line of the **Orders.inv** file. The **InputFields** method of the File control is used to retrieve the five fields of information. The fields are, again:

- Order number
- Item number
- Book title
- Barcode
- Location

```
' Build a list of the orders to be processed.
  On Error Resume Next

  Do While Not ceFileInput.EOF
    avntOrderRecord = ceFileInput.InputFields(5)
```

A check is then made to verify that no error has occurred. If one has, then the read loop is exited:

```
If (Err.Number <> 0) Then
  Exit Do
End If
```

The details of this record are loaded into an array, **mavntOrderInformation**. This array will be used throughout the program as a source for the order information. Note the use of the **Preserve** keyword when resizing the array. This maintains the existing contents of the array:

```
mintNumberOfItems = mintNumberOfItems + 1
ReDim Preserve mavntOrderInformation(5, mintNumberOfItems)

' Order #
mavntOrderInformation(0, mintNumberOfItems) = avntOrderRecord(0)

' Item #
mavntOrderInformation(1, mintNumberOfItems) = avntOrderRecord(1)

' Title of the book
mavntOrderInformation(2, mintNumberOfItems) = avntOrderRecord(2)

' Barcode of the book
mavntOrderInformation(3, mintNumberOfItems) = avntOrderRecord(3)

' Location of where the book is stored.
mavntOrderInformation(4, mintNumberOfItems) = avntOrderRecord(4)

' Has this item been processed?
mavntOrderInformation(5, mintNumberOfItems) = "N"
```

Next a bit of software slight-of-hand is used to build a list of orders. Since there is no separate list of orders provided to Inventory Manager, it must build the list by monitoring the orders it encounters while reading in the orders file. To aid this process the desktop application used to generate **Orders.inv** could be designed to write the order items out sorted by their respective order numbers.

Take a look at the following excerpt from the **Orders.inv** example file included with this application. Note how the records are sorted by their order number, which is the first field of each record:

```
 Orders.inv - Notepad
File  Edit  Search  Help
"11111","1","Beginning Visual Basic 5","9781861000392","W5"
"22222","2","Professional Active Server Pages 2.0","9781861001269","W2"
"22222","3","Instant VBScript","9781861000446","W9"
"33333","4","Instant Visual Basic 5 ActiveX Control Creation","9781861000231","W4"
"44444","5","Beginning ATL COM Programming","9781861000118","W7"
"44444","6","Visual C++ 5 ActiveX COM Control Programming","9781861000378","W8"
"55555","7","Instant IE4 Dynamic HTML Programming","9781861000682","W3"
"66666","8","Professional Active Server Pages 2.0","9781861001269","W2"
"66666","9","Instant IE4 Dynamic HTML Programming","9781861000682","W3"
"66666","10","Instant Visual Basic 5 ActiveX Control Creation","9781861000231","W4"
"66666","11","Beginning ATL COM Programming","9781861000118","W7"
"66666","12","Visual C++ 5 ActiveX COM Control Programming","9781861000378","W8"
"66666","13","Instant VBScript","9781861000446","W9"
"77777","14","Professional Active Server Pages 2.0","9781861001269","W2"
```

The variable **strLastOrder** is used to track the changes in order numbers. It's simply used to remember the last order number. If the current order number doesn't match the last order number it's added to the list of orders in the combo box, since a different order number represents the start of another order:

```
' If this is a new order add it to the list.
   If (strLastOrder <> avntOrderRecord(0)) Then
      cboOrders.AddItem avntOrderRecord(0)
   End If
```

The variable **strLastOrder** is then updated to reflect the last order number that was encountered and the end of the loop occurs:

```
' Set the variable used to track order # changes.
   strLastOrder = avntOrderRecord(0)

Loop
```

After all of the records have been read in from the orders file the first order in the combo box is selected and the contents of that order are displayed by invoking the **DisplayOrder** procedure. This procedure will be examined after the **OpenDataFiles** procedure below.

```
' Select the first order and display its order.
   cboOrders.ListIndex = 0
   DisplayOrder

End Sub
```

The OpenDataFiles Procedure

This procedure handles the opening of both the **Orders.inv** and **Completed.inv** items files. It begins by verifying that the **Orders.inv** file exists using the **Dir** method of the File System control.

> *The File System **Dir** function returns a filename matching the criteria that you provide. It can be used to check to see if a file exists by specifying the exact name of the file as the criteria. If the file does not exist an empty string will be returned.*

```
Private Sub OpenDataFiles()

' This routine opens the two files used by this application.
  Dim strCompletedFilename
  Dim strOrderFilename
  Dim intUsersResponse

' Check to see if the order file exists.
  strOrderFilename = ceFileSystem.Dir("\My Documents\Synchronized
    ⤷ Files\Orders.inv")
```

If the file exists (i.e. the value returned from the **Dir** method of the **ceFileSystem** control is not empty) then it opens the orders file:

```
' If the order file is present so open it.
  If (strOrderFilename <> "") Then
    ceFileInput.Open "My Documents\Synchronized Files\Orders.inv",
      ⤷ lrFileModeInput
```

If the `Orders.inv` file doesn't exist then exit that application because there is nothing that we can do:

```
' Order file is not present so exit the application.
  Else
    MsgBox "Order file not found. Program exiting.", vbCritical,
        ↳ "Fatal Error"
    App.End

  End If
```

Next check to see if there is a `Completed.inv` file present in the `Synchronized Files` folder. If there is prompt the user to see what should be done. This file would normally be deleted by the order processing software on the desktop PC when it does its part of the processing:

```
' Check to see if the completed file exists.
  strCompletedFilename = ceFileSystem.Dir("\My Documents\Synchronized
        ↳ Files\Completed.inv")

' A completed file is already on the system. Prompt the user to see
' what they want to do.

  If (strCompletedFilename <> "") Then
    intUsersResponse = MsgBox("A completed file already exists. Do
        ↳ you want to add to this file?", vbQuestion + vbYesNo +
        ↳ vbDefaultButton1, "Continue Processing?")

    Select Case intUsersResponse

      Case vbYes
        ceFileOutput.Open "\My Documents\Synchronized
          ↳ Files\Completed.inv", lrFileModeAppend

      Case vbNo
        App.End

    End Select
```

We then open the `Completed.inv` file for output. This file will be updated as individual order items are processed. See the **Change** event procedure for the **txtBarcode** text box for additional information on this functionality:

```
  Else
    ceFileOutput.Open "\My Documents\Synchronized
        ↳ Files\Completed.inv", lrFileModeAppend

  End If

End Sub
```

The DisplayOrder Procedure

As the user of the Inventory Manager selects individual orders, the items that comprise that order will be displayed in the list box control that dominates the interface. The procedure providing this functionality is **DisplayOrder**.

The procedure begins by emptying out any items that may be in the list box using the **Clear** method:

```
Private Sub DisplayOrder()

  Dim intCounter

' This routine displays the items for the selected order.
' First clear out the previous list.
  lstOrderItems.Clear
```

Next, a loop is used to run through the array of order items looking for items that are part of the selected order. As you recall, this array was loaded with the order information in the **LoadOrders** procedure that's called from the **Form_Load** procedure.

Items that are part of the selected order are first checked to see if they've already been processed (details on this can be found in the **ProcessThisItem** procedure) before being loaded into the list box. The item number for each order item is then loaded into the **ItemData** property of the list box control. This will be used by the **ProcessThisItem** procedure to identify the selected item:

```
' Now loop through the array of order items and select all
' of the items for the current order.

  For intCounter = 1 To mintNumberOfItems
    If (mavntOrderInformation(0, intCounter) = cboOrders.Text) Then

      If (mavntOrderInformation(5, intCounter) <> "Y") Then
        lstOrderItems.AddItem mavntOrderInformation(2, intCounter)
        lstOrderItems.ItemData(lstOrderItems.NewIndex) = _
                   mavntOrderInformation(1, intCounter)

      End If

    Else

      If (mavntOrderInformation(0, intCounter) > cboOrders.Text) Then
        Exit For
      End If

    End If

  Next
```

Once all of the items for the selected order have been loaded into the list box control, the first item from the list is selected. The purpose in selecting the first item is to minimize the interaction required from the user as they work with this application:

```
' Select the first item in the list.
  lstOrderItems.ListIndex = 0
  lstOrderItems_Click

End Sub
```

The cboOrders_Click Event Procedure

The code for this event procedure is minimal. All that it does is invoke the **DisplayOrder** procedure to display the items that comprise this order:

```
Private Sub cboOrders_Click()

' Display all of the order items for the selected order.
  DisplayOrder

End Sub
```

The lstOrderItems_Click Event Procedure

The purpose of this procedure is to display details on a particular order item as it's selected in the list box control. This is accomplished by looping through the order array comparing each item to the **ItemData** property of the selected list box item. If you remember, the **ItemData** property was loaded with the item number of each item. Here it's used to locate the appropriate order item:

```
Private Sub lstOrderItems_Click()

  Dim intCounter

' Loop through all of the orders to find the information on this item.
  For intCounter = 1 To mintNumberOfItems
    If (CInt(mavntOrderInformation(1, intCounter)) = _
          lstOrderItems.ItemData(lstOrderItems.ListIndex)) Then
```

When the selected order item's information has been located in the order array display the location (where the item is stored):

```
        lblLocation.Caption = mavntOrderInformation(4, intCounter)

      Exit For

    End If

  Next
```

Once the information on this item has been displayed, the text box control is cleared, and then focus is set to the text box control. Both of these steps are intended to simplify the user interface.

```
' Clear out the TextBox used to enter barcodes and set
' focus there so that the user doesn't have to.
  txtBarcode.Text = ""
  txtBarcode.SetFocus

End Sub
```

The txtBarcode_Change Event Procedure

At the heart of the Inventory Manager application is this procedure. It's here that the items are physically processed. When the user scans in a barcode this procedure is fired. Its purpose is to process the order item that is presently selected in the list box.

The procedure starts by confirming that the barcode text box contains something. After all, the text box **Change** event fires every time that the **Text** property of the control changes, whether that be for an addition or subtraction of text:

```
Private Sub txtBarcode_Change()

' Check to see if the barcode that has been entered
' matches the selected book. If so then process this item.

   Dim intCounter

' Ignore situations where the control is empty.
   If (txtBarcode.Text = "") Then
     Exit Sub
   End If
```

If the text box is not empty, a loop is initiated to run through the order array looking for the selected order item. When it is found, a comparison is made between the barcode that was entered by the user (either manually or via a scan) and the barcode that was sent with in the **Orders.inv** file. If there is a match then this order item is processed by calling the **ProcessThisItem** procedure, which we'll code in a minute:

```
' Find the item to process in the order array.
   For intCounter = 1 To mintNumberOfItems

     If (CInt(mavntOrderInformation(1, intCounter)) = _
     lstOrderItems.ItemData(lstOrderItems.ListIndex)) Then

       If (txtBarcode.Text = mavntOrderInformation(3, intCounter)) Then
          ProcessThisItem
       End If

       Exit For

     End If

   Next

End Sub
```

The ProcessThisItem Procedure

This procedure could be thought of as the packaging part of our ordering process. For it is here that an item is 'packed up' and 'shipped out' to the **Completed.inv** file.

It begins by adding the item number from this order to the completed file. This number will eventually be used by an application on the desktop PC to mark this item as being processed:

```
Private Sub ProcessThisItem()

   Dim intCounter

' This routine processes the current item, removing it from the pull
' list and adding it to a processed items file.
```

```
' First add this item to the processed order file.
For intCounter = 1 To mintNumberOfItems

    If (CInt(mavntOrderInformation(1, intCounter)) = _
                        lstOrderItems.ItemData(lstOrderItems.ListIndex)) Then
        ceFileOutput.LinePrint mavntOrderInformation(1, intCounter)

        Exit For

    End If

Next
```

Next this order item is marked as being processed so that it will not reappear in the order list as it's displayed to the user. I could have done some software gymnastics at this point to remove the processed item from the order array, but this method is just far simpler and more efficient:

```
' Mark this item as processed.
mavntOrderInformation(5, intCounter) = "Y"
```

The item is then removed from the list box. If it was the last item in this order, the order is in turn removed from the orders combo box and a new order is displayed. If this was the last item of the last order, the user is informed that they have processed all of the orders:

```
' Finally remove it from the item ListBox.
lstOrderItems.RemoveItem lstOrderItems.ListIndex

If (lstOrderItems.ListCount = 0) Then
    cboOrders.RemoveItem cboOrders.ListIndex

    If (cboOrders.ListCount <> 0) Then
        cboOrders.ListIndex = 0
        DisplayOrder

    Else
        MsgBox "All orders have been processed.", vbInformation, _
               "Processing Complete"

    End If
```

If there are still items to select with this order, select the next item in the list box and clear out the barcode text box:

```
    Else
        lstOrderItems.ListIndex = 0

    End If

    txtBarcode.Text = ""

End Sub
```

We set up an alternative method of removing items from the list by adding the Pull Item command button. In order for this to work we need to simply call the **ProcessThisItem** procedure:

```
Private cmdPullItem_Click()

' Allow items to be pulled with the command button
  ProcessThisItem

End Sub
```

The txtBarcode_KeyUp Event Procedure

The whole purpose behind this procedure is to prohibit the user from entering any barcode before selecting an order item from the list box. A simple check is made to verify that an item is selected before allowing any keyboard input. If an item is not selected a message box is displayed and the keyboard character is thrown away by setting the **KeyCode** argument equal to **0**:

```
Private Sub txtBarcode_KeyUp(KeyCode, Shift)

' Do not allow the user to enter anything unless an item is selected.
  If (lstOrderItems.ListIndex = -1) Then
    MsgBox "You must select an item from the list before entering a
           barcode."
    KeyCode = 0

  End If

End Sub
```

Implementing the Operation Menu

The Inventory Manager menu structure is comprised of two menus: Operation and Help. In this section we will walk through each, examining the code used to provide functionality to the menus.

The Operation menu is used to hold the Error (used for debugging) and Exit menu items. A brief discussion of each of these event procedures is provided below:

The Error Menu Item

The Error menu item is intended for development use only. It displays the number and description of the last runtime error that was encountered. Before releasing Inventory Manager to users set the Visible property of the Error menu item to False:

```
Private Sub mnuOperationError_Click()

' This procedure is for debugging purposes only.
  MsgBox Err.Number & " - " & Err.Description

End Sub
```

The Exit Menu Item

The Exit menu item event procedure contains only a single statement that uses the **End** method of the **App** object to exit the application:

```
Private Sub mnuOperationExit_Click()

  App.End

End Sub
```

Implementing the Help Menu

The Help menu provides access to the Inventory Manager help system. It uses the Common Dialog control with some minimal coding to implement this functionality. A brief discussion of each of the items found in the Help menu follows.

You can simply use the help files from the source code if you don't want to create them yourself. If you create them then you will still need a copy of the **Inventory Manager.bmp** file which you should copy to your handheld's **\Windows** directory.

Using the Inventory Manager Menu Item

Only two statements are required to display the Using Inventory Manager help file. The first statement sets the **HelpFile** property of the Common Dialog control to the name of the file to display. The second statement makes use of the Common Dialog control's **ShowHelp** method to display the desired help file:

```
Private Sub mnuHelpUsing_Click()

' Display the contents, or using help.
  ceCommonDialog.HelpFile = "Inventory Manager.htc"
  ceCommonDialog.ShowHelp

End Sub
```

The HTML to construct this file is simple. Just use a simple text editor such as EasyEdit or Notepad to create the file and save it as **Inventory Manager.htc**:

*Remember to save it in the handheld's **\Windows** directory otherwise it won't work.*

```
<HTML>
<BODY>
<TABLE>
<TR>
<TD><IMG SRC="Inventory Manager.bmp" ></TD>
<TD><H2>Inventory Manager Help</H2></TD>
</TR>
<TR>
<TD></TD>
<TD><FONT SIZE=+2>
<A HREF="FILE:Inventory Manager Quick Start.htp">A quick start to
  using Inventory Manager</A>
</FONT></TD>
</TR>
```

```
<TR>
<TD></TD>
<TD><FONT SIZE=+2>
<A HREF="FILE:Inventory Manager About.htp">About Inventory
   Manager</A>
</FONT></TD>
</TR>
<TR>
<TD></TD>
<TD><FONT SIZE=+2>
<A HREF="FILE:Inventory Manager Operation Menu.htp">Operation menu
   commands</A>
</FONT></TD>
</TR>
<TABLE>
</BODY>
</HTML>
```

The Quick Start for the Inventory Manager Menu Item

The code used to display the Quick Start For Inventory Manager help file is nearly identical to that used shown above. The only difference is the name of the help file that will be displayed:

```
Private Sub mnuHelpQuickStart_Click()

' Display the Quick Start help.
ceCommonDialog.HelpFile = "Inventory Manager Quick Start.htp"
ceCommonDialog.ShowHelp

End Sub
```

Again the help file itself is simple, but remember to save this as a **.htp** file:

```
<HTML>
<BODY>
<TABLE>
<TR>
<TD WIDTH=70>
<IMG SRC="Inventory Manager.bmp">
</TD>
<TD><H2>Quick Start</H2></Td>
</TR>
<TR><FONT SIZE=+1>
<TD></TD>
</FONT></TD>
<TD><FONT SIZE=+1>
The following set of instructions provide a brief introduction in
   the use of Inventory Manager.
</FONT></TD>
</TR>
<TR><FONT SIZE=+1>
<TD><B>Getting Orders</B></TD>
</FONT></TD>
<TD><FONT SIZE=+1>
```

```
    Orders are loaded onto your H/PC from your desktop computer. To
       generate a set of orders run the <I>Order Dispatch</I>
       application on your desktop computer. This will generate an
       order file. Next connect up your H/PC to your desktop. The
       order file will automatically be copied to your H/PC as part
       of the synchronisation process.
    </FONT></TD>
    </TR>
    <TR><FONT SIZE=+1>
    <TD><B>Selecting an Order</B></TD>
    </FONT></TD>
    <TD><FONT SIZE=+1>
    To process an order simply select the order from the list of orders
       presented in combo box found in the upper left corner of this
       application's interface. The items that comprise this order
       will be displayed.
    </FONT></TD>
    </TR>
    <TR><FONT SIZE=+1>
    <TD><B>Processing an Order</B></TD>
    </FONT></TD>
    <TD><FONT SIZE=+1>
    To process an order simply select a book title from the item list
       and then scan the barcode off of the book. The book will be
       processed and removed from the list. As an alternative you
       can type the barcode in or click on the "Pull Item" button.
    </FONT></TD>
    </TR>
    <TR><FONT SIZE=+1>
    <TD><B>Completing Orders</B></TD>
    </FONT></TD>
    <TD><FONT SIZE=+1>
    As orders are completed they will automatically be removed from the
       order list.
    </FONT></TD>
    </TR>
    <TR><FONT SIZE=+1>
    <TD><B>Processing Completed Orders</B></TD>
    </FONT></TD>
    <TD><FONT SIZE=+1>
    Once you have completed all of your orders you need to perform the
       following steps to process the completed orders. First exit
       the Inventory Manager application. Next connect you H/PC up
       to your desktop computer. The synchronization process will be
       performed and as part of this process your completed orders
       will be transferred to your desktop computer. Finally run the
       <I>Process Orders</I> application on your desktop computer.
       This will update the order database with your completed
       orders.
    </FONT></TD>
    </TR>
    </TABLE>
    </BODY>
    </HTML>
```

The About Inventory Manager Menu Item

As with the previous procedure, the code used to display the <u>A</u>bout Inventory Manager help file only differs from the previous two examples in the name of the help file that it will display:

```
Private Sub mnuHelpAbout_Click()

' Display the About help.
  ceCommonDialog.HelpFile = "Inventory Manager About.htp"
  ceCommonDialog.ShowHelp

End Sub
```

Finally here's the HTML for this help file:

```
<HTML>
<BODY>
<TABLE>
<TR>
<TD><IMG SRC="Inventory Manager.bmp" ></TD>
<TD><H2>About Inventory Manager</H2></TD>
</TR>
<TR>
<TD></TD>
<TD><FONT SIZE=+2>
Larry Roof's Inventory Manager version 1.0
</FONT></TD>
</TR>
<TR>
<TD></TD>
<TD><FONT SIZE=+2>
Copyright &copy; 1998 Larry Roof<BR>
</FONT></TD>
</TR>
<TR>
<TD></TD>
<TD><FONT SIZE=+2>
All rights reserved.
</FONT></TD>
</TR>
</TABLE>
</BODY>
</HTML>
```

And that's it – everything that is required to implement a fully functional order processing application. As I said at the beginning of this case study, this application takes the simplest approach at constructing a CE application.

Step 6 - Testing in the CE Emulator

Set the Run on <u>T</u>arget project property to Emulator and run your project. While you will not be able to test a barcode scanner out from the emulator environment you can test Inventory Manager's functionality by entering barcodes directly into the text box. The table below provides the barcodes for each of the books included in the **Orders.inv** file:

Title	Barcode
Beginning Visual Basic 5	9781861000392
Professional Active Server Pages 2.0	9781861001269
Instant VBScript	9781861000446
Instant Visual Basic 5 ActiveX Control Creation	9781861000231
Beginning ATL COM Programming	9781861000118
Visual C++ 5 ActiveX COM Control Programming	9781861000378
Instant IE4 Dynamic HTML Programming	9781861000682

> You will need to copy the file Orders.inv to the Synchronized Files folder on both the emulator and your H/PC before testing the Inventory Manager application. You will also need to copy the help files into the same directory as the .pvb file.

Try working through a few orders. Note how each order item is removed from the list as you enter its barcode. When you complete each order it in turn will be removed from the list of orders displayed in the combo box. After you exit, examine the contents of the **Completed.inv** file under the **Synchronized Files** folder on your emulator. You can use the EasyEdit application from Chapter 6 to view the file.

You will need to use the Control Manager to install the File, File System and Common Dialog controls onto both the emulator and your H/PC before running this test. See Chapter 4 for further details on using this utility.

Step 7 - Testing on a Handheld Computer

Set the Run on Target project property to Remote Device and run your project. As you did in the emulator, test out the functionality of the Inventory Manager application. If you have a barcode scanner configured for use with your H/PC you can test it out now using the barcodes that were provided earlier in this chapter.

Testing the Complete Process

The Inventory Manager application is designed to demonstrate a complete process, transferring data from desktop to H/PC and back to the desktop. Try testing out this complete process using the following steps:

- Disconnect your H/PC from your desktop PC
- Delete both the **Orders.inv** and **Completed.inv** files from the **Synchronized Files** folder on your H/PC
- Place a copy of **Orders.inv** in the **Synchronized Files** folder on your desktop PC. Make sure that there is not a copy of the **Completed.inv** file in this folder.
- Attach your H/PC to your desktop PC, establish a connection to your desktop PC and let the ActiveSync feature copy the **Orders.inv** file from your desktop PC to your H/PC

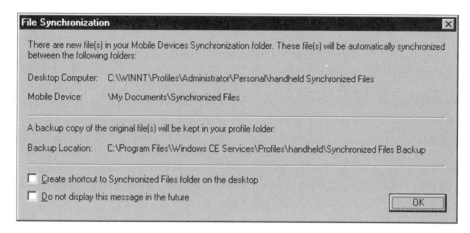

Confirm that a copy of **Orders.inv** has been added to the **Synchronized Files** folder on your H/PC

▲ Disconnect your H/PC from your desktop PC

▲ Run Inventory Manager and process a few orders

▲ Exit Inventory Manager

▲ Confirm that the **Completed.inv** file has been added to the **Synchronized Files** folder

▲ Attach your H/PC to your desktop PC, establish a connection to your desktop PC and let the ActiveSync feature copy the **Completed.inv** file from your H/PC to your desktop

▲ Confirm that a copy of **Completed.inv** has been added to the **Synchronized Files** folder on your desktop PC

If all of this happened as designed all you would have to do is to write a program to generate the **Orders.inv** file and process the returning **Completed.inv** file on your desktop PC.

Step 8 - Creating an Installation Program

Use the Application Install Wizard to generate an installation program for Inventory Manager. Make sure to include the help files. If you need help with this wizard refer to Chapter 2 where a detailed explanation of the process is provided.

Step 9 - Test the Installation Program

As with previous examples, it's important that you test your installation program. It should install without error and allow you to completely remove the program. Make sure to test both the complete operational cycle as detailed in Step 7, and each of the individual functions that Inventory Manager provides.

Other Uses for the Inventory Manager

The Inventory Manager application demonstrates how easy it is to develop portable applications for processing information that incorporate the use of a barcode scanner. This technology has use in such fields as manufacturing, health care, sales, retail, help desks and shipping.

You could enhance this application to:

- Use a database instead of sequential files. This would provide a far more functional base on which to build an application.

- Use the ActiveSync feature built into the ADO CE to handle the transferring of data between the desktop PC and H/PC. What can I say – all of the benefit of a database without the hassles that synchronization holds.

- Add a database on the H/PC that would use a scanned barcode to retrieve and display information. This function opens all kinds of avenues where the H/PC can be used as a comprehensive information source.

- Develop a smart-processing module that would organize an order to optimize its processing. This routine would evaluate orders and determine the best method for retrieval.

Barcode Scanners for Windows CE

If you are in the market for a barcode scanner to use with your H/PC, I particularly like Socket's Bar Code Wand Card. This unit combines a barcode scanner along with a PC card as a single unit so you don't have to worry about the connection between the card and the scanner. Along with supporting software this product allows you to scan barcode data directly into any Windows CE application – including your own.

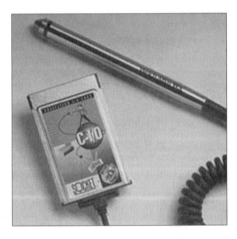

The supporting software that is provided with this product acts as a "keyboard wedge". By making CE programs think that the data was typed in via the keyboard it does not require any additional programming to use. Simply load the barcode wand software that is provided along with the scanner, plug in the card and you are ready to go.

An added feature is the translation software that is bundled with this scanner. This software allows you to create a custom translation table that will convert any barcode character to any Windows CE key including combination keys involving the *Shift*, *Alt* and *Ctrl* keys.

For more information on this product visit Socket's web site at **www.socketcom.com**.

Summary

What does it take to add barcode scanning to your Windows CE applications? As this chapter showed the answer is next to nothing. Through the use of "keyboard wedge" technology there is nothing that you need to do to incorporate scanned input into your programs. The result is a pretty powerful combination – the portability of an H/PC combined with the ease of date input provided by a barcode scanner.

The application that I selected to demonstrate CE-based barcode technologies is purposefully simple. It has a simple interface and makes use of a very simple method for transferring data to and from the H/PC. I took this approach to demonstrate that you can quickly construct easy-to-use applications using the built-in features of Windows CE and the functionality provided by third-party products. And after all, isn't that what we're all looking for?

The Note Manager

Have you ever wanted a simple utility that makes it easy to keep track of your daily tasks? A program that allows you to organize and quickly view notes from meetings, phone calls that need to be made, errands to run and events to attend? Well that's exactly what Note Manager offers. With its Explorer-like interface, Note Manager provides you with a note storage and retrieval tool that can be used for a variety of tasks. More than that, though, it demonstrates how Visual Basic for Windows CE can be used to create fully functional Windows CE utilities.

The Application Specifications

Note Manager is a moderately easy case study. It's built upon a single form and maintains all of its data locally using the ADO CE. The specifics on this application are:

Level of application:	INTERMEDIATE – sound understanding of VB and database fundamentals, minimal understanding of CE
Data storage – Local:	ADO CE tables
Data storage – Desktop:	None
Transferal method:	None
Desktop update method:	None
Controls used:	TreeView, ImageList, FileSystem, Utility and Common Dialog
Unique features:	Self creating database and use of initialization file.

Note Manager – Step-by-Step

In the following sections, I will lead you through the process that I used to create the Note Manager application. This application demonstrates how the VBCE Toolkit can be used to create feature-rich commercial quality applications. By making use of ADO for data storage, and an interface built upon the TreeView control, Note Manager provides a simple to use, yet powerful application for managing your notes. I think you'll be pleasantly surprised how easy it is to build.

> *There is no synchronization feature built into Note Manager. It is a H/PC based application only. That's not to say that you couldn't extend the functionality of this application to provide a corresponding desktop application.*

Using Note Manager

We will begin our examination of Note Manger by looking at the finished product.

Installing Note Manager

To install Note Manager on your handheld computer follow these steps:

- ▲ Establish a connection between you desktop and handheld computers
- ▲ Using the instructions laid out in Appendix A find the setup program for Note Manager
- ▲ Follow the installation directions.

> **You also need to install the ADO CE to run this application. Please refer to Chapter 7 for further details on this process.**

Running Note Manager

Once you have completed the installation of this example, run it on your handheld computer by selecting the Note Manager item from the Start menu. The Note Manager interface should be displayed as shown in the screenshot below:

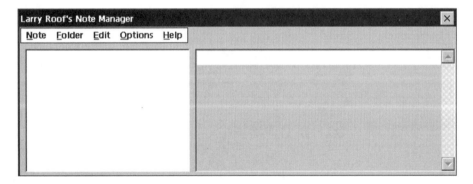

Let's run Note Manager through its paces. Follow the steps below to see how easy Note Manager is to use and just what it has to offer:

Start by creating a new note. Under the Folder menu select Add a Folder. The Create Folder dialog will be displayed as shown in the screenshot below. Type in * Today for the name of the folder. Why is the first character of our folder's name an asterisk? Because we are using Note Manager's sort feature to have this note always appear first in the list of folders:

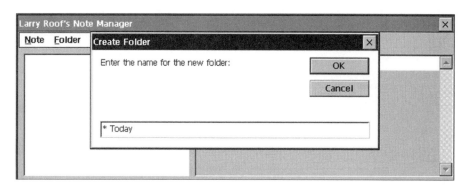

Add two more folders. One titled Status meetings. The other with the title of VBCE Project.

The screenshot below displays how the Note Manager interface will appear with the addition of the three folders:

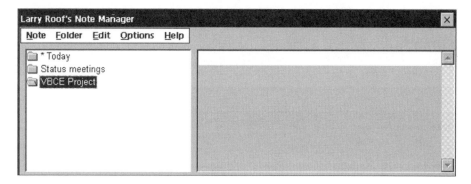

Now let's add a note. First select the * Today folder. With Note Manager you must always select the folder in which you want the note to reside before creating the note. Under the Note menu pick Add a Note. The Create Note dialog will be displayed as shown below. Enter the note title of Call builder 555 - 1212. When you click the OK button the note will be added:

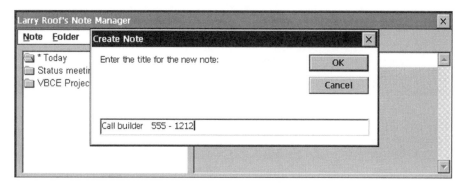

Now you are ready to add content to the note. Content is displayed in the right-hand window of the Note Manager display. As you select each note its content is retrieved from a database and displayed. Enter the contents for our first note as shown in the screenshot below:

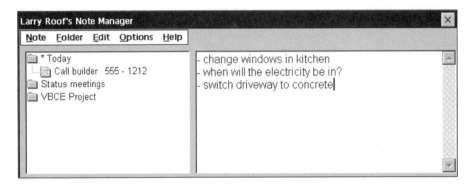

You should begin to see some of the beauty of Note Manager. Information is readily available with a simple tap of a note title. By selecting the Call builder note you have his phone number plus all of the questions that you want to ask him right there in front of you.

Add two more notes to the * Today folder so that you can see how easy it is to work with multiple notes. The first note is titled Grocery list and the second Get car serviced. To the content of the second note add - oil changed and - tires rotated. Your screen should now look like the screenshot below:

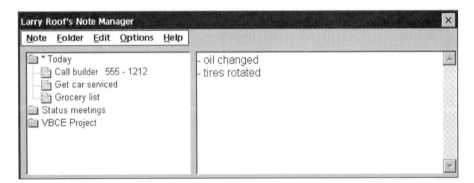

Need to change the name of a folder or title to a note? Simply tap on the item that you wish to change and then tap once more to activate in-place editing.

How easy is it to get rid of a note? Simply select the note that you wish to delete and then select the Delete This Note item from under the Note menu. Depending upon how you have Note Manager's options configured you may be prompted to confirm your deletion request. Select the Get car serviced note and delete it.

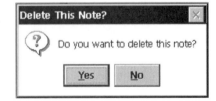

Deleting a folder will also delete all of its notes. To delete a folder, first select the folder and then use the Delete This Folder item under the Folder menu. Try this out by selecting the Status meetings folder and deleting it:

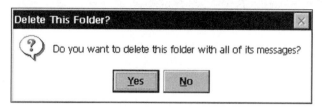

Your screen should now appear as shown in the screenshot below:

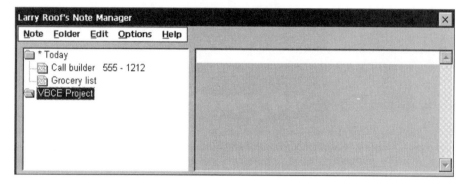

Using Note Manager's Options menu you can set the font of the contents display and whether or not you are prompted to confirm deletions. To try out the font configuration feature first select the Call builder note and then select Select Font Size For Note... from the Options menu. The Font dialog will be displayed as shown:

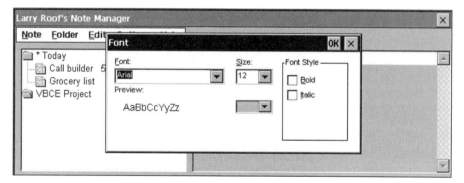

Change the font size to 14 and tap the OK button. An example of how the contents should now appear is shown below:

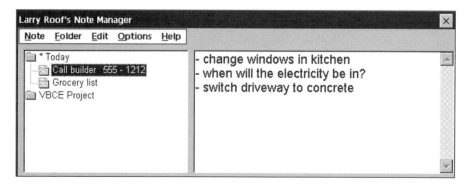

That concludes our brief tutorial in the use of Note Manager. For additional information refer to the Quick Start for Note Manager menu item under the Help menu.

Removing Note Manager

You may want to remove the Note Manager application from your H/PC after you have finished evaluating the finished product. This can be accomplished via the Start menu by selecting Settings, then Control Panel and finally Remove Programs. Select Note Manager from the Remove Programs interface.

Removing the Note Manager application does not remove the databases used by this application.

Note Manager – The Requirements

The purpose for Note Manager is to provide an easy to use utility for managing information. The requirements for this application are to:

- Make use of a single form, 'right in front of you' interface
- Use a familiar Explorer type interface to minimize the users' learning curve
- Provide quick access to information with a single tap
- Require no additional steps to save and retrieve notes
- Give a simple method for organizing notes

Note Manager – The Design

The design of the Note Manager application is only slightly more complex than that of Inventory Manager. Note Manager offers an interface that is comprised of a single form that is made up of only a handful of controls. At its foundation is ADO, which is used to store folder and note information. As you will see, ADO is no more difficult to use than the sequential files used by Inventory Manager. In fact, the most complex component of Note Manager is its manipulation of the TreeView control.

The User Interface

Note Manager's interface is comprised of a single form. This is a goal of mine with every CE application that I create. Why? First, because unlike desktop applications there is only room enough on an H/PC to display one form at a time. Second, because switching between forms requires time and makes it more difficult for the user to follow the flow of your application. An example of the interface is shown in the screenshot below:

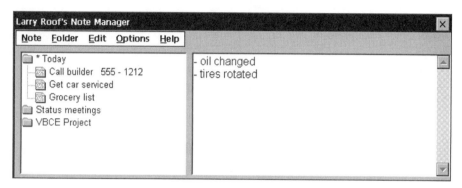

I also believe that you should build user-friendly interfaces that act the way the user expects. That's why I chose to use the TreeView control with its Explorer-like look and feel.

Finally inputting data and interacting with an application can be difficult on an H/PC. So in the design of Note Manager I tried to minimize the actions that a user had to perform to create, store and retrieve notes. That includes:

▲ Automatically saving and retrieving note contents

▲ Selecting new folders and notes as they are created

▲ Expanding the contents of folders as notes are added to them

▲ Provide common cut, copy and paste functions that the user would expect to find in a text editing application

Data Storage

Note Manager makes use of ADO for storing folder and note data. It uses three CE databases, or tables, as they would more commonly be thought of. These are:

nmFolders – Used to store folder information. Each record is comprised of the following fields:

Field	Type
FolderID	Integer
FolderName	50 character string

nmManagement – This database is used to mimic the autonumber feature found in an Access database. Since the Windows CE implementation of ADO does not provide for automatically assigning an identification number to a new record we have to provide a workaround. The **nmManagement** table is used to store the last ID number used for both the **nmFolders** and **nmNotes** tables. It will only have a single record that has the following fields:

Field	Type
RecordID	Integer
LastFolderID	Integer
LastNoteID	Integer

nmNotes – Used to store note information. Each record is comprised of the following fields:

Field	Type
NoteID	Integer
FolderID	Integer
LastModified	Date
Title	50 character string
Note	Text

These databases are created the first time that Note Manager runs. Reference the **InitializeDatabase** procedure later in this chapter for a detailed description of this process.

Now that you have an understanding of what the Note Manager application is and what capabilities it has to offer we will turn our attention to the process of constructing the application.

Note Manager – The Construction

In the pages that follow you will be led through all nine steps of the creation process for the Note Manager application. As with previous examples you may want to work along with the instructions to create your own copy of Note Manager. You will note that for many of the steps I no longer provide step-by-step instructions.

> *The file* **Note Manager.vbp** *contains a completed version of this project. Refer to Appendix A for instructions on downloading and installing the examples included in this book.*

Step 1 - Starting a New Project
Start Visual Basic and create a new Windows CE project.

Step 2 - Setting the Project Properties
Set the Project Name, Form Width, Remote Path and Run on Target properties to the values shown in the screenshot below:

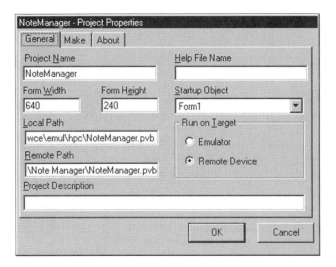

The setting for Remote Path is **\Program Files\Note Manager\Note Manager.pvb**. This is the location on your H/PC where the application program will be created. If you didn't run the setup program earlier then you will need to create this directory.

This application does not support the 'narrow screen' H/PCs. It could be easily modified though to incorporate the auto resizing techniques demonstrated with the Time Manger application.

Step 3 - Constructing the User Interface

Add the following items to the Note Manager form:

- TreeView control for displaying the folders and notes
- Text box control that will be used for displaying and editing the contents of notes
- ImageList control for storing the images that will be used by the TreeView control
- Common Dialog control used to display help
- Utility control used to work around text box bug
- File control used to access the **.INI** file used with Note Manager

The user interface should look something like this:

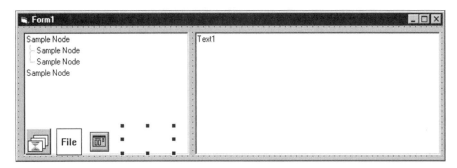

Construct a menu using the following information:

Menu Caption	Object Name	Enabled
&Note	MnuNote	True
&Add a Note	MnuNoteAdd	True
&Delete This Note	MnuNoteDelete	True
-	MnuNoteBar1	n/a
&Error	MnuNoteError	False
E&xit	MnuNoteExit	True
&Folder	MnuFolder	True
&Add a Folder	MnuFolderAdd	True
&Delete This Folder	mnuFolderDelete	True
&Edit	mnuEdit	True
Cu&t *Ctrl+X* shortcut key	mnuEditCut	True
&Copy *Ctrl+C* shortcut key	mnuEditCopy	True
&Paste *Ctrl+V* shortcut key	mnuEditPaste	True
&Options	mnuOptions	True
&Set Font Size For Note...	mnuOptionsFont	True
&Prompt Before Deleting	mnuOptionsPrompt	True
&Help	mnuHelp	True
&Using Note Manager	mnuHelpUsing	True
&Quick Start For Note Manager	mnuHelpQuickStart	True
-	mnuHelpBar1	n/a
&About Note Manager	mnuHelpAbout	True

Also select the <u>C</u>hecked property for the &Prompt Before Deleting menu item as well

Step 4 - Setting the Form and Control Properties

Set the properties for the form and controls to match the following table:

Object	Property	Value
Form	Name	frmNoteManager
	Caption	Larry Roof's Note Manager
	WindowState	2 – Maximized
TreeView	Name	treNotes
Text box	Name	txtNote
	MultiLine	True
	ScrollBars	2 – Vertical
	Text	<blank>

Object	Property	Value
ImageList	Name	**ilsNotes**
Common Dialog	Name	**ceCommonDialog**
File	Name	**ceFile**
Utility	Name	**ceUtility**

The completed user interface should be not dissimilar to this:

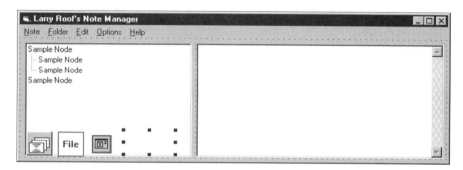

Finish this step by saving your project.

Step 5 - Adding Your Coding

The next step in our development process is to add the code that will define how the Note Manager application performs. I've broken this step down into logical components starting with the declarations.

The ADO Declarations File

There is a declaration file included with the ADO CE SDK, **ADOdeclarations.bas**, which defines values of constants used when working with ADO. It needs to be included in this project, and any other projects that you create that make use of ADO in order to use the constants prefixed with **ad** that you will use throughout the code.

The General Declarations Section

In the General Declarations section of the Note Manager application there is the definition of the following constants and procedure level variables. The constants are used by the Utility control to provide a workaround for the text box navigation bug. The variables are used for various control and data management tasks in the application:

```
Option Explicit

Const EM_GETLINECOUNT = &HBA
Const EM_LINEFROMCHAR = &HC9
Const EM_LINEINDEX = &HBB
Const EM_LINELENGTH = &HC1
Const EM_SCROLLCARET = &HB7
```

```
Private mblnControlledDelete
Private maobjFolders()
Private mrecFolders
Private mblnLoading
Private mblnNoteIsDirty
Private maojbNotes()
Private mrecNotes
Private mintNumberOfFolders
Private mintNumberOfNotes
Private mintPreviousIndex
Private mstrPreviousNote
Private mrecRecord
```

Starting Note Manager – The Form_Load Procedure

As you would expect, this procedure performs the initialization steps necessary to get Note Manager up and running.

It begins by initializing a variable that is used to track which item was last tapped in the TreeView control. It then calls the **ConfigureControls** procedure that sets properties, most notably the images that will be used by the TreeView control. Next it calls **GetSettings** which loads in user preference settings from an initialization file. Finally a call is made to **LoadNotes**, the routine that is responsible for loading folder and note information:

```
Private Sub Form_Load()

' Initialize values.
  mintPreviousIndex = -1

' Setup the interface.
  ConfigureControls

' Initialize the database.
  InitializeDatabase

' Get the configuration settings.
  GetSettings

' Load existing content.
  LoadNotes

End Sub
```

The ConfigureControls Procedure

The function of this procedure is to configure the ImageList control, which is subsequently used by the TreeView control, to display the images that are shown for folders and notes.

Unlike the ImageList control that is used by Visual Basic, the VBCE ImageList control cannot be configured with images at design time. Instead they are set at runtime as shown in this code fragment. First the **ImageHeight** and **ImageWidth** properties are set to the size of the images. Next the images are loaded into the control. Here the **App.Path** property is used to specify the location of the graphical files. The routine ends by setting the **ImageList** property of the TreeView control to our freshly configured ImageList control:

```
     Private Sub ConfigureControls()

     ' Set some default control configurations.
       treNotes.FontSize = 10
       ilsNotes.ImageHeight = 16
       ilsNotes.ImageWidth = 16
       ilsNotes.Add App.Path & "\closed folder.bmp"
       ilsNotes.Add App.Path & "\open folder.bmp"
       ilsNotes.Add App.Path & "\note.bmp"
       treNotes.ImageList = ilsNotes.hImageList

     ' Fill the remaining space of the form with the txtNote control
       txtNote.Width = Me.Width - txtNote.Left - 30

     End Sub
```

If you're using the ImageList control with one of your applications, you will need to ship the graphical files with the application - since they need to be resident on the user's H/PC in the same folder as the application.

The InitializeDatabase Procedure

The purpose of this procedure is primarily to check to see if the tables used by Note Manager are present. If not, the tables will be created.

The **InitializeDatabase** procedure begins by creating recordset objects for primary tables:

```
     Private Sub InitializeDatabase()

     ' Create recordset objects for both tables.
       Set mrecFolders = CreateObject("adoce.recordset")
       Set mrecNotes = CreateObject("adoce.recordset")
       Set mrecRecord = CreateObject("adoce.recordset")
```

Next an attempt is made at opening the **nmFolders** table for the purpose of determining whether or not the table exists. An error generated when opening the table is a signal that the table does not exist. The response to this error is to issue two commands to ADO. The first command creates the **nmFolders** table. The second command creates an index for the table using the **FolderID** field:

```
     ' Check to make sure the Folders table is present.
     ' If it is not, create it.

       On Error Resume Next

       mrecFolders.Open "nmFolders"

       If (Err <> 0) Then
         Err.Clear
         mrecFolders.Open "CREATE TABLE nmFolders (FolderID INTEGER,
              ⤷ FolderName VARCHAR(50))"
```

```
    If Err.Number <> 0 Then
      MsgBox "Error creating Folders table." & vbCrLf & Err.Number _
            & " - " & Err.Description
      App.End

    End If

    mrecFolders.Open "CREATE INDEX PrimaryKey ON nmFolders (FolderID)"

  End If

  mrecFolders.Close
```

The same technique is used with the **nmNotes** table. An attempt is made at opening the table. If the open failed, two commands are used to create the table and its index:

```
' Check to make sure the Notes table is present.
' If it is not, create it.

mrecNotes.Open "nmNotes"

If (Err <> 0) Then
  Err.Clear
  mrecNotes.Open "CREATE TABLE nmNotes (NoteID INTEGER, FolderID
          ⮡ INTEGER, LastModified DATETIME, Title VARCHAR(50),
          ⮡ Note Text)"

  If Err.Number <> 0 Then
    MsgBox "Error creating Notes table." & vbCrLf & Err.Number _
          & " - " & Err.Description
    App.End

  End If

  mrecNotes.Open "CREATE INDEX PrimaryKey ON nmNotes (NoteID)"

Else
  mrecNotes.Close

End If
```

Finally, a check is made to see if the **nmManagement** table is present. This table is used to mimic the autonumbering feature found in Access. As with the two previous tables, if the **nmManagement** table is not present then it is created:

```
' Check to make sure the Management table is present.
' If it is not, create it.

mrecRecord.Open "nmManagement"

If (Err <> 0) Then
  Err.Clear
  mrecRecord.Open "CREATE TABLE nmManagement (RecordID INTEGER,
          ⮡ LastFolderID INTEGER, LastNoteID INTEGER)"
```

```
      If Err.Number <> 0 Then
        MsgBox "Error creating Management table." & vbCrLf & _
            Err.Number & " - " & Err.Description
      App.End

    End If

    mrecRecord.Open "CREATE INDEX PrimaryKey ON nmNotes (NoteID)"

  Else
    mrecRecord.Close

  End If

End Sub
```

At this point the databases that are used by Note Manager have been confirmed.

The GetSettings Procedure

This procedure mimics the functionality of an initialization, or **.INI** file. I say mimics because unlike the **GetSettings** and **SaveSettings** functions found in Visual Basic, the VBCE Toolkit does not provide any method for either working with the system registry or with initialization files.

Instead the technique that I use here is to save and load settings by making use of a standard text file. This procedure, **GetSettings**, is responsible for reading in the settings. The **SaveSettings** procedure handles saving the settings (we'll code this later).

GetSettings starts by opening up the **Note Manager.ini** file, which is stored in the same directory as the Note Manager application:

```
Private Sub GetSettings()

  Const lrFileInput = 1
  Dim intEndLocation
  Dim intStartLocation
  Dim strSettingsFile
  Dim strInputString

' Setup the error handler.
  On Error Resume Next

' This procedure provides a crude INI file functionality
' by reading in settings.
  strSettingsFile = App.Path & "\Note Manager.ini"

' Open the selected file.
  On Error Resume Next
  ceFile.Open strSettingsFile, lrFileInput

  If Err Then
    Err.Clear
    mblnControlledDelete = True
    Exit Sub

  End If
```

Once the file is opened, its contents are read all at once into a string variable:

```
' Read in the file.
' Note - the "ceFile.LOF - 2" removes the trailing CrLf
'        added during the saving of the file.
  strInputString = ceFile.Input(ceFile.LOF)

  If Err Then
    Err.Clear
    ceFile.Close
    mblnControlledDelete = True
    Exit Sub

  End If

  strInputString = Mid(strInputString, 1, ceFile.LOF - 2)

' Done with the INI file so close it.
  ceFile.Close
```

The string is first parsed to locate the **Controlled Delete** setting. Both a module level variable and the controlled delete menu selection are then configured accordingly:

```
' Find the setting for mblnControlledDelete.
  intStartLocation = InStr(1, strInputString, _
                           "Controlled Delete=", vbTextCompare)
  intStartLocation = InStr(intStartLocation, strInputString, "=", vbTextCompare)

  If (Mid(strInputString, intStartLocation + 1, 1) = "T") Then
    mblnControlledDelete = True

  Else
    mblnControlledDelete = False

  End If

  mnuOptionsPrompt.Checked = mblnControlledDelete
```

Next the font configuration is retrieved from the string variable. This includes the **Font Name** and **Size** as well as the **Bold** and **Italics** attributes:

```
' Get the Font name setting.
  intStartLocation = InStr(intStartLocation + 1, strInputString, _
                   "Font Name=", vbTextCompare)
  intStartLocation = InStr(intStartLocation, strInputString, "=", vbTextCompare)
  intEndLocation = InStr(intStartLocation + 1, strInputString, vbCr, vbTextCompare)
  txtNote.FontName = Mid(strInputString, intStartLocation + 1, _
                          intEndLocation - intStartLocation - 1)

' Get the Font size setting.
  intStartLocation = InStr(intStartLocation + 1, strInputString, _
                   "Font Size=", vbTextCompare)
```

```
        intStartLocation = InStr(intStartLocation, strInputString,  "=", vbTextCompare)
        intEndLocation = InStr(intStartLocation + 1, strInputString, vbCr, vbTextCompare)
        txtNote.FontSize = Mid(strInputString, intStartLocation + 1, _
                           intEndLocation - intStartLocation - 1)

    ' Get the Font bold setting.
        intStartLocation = InStr(intStartLocation + 1, strInputString, _
                           "Font Bold=", vbTextCompare)
        intStartLocation = InStr(intStartLocation, strInputString, "=", vbTextCompare)

        If (Mid(strInputString, intStartLocation + 1, 1) = "T") Then
          txtNote.FontBold = True

        Else
          txtNote.FontBold = False

        End If

    ' Get the Font italic setting.
        intStartLocation = InStr(intStartLocation + 1, strInputString, _
                              "Font Italic=", vbTextCompare)
        intStartLocation = InStr(intStartLocation, strInputString, "=", vbTextCompare)

        If (Mid(strInputString, intStartLocation + 1, 1) = "T") Then
          txtNote.FontItalic = True

        Else
          txtNote.FontItalic = False

        End If

    End Sub
```

The LoadNotes Procedure

The purpose behind this procedure is to load all of the folder and note information into the Note Manager application. While the complete notes are not kept within this application, the folder details and the note titles are kept both in the TreeView control and in an array.

The loading process begins by creating a recordset of all the folders in **nmFolders**.

```
Private Sub LoadNotes()

  Dim intCount

' Setup error handler.
  On Error Resume Next

' Set flag used to control event procedures.
  mblnLoading = True
```

```
' Create a recordset of the folders.
  mrecFolders.Open "SELECT * FROM nmFolders", , adOpenKeyset, adLockOptimistic

  If Err Then HandleError
```

This recordset is then navigated to build a list of folders, loading them into the TreeView control. The loop used to process these records will continue until the end of file is reached as determined by the **EOF** property of the recordset.

The key that is used to reference each folder in the TreeView control is the word **Folder –** followed by the folder's **FolderID**. This combination produces a unique key for each item.

The **MoveNext** method of the recordset is used to move through the records:

```
' Load the display with the folders.
  mintNumberOfFolders = 0

  Do Until (mrecFolders.EOF)
    mintNumberOfFolders = mintNumberOfFolders + 1
    ReDim Preserve maobjFolders(mintNumberOfFolders)
    Set maobjFolders(mintNumberOfFolders) = treNotes.Nodes.Add(, , _
          "Folder - " & mrecFolders.Fields("FolderID"), _
          mrecFolders.Fields("FolderName"), 1, 2)

    If Err Then HandleError

    mrecFolders.MoveNext

  Loop
```

Once the folders have been loaded, we're ready to add the notes. You should note, here, that the folders had to be processed first because the notes become 'children' of the folders in the hierarchy that is created within the TreeView control.

Creating a recordset of all the notes starts this part of the process. This recordset is then processed to load each note into the TreeView control. Note that a reference to the parent folder is established as each note is added. Just as we saw with the folder recordset, the **EOF** property and **MoveNext** method are used to work through the recordset. The **Key** property for a note will be calculated as the **NoteID** for the containing folder, a dash and then the ID for the note itself:

```
' Create a recordset of the notes.
  mrecNotes.Open "SELECT * FROM nmNotes", , adOpenKeyset, adLockOptimistic

' Load the display with the notes.
  mintNumberOfNotes = 0

  Do Until (mrecNotes.EOF)
    mintNumberOfNotes = mintNumberOfNotes + 1
    ReDim Preserve maobjNotes(mintNumberOfNotes)
    Set maobjNotes(mintNumberOfNotes) = treNotes.Nodes.Add("Folder - " _
          & mrecNotes.Fields("FolderID"), 4, mrecNotes.Fields("FolderID") _
          & " - " & mrecNotes.Fields("NoteID"), mrecNotes.Fields("Title"), _
          3, 3)
```

```
      If Err Then HandleError

      mrecNotes.MoveNext

   Loop
```

Finally the folders are sorted within the TreeView control:

```
' Sort the entries in the TreeView control.
treNotes.Sorted = True

For intCount = 1 To mintNumberOfFolders
   maobjFolders(intCount).Sorted = True
Next

' Reset flag used to control events.
mblnLoading = False

End Sub
```

At this point the Note Manager application is ready for the user.

The Form_Unload Procedure

This procedure has two purposes. First, to save the contents of the active note and second, to save the user configuration settings. If you are unfamiliar with the **Form_Unload** event, it will get fired when the user selects Exit from the Note menu or clicks on the X in the upper-right corner of the form.

The **mblnNoteIsDirty** flag is used to check whether of not the active note has been changed. This flag is set to **True** in the **Change** event of the note text box. If the note has changed, then it needs to be saved before exiting the application. The **SaveNote** procedure is called to perform this function:

```
Private Sub Form_Unload(Cancel)

' Make sure that any changes to the previous note were saved.
If (mblnNoteIsDirty) Then
   SaveNote
End If
```

The user configuration settings are saved using a call to the **SaveSettings** procedure:

```
' Save configuration settings.
SaveSettings
```

Finally the application is terminated:

```
' Everything is cleaned up so exit.
App.End

End Sub
```

The SaveNote Procedure

The purpose of this procedure is to save the contents of the active note. Note that this procedure is not concerned with whether or not the note has changed. That situation is being tracked by other parts of the Note Manager application.

The first step to this procedure is to find the record for the active note in the **nmNotes** table. The variable **mstrPreviousNote** contains the **NoteID** for the note. This variable is set when a note is selected from the TreeView control:

```
Private Sub SaveNote()

  Dim strThisNoteID

' Save the note that was changed.
' First retrieve the record for the note.
  strThisNoteID = Right(mstrPreviousNote, Len(mstrPreviousNote) - _
                   InStr(1, mstrPreviousNote, "-"))
  mrecRecord.Open "SELECT * FROM nmNotes WHERE NoteID = " & _
                   strThisNoteID, , adOpenKeyset, adLockOptimistic
```

If there's a problem accessing the record for this note a call is made to the **HandleError** procedure to process the error:

```
    If Err Then HandleError
```

The record for the active note is updated with the contents of the text box control and then saved:

```
' Then store the updated text for that note.
  mrecRecord.Fields("Note").Value = txtNote.Text
  mrecRecord.Update
  mrecRecord.Close

End Sub
```

The HandleError Procedure

This is a general error handling procedure, offering only minimal functionality by displaying the number and description of the error that is encountered:

```
Private Sub HandleError()

' Display errors that are encountered.
  If (Err.Number <> 13) Then
    MsgBox "The following error has occurred:" & vbCrLf & _
            "Error number: " & Err.Number & vbCrLf & "Error description: " _
            & Err.Description, vbCritical, "Larry Roof's Note Manager"
  End If

' Reset this error.
  Err.Clear

End Sub
```

The SaveSettings Procedure

The purpose of this procedure is to save the user configurations so that they may be reapplied the next time Note Manager is run. As was stated in the discussion of the **GetSettings** procedure, the VBCE Toolkit doesn't provide any method for reading and writing to the System Registry or initialization files. **SaveSettings** fills this void by writing configurations to a standard sequential file.

The procedure begins by opening the file **Note Manager.ini**. This file is stored in the application directory:

```
Private Sub SaveSettings()

  Const lrFileOutput = 2
  Dim strOutput
  Dim strSettingsFile

' Setup the error handler.
  On Error Resume Next

' This procedure provides a crude INI file functionality
' by reading in settings.
  strSettingsFile = App.Path & "\Note Manager.ini"

' Open the selected file.
  On Error Resume Next
  ceFile.Open strSettingsFile, lrFileOutput

  If Err Then
    MsgBox Err.Number & " - " & Err.Description
    Err.Clear
    Exit Sub

  End If
```

Next a string is constructed containing all of the user configuration settings:

```
' Build the string to write to the file.
' First the mblnControlledDelete setting.
  strOutput = "Controlled Delete="

  If mblnControlledDelete Then
    strOutput = strOutput & "True"

  Else
    strOutput = strOutput & "False"

  End If

  strOutput = strOutput & vbCrLf

' Then the Font settings.
  strOutput = strOutput & "Font Name="
  strOutput = strOutput & txtNote.FontName & vbCrLf
  strOutput = strOutput & "Font Size="
  strOutput = strOutput & txtNote.FontSize & vbCrLf
  strOutput = strOutput & "Font Bold="
```

```
    If (txtNote.FontBold = True) Then
      strOutput = strOutput & "True"

    Else
      strOutput = strOutput & "False"

    End If

    strOutput = strOutput & vbCrLf

    strOutput = strOutput & "Font Italic="

    If (txtNote.FontItalic = True) Then
      strOutput = strOutput & "True"

    Else
      strOutput = strOutput & "False"

    End If

    strOutput = strOutput & vbCrLf
```

Finally the string is written out to the file using a single write:

```
  ' Write out the file.
    ceFile.LinePrint strOutput

    If Err <> 0 Then
      MsgBox Err.Number & " - " & Err.Description
      Err.Clear
      Exit Sub

    End If

  ' File has been saved so perform final cleanup.
    ceFile.Close

  End Sub
```

The TreeView Control Event Procedures

At the heart of the Note Manager application is the TreeView control. While much of the functionality that's provided by this part of the user interface is built into the control itself, it is supplemented with two key event procedures. The first, **AfterLabelEdit**, saves changes to folder and note titles as they are made. The second, **NodeClick**, handles the retrieval and display of note details.

The treNotes_AfterLabelEdit Procedure

While the ability to change folder and note titles is an inherit feature of the TreeView control, it is still necessary to save these changes to the underlying tables.

The `treNotes_AfterLabelEdit` procedure is fired after the user has completed any change to a title. This procedure begins by first confirming that an acceptable change has occurred:

```
Private Sub treNotes_AfterLabelEdit(ByVal NewString)

  Dim strThisFolderID
  Dim strThisNoteID

' Exit this routine if no change was made or
' If this is an empty string.

  If (treNotes.SelectedItem.Text = NewString) Then Exit Sub

  If (NewString = "") Then Exit Sub
```

Next a check is made to see if it was a folder or note title that was changed. This is determined by checking the **Key** property of the **SelectedItem** node of the TreeView control. Remember, if it's a folder node then the **Key** was loaded with either the word **Folder** – combined with the ID number for the record in which it is stored. If it's a note node it's stored as the ID of the parent followed by a dash followed by the ID of the note.

If it is a note, or at least **Not** a folder, then the record for the note is retrieved from the **nmNotes** table and updated:

```
' Update the name of the note.
  If (Mid(treNotes.SelectedItem.Key, 1, 6) <> "Folder") Then
    strThisNoteID = Right(treNotes.SelectedItem.Key, _
        Len(treNotes.SelectedItem.Key) - _
        InStr(1, treNotes.SelectedItem.Key, "-"))

    mrecRecord.Open "SELECT * FROM nmNotes WHERE NoteID = " & _
                    strThisNoteID, , adOpenKeyset, adLockOptimistic

    If Err Then HandleError

    mrecRecord.Fields("Title").Value = NewString
```

If it is a folder then its record is retrieved from the **nmFolders** table and updated:

```
' Update the name of the folder.
  Else
    strThisFolderID = Right(treNotes.SelectedItem.Key, _
      Len(treNotes.SelectedItem.Key) - _
      InStr(1, treNotes.SelectedItem.Key, "-") - 1)
    mrecRecord.Open "SELECT * FROM nmFolders WHERE FolderID = " & _
      strThisFolderID, , adOpenKeyset, adLockOptimistic

    If Err Then HandleError

    mrecRecord.Fields("FolderName").Value = NewString

  End If
```

Finally, the record is written to the table and the recordset is closed:

```
' Clean up the temporary recordset.
  mrecRecord.Update
  mrecRecord.Close

End Sub
```

The treNotes_NodeClick Procedure

It's in this procedure that the saving, retrieval and displaying of notes is performed.

The procedure begins by comparing the value of the **Index** argument, which tells which item in the TreeView control was tapped, against **mintPreviousIndex**, which tells the last item that was tapped. If they match then there is nothing to do so the procedure is exited. If they don't match then the new index is saved for future reference:

```
Private Sub treNotes_NodeClick(ByVal Index)

  Dim strThisNoteID

' Make sure that the user didn't just click on the same note again.
  If (mintPreviousIndex = Index) Then
    Exit Sub

  Else
    mintPreviousIndex = Index

  End If
```

Next a check is made to determine if there are unsaved changes from the current note to save before the new note or folder is displayed. The variable **mblnNoteIsDirty** is set in the **Change** event procedure for the text box **txtNote**. The **SaveNote** procedure was discussed earlier in this chapter:

```
' Make sure that any changes to the previous note were saved.
  If (mblnNoteIsDirty) Then
    SaveNote
  End If
```

The **Index** to the presently selected item in the TreeView control is saved for use later in this routine and a check is made to see what was tapped - a folder or a note. As was shown earlier, the **Key** value is used for this, which will begin with the word **Folder** – for a folder node:

```
' Store the index to this note so that it can
' be used to save the note later.
  mstrPreviousNote = treNotes.Nodes(Index).Key

' Check what was clicked, a folder or a note.
  If (Not mblnLoading) And _
     (Mid(treNotes.Nodes(Index).Key, 1, 6) <> "Folder") Then
```

A note was tapped so retrieve its record:

```
' Find the record for this note.
    strThisNoteID = Right(treNotes.Nodes(Index).Key, _
        Len(treNotes.Nodes(Index).Key) - _
        InStr(1, treNotes.Nodes(Index).Key, "-"))
    mrecRecord.Open "SELECT * FROM nmNotes WHERE NoteID = " & _
        strThisNoteID, , adOpenKeyset, adLockOptimistic

    If Err Then HandleError
```

Display the new note, reset the flag used to make changes (**mblnNoteIsDirty**), and set the focus to the note part of the interface to simplify user interaction:

```
    txtNote.Text = mrecRecord.Fields("Note")
    mblnNoteIsDirty = False
    txtNote.Locked = False
    txtNote.SetFocus
```

Finally close the recordset used to retrieve the note:

```
' Clean up the recordset.
    mrecRecord.Close
```

Folders are much easier to handle. The following code takes care of the situation where a folder was tapped. All that needs to occur is to clear the note, configure the text box control so that no text may be entered and reset the flag used to track changes to notes:

```
' The user clicked on a folder so clear the note display.
    Else
        txtNote.Text = ""
        txtNote.Locked = True
        mblnNoteIsDirty = False

    End If

End Sub
```

The txtNote Text Box Control Event Procedures

The event procedures that are used by the **txtNote** text box control are used to identify that changes have occurred to the contents of the control and to work around a text box navigation bug that the control suffers from.

The txtNote_Change Procedure

Every time that the user modifies the contents of a note, the **Change** event for the text box control is fired. In this event the **mblnNoteIsDirty** flag is set to record that there have been changes made to the note. This flag is used by other procedures within the Note Manager application to determine when a note needs to be saved:

```
Private Sub txtNote_Change()

' Set the flag used to track note changes.
  mblnNoteIsDirty = True

End Sub
```

The txtNote_KeyUp Procedure

This procedure is used to initiate a set of routines used to work around a bug that is present in the VBCE Toolkit text box control. See the discussion of this control in Chapter 5 for a detailed description of the code used to address this problem.

Implementing the Note Manager Menu

The Note Manager menu structure is comprised of five menus: Note, Folder, Edit, Options and Help. In this section we will walk through each one, examining the code used to provide functionality to all the menus.

The Note menu is divided into two parts. The first part contains items for adding and deleting notes. The second part offers more general items used for debugging and exiting the application. A brief discussion of each of these event procedures is provided in the following section.

The Add a Note Menu Item

This procedure handles the adding of notes to Note Manager. It begins by first verifying that the user has selected the folder in which the new note will reside. If the user hasn't selected a folder, they are informed of their error:

```
Private Sub mnuNoteAdd_Click()

  Dim lngSelectedFolderID
  Dim strNoteTitle

  On Error Resume Next

' A folder must be selected before adding a note.
  If (Mid(treNotes.SelectedItem.Key, 1, 6) <> "Folder") Then
    MsgBox "You must select a folder first before adding a new note.", _
           vbExclamation, "Error Adding Note"
    Exit Sub
```

If they have selected a folder, its ID is saved for future use:

```
  Else
    lngSelectedFolderID = CLng(Right(treNotes.SelectedItem.Key, _
        Len(treNotes.SelectedItem.Key) - _
        InStr(1, treNotes.SelectedItem.Key, "-") - 1))

  End If
```

Next the user is prompted to enter the title for the new note. Here I chose to use a simple **InputBox** function instead of an additional form, opting for the efficiencies that this approach offered. A check is made of the user's response. An empty response results in an exit from this procedure:

```
' Prompt for the title to the new note.
strNoteTitle = InputBox("Enter the title for the new note: ", _
              "Create Note", "")

If (Len(strNoteTitle) = 0) Then
  Exit Sub
End If
```

With the title for the note in hand we can create the new note. This is accomplished by using the ADO recordset's **AddNew** method, followed by the loading of the fields for the record and finally completed with the recordset **Update** method. Note the use of the **NextNoteID** function here that returns a unique Node ID to associate with this new note record. This routine is discussed later in this chapter:

```
' Create the note in the Notes table.
mrecRecord.Open "nmNotes", , adOpenKeyset, adLockOptimistic

mrecRecord.AddNew
mrecRecord.Fields("NoteID").Value = NextNoteID
mrecRecord.Fields("FolderID").Value = lngSelectedFolderID
mrecRecord.Fields("Title").Value = strNoteTitle

mrecRecord.Fields("Note").Value = ""
mrecRecord.Update
```

Now that the record has been added to the **nmNotes** table, it can be entered into the TreeView display:

```
' Add the note to the TreeView display.
mintNumberOfNotes = mintNumberOfNotes + 1
ReDim maobjNotes(mintNumberOfNotes)
Set maobjNotes(mintNumberOfNotes) = _
    treNotes.Nodes.Add(treNotes.SelectedItem.Index, 4, _
    mrecRecord.Fields("FolderID") & "-" & _
    mrecRecord.Fields("NoteID"), strNoteTitle, 3, 3)

If Err Then HandleError
```

Now it's time to perform a bit of user interface manipulation to make it easy for the user to work with Note Manager.

We start by making sure that the folder in which the new note was added in is expanded. This will allow the user to see the new note that they added without having to manually expand the folder:

```
' Make sure that the folder is expanded so
' that you can see the new note.
treNotes.SelectedItem.Expanded = True
```

Next the notes in the folder are resorted so that all of the notes, including the new one, are in alphabetical order:

```
' The Notes for this folder must be resorted when a
' new note is added to the TreeView control.
treNotes.SelectedItem.Sorted = True
```

Finally the new note is selected, again with the intention of simplifying the use of Note Manager. If we did not perform this step then every time that a user added a note they would then have to manually select the note before they could begin working with it:

```
' Select and setup the new note.
  treNotes.SelectedItem.Child.LastSibling.Selected = True
  mstrPreviousNote = treNotes.Nodes(treNotes.SelectedItem.Index).Key
  mintPreviousIndex = treNotes.SelectedItem.Index
```

The final parts of this procedure setup the **txtNote** text box and reset the flag used to track note changes:

```
  txtNote.Text = ""
  txtNote.Locked = False
  mblnNoteIsDirty = False
  txtNote.SetFocus
```

The procedures end with the closing of the recordset used to add the new record:

```
' Clean up the temporary recordset.
  mrecRecord.Close

End Sub
```

Providing a Unique Note ID – The NextNoteID Procedure

As was discussed in Chapter 7, the ADO CE doesn't support the automatic numbering feature found in Microsoft Access. Since I need a way to uniquely identify each record I wrote the **NextNoteID** function which creates new IDs as they are needed.

There is nothing tricky about this procedure. It simply makes use of another table, **nmManagement**, to store the last **NoteID** that was used.

When a request is made for a new ID, the last ID is retrieved from the table:

```
  Private Function NextNoteID()

    Dim recTemp

' Retrieve the Managment record.
  Set recTemp = CreateObject("adoce.recordset")
  recTemp.Open "SELECT * FROM nmManagement", , adOpenKeyset, adLockOptimistic
```

Then it's simply incremented by one and written back to the table:

```
' Increment the Note counter by 1 and write it to the database.
  recTemp.Fields("LastNoteID").Value = recTemp.Fields("LastNoteID") + 1
  recTemp.Update
```

Before being sent back to the user:

```
NextNoteID = recTemp.Fields("LastNoteID")
```

All that is left to do is to close the recordset used with this operation:

```
' Clean up the temporary recordset.
recTemp.Close
Set recTemp = Nothing

End Function
```

The Delete This Note Menu Item

The process of deleting a note begins by confirming that the user has selected the note that they wish to delete. If a note is not selected, the user is notified of their error and this procedure exits:

```
Private Sub mnuNoteDelete_Click()

   Dim strThisNoteID
   Dim intUsersResponse

' Setup error handler.
   On Error Resume Next

' A note must be selected before it can be deleted.
   If (Mid(treNotes.SelectedItem.Key, 1, 6) = "Folder") Then
      MsgBox "You must select the note you want to delete.", _
            vbExclamation, "Error Deleting Note"
      Exit Sub

   End If
```

Next a check is made of the delete confirmation configuration setting. If it's configured to prompt the user before deleteing we use the **MsgBox** function to confirm the user's intention. This configuration is set in the **mnuOptionsPrompt** event procedure:

```
' Confirm that the user wants to delete this note.
   If (mblnControlledDelete) Then
      intUsersResponse = MsgBox("Do you want to delete this note?", _
         vbQuestion + vbYesNo + vbDefaultButton1, "Delete This Note?")
      Select Case intUsersResponse

' Do nothing but continue.
         Case vbYes

' Exit the routine.
         Case vbNo
            Exit Sub

      End Select

   End If
```

The note is then deleted and removed from the TreeView control via the **Remove** method. Note the use of **SelectedItem**, which identifies which record to remove:

```
' Find the record for this note.
strThisNoteID = Right(treNotes.SelectedItem.Key, _
                  Len(treNotes.SelectedItem.Key) - _
                  InStr(1, treNotes.SelectedItem.Key, "-"))
mrecRecord.Open "DELETE FROM nmNotes WHERE NoteID = " & strThisNoteID

If Err Then HandleError

treNotes.Nodes.Remove treNotes.SelectedItem.Index

If Err Then HandleError
```

Finally a call is made to the **NodeClick** event of the TreeView control to update the user interface:

```
' Clean up the interface.
mblnNoteIsDirty = False
treNotes_NodeClick (treNotes.SelectedItem.Index)

End Sub
```

The Error Menu Item

The Error menu item is intended for development use only. It displays the number and description of the last runtime error that was encountered. Before releasing Note Manager to users, set the Visible property of the Error menu item to False:

```
Private Sub mnuNoteError_Click()

' This is a debug function that is hidden when the product is
' released.
MsgBox "Error #: " & Err.Number & " Error Description: " & Err.Description

End Sub
```

The Exit Menu Item

The Exit menu item **Click** event procedure is the same as the **Form_Unload** procedure. Normally you would only need this code in the **Unload** event, but I've encountered situations where the **Unload** procedure is not fired using the VBCE Toolkit:

```
Private Sub mnuNoteExit_Click()

' Make sure that any changes to the previous note were saved.
If (mblnNoteIsDirty) Then
  SaveNote
End If

' Save configuration settings.
SaveSettings

' Everything is cleaned up so exit.
```

```
      App.End

   End Sub
```

The Folder Menu

This menu contains two items: one for adding a new folder and the other for deleting an existing folder.

The Add a Folder Menu Item

This procedure handles the adding of folders to Note Manager. It begins by performing a bit of software slight of hand, making sure that a folder is selected so that later we will be able to select the new folder.

The selection of a folder from code differs depending upon whether a folder, a note, or nothing is currently selected.

Selecting a folder when nothing is selected is a bit tricky. The TreeView control will tell you that a folder is selected even when nothing is selected. You can get around this by forcing an error by trying to reference the selected value and then responding to the error accordingly:

```
   Private Sub mnuFolderAdd_Click()

      Dim strFolderName
      Dim blnErrorTrap

      On Error Resume Next

   ' We need to select a folder here so that
   ' the selection below will work correctly.
   ' The first part of this IF statement handles
   ' the situation when Note Manager has
   ' just started up and nothing has been selected.

      If (Mid(treNotes.SelectedItem.Key, 1, 6) = "Folder") Then
         blnErrorTrap = treNotes.SelectedItem.Selected

         If (Err.Number <> 0) Then
```

To select a folder when nothing is selected you must perform the following three actions:

```
            treNotes.Nodes(0).EnsureVisible = True
            treNotes.Nodes(0).Selected = True
            treNotes.SetFocus

         End If
```

Selecting a folder when either a folder or note is selected is simple. Simply reference the **Parent** of the selected item:

```
   ' Something is selected so select its folder.
      Else
         treNotes.SelectedItem.Parent.Selected = True

      End If
```

Now that a folder is selected we can prompt the user for the name of the new folder. Here again I chose to use the **InputBox** because of its efficiency:

```
' Prompt for the name to the new folder.
strFolderName = InputBox("Enter the name for the new folder: ", "Create Folder", "")

If (Len(strFolderName) = 0) Then
  Exit Sub
End If
```

A new folder is added to the recordset, its fields are filled and the record is written to the table using the **Update** method. Note the use of the **NextFolderID** function that provides a work around to the lack of autonumbering support in ADO CE. This procedure is discussed later in the chapter:

```
' Create the folder in the Folders table.
Err.Clear
mrecRecord.Open "nmFolders", , adOpenKeyset, adLockOptimistic
mrecRecord.AddNew
mrecRecord.Fields("FolderID").Value = NextFolderID
mrecRecord.Fields("FolderName").Value = strFolderName
mrecRecord.Update
```

The new folder is then added onto the TreeView display:

```
' Add the folder to the TreeView display.
mintNumberOfFolders = mintNumberOfFolders + 1
ReDim maobjFolders(mintNumberOfFolders)
Set maobjFolders(mintNumberOfFolders) = treNotes.Nodes.Add(, , _
        "Folder - " & mrecRecord.Fields("FolderID"), _
          mrecRecord.Fields("FolderName"), 1, 2)

  If Err Then HandleError
```

The new folder is selected for ease of user interaction:

```
' Select the new folder.
treNotes.SelectedItem.LastSibling.Selected = True
```

The recordset is no longer needed so it is closed:

```
' Clean up the temporary recordset.
mrecRecord.Close
```

And finally the folders are resorted to account for the new folder.

```
' The Folders have to be resorted when a Folder is added to the
' Treeview control.
treNotes.Sorted = True
```

We finish up this routine by calling the **NodeClick** event procedure of the TreeView control to update the user display:

```
' Set the appropriate display.
  treNotes_NodeClick (treNotes.SelectedItem.Index)

End Sub
```

Providing a Unique Folder ID – The NextFolderID Procedure

As I mentioned earlier in this chapter, the ADO CE doesn't support the automatic numbering feature found in Microsoft Access. Since I need a way to uniquely identify each record, I wrote the **NextFolderID** function - which creates new IDs as they're needed.

This procedure, like the **NextNoteID** procedure, simply makes use of another table, **nmManagement**, to store the last **FolderID** that was used.

When a request is made for a new ID, the last ID is retrieved from the table:

```
Private Function NextFolderID()

  Dim recTemp

' Retrieve the Management record.
  Set recTemp = CreateObject("adoce.recordset")
  recTemp.Open "SELECT * FROM nmManagement", , adOpenKeyset, _
    adLockOptimistic

' There should be a single record in the Management file.
' If there is not a record create one here and initialize
' the values for both the Folder and Note counters.
  If (recTemp.EOF) And (recTemp.bof) Then
    recTemp.AddNew
    recTemp.Fields("LastFolderID").Value = 0
    recTemp.Fields("LastNoteID").Value = 0
    recTemp.Update

  End If
```

Then it is simply incremented by one, written back to the table and the new value returned:

```
' Increment the Folder counter by 1 and write it to the database.
  recTemp.Fields("LastFolderID").Value = _
            recTemp.Fields("LastFolderID") + 1
  recTemp.Update
  NextFolderID = recTemp.Fields("LastFolderID")
```

All that is left to do is to close the recordset used with this operation:

```
' Clean up the temporary recordset.
  recTemp.Close
  Set recTemp = Nothing

End Function
```

The Delete This Folder Menu Item

Deletion of a folder begins by checking to see if the user has selected the folder to delete. If a folder is not selected then a message is displayed and the procedure is exited:

```
Private Sub mnuFolderDelete_Click()

  Dim strThisFolderID
  Dim strThisNoteID
  Dim intUsersResponse
  Dim strNoteKey
' Setup error handler.
  On Error Resume Next

' A folder must be selected before it can be deleted.
  If (Mid(treNotes.SelectedItem.Key, 1, 6) <> "Folder") Then
    MsgBox "You must select the folder you want to delete.", _
    vbExclamation, "Error Deleting Folder"
    Exit Sub

  End If
```

Depending upon the user configuration setting, the user may be prompted to confirm the deletion of the folder:

```
' Confirm that the user wants to delete this folder
' with all of its notes.
  If (mblnControlledDelete) Then
    intUsersResponse = MsgBox("Do you want to delete this folder " _
        & "with all of its messages?", vbQuestion + _
        vbYesNo + vbDefaultButton1, "Delete This Folder?")

    Select Case intUsersResponse

' Do nothing but continue.
      Case vbYes

' Exit the routine.
      Case vbNo
        Exit Sub

    End Select

  End If
```

At this point we are ready to delete the folder. First we need to delete all of the notes that are held by this folder. Note the use of **Child** and **FirstSibling** properties to work through the TreeView hierarchy identifying all of the notes associated with this folder:

```
' Loop through and delete all of the childer (notes) for this folder.
  Do While Err.Number = 0
    strNoteKey = treNotes.Nodes(treNotes.SelectedItem.Index).Child.FirstSibling.Key
```

```
        strThisNoteID = Right(strNoteKey, Len(strNoteKey) - InStr(1,strNoteKey, "-"))

    If Err Then

      Select Case Err.Number

        Case 424 ' No more children to delete.
          Err.Clear
          Exit Do

        Case Else
          HandleError

      End Select

    End If
```

This note is first deleted from the underlying table and then from the TreeView control. These two steps will be performed for each note in the selected folder:

```
' Delete the note from the table and from the TreeView control.
  mrecRecord.Open "DELETE FROM nmNotes WHERE NoteID = " & strThisNoteID

    If Err Then HandleError

    treNotes.Nodes.Remove _
          treNotes.Nodes(treNotes.SelectedItem.Index).Child.FirstSibling.Index

    If Err Then HandleError

  Loop
```

At this point the notes contained by this folder have been deleted. Now we can delete the folder itself. We start by removing it from the **nmFolders** table followed by taking it out of the TreeView control:

```
' The children have been deleted so remove the folder.
  strThisFolderID = Right(treNotes.SelectedItem.Key, _
          Len(treNotes.SelectedItem.Key) - _
          InStr(1, treNotes.SelectedItem.Key, "-"))

  mrecRecord.Open "DELETE FROM nmFolders WHERE FolderID = " & strThisFolderID

  If Err Then HandleError

  treNotes.Nodes.Remove treNotes.SelectedItem.Index

  If Err Then HandleError

End Sub
```

The Edit Menu

This menu provides simple cut, copy and paste functionality for the Note Manager application. It's built upon the CE Clipboard.

The Cut Menu Item

This event procedure simply takes any text that is selected in the active note and copies it to the Clipboard using the **SetText** method. The **SelText** property of the text box control is used to identify the text that the user has selected.

Note that since this is a 'Cut' operation, the selected text is removed (by setting it to an empty string):

```
Private Sub mnuEditCut_Click()

' Send a copy of the selected text to the Clipboard and
' delete the text from the note.
  If (txtNote.SelText <> "") Then
    Clipboard.SetText txtNote.SelText
    txtNote.SelText = ""

  End If

End Sub
```

The Copy Menu Item

This procedure is nearly identical to the **mnuEditCut_Click** procedure with the exception that the original contents of the text box control are not altered:

```
Private Sub mnuEditCopy_Click()

' Send a copy of the selected text to the Clipboard.
  If (txtNote.SelText <> "") Then
    Clipboard.SetText txtNote.SelText
  End If

End Sub
```

The Paste Menu Item

The corresponding procedure to the Cut and Copy procedures is the Paste procedure. In this procedure the contents of the Clipboard are copied to the active note using the **GetText** method of the Clipboard:

```
Private Sub mnuEditPaste_Click()

' Paste whatever is on the Clipboard into the current note.
  txtNote.SelText = Clipboard.GetText

End Sub
```

The Options Menu

This menu provides some minimal user configuration capabilities to the Note Manager application. It allows the user to set the size of the font used to display a note and to specify whether or not they should be prompted when deleting a folder or note.

The Set Font Size For Note... Menu Item

I always try to give the user the ability to adjust the font size of my CE applications. Given the size of the H/PC screen and how well the screen can be viewed in a variety of situations I think that this is a necessary feature.

This procedure is built around the Common Dialog control. It begins by configuring the control:

```
Private Sub mnuOptionsFont_Click()

' Define font constants
  Const cdlCFScreenFonts = &H1
  Const cdlCFLimitSize = &H2000
  Const cdlCFForceFontExist = &H10000

' Set the minimum and maximum font sizes.
  ceCommonDialog.Max = 30
  ceCommonDialog.Min = 8
```

Next it loads the current values used by the **txtNote** text box control:

```
' Set the dialog from the control.
  ceCommonDialog.FontBold = txtNote.FontBold
  ceCommonDialog.FontItalic = txtNote.FontItalic
  ceCommonDialog.FontName = txtNote.FontName
  ceCommonDialog.FontSize = txtNote.FontSize
```

Some software manipulation must then be performed to work around the habit of the Common Dialog control of setting fonts a half size too small:

```
' Handle bug where Common Dialog returns font a half less than what
' the user selected.
  If ceCommonDialog.FontSize <> txtNote.FontSize Then
    ceCommonDialog.FontSize = ceCommonDialog.FontSize + 1
  End If
```

Select what features of the Font dialog to use:

```
' Define what the font dialog should show. In this case we only want
' the Bold and Italic options displayed.
  ceCommonDialog.Flags = cdlCFForceFontExist Or cdlCFLimitSize Or _
    cdlCFScreenFonts
```

And finally display the dialog using the **ShowFont** method. When this dialog returns, it will contain the font configuration selected by the user:

```
' Display the dialog.
  ceCommonDialog.ShowFont
```

Finally, retrieve the new configurations from the Common Dialog control and assign them to the **txtNote** text box control:

```
' Set the control from the dialog.
  txtNote.FontBold = ceCommonDialog.FontBold
  txtNote.FontItalic = ceCommonDialog.FontItalic
  txtNote.FontName = ceCommonDialog.FontName
  txtNote.FontSize = ceCommonDialog.FontSize

End Sub
```

The Prompt Before Deleting Menu Item

I like to give the user the capability to configure how much prompting they must deal with in performing the key functions that an application offers. In the case of the Note Manager application, both the deleting of a folder and a note would normally merit a message box to confirm the user's intention. What I've provided them with is the capability to "turn off" this warning.

The procedure that provides this functionality is simple. It begins by toggling the **mnuOptionsPrompt Checked** property. The use of the **Not** keyword here says, "If this item is checked, uncheck it. If it is unchecked, check it."

```
Private Sub mnuOptionsPrompt_Click()

' Toggle the Controlled Delete option.
  mnuOptionsPrompt.Checked = Not mnuOptionsPrompt.Checked
```

The new value of the **Checked** property is then saved to a procedure level variable. This variable is evaluated when the user selects to delete a folder or a note:

```
    mblnControlledDelete = mnuOptionsPrompt.Checked

End Sub
```

The Help Menu

The Help menu provides access to the Note Manager help system. It uses the Common Dialog control with some minimal coding to implement this functionality. A brief discussion of each of the items found in the Help menu follows:

The Using Note Manager Menu Item

Only two statements are required to display the Using Note Manager help file. The first statement sets the **HelpFile** property of the Common Dialog control to the name of the file to display. The second statement uses the Common Dialog control's **ShowHelp** method to display the desired help file:

```
Private Sub mnuHelpUsing_Click()

' Display the contents, or using help.
  ceCommonDialog.HelpFile = "Note Manager.htc"
  ceCommonDialog.ShowHelp

End Sub
```

The `.htc` file itself is easy to create using a simple text editor such as Notepad or my EasyEdit. I won't bother to explain what is going on in this HTML as it should be second nature to you by now. Just remember to save the help files in the handheld's `\Windows` directory:

If you don't want to build these files yourself then simply copy those from the source code for this chapter into the handhelds `\Windows` directory. Whichever method you chose to implement the help files, you'll also need a copy of the **Note Manager.bmp** file, which can be found in the source code.

```
<HTML>
<BODY>
<TABLE>
<TR>
<TD><IMG SRC="Note Manager.bmp" ></TD>
<TD><H2>Note Manager Help</H2></TD>
</TR>
<TR>
<TD></TD>
<TD><FONT SIZE=+2>
<A HREF="FILE:Note Manager Quick Start.htp">A quick start to using
  Note Manager</A>
</Font></TD>
</TR>
<TR>
<TD></TD>
<TD><FONT SIZE=+2>
<A HREF="FILE:Note Manager About.htp">About Note Manager</A>
</FONT></TD>
</TR>
<TR>
<TD></TD>
<TD><FONT SIZE=+2>
<A HREF="FILE:Note Manager Note Menu.htp">Note menu commands</A>
</FONT></TD>
</TR>
<TR>
<TD></TD>
<TD><FONT SIZE=+2>
<A HREF="FILE:Note Manager Folder Menu.htp">Folder menu
   commands</A><BR>
</FONT></TD>
</TR>
<TR>
<TD></Tcd>
<TD><FONT SIZE=+2>
<A HREF="FILE:Note Manager Edit Menu.htp">Edit menu commands</A><BR>
</FONT></TD>
</TR>
<TR>
<TD></TD>
<TD><FONT SIZE=+2>
<A HREF="FILE:Note Manager Options Menu.htp">Options menu
   commands</A><BR>
</FONT></TD>
</TR>
<TABLE>
</BODY>
</HTML>
```

This contents help file requires the presence of six other files. Create this in the same way as the `.htc` file.

The `Note Manager Note Menu.htp` file:

```
<HTML>
<BODY>
<TABLE>
<TR>
<TD WIDTH=70>
<IMG SRC="Note Manager.bmp">
</TD>
<TD><H2>Note Menu</H2></TD>
</TR>
<TR><FONT SIZE=+1>
<TD><B>Add a note</B></TD>
</FONT></TD>
<TD><FONT SIZE=+1>
Creates a new note.
</FONT></TD>
</TR>
<TR><FONT SIZE=+1>
<TD><B>Delete this note</B></TD>
</FONT></TD>
<TD><FONT SIZE=+1>
Deletes the selected note.
</FONT></TD>
</TR>
<TR><FONT SIZE=+1>
<TD><B>Exit</b></TD>
</FONT></TD>
<TD><FONT SIZE=+1>
Exits the Note Manager application.
</FONT></TD>
</TR>
</TABLE>
</BODY>
</HTML>
```

The `Note Manager Folder Menu.htp` file:

```
<HTML>
<BODY>
<TABLE>
<TR>
<TD WIDTH=70>
<IMG SRC="Note Manager.bmp">
</TD>
<TD><H2>Folder Menu</H2></TD>
</TR>
<TR><FONT SIZE=+1>
<TD><B>Add a folder</B></Td>
</FONT></TD>
```

```
<TD><FONT SIZE=+1>
Creates a new folder.
</FONT></TD>
</TR>
<TR><FONT SIZE=+1>
<TD><B>Delete this folder</B></TD>
</FONT></TD>
<TD><FONT SIZE=+1>
Deletes the selected folder.
</FONT></TD>
</TR>
</TABLE>
</BODY>
</HTML>
```

The **Note Manager Edit Menu.htp** file:

```
<HTML>
<BODY>
<TABLE>
<TR>
<TD WIDTH=70>
<IMG SRC="Note Manager.bmp">
</TD>
<TD><H2>Edit Menu</H2></TD>
</TR>
<TR><FONT SIZE=+1>
<TD><B>Cut</B></TD>
</FONT></TD>
<TD><FONT SIZE=+1>
Removes the selected text and places it on the clipboard.
</FONT></TD>
</TR>
<TR><FONT SIZE=+1>
<TD><B>Copy</B></TD>
</FONT></TD>
<TD><FONT SIZE=+1>
Copies the selected text to the clipboard.
</FONT></TD>
</TR>
<TR><FONT SIZE=+1>
<TD><B>Paste</B></TD>
</FONT></TD>
<TD><FONT SIZE=+1>
Pastes the contents of the clipboard into the current file.
</FONT></TD>
</TR>
</TABLE>
</BODY>
</HTML>
```

The **Note Manager Options Menu.htp** file:

```
<HTML>
<BODY>
<TABLE>
<TR>
<TD WIDTH=70>
<IMG SRC="Note Manager.bmp">
</TD>
<TD><H2>Options Menu</H2></TD>
</TR>
<TR><FONT SIZE=+1>
<TD><B>Set font size for this note</B></TD>
</FONT></TD>
<TD><FONT SIZE=+1>
Adjusts the size of the font being used.
</FONT></TD>
</TR>
<TR><FONT SIZE=+1>
<TD><B>Prompt before deletes</B></TD>
</FONT></TD>
<TD><FONT SIZE=+1>
Prompts you to confirm before deleting a folder or note.
</FONT></TD>
</TR>
</TABLE>
</BODY>
</HTML>
```

The Quick Start For Note Manager Menu Item

The code used to display the Quick Start For Note Manager help file is nearly identical to that used shown above. The only difference is the name of the help file that will be displayed:

```
Private Sub mnuHelpQuickStart_Click()

' Display the Quick Start help.
  ceCommonDialog.HelpFile = "Note Manager Quick Start.htp"
  ceCommonDialog.ShowHelp

End Sub
```

The **Note Manager Quick Start.htp** file:

```
<HTML>
<BODY>
<TABLE>
<TR>
<TD WIDTH=70>
<IMG SRC="Note Manager.bmp">
</TD>
<TD><H2>Quick Start</H2></TD>
</TR>
<TR><FONT SIZE=+1>
<TD></TD>
</FONT></TD>
```

```
<TD><FONT SIZE=+1>
The following set of instructions provide a brief introduction in
   the use of Note Manager.
</FONT></TD>
</TR>
<TR><FONT SIZE=+1>
<TD><B>Adding Folders</B></TD>
</FONT></TD>
<TD><FONT SIZE=+1>
All of the notes that you create within the Note Manager application
   are stored in folders. Folders provide a simple way to organize
   your notes. To create a folder select <I>Add a folder</I> from
   the <I>Folder</I> menu. You will be prompted to enter the title
   for your new folder.
</FONT></TD>
</TR>
<TR><FONT SIZE=+1>
<TD><B>Renaming a Folder</B></TD>
</FONT></TD>
<TD><FONT SIZE=+1>
Don't get too concerned on what you name your folders as you can
   easily change the name of any folder. To change the name of a
   folder first tap on the folder to select it, pause for a second
   and then tap the folder again. The folder name will switch in
   edit mode. Make the changes that you want and hit the [ENTER]
   key to save the new name.
</FONT></TD>
</TR>
<TR><FONT SIZE=+1>
<TD><B>Deleting a Folder</B></TD>
</FONT></TD>
<TD><FONT SIZE=+1>
When you delete a folder you will also be deleting all notes that
   are stored within that folder. To delete a folder first tap on
   the folder and then select <I>Delete This folder</I> from the
   <I>Folder</I> menu. You may be prompted to confirm the deletion
   depending upon how you have set the <I>Prompt before
   deleting</I> option which can be found under the <I>Options</I>
   menu.
</FONT></TD>
</TR>
<TR><FONT SIZE=+1>
<TD><B>Adding Notes</B></TD>
</FONT></TD>
<TD><FONT SIZE=+1>
To add a note simply tap the folder in which you wish to add the
   note and then select <I>Add a note</I> from the <I>Note</I>
   menu. You will be prompted to enter the title for your new note.
</FONT></TD>
</TR>
<TR><FONT SIZE=+1>
<TD><B>Renaming a Note</B></TD>
</FONT></TD>
<TD><FONT SIZE=+1>
You can easily rename, or change the title to a note. First tap on
   the note title to select it, pause for a second and then tap on
   the note title again. The note title will switch into edit mode.
```

```
    Make the changes that you want and hit the [ENTER] key to save
    the new name.
</FONT></TD>
</TR>
<TR><FONT SIZE=+1>
<TD><B>Writing the Note</B></TD>
</FONT></TD>
<TD><FONT SIZE=+1>
To create or modify the contents of a note first tap on the title
    to the note, then tap in the note panel that comprises the right
    part of Note Manager's form. You can then add or modify the
    text.
</FONT></TD>
</TR>
<TR><FONT SIZE=+1>
<TD><B>Viewing a Note</B></TD>
</FONT></TD>
<TD><FONT SIZE=+1>
To view a note tap on the title to the note. The contents of that
    note will be displayed in the note panel on the right of Note
    Manager's form.
</FONT></TD>
</TR>
<TR><FONT SIZE=+1>
<TD><B>Deleting a Note</B></TD>
</FONT></TD>
<TD><FONT SIZE=+1>
To delete a note first tap on the note title and then select
    <I>Delete this note</I> from the <I>Note</I> menu. You may be
    prompted to confirm the deletion depending upon how you have
    set the <I>Prompt before deletes</I> option which can be found
    under the <I>Options</I> menu.
</FONT></TD>
</TR>
<TR><FONT SIZE=+1>
<TD><B>Cut, Copy and Paste Note Text</B></TD>
</FONT></TD>
<TD><FONT SIZE=+1>
Note Manager provides the standard set of text manipulation tools
    including Cut, Copy and Paste. These functions can be found
    under the <I>Edit</I> menu.
</FONT></TD>
</TR>
<TR><FONT SIZE=+1>
<TD><B>Changing the Note's Display Font</B></TD>
</FONT></TD>
<TD><FONT SIZE=+1>
You can change the font of the note display to suit your needs. You
    do this by selecting <I>Set Font Size For Note...</I> from the
    <I>Options</I> menu.
</FONT></TD>
</TR>
</TABLE>
</BODY>
</HTML>
```

The About Note Manager Menu Item

As with the previous procedure, the code used to display the <u>A</u>bout Note Manager help file only differs from the previous two examples in the name of the help file that it will display:

```
Private Sub mnuHelpAbout_Click()

' Display the About help.
  ceCommonDialog.HelpFile = "Note Manager About.htp"
  ceCommonDialog.ShowHelp

End Sub
```

Finally the **Note Manager About.htp** file:

```
<HTML>
<BODY>
<TABLE>
<TR>
<TD><IMG SRC="Note Manager.bmp" ></TD>
<TD><H2>About Note Manager</H2></TD>
</TR>
<TR>
<TD></TD>
<TD><FONT SIZE=+2>
Larry Roof's Note Manager version 1.0
</FONT></TD>
</TR>
<TR>
<TD></TD>
<TD><FONT SIZE=+2>
Copyright &copy; 1998 Larry Roof<BR>
</FONT></TD>
</TR>
<TR>
<TD></TD>
<TD><FONT SIZE=+2>
All rights reserved.
</FONT></TD>
</TR>
</TABLE>
</BODY>
</HTML>
```

That wraps up the discussion on the code behind Note Manager. As you saw adding the ADO CE to your applications is easy and requires minimal code. The functionality it provides though can greatly enhance your applications.

Step 6 - Testing in the CE Emulator

Set the Run on <u>T</u>arget project property to Emulator and run your project. Try creating a few folders and notes to confirm the functionality in this environment.

You'll need to use the Control Manager to install the ImageList, TreeView, File, Utility and Common Dialog controls onto both the emulator and your H/PC before running this test. See Chapter 4 for further details on using this utility. Also, you will need to ensure that the ADO components are installed on the emulator. This is an optional part of the setup for ADO CE.

You will need to copy the three bitmaps that the Note Manager application uses over to the emulator. Place them in the same folder as used by Note Manager runtime. The files that are needed are `closed folder.bmp`, `note.bmp` and `open folder.bmp`. These files are the images used in the TreeView display. The empfile utility can be used to copy the files to the emulator.

You will also need to copy the Note Manager help files to the `\Windows` directory on the emulator for the help system to work.

Step 7 - Testing on a Handheld Computer

Set the Run on Target project property to Remote Device and run your project. As you did in the emulator test out the functionality of the Note Manager application. Make sure to test all of the functionality provided by Note Manager including add, modifying and deleting folders and notes. You can use the instructions given at the beginning of this chapter on using Note Manager for assistance.

Don't forget to copy the controls and files listed in Step 7 to the H/PC. You can use the Mobile Devices application to perform the copy.

Step 8 - Creating an Installation Program

Use the Application Install Wizard to generate an installation program for Note Manager. Make sure to include both the help files and the three bitmaps used by the TreeView display. If you need help with this Wizard, refer to Chapter 2 - where a detailed explanation of the process is provided.

Step 9 - Test the Installation Program

As with previous examples, it's important that you test your installation program. It should install without error and allow you to completely remove the program.

Note Manager – The Final Word

Just because we're at the end of the chapter, it doesn't mean that Note Manager and the techniques presented as part of its construction are finished, or final. My purpose in presenting case studies is to provide you with a starting point, the ideas and skills from which you can build your own applications. So before we exit this chapter let's take a quick look at how you can build upon Note Manager, either by constructing your own enhanced version of Note Manger or through the reuse of techniques that Note Manager demonstrated.

Enhancing Note Manager

Note Manager is by no means feature exhausted. In fact, it's just the opposite. I purposefully limited its features to demonstrate how useful a Windows CE application could be even in a very simple implementation. So what might you consider adding to Note Manager? The following is just a few ideas that I came up with:

- A filtering mechanism that would allow you to restrict which records are displayed.
- Allow notes to be copied between folders.
- Be able associate alarms, or reminders with notes.
- Provide support for importing and exporting notes to and from files.
- Display the date that each note was created and last updated.
- Create a desktop version of Note Manager for accessing and modifying notes. Notes would need to be synchronized between the desktop computer and the handheld computer.

Reusing Note Manager Techniques

While Note Manager doesn't contain a very large sampling of techniques it does include some examples of general-purpose features or skills that you can readily incorporate into your own applications.

Table naming criteria – The name of the tables used by Note Manager all began with the letters **nm**, for Note Manager. The use of a prefix with the table's name cuts down on the possibility of creating tables that have been created by a different application with a different data structure.

Auto-numbering – Those of you that have grown dependent upon the auto-number feature found in Microsoft Access tables will be disappointed to find out that the ADO CE doesn't provide this functionality. I get around this limitation in Note Manager by implementing a table that contains a single record that holds the last-used numbers for each of the auto-numbered fields I wish to include. Any time I add a new record I simply increment the appropriate auto-counter field.

Database creation – Any application that is built upon a database must deal with the 'startup' situation where the database is either not present or empty. Note Manager addresses this problem by creating the necessary table the first time it's run. This removes the necessity of shipping and installing an empty database with your application.

Summary

Hopefully what you came away with from this chapter is that VBCE can be used to create useful, full-feature Windows CE applications and how a simple application, like Note Manager, can often be more useful than a far more feature-filled application, like Pocket Outlook.

The Note Manager application demonstrates a key trait that I look for in a Windows CE application. A trait that I refer to as **Clean**. This is the term that I use for applications that are easy to use and just 'feel' right. Clean is a goal that you should always reach for when developing applications for a handheld computer. Handheld computers and the software that runs on them should make the user's life easier, not more complicated.

So remember, when developing Windows CE applications, keep it clean.

The Examples

Throughout this book, you've been asked to look at various sample files and installation programs so that you can examine the sample applications yourself. However, you first need to download these samples.

Getting the Samples and Examples

The compiled demonstration applications setups and the sample code used in the book is all available from the Wrox web site at:

`http://www.wrox.com/`

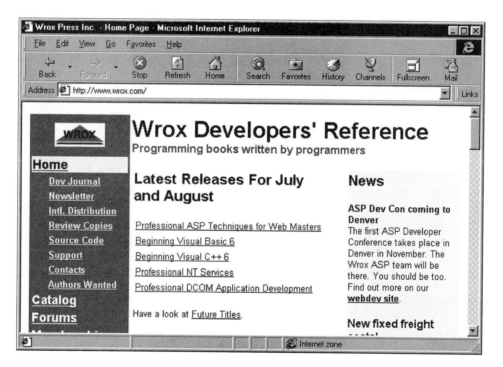

From the Wrox home page, you'll need to navigate to the book catalog for this book. Click on the hyperlink <u>Catalog</u> in the red navigation bar on the left:

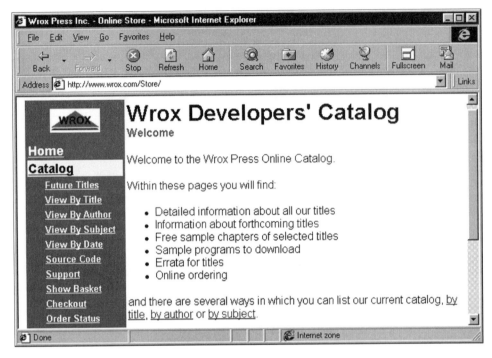

From the catalog's front page you should find the entry for this book. Clicking the <u>by title</u> link will get you to an alphabetical listing of all the Wrox books available. You should then select the hyperlink for this book, which will give you some information about the book.

In the upper right area of the web page is a yellow box with links to various topics relevant to the book. You should select the <u>source code</u> link. This will take you to a page where all the resources for this book's sample files may be downloaded:

> Add to <u>shopping basket</u>.
> Join in <u>discussion forum</u>.
> Read <u>reviews</u> and post your own.
> Download the <u>source code</u>.
> View the <u>errata sheets</u>.
> View the <u>sample chapter</u>.

There are many individual downloads available. Working sample programs that are ready to be installed on your H/PC have two download files, one each for Hitachi SH3 machines and those using the MIPS processors. These files are PKZIP compressed and contain a setup program for the examples. You should select a link to download the particular example appropriate to your H/PC.

Unsure of what processor your H/PC has? To find out, tap the Start button on the task bar and then select the Settings, Control Panel option. From the control panel open the system icon. This has two tabs of information. The General tab has two frames of text. The right-hand frame is entitled System. In this frame is a label, Processor Type:, which tells you what sort of H/PC you are using.

Extracting the Setup

Having downloaded the compressed example setup files, you need to extract them to an empty directory on your hard disk. The easiest way is with one of the popular Windows ZIP file utilities such as ZIPBack® from **www.stonebroom.com** or WinZip® from **www.winzip.com**. If you're using the PKUNZIP command line utility, be sure to use the **-d** option because the files in the archive are stored in a directory structure.

Installing the Example Files

Once you have downloaded and extracted the sample setup, you need to run it. Either double-click its icon in the Explorer window, or use the Windows Start button and select Run... entering the full path to the installation file **Setup.exe** program. If you extracted the sample to the folder **C:\Temp\CEexample** then the setup program will be found at **C:\Temp\CEexample\CD1\Setup.exe**.

> If you look at the files which get produced by the installation wizard and the files that are in the example archive, you'll notice one exception. In the downloads, we have removed the MSVBM50.DLL file from the CD1 folder. Since you're expected to have this file in your Windows System32 folder already present, it seemed a bit unfriendly to give you a 1.3MB DLL that you already have!
>
> However, the version of this file may not be the exact same as the one you already have, depending on which service pack you have installed. If the Setup.exe doesn't work, you will need to get the correct DLL that it was created for and place it in the same folder as the Setup.exe. In this case, the file will be available from the download web page. You will also need this file if you intend giving the demonstration to someone who doesn't have this file on their system.

To complete the setup just follow the on-screen instructions.

Using the Sample Code

Apart from the various applications setups available for download, the most important item available is the completed source code samples. You can, of course, go through the book page by page and recreate the code yourself; but after all, who wants to type everything? When you download the samples item from the book's web page at Wrox, you'll have a single executable installation program called **1622VBCE.exe**.

When you run the installation you will have one choice to make, where should the files be installed? By default this will be **C:\Wrox VB for CE**:

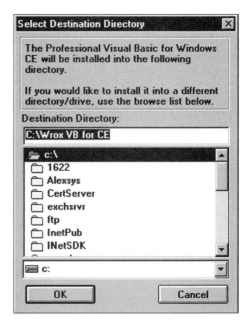

If you decide to place the files elsewhere then you'll have to remember to modify the Local Path property for each of the projects before you try and build them. The local path property name is stored in each of the project files (**.VBP**) themselves.

If you install to a directory other than the default and do not modify the Local Path property to match your location you will receive an error when you attempt to Run the program from the environment or attempt to Build the **.PVB** file

The installation program will place all the source code files onto your PC in a folder structure below the folder you selected. Under this folder will be a sub folder for each chapter where there is code available, basically every chapter except the first plus the two case studies:

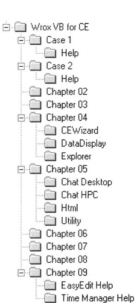

Generally, all the sample project files will be in their respective chapter folders. In chapters 4 and 5, the individual sample apps have their own folders - plus any help files can be found in a separate **\Help** folder.

Shortcuts to Projects

In addition to making the folder structure on your hard disk, the setup program will create shortcuts to each of the project files. From the Windows Start button select Programs and then Wrox VB for CE. From here you can select any of the project samples installed.

> *To keep things tidy, you may find it beneficial to unzip any examples you may have downloaded into the structure created by the sample setup.*

Uninstalling the Samples

When the time comes that you want to clean up your Windows start menus and you no longer feel the need to have these samples, there will be an uninstall utility placed in the folder where you specified the installation to take place. It's called **Unwise.exe**.

Copying Files to the Emulator

Many of the examples in the book use files (such as bitmap files to be used with an image list control) that are expected to be found in the same folder as the running program, or, in the case of help files, the **\Windows** folder of the emulator. Copying those files is not as simple as it may sound. You cannot drag and drop to the Mobile Devices folder like you can with your physical device. Instead you have to use the command line utility, **EMPFILE.EXE**.

This program is likely to be found at `C:\Program files\Windows CE Platform SDK\emil\hpc\windows\empfile.exe`. If that seems a lot to type from your command prompt there is a convenient shortcut to this from the Start menu. The easiest way to copy many files to the emulation environment is to copy the files to an appropriate structure under the `....\emul\hpc` folder and use the utility with its **Synchronize** option:

```
Empfile.exe -s
```

This command takes quite a while to complete but it synchronizes the entire directory structure from the disk with what the emulator represents. If you're just copying a single file from your hard disk to the emulation object store you would use the **-c** option. For example:

```
empfile.exe -c "C:\Temp\coolsnd.wav" "wce:windows\coolsnd.wav"
```

You can get more help on these commands with the **/?** option.

The Bugs

In an ideal world, all software would work as it should, and it would be documented perfectly. In reality, of course, this is not the case - and we have to contend with **bugs**. The VBCE Toolkit has its fair share of these, so in this appendix I will discuss a few of the more apparent bugs. There are actually quite a large number of small problems, and I'll only be able to scratch the surface. If you want to get a comprehensive list then you should point your browser to the Microsoft Knowledge base or Newsgroups dedicated to Visual Basic development for CE - such as **microsoft.public.vb.vbce** on the **msnews.micorsoft.com** Internet news server.

Bugs and Solutions

This appendix is not the Oracle of knowledge for all VBCE problems. However, I do propose to take you through a couple of the more annoying bugs found in the Toolkit. The bugs covered here are:

- ▲ The Left function failure
- ▲ The text box cursor keys failure
- ▲ The VBCE Utility control loading failure
- ▲ Lost Events in Framed Controls
- ▲ The WinSock control problems

The Left Function Failure

Throughout this book I have done quite a lot of string parsing. Something that you may have noticed is that I tend to use the **Mid** function for extracting text from the beginning of a string. You may be wondering why I don't just use the **Left** function, which achieves the same result while being easier to read. The reason is that it doesn't work in a form!

When the runtime interpreter for your **PVB** files comes across the **Left** function in form code, it mistakenly identifies it with the **Left** property of the form object. For example, look at the following code:

```
strMyData = Left(strYourData,4)
```

This line gives an error when found in a form module reporting that the Object is not a collection. The **Object** in this case is in fact the **Left** property of the form, which definitely isn't a collection. So, we have to use an alternate mechanism to get characters from the left-hand part of a string. The code to use is the **Mid** function. The code snippet above can be rewritten as:

```
strMyData = Mid(strYourData, 1, 4)
```

This code is not so clean to read, of course: you would rarely expect to see **1** hard coded as the start position when getting the characters from the middle of a string. But right now, that's what we need to do to get around this bug.

You can use **Left** in a standard code module, but since you may not always want to write a routine and have it in your single allowed module you had better get used to using **Mid**, at least until the Toolkit gets a fix!

The Text Box Cursor Keys Failure

This has to be one of the most annoying of the bugs of the toolkit. A text box has to be one of the most widely used methods of gathering input from a user. For users of an H/PC machine you can expect quite a high rate of keyboard typos and so when someone tries to move the caret back a few places to correct some typing error they are going to be really annoyed that the cursor keys don't work. They will be forced to either delete their way back to the error or use the stylus. The last thing you want to do with an application is force the user to do things in a way that is unfriendly.

To the rescue comes the CEUtility control. This is a freeware control designed for use with the VBCE toolkit. It has numerous uses, not least of which is the ability to use the Windows **SendMessage** API function. In fact, this has two such methods, **SendMessageLong** for messages that have numeric arguments and **SendMessageString** for messages that need character arguments.

You can get this control from the Web at **http://www.vbce.com/**

> There are also problems with the control itself, but the pros far outweigh the cons for this versatile tool.

To get around the cursor key failure, you'll have to write a **KeyUp** event handler for the text box. You have to use the **KeyUp** event, since there's another bug that prevents you from using the **KeyDown** event. You'll need to have a Utility control on the form, in this example that is called **ceUtility**.

> It's important to take action only when the *Shift* key is not pressed - because changing the selection of text in a text box is not affected by the bug!

The routines described here are not perfect - they don't take into consideration the font for example. If you have two lines of text, one of letter i's, and one of letter m's, then you will notice a considerable jump horizontally as you move between them. This is because the code simply uses the relative character position of the caret in a line and not the real distance. You could develop these routines further, but the extra gain would not be likely to justify the extra effort required:

```
Private Sub txtControl_KeyUp(KeyCode, Shift)

    'Detect cursor key presses with no Shift
    If (Shift = 0) Then
```

```
        Select Case KeyCode

            Case 37
                ArrowLeft(txtControl, ceUtility)

            Case 38
                ArrowUp(txtControl, ceUtility)

            Case 39
                ArrowRight(txtControl, ceUtility)

            Case 40
                ArrowDown(txtControl, ceUtility)

        End Select

    End If

End Sub
```

Having determined that a cursor key has been pressed, you need to have an appropriate Arrow move routine. This could be either in the form or as public routines in a **bas** module. The following code is for a private form routine. The routines make use of message constants defined as follows:

```
Const EM_GETLINECOUNT = &HBA
Const EM_LINEFROMCHAR = &HC9
Const EM_LINEINDEX = &HBB
Const EM_LINELENGTH = &HC1
Const EM_SCROLLCARET = &HB7
```

```
Private Sub ArrowDown(Textbox, Utility)

    Dim intCharPos
    Dim intCharsPriorToLine
    Dim intCurLine
    Dim intCursorPosOnLine
    Dim intNextLineLen
    Dim intTotalLines

    On Error Resume Next

' Find out where the cursor is presently at in the textbox.
    intTotalLines = Utility.SendMessageLong(Textbox.hWnd, _
            EM_GETLINECOUNT, 0, 0)
    intCharPos = Utility.SendMessageLong(Textbox.hWnd, EM_LINEINDEX, -1, 0)
    intCurLine = Utility.SendMessageLong(Textbox.hWnd, _
            EM_LINEFROMCHAR, intCharPos, 0)

' The cursor is already at the last line. It can't move down.
    If intCurLine = (intTotalLines - 1) Then Exit Sub

' Get more information on the cursor position.
    intCharsPriorToLine = Utility.SendMessageLong(Textbox.hWnd, _
            EM_LINEINDEX, intCurLine, 0)
```

```vb
        intCursorPosOnLine = Textbox.SelStart - intCharsPriorToLine
        intCharsPriorToLine = Utility.SendMessageLong(Textbox.hWnd, _
                EM_LINEINDEX, intCurLine + 1, 0)
        intNextLineLen = Utility.SendMessageLong(Textbox.hWnd, _
                EM_LINELENGTH, intCharsPriorToLine, 0)

    ' Set the new cursor position.
        If (intCursorPosOnLine <= intNextLineLen) Then
            Textbox.SelStart = intCharsPriorToLine + intCursorPosOnLine

        Else
            Textbox.SelStart = intCharsPriorToLine + intNextLineLen

        End If

    ' Make sure that the cursor is visible.
        Utility.SendMessageLong  Textbox.hwnd, EM_SCROLLCARET, 0, 0

    End Sub


    Private Sub ArrowLeft(Textbox, Utility)  Dim intCharPos

        Dim intCharsPriorToLine
        Dim intCurLine

        On Error Resume Next

    ' The cursor is already at the first character. It can't move left.
        If (Textbox.SelStart = 0) Then Exit Sub

    ' Get move information on the cursor position.
        intCharPos = Utility.SendMessageLong(Textbox.hWnd, EM_LINEINDEX, -1, 0)

        intCurLine = Utility.SendMessageLong(Textbox.hWnd, _
                EM_LINEFROMCHAR, intCharPos, 0)
        intCharsPriorToLine = Utility.SendMessageLong(Textbox.hWnd, _
                EM_LINEINDEX, intCurLine, 0)

    ' Set the new cursor position.
        If Textbox.SelStart - intCharsPriorToLine = 0 Then
            Textbox.SelStart = intCharsPriorToLine - 2

        Else
            Textbox.SelStart = Textbox.SelStart - 1

        End If

    ' Make sure that the cursor is visible.
        Utility.SendMessageLong  Textbox.hwnd, EM_SCROLLCARET, 0, 0

    End Sub

    Private Sub ArrowRight(Textbox, Utility)

        Dim intCharPos
        Dim intCharsPriorToLine
```

```
        Dim intCurLine
        Dim intCursorPosOnLine
        Dim intLineLen
        Dim intTotalLines

        On Error Resume Next

    ' Find out where the cursor is presently at in the textbox.
        intTotalLines = Utility.SendMessageLong(Textbox.hWnd, _
                EM_GETLINECOUNT, 0, 0)
        intCharPos = Utility.SendMessageLong(Textbox.hWnd, EM_LINEINDEX, -1, 0)

        intCurLine = Utility.SendMessageLong(Textbox.hWnd, _
                EM_LINEFROMCHAR, intCharPos, 0)

    ' The cursor is already at the last line. It can't move down.
        If intCurLine = (intTotalLines - 1) Then

            If (Textbox.SelStart < Len(Textbox.Text)) Then
                Textbox.SelStart = Textbox.SelStart + 1
            End If

            Exit Sub

        End If

    ' Get more information on the cursor position.
        intCharsPriorToLine = Utility.SendMessageLong(Textbox.hWnd, _
                EM_LINEINDEX, intCurLine, 0)

        intCursorPosOnLine = Textbox.SelStart - intCharsPriorToLine
        If (intCurLine = 0) Then
          intLineLen = Utility.SendMessageLong(Textbox.hWnd, _
                EM_LINELENGTH, 0, 0)

        Else
          intLineLen = Utility.SendMessageLong(Textbox.hWnd, _
                EM_LINELENGTH, intCharsPriorToLine + 2, 0)

        End If

    ' Set the new cursor position.
        If intCursorPosOnLine < intLineLen Then
            Textbox.SelStart = Textbox.SelStart + 1

        Else
            Textbox.SelStart = Textbox.SelStart + 2

        End If

    ' Make sure that the
    cursor is visible.
        Utility.SendMessageLong  Textbox.hwnd, EM_SCROLLCARET, 0, 0

    End Sub
```

```vb
Private Sub ArrowUp(Textbox, Utility)

    Dim intCharPos
    Dim intCRLFOffset
    Dim intCurLine
    Dim intCharsPriorToLine
    Dim intCursorPosOnLine
    Dim intPrevLineLen

    On Error Resume Next

' Find out where the cursor is presently at in the textbox.
    intCharPos = Utility.SendMessageLong(Textbox.hWnd, _
            EM_LINEINDEX, -1, 0)
    intCurLine = Utility.SendMessageLong(Textbox.hWnd, _
            EM_LINEFROMCHAR, intCharPos, 0)

' The cursor is already at the first line. It can't move up.
    If (intCurLine = 0) Then Exit Sub

    ' Get more information on the cursor position.
    intCharsPriorToLine = Utility.SendMessageLong(Textbox.hWnd, _
            EM_LINEINDEX, intCurLine, 0)
    intCursorPosOnLine = Textbox.SelStart - intCharsPriorToLine
    intPrevLineLen = Utility.SendMessageLong(Textbox.hWnd, _
            EM_LINELENGTH, Textbox.SelStart - intCursorPosOnLine - 2, 0)

' Handle carriage return / line feed combinations that are encountered.
    If (Mid(Textbox.Text, intCharsPriorToLine - 1, 2) = vbCrLf) Then
        intCRLFOffset = 2
    End If

    ' Set the new cursor position.
    If (intPrevLineLen < intCursorPosOnLine) Then
        Textbox.SelStart = intCharsPriorToLine - intCRLFOffset

    Else
        Textbox.SelStart = intCharsPriorToLine - _
                (intPrevLineLen - intCursorPosOnLine) - intCRLFOffset

    End If

    ' Make sure that the cursor is visible.
    Utility.SendMessageLong Textbox.hwnd, EM_SCROLLCARET, 0, 0

End Sub
```

The VBCEUtility Control Loading Failure

Having used the VBCEUtility control to fix some of the text box problems, you may run into another bug. You'll probably only discover this particular bug if you open VBCE projects from the Windows Explorer by double-clicking the project file in order to launch Visual Basic. What happens is that your forms take a very long time to load and then you get a pair of message boxes warning that the FILESYS.EXE could not be initialized. In fact you get two such message boxes for each VBCE utility control. After these messages you get a further message from VB informing you that there were problems loading and that a log file has been generated.

Once the project is loaded, you'll find that you no longer have a utility control on your form. What you have to do is select the File, Open Project... menu item, selecting not to save any changes and reopen the project file. This second time it will load without problem.

The control authors at VBCE are aware of the problem. You should check back to their web site at `www.vbce.com` frequently in case there are improvements or new versions available.

Lost Events in Framed Controls

When you want to use a frame control to group related controls together, you lose the **Click** and **Change** events for combo boxes and text boxes. The suggested workaround from the Microsoft Knowledge Base is to use the Frame control only for its graphical appearance and then place the controls on top of the frame. However, this is not always an acceptable solution. In the Chapter 4 example, CEWizard, frame controls were used to group controls associated with different tabs on a tab strip control.

In that particular example I have been forced to use **LostFocus** events for the affected controls to invoke necessary application logic. This is not a fix, but you have been warned.

The WinSock Control Problems

Working with the current version of the CE Winsock control can be a real challenge. Not only does it offer less functionality than the Visual Basic version of this control - but it's also hindered by several significant bugs.

The most noticeable of these bugs involves the **DataArrival** event. How a normal Winsock request should progress is:

- ▲ Open a connection using the Connect method. Processing will pause while the connection is established.
- ▲ Issue a request using the **SendData** method.
- ▲ The **DateArrival** event will fire when the request has been fulfilled.
- ▲ The **GetData** method is used to retrieve the data.

The bug with the Winsock control is that the connection between the two systems is closed *BEFORE* the **DataArrival** event fires. Therefore when you try to retrieve the data a runtime error is generated. The workaround for this problem is in the **DataArrival** event perform the following steps:

- ▲ Close the connection using the **Close** method
- ▲ Connect again using the **Connect** method
- ▲ Use the **GetData** method to retrieve the data
- ▲ Close the connection again

The second bug is that you can't use the Winsock control to access another machine over an Ethernet connection. I'm not sure if this is a bug in the network driver or in the Winsock control. For now though, your Winsock adventures are limited to a modem connection.

The third bug is that the Winsock control only returns the correct data once in every 3 to 5 attempts. You can request the exact same data again and again - only to receive different results. In none of the cases does it generate any kind of runtime errors.

On the desktop version of the Visual Basic Winsock control, you can set the **RemoteHost** property to an IP address. That way you can connect to another system using either a URL or a TCP/IP address. With the CE Winsock control only the URL method works.

Further Information

Web Sites

The newness of the Visual Basic for Windows CE Toolkit is apparent in the fact that there are currently only three web sites that focus on this product.

VBforCE.com

At VBforCE.com you will find tips, techniques and training. It offers sections on:

- ActiveX controls to use with your CE applications
- Both desktop and H/PC tools to aid the developer
- Frequently asked questions on using the Toolkit and building on CE applications
- Reviews of software and hardware products that can be used with Windows CE
- Tips and tricks that will enhance your development skills
- A number of online training classes on the Visual Basic for Windows CE Toolkit

VBCE.com

This is the first web site on the Visual Basic for Windows CE Toolkit. It provides a wealth of information including:

▲ An extensive bug list including suggested workarounds

▲ Code samples for some common programming problems

▲ A questions and answer section

▲ Tips and tricks on a variety of topics

▲ A Visual Basic for Windows CE Toolkit mailing list

▲ A bookstore on CE related books

▲ A section on freeware and shareware controls

▲ The CEUtility control

▲ and much more...

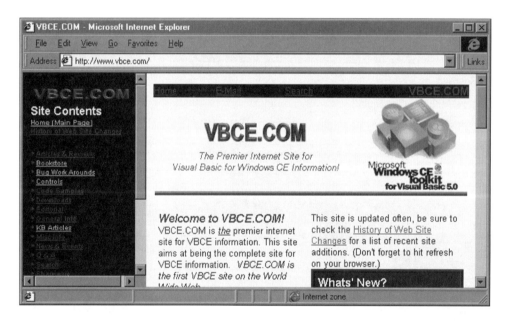

Microsoft.com/windowsce/developer

This is Microsoft's site for developers working with Windows CE, this site provides information on the Visual Basic, Visual C++ and Visual J Toolkits for CE. The download area contains updates, patches and tools to use with the Visual Basic for Windows CE Toolkit.

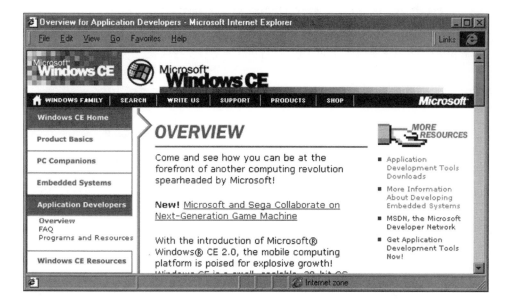

Wrox.com

Although this site isn't specific to the VBCE Toolkit, it does offer additional support for this book. Here you'll be able to access source code for all the applications in this book, the CEUtility control plus a few bits and pieces not in the book itself. For example, there'll some more example apps, such as a GPS program, to help demonstrate some more features of the Toolkit.

Newsgroups

As was with the web sites, the newsgroups focusing on the Visual Basic for Windows CE Toolkit are limited.

microsoft.public.vb.vbce

At the time this book went to press, this was the only newsgroup that catered to the Visual Basic for Windows CE Toolkit. While it's not a very active newsgroup, the discussions typically cover topics that will benefit most CE developers.

microsoft.public.ado.wincebeta

While this newsgroup does not focus on the Visual Basic for Windows CE Toolkit, it does offer a wealth of database information that can be leveraged in your CE applications.

microsoft.public.win32.programmer.wince

A general purpose newsgroup for CE developers. Normally, the topics are more on C++ related but you will find threads that will help your VB efforts as well.

microsoft.public.windowsce.developer.betas

Looking for information (or help with) the latest Windows CE beta products? This is the newsgroup for just that! You will find discussions run from the Visual Basic for Windows CE Toolkit to VC++, Visual J and the ADO.

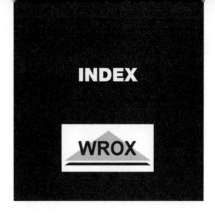

INDEX

WROX

A

About file (CE help systems) 311
EasyEdit example 312
Time Manager example 320
Inventory Manager example 347
Note Manager example 397
Access databases
copying tables to/from 224-228
Access mode 177, 182
ActiveX Control Pack. *see* **ActiveX controls**
ActiveX controls 27, 28, 88
adding to projects 91
Comm 133, 134, 139-141
clearing receive box 145
closing ports 144
communicating instructions 289
confirming data transfers 290
connecting devices 289, 290
data transfers using 288
handling errors 290
opening ports 142, 143
passing data 289
receiving messages 144, 145
Rthreshold 141
sending messages 143, 144
Common Dialog 134
accessing help with 301, 302
copying
Using Control Manager for 92, 93
creating 13, 27
data management tools 133, 134
File System 89, 134, 184
Comm 133, 134, 139, 140, 141
Winsock 134, 280, 282
distributing with applications 95
Finance 134
File 29, 168
Close method 176, 180, 184
Get method 179, 180, 183, 184
Input method 173, 175
InputFields method 175, 176
LineInputString method 175
LinePrint method 172, 173, 175
Open method 169, 177, 181
Put method 178, 179, 182, 183
WriteFields method 172, 173, 175
File System 89, 134, 184
Dir method 126, 129, 185
FileCopy method 187
FileDateTime method 188, 189
FileLen method 189
GetAttr method 190, 191
Kill method 188
MkDir method 186
MoveFile method 187, 188
RmDir method 186
SetAttr method 191, 192
Grid 89
basics 114
benefits/limitations 114, 120
displays 117, 118
formatting 115, 116
loading data 118-120
Image 89
ImageList 90, 123
Add method 124, 125
size/color limitations 123
installing on CE emulator 93, 94
installing on handheld computer 94

interface-enhancing 89
   Grid 89
   Image 89
   ImageList 90
   ListView 90
   PictureBox 90
   TabStrip 90, 98-100
   TreeView 90, 122, 123
ListView 90, 123
Picture Box 90
removing 94
TabStrip 90, 98-100
   basics 98
   benefits/limitations 112
   CEWizard example 95-97
TreeView 90, 122, 123
Utility control 91, 135, 145
   AlwaysOnTopOn method 150
   accessing help with 301
   MsgBox method 149
   PlayWaveFile method 151
   SendMessageLong method 151
   SendMessageString method 156, 157
   Shell method 129, 131
   WaitCursor method 158, 159
Winsock 134
   bugs 159, 280
   error handling 163
   forms 161, 162
   initializing 162
   parsing HTML 285-287
   receiving documents 163, 164
   requesting data from ASP 283-285
   requesting documents 162
   sending data to ASP 282, 283
working with 135

ActiveX Data Objects for Windows CE.
see **ADO CE**
Add method (ImageList control) 124, 125
Add method (ListView control) 127

AddItem method (Grid control) 117
AddNew method 241
ADO CE (CE ActiveX data objects)
adding to Mobile Devices 274, 275
   manual method 275
   programmatic method 275-280
applications. *see* ADO CE
copying tables 274
databases. *see* ADO CE
features 219, 220
limitations 220
SDK tools 219, 220
   downloading 220
   for copying databases 224
   for copying desktop databases 224-226
   for copying H/PC databases 227, 228
   for copying to ODBC databases 228, 229
   installing 220, 221, 222
   programming-related 229, 230
setup bugs 223
system requirements
   clients' system 221
   developer's system 221

ADO CE (CE ActiveX data objects)
applications
distributing 251, 252
Note Manager 353
TableView example 244
ADO CE (CE ActiveX data objects)
databases
adding records 240, 241
adding to Time Manager 252
auto numbering 242
checking pre-existing tables 233, 234
creating indexes 232
creating tables 230, 231
deleting records 243, 244
dropping tables 234

information about 264
managing recordsets 237, 238
modifying records 242
navigating recordsets 238, 239, 240
opening tables 235, 236
SQL queries 236, 237, 238, 241, 243

ADO declarations file 363

ADO Help 236-238

ADO SDK (ADO Software Development Kit). *see* **ADO CE**

ADOfiltr.dll 276

AlwaysOnTopOff method 150

AlwaysOnTopOn method 150

API calls 28

Append mode 171

Application Install Wizard 47-52

applications. *see* **CE applications**

arrow keys, bug work around
Utility example 152-156

ASP Client application 280

attributes, file
retrieving 190, 191
setting 191, 192

auto numbering 273
adding to databases 242

auto-sizing forms 77, 78

B

barcode scanners 350

barcode-related procedures (Inventory Manager) 340-343

beep function, adding to CE applications 151

binary files
Access mode 182
closing 184
features 180, 181
opening 181, 182
reading 183, 184
writing 182, 183

bitmap images
displaying 89

bitwise comparisions 190

BOF/EOF properties 239, 240

Books Online 23

bugs
ADO CE SDK setup 223
Comm control 141
Winsock control 159, 280

buttons. *see* **command buttons**

C

CE ADO (ActiveX data control). *see* ADO CE

CE Application Installation Wizard 95

CE applications
  accessing help 301, 302
    ActiveX controls for 28
  ActiveX controls
    see also ActiveX Controls
    adding 91
    distributing 95
  ADO CE
    see also ADO CE
    distributing 251, 252
    features 219, 220
    limitations 220
    limitations of 220
    requirements for using 220, 221
  ADO CE data transfers 273
  ASP Client 280
  barcode scanners for 350
  CEWizard. *see* CEWizard application
  Chat. *see* Chat application
  Check Files. *see* Check Files application
  communication-enabled 288
    Comm control 288-290
  converting desktop applications to 78, 79
  Copy Tables. *see* Copy Tables application
  creating 31
  databases 167
    adding records 240, 241
    auto numbering 242
    checking pre-existing tables 233, 234
    creating indexess 232
    creating tables 230, 231
    deleting records 243, 244
    dropping tables 234
    managing recordsets 236-238
    modifying records 242
    navigating recordsets 238-240
    opening tables 235, 236
    SQL queries 237, 238, 241, 243
  DataDisplay. *see* DataDisplay application
  designing 57, 58
    displays 58, 60, 61
    handheld displays 58
    input methods 61, 62, 63
    usage considerations 63, 64
  developing
    system requirements 10, 11
  EasyEdit. *see* EasyEdit
  error handling 79, 80
    first Err.Number example 80
    runtime errors 81, 82
    second Err.Number example 81
  exiting 27
  Explorer. *see* Explorer application
  file I/O 167, 168
  file management controls 184
  HTML Viewer. *see* HTML Viewer application
  installing 23
  Inventory Manager. *see* Inventory Manager
  Note Manager. *see* Note Manager
  path names 170
  removing 34, 55
  TableView. *see* TableView application
  testing 40
    CE emulator for 77
    on handheld computers 62, 77, 78
    hardware variability 64
    usage conditions 64
  Time Manager. *see* Time Manager
  Utility. *see* Uitlity application
  Winsock-compatible 162
    developing 280-287

CE Debugger 26

CE emulator 10, 43, 44, 45
  ADO for 222
  installing controls 93, 94
  removing controls 94
  testing CE applications
    Easy Edit example 216
    Inventory Manager example 347, 348

Note Manager example 397
TableView example 250
testing help system files on 312

CE help systems 293

accessing 294
Common Dialog control for 301, 302
Utility control for 301
components
Contents file 295-297
Topic files 297, 298
designing 300
Easy Edit example 302
HTML tags 299
Time Manager example 313
using 294, 295

CE Platform SDK (Systems Development Kit) 10

installing 14

CE Project Type 21

CE Services 10, 14, 18, 19

components 16
installing 15, 16, 17
Synchronized Files folder 268, 269
Check Files example 269-272

CE Toolkit 9

Books Online 23
Control Manager 23
Debug menu 22
Debugger dialog window 26
Download Runtime Files 23
features 20
File menu 22
Heap Walker 24
Installation Wizard 23
installing 12, 13
menu structure 21
Process Viewer 24
Project menu 22
Project Type 21
Registry Editor 24
Run menu 22

Spy 25
toolbar 26
Tools menu 22
Windows CE menu 22
Zoom 25

CeCreateDatabase function 220

CEWizard application 95

adjusting interface 101-103
building 98-112
enabling command buttons 105-107
enabling tabs 108, 109
features 96
frame control reference 104, 105
housekeeping code 112
initializing 101
navigating with command buttons 110
saving data 111
TabStrip control 98
updating display 103, 104
using the interface 96, 97

Chat application

clearing receive box 145
closing ports 144
Comm control 139
forms 140, 141
features 136
initializing 141, 142
opening ports 138, 142, 143
receiving messages 144, 145
sending messages 138-144
using 136-138

Check Files application

features 270
installing 269, 270
using 272

class modules 28

Clear method (Err object) 81

Close method (File control) 176, 180, 184

closing

binary files 184

communication ports 144
random access files 180
sequential files 176

code. *see* **programming**
code modules,, VB vs. VBCE 28
Comm control 133, 139-141
clearing receive box 145
closing ports 144
communicating instructions 289
confirming data transfers 290
connecting devices 289, 290
data transfers using 288
handling errors 290
opening ports 142, 143
passing data 289
receiving messages 144, 145
Rthreshold 141
sending messages 143, 144

comma-delimited data
reading into sequential files 175, 176
storing 172, 173

Common Dialog control   134
accessing help with 301, 302

communication ports
closing 144
opening 142, 143

communications ports, serial. *see* **Serial ports**

connecting
devices
Comm control 289
handhelds to desktops 10
Windows CE Services for 17

Contents file   (CE help systems)   295-297
coding 307
EasyEdit example 305, 306
Inventory Manager 344
Note Manager 390
Time Manager example 313, 314

Control Manager   23, 92, 93

controls
see also ActiveX controls
ActiveX controls. *see* ActiveX controls
ADO CE 219
features 219, 220
limitations 220
requirements for using 220, 221
CE File System 168
Comm 133, 134, 139, 140, 141
clearing receive box 145
closing ports 144
communicating instructions 289
confirming data transfers 290
connecting devices 289, 290
data transfers using 288
handling errors 290
opening ports 142, 143
passing data 289
receiving messages 144, 145
Rthreshold 141
sending messages 143, 144
Common Dialog 134
accessing help with 301, 302
configuring
Explorer example 124, 125
copying
Control Manager for 92, 93
data management tools 133, 134
File System 89, 134, 184
Comm 133-141
Winsock 134, 280, 282
EasyEdit 197
File 29, 168
Close method 176, 180, 184
Get method 179-184
Input method 173, 175
InputFields method 175, 176
LineInputString method 175
LinePrint method 172, 173, 175
Open method 169, 177, 181
Put method 178, 179, 182, 183
WriteFields method 172-175
File System 89, 134, 184
Dir method 126, 129, 185
FileCopy method 187

FileDateTime method 188, 189
FileLen method 189
GetAttr method 190, 191
Kill method 188
MkDir method 186
MoveFile method 187, 188
RmDir method 186
SetAttr method 191, 192
Finance 134
Grid 89
  basics 114
  benefits/limitations 114, 120
  displays 117, 118
  formatting 115, 116
  loading data 118-120
I/O 29
Image 89
ImageList 90, 123
  Add method 124, 125
  size/color limitations 123
interface-enhancing 89
  Grid 89
  Image 89
  ImageList 90
  ListView 90
  PictureBox 90
  TabStrip 90, 98-100
  TreeView 90, 122, 123
installing on CE emulator 93, 94
installing on handheld computer 94
ListView 90, 123
  form for 123
PictureBox 90
placing 69
properties
  setting 38, 39
removing 94
TableView example 247
TabStrip 90
  basics 98
  benefits/limitations 112
  CEWizard example 95, 96, 97
  form for 98, 99, 100
text box
  fixing bugs in 203-207

TreeView 90, 122
  form for 123
Utility control 91, 135, 145
  AlwaysOnTopOn method 150
  accessing help with 301
  MsgBox method 149
  PlayWaveFile method 151
  SendMessageLong method 151
  SendMessageString method 156, 157
  Shell method 129, 131
  WaitCursor method 158, 159
Winsock 134
  bugs 159, 280
  error handling 163
  forms 161, 162
  initializing 162
  parsing HTML 285-287
  receiving documents 163, 164
  requesting data from ASP 283-285
  requesting documents 162
  sending data to ASP 282, 283
working with 135
Copy Tables application
  copying from H/PC 278, 279
  copying to H/PC 276-278
  installing 275
  using 275, 276
copying files 187. *See also* see also data transfer
creating CE applications 31
  adding code 40-43, 70-76
  creating user interface 37, 38
  installation program 47-52
  reworking user interface 68-70
  setting form and control properties 38, 39
  setting project properties 36, 37
  starting new projects 35
  testing installation program 52-54
  testing on handheld computers 77, 78
  testing on handlheld computer 46, 47
  testing uninstall program 55
  testing with CE emulator 43-45, 77

D

data
displaying
  DataDisplay example 112-120
loading
  DataDisplay example 115-120
saving
  CEWizard example 111
scanning/recording
  Inventory Manager application 327

data controls
ActiveX. working with 135

data entry
enhancing
  CEWizard example 95, 96
updating display following
  CEWizard example 108

data files
comma-delimited
  storing 172, 173
reading into sequential files 175, 176
writing to sequential files 171, 172

data handling
Grid control for 114

data input. *see* **input**

data management ActiveX tools 133
Comm control 133, 134, 139-141
  clearing receive box 145
  closing ports 144
  communicating instructions 289
  confirming data transfers 290
  connecting devices 289, 290
  data transfers using 288
  handling errors 290
  opening ports 142, 143
  passing data 289
  receiving messages 144, 145

Rthreshold 141
sending messages 143, 144
Common Dialog 134
  accessing help with 301, 302
File 29, 168
  Close method 176, 180, 184
  Get method 179, 180, 183, 184
  Input method 173, 175
  InputFields method 175, 176
  LineInputString method 175
  LinePrint method 172, 173, 175
  Open method 169, 177, 181
  Put method 178-183
  WriteFields method 172-175
File System 89, 134, 184
  Dir method 126, 129, 185
  FileCopy method 187
  FileDateTime method 188, 189
  FileLen method 189
  GetAttr method 190, 191
  Kill method 188
  MkDir method 186
  MoveFile method 187, 188
  RmDir method 186
  SetAttr method 191, 192
Finance control 134
Utility control 91, 135, 145
  accessing help with 301
  AlwaysOnTopOn method 150
  MsgBox method 149
  PlayWaveFile method 151
  SendMessageLong method 151
  SendMessageString method 156, 157
  Shell method 129, 131
  WaitCursor method 158, 159
Winsock 134
  bugs 159, 280
  error handling 163
  forms 161, 162
  initializing 162
  parsing HTML 285-287
  receiving documents 163, 164
  requesting data from ASP 283-285

requesting documents 162
sending data to ASP 282, 283

data storage

ADO CE applications

Note Manager example 359, 360

data transfers

ADO CE 273-275

Copy Table example

copying from H/PC 278, 279

copying to H/PC 276-278

installing 275

using 275, 276

inter-device 267, 68

Internet method 280-287

serial ports for 288

Comm control 288-290

synchronized 269-272

Winsock control for 281

databases (ADO CE)

Access

copying tables to/from 224-228

accessing, ADO tools for 219

connecting to in VBCE 29

managing

ADO tools for 224

ODBC

copying tables to/from 228, 229

programming 229, 230

adding records 240, 241

auto numbering 242

checking pre-existing tables 233, 234

creating indexes 232

creating tables 230, 231

deleting records 243, 244

dropping tables 234

managing recordsets 236-238

modifying records 242

navigating recordsets 238-240

opening tables 235, 236

synchronization requirements 229, 232

DataDisplay application 112

building 114-120

features 112, 113

initializing 115

using 113

date stamps, retrieving 188, 189

Debug Menu 22

debug object 28

Debugger dialog window 26

Delete method 243

deleting

files 188

records 243, 244

tables 234

designing applications 57, 58

handheld displays 58, 60, 61, 65

hardware variability 64

input methods 61-63

usage considerations 63, 64

desktop computers

applications, converting to VBCE 78, 79

communicating with H/PCs, Chat example 136-145

connecting to H/PC, Comm control 289

connecting to handhelds, Windows CE Services for 17

connecting with handheld, Windows CE Services for 10

copying databases from 224-226

data transfers 267, 268

ADO CE 273-275

Synchronized Files folder 268-272

establishing partnership with handheld 18, 19

DesktopToDevice function 276-278

DeviceToDesktop function 278, 279

Dir method (File System control) 126, 129, 185

directories
    creating 120, 186
    deleting 186
    retrieving 185

displays. see user interfaces
    designing 58, 60, 61
    font sizes 60, 69
    placing controls 69

distributing
    ActiveX controls with applications 95
    ADO CE applications 251, 252

DLLs
    ADOfiltr.dll 276

Download Runtime Files 23

downloading, ADO SDK 220

dropping tables 234

E

EasyEdit application 192
    building 195
    coding 197
    control forms 197
    creating user interface 195, 196
    design 194, 195
    features 194
    help system 302
    installation program for 216
    menu structure 207
    setting properties 195
    testing, 216
    using 193, 194

emulator. see CE emulator

End method 27

Err object 80
    Clear method 81
    Number property 80
        first Err.Number example 80
        second Err.Number example 81

errors.
    see also troubleshooting
    data transfer errors 290
    handling 28, 79, 80
        first Err.Number example 80
        formatting errors 84
        runtime errors 81, 82
        second Err.Number example 81
    startup 92

Exchange/Outlook Extensions for Pocket Outlook 16
exiting CE applications 27
Explorer application 120, 131
  building 122-131
  changing views 130, 131
  configuring controls 124, 125
  control forms 123
  displaying directory 129
  features 120
  gathering folder/file details 125-128
  ImageList control 123
  initializing 124
  navigating forms 129
  renaming directories 129
  renaming files 129
  using 121, 122

F

File control 29, 168
  Close method 176, 180, 184
  Get method 179-184
  Input method 173, 175
  InputFields method 175, 176
  LineInputString method 175
  LinePrint method 172-175
  Open method 169, 177, 181
  Put method 178-183
  WriteFields method 172-175
File object 89
File System control 89, 134, 184
  Dir method 126, 129, 185
  FileCopy method 187
  FileDateTime method 188, 189
  FileLen method 189
  GetAttr method 190, 191
  Kill method 188
  MkDir method 186
  MoveFile method 187, 188
  RmDir method 186
  SetAttr method 191, 192
FileCopy method (File System control) 187
FileDateTime method (File System control) 188, 189
FileLen method (File System control) 189
files
  attributes
    retrieving 190, 191
    setting 191, 192

.BAS 27

binary

closing 184

features 180, 181

opening 181, 182

reading 183, 184

writing 182, 183

comparing random and binary 181

copying 187

date and time stamps 188, 189

deleting 188

determining length 189

I/O tools 29 167, 168

making 48

management controls 184

moving 187, 188

random access

closing 180

opening 177

reading 179, 180

record length 177

when to use 176

writing to 178, 179

runtime, downloading 23

sequential

Append mode 171

closing 176

comma-delimited data 172, 173

managing 192-194

opening 169

opening for input 169, 170

opening for output 170, 171

reading data 175, 176

reading text 173-175

when to use 168, 172

writing to 171, 172

Finance control 134

folders

listings of, loading into Explorer 125-128

setup 52

font sizes 69

handheld displays 60

form modules, VB vs. VBCE 28

formatting errors

handling in Time Manager 84

formatting Grid control

DataDisplay example 115, 116

forms

auto-sizing 77, 78

controlling, frame control reference 104, 105

properties, setting 38, 39

setting width 47

unloading 28

unloading QueryUnload procedure 202, 203

frames. see forms

functions, Is 27

G

Get method (File control) 179-184

GetAttr method (File System control) 190, 191

Grid control 89, 112

   AddItem method 117

   basics 114

   benefits/limitations 114, 120

   displays, DataDisplay example 117, 118

   form for 114

   formatting, DataDisplay example 115, 116

   loading data, DataDisplay example 118-120

   RemoveItem method 117

   TableView example 244-250

Guided Tour 16

H

H/PC. see handheld computers

handheld computers

   application design 57, 58

      displays 58-61

      input methods 61-65

      testing on hardware 64

      testing usage conditions 64

      usage considerations 63, 64, 65

   connecting to desktops, Comm control 289

   connecting, Windows CE Services for 10, 17

   converting desktop applications for 78, 79

   copying controls to 92, 93

   copying desktop databases to 224-226

   copying H/PC databases to 227, 228

   data transfers 267, 268

      ADO CE 273, 274, 275

      Synchronized Files folder 268-272

   establishing partnership with desktop 18, 19

   installing controls 94

   removing controls 94

   removing programs 34

   testing applications on 46, 47, 62, 77, 78

   testing help systems on 312

hardware requirements 10

hardware variability 64

Heap Walker 24

help systems 293

   accessing 294

      Common Dialog control for 301, 302

      Utility control for 301

   components

      Contents file 295-297

      Topic files 297, 298

   designing 300

Easy Edit example 302
HTML tags 299
Inventory Manager example 344, 345
Note Manager example 390
Time Manager example 314, 318, 319
using 294, 295

HTML
parsing, ASP Client example 285-287
tags, 299

HTML Viewer application 159
features 160
initializing 162
receiving documents 163, 164
requesting documents 162, 163
using 160

I

I/O (input/output) tools 167, 168
icons, CE help 294
Image control 89
ImageList control 90, 123
Add method 124, 125
size/color limitations 123

importing. *see* **loading**
indexes, creating 232
initializing
ADO CE applications
TableView example 248
Note Manager example 364
CE applications
CEWizard 101
Chat example 141, 142
DataDisplay 115
Explorer 124
HTML Viewer example 162
Inventory manager example 335
Utility example 149

input. *see also* **I/O (input/output)**
opening text files for 169, 170
Input method (File control) 173, 175
input methods
designing 61
control size 61
incorporating flexibility 62
preventing input errors 63
InputFields method (File control) 175, 176
installation programs
creating 47-52
testing 52-54

Installation Wizard 23
installing
  ADO SDK 220-222
    setup bugs 223
  controls
    on CE emulator 93, 94
    on handhelds 94
  VBCE Toolkit 12, 13
  Windows CE Platform SDK 14
  Windows CE Services 14-19
  Windows NT Remote Access Service (RAS) 14
InStr function 213
interfaces. *see* **user interfaces**
Internet connectivity
  ActiveX tools, Winsock control 159-165
Internet files
  data transfer method 280-287
  handling, Winsock applications 281
Inventory Manager application 327
  barcode procedure 340-343
  features 330, 331
  form/control properties 333, 334
  initializings 335
  installation program 349
  installing 328
  project properties 332-334
  removing 330
  starting project 332
  testing application 347-349
  testing installation 349
  uses for 349, 350
  using 328, 329
Is functions 27

K

Kill method (File System control) 188

L

Larry Roof's Time Manager. *see* **Time Manager**
LineInputString method (File control) 175
LinePrint method (File control) 172-175
listings
  directories
    creating new 186
    deleting 186
    retrieving 185
ListView control 90, 123
  Add method 127
  form for 123
loading. *see* **initializing**
  folder/file details
    Explorer example 125-128
loading data
  DataDisplay example 115, 116

M

making files 48

managing

  databases, ADO tools for 224

  recordsets 236-238

MDI forms 28

messages

  receiving, Comm control for 144, 145

  sending

    Chat example 138, 139

    Comm control for 143, 144

methods

  AddNew 241

  AlwaysOnTopOn (Utility) 150

  Clear (Err object) 81

  database navigation-related 238, 239

  Delete 243

  End 27

  File control

    Close 176, 180

    Closet 184

    Get 179-184

    Input 173, 175

    InputFields 175, 176

    LineInputString 175

    LinePrint 172, 173, 175

    Open 169, 177, 181

    Put 178, 179-183

    WriteFields 172-175

  File System control

    Dir 126, 129, 185

    FileCopy 187

    FileDateTime 188, 189

    FileLen 189

    GetAttr 190, 191

    Kill 188

    MkDir 186

    MoveFile 187, 188

    RmDir 186

    SetAttr 191, 192

  Grid control

    AddItem 117

    RemoveItem 117

  ImageList control

    Add 124, 125

  ListView control

    Add 127

  MsgBox (Utility) 149

  Open

    ADO databases 235, 236

  PlayWaveFile (Utility) 151

  SendMessageLong (Utility) 151

  SendMessageString (Utility) 156, 157

  Shell (Utility) 158

  Utility control

    AlwaysOnTopOn (Utility) 150

    MsgBox 149

    PlayWaveFile (Utility) 151

    SendMessageLong (Utility) 151

    SendMessageString (Utility) 156, 157

    Shell 129, 131

    WaitCursor 158, 159

  WaitCursor (Utility) 158, 159

Mips folders 52

MkDir method (File System control) 186

Mobile Devices application 17, 274

  adding ADO CE to 274, 275

  manual method, using 275

  programmatic method, using 275-280

modifying records 242

MoveFile method (File System control) 187, 188

moving data

  inter-device 267, 268

    ADO CE 273, 274, 275

    Synchronized Files folder 268-272

moving files 187, 188

MsgBox method 149

N

navigating

CE applications

Utility example 152-156

directories

Explorer example 129

navigating recordsets 238-240

New Partnership Wizard 18, 19

Note Manager application

data storage 359, 360

design 358

enhancing 399

features 358

form/control properties 362, 363

initializing 364

installing 354, 398

menu structure 362

project properties 360, 361

removing 358

reusing techniques in 399

specifications 353

starting project 360

testing 397, 398

testing installation 398

user interface 359, 361

using 354-358

Number property (Err object) 80

first Err.Number example 80

second Err.Number example 81

numbering, automatic

adding to databases 242

O

objects

Err 80

Clear method 81

Number property 80, 81

Err (Number property) 80

File 89

File System 89

ODBC databases

copying tables to/from 228, 229

OLE support 28

On Error Resume Next statement 79, 80

first Err.Number example 80

second Err.Number example 81

Open method

ADO databases 235, 236

File control 169, 177, 181

opening

binary files 181, 182

communication ports 138, 142, 143

random access files 177

sequential files 169-171

tables 235, 236

output.

see also I/O (input/output)

opening text files for 170, 171

P

partnerships
  handheld-to-desktop, establishing 18, 19

path names 170

PictureBox control 90

PlayWaveFile method 151

ports, communications
  opening, 138

primary keys 273

Process Viewer 24

programming
  ADO CE databases 229, 230
    adding records 240, 241
    auto numbering 242
    checking pre-existing tables 233, 234
    creating indexess 232
    creating tables 230, 231
    deleting records 243, 244
    dropping tables 234
    managing recordsets 236-238
    modifying records 242
    navigating recordsets 238-240
    opening tables 235, 236
  ASP Client. *see* **ASP Client application**
  Check Files *see* **Check Files application**
  Copy Table *see* **Copy Tables application**
  EasyEdit *see* **EasyEdit**
  HTML Viewer *see* **HTML Viewer application**
  Inventory Manager *see* **Inventory Manager**
  Note Manager *see* **Note Manager**
  text box work-around 203-207
  Time Manager *see* **Time Manager**
  Utility *see* **Utility application**

programs
  removing from handheld computers 34

Project Menu 22

properties
  BOF/EOF 239, 240
  Number (Err object) 80, 81

Put method (File control) 178-183

R

random access files
  closing 180
  opening 177
  reading 179, 180
  record length 177
  when to use 176
  writing to 178, 179

RAS (Remote Access Service)
  installing 14, 16

reading
  binary files 183, 184
  random access files 177-180
  sequential files
    data 175, 176
    text 173-175

recording data
  Inventory Manager example 327

records
  adding to databases 241
  deleting 243, 244
  modifying 242

recordsets. *see also* **tables**
  managing 236-238
  navigatings 238-240

Registry Editor 24

Remote Access Service (RAS)
  installing 14, 16

RemoveItem method (Grid control) 117

removing applications 34
  testing program for 55
  testing uninstall program 55

removing controls 94

removing directories 186

requirements

hardware 10

software 11, 12, 16

using ADO CE controls

clients' system 221

developer's system 221

RmDir method (File System control) 186

Run Menu 22

runtime errors

avoiding 79, 80

handling

adding to Time Manager 82-84

VB vs. VBCE 81, 82

handling with VBCE 28

runtime files, downloading 23

S

saving data

CEWizard example 111

saving files

SaveFile function 200-202

scanning data

Inventory Manager example 327

SDK (Systems Development Kit)

Windows CE Platform 10

installing 14

search capability

Utility example 157, 158

SendMessageLong method 151

SendMessageString method 156, 157

sequential files

closing 176

comma-delimited data 172, 173

managing

EasyEdit example 192-195

opening 169

Append mode 171

for input 169, 170

for output 170, 171

reading data 175, 176

reading text 173-175

when to use 168, 172

writing to 171, 172

serial ports

data transfers using 288

Comm control 288-290

Service Pack 3

installing 12

SetAttr method (File System control) 191, 192

setup folders 52

SH 3 folders 52

Shell method (Utility control) 129, 131, 158

shortcut keys, testing 63

snapshot test 61

software requirements 11
  RAS 16
  Visual Basic 12
  Windows NT 11
  Windows Service Pack 3 12

sorting databases 238

Spy 25

SQL queries, ADO CE-supported 236-238
  adding records 241
  deleting records 243

starting. *see* initializing

starting new projects 35

storing comma-delimited data 172, 173

surveying programs
  CEWizard example 96

Synchronized Files folder 268, 269
  Check Files example 269-272

synchronizing databases, 274
  requirements 229, 232

T

tables. *see also* recordsets
  checking for pre-existing 233, 234
  copying, ADO CE tools for 274, 275
  creating 230, 231
  dropping 234
  opening 235, 236

TableView application 244
  building 245
  coding 247-250
  design 245
  features 245
  form/control properties 247
  installation program 251
  installing 244
  setting properties 245
  testing, 250
  user interface 246
  using 244

tabs
  CEWizard example
    enabling 108, 109
    TabStrip control for 98-100

TabStrip control 90
  basics 98
  benefits/limitations 112
  CEWizard example 95-97
  form for 98-100

testing
  applications, 40
    CE emulator for 43-45
    on handheld computer 46, 47
  for pre-existing tables 233, 234
  installation program 52-54
  shortcut keys 63
  uninstall programs 55

text box control

fixing bugs in 203-207

text files

Append mode 171

opening for input 169, 170

opening for output 170, 171

reading 173-175

writing to 171, 172

Time Manager 32

adding database functionality 252

help system 313, 316

About menu 320

accessing files 321

Function menu 314-316

Options menu 316

Overview menu 317

Quick Start menu 318-320

using 33

Version 1 34

adding code 40-43

construction 34, 35

creating installation program 47-52

creating user interface 37, 38

design 34

display problems 65

input problems 65

setting form and control properties 38, 39

setting project properties 36, 37

testing installation program 52-55

testing on handheld computer 46, 47

testing with CE emulator 43-45

usage problems 65

Version 2 (Chapter 3) 65

adding code 70-76

construction 68

design 67, 68

final product 66

requirements 67

reworking user interface 68-70

testing on handheld computer 77, 78

testing with CE emulator 77

using 66

Version 3 (Chapter 7) 253, 254

coding 254-263

design 253, 254

features 253

installation program 264

testing installation 264

testing on handheld computer 263

testing with CE emulator 263

time stamps, retrieving 188, 189

toolbar, VBCE Toolkit 26

tools

ADO SDK 219, 220, 224

copying desktop databases 224-226

copying H/PC databases 227, 228

copying to OBDC databases 228, 229

programming-related 229, 230

connectivity

Winsock control 159-165

data management

ActiveX 133, 134

VBCE.com Utility 135, 145-159

file I/O (input/output) 167, 168

VBCE Toolkit 9

installing 12, 13

Windows CE Platform SDK 10

installing 14

Windows CE Services

components 16

installing 14-19

Tools Menu 22

Topic files (CE help systems) 297, 298

TreeView control 90, 122

form for 123

troubleshooting, handheld-desktop connections 20

U

uninstall programs, testing 55
unloading forms 28
uploading. *see* loading
usage considerations
  Time Manager example 65
user interfaces
  accomodating individuality 62
  ADO CE applications
    Note Manager example 359, 361
  constructing 37, 38
  data displays
    DataDisplay example 90, 112-120
  data survey forms
    CEWizard example 95, 96, 101-112
  directories
    Explorer example 120-131
  enhancing
    ActiveX controls 89, 90
    Utility control 91
  error-prevention 63
  help systems 304
    accessing 294
    components 295-298
    using 294, 295
  setting form width 47
  spreadsheets
    Grid control for 114
  TableView example 246
  text editors
    EasyEdit example 195, 196
  Time Manager example
    revising 68, 69, 70
    reworking 70-76

utilities
  Control Manager 92, 93
  Mobile Devices 17
  Windows CE menu
    Application Install Wizard 23
    Books Online 23
    Control Manager 23
    Download Runtime Files 23
    Heap Walker 24
    Process Viewer 24
    Registry Editor 24
    Spy 25
    Zoom 25
Utility application 145, 159
  AlwaysOnTopOff 150
  AlwaysOnTopOn 150
  arrow keys 152-156
  features 145
  initializing 149
  MsgBox 149
  PlayWaveFile 151
  program forms 147, 148
  search capability 157, 158
  SendMessageLong 151
  SendMessageString 156, 157
  Shell 158
  using 146, 147
  WaitCursor 158, 159
Utility control 91, 135, 145
  AlwaysOnTopOn method 150
  accessing help with 301
  MsgBox method 149
  PlayWaveFile method 151
  SendMessageLong method 151
  SendMessageString method 156, 157
  Shell method 129, 131
  WaitCurso method 158, 159

V

variant data type 27
VBCE (Visual Basic for Windows CE)
accessing help
ActiveX controls for 28
ActiveX controls 27
creating 13
API calls 28
.BAS files in 27
class modules 28
comparison with VB 27-29
data type 27
database support 29
debug object 28
error-handling 28
File I/O controls 29
MDI forms 28
OLE support 28
unloading forms 28
VBCE Toolkit 9, 88
ActiveX Control Pack 88 *see also* ActiveX controls
Application Installation Wizard 23
Books Online 23
Control Manager 23
converting desktop applications using 78, 79
Debug menu 22
Debugger dialog window 26
developing applications using 31-37
Download Runtime Files 23
error handling method 79, 80
first Err.Number example 80
second Err.Number example 81
features 20
file I/O tools 167, 168
File menu 22
Heap Walker 24
installing 12, 13
menu structure 21
Process Viewer 24
Project menu 22
Project Type 21
Registry Editor 24
Run menu 22
Spy 25
toolbar 26
Tools menu 22
Windows CE menu 22
Zoom 25
VBCE.com Utility control 91 *see* **Utility control**
views, changing
Explorer example 130, 131
Visual Basic
comparison with VBCE 27-29
required editions 12
Visual Basic for Windows CE. **see** VBCE
Visual Basic IDE (integrated design environment)
CE Toolkit modifications 20
Debugger dialog window 26
menu structure 21
toolbar structure 26
Visual C++ 27
creating custom ActiveX controls 88

W

WaitCursor method 158, 159
web server connections
    HTML Viewer example 159-164
web servers, data transfers to/from 280
web sites, ADO CE information 264
Windows CE help system 293. *see* CE
help
Windows CE Menu 22
**Windows CE Platform SDK (Systems
Development Kit)** 10
    installing 14
Windows CE Services 10..
    see also CE Services
    components 16
    installing 14-19
Windows NT 11
    installing 11
    Remote Access Service (RAS)
      installing *14, 16*
    Service Pack 3 12
Winsock control 134, 280, 282
    bugs 159, 280
    error handling 163
    forms 161, 162
    initializing 162
    parsing HTML 285, 286, 287
    receiving documents 163, 164
    requesting data from ASP 283-285
    requesting documents 162
    sending data to ASP 282, 283

Winsock-compatible applications 162
wizards
    Application Install Wizard 23, 47-52
    CE Application Installation Wizard 95
    New Partnership Wizard 18, 19
WriteFields method (File control) 172-175
writing
    binary files 182, 183
    random access files 178, 179
    sequential files 171, 172

Z

Zoom 25